Ockwells Manor

A history of the house and its occupants

Ann Darracott 12th May 2025

by

Ann Darracott

Maidenhead Civic Society

Ockwells Manor

A history of the house and its occupants

By Ann Darracott

First published in 2023 by ABD Titles
6 Medallion Place, Maidenhead, SL6 1TF, UK

Printed edition: ISBN 978 0 9544919 5 6

Printed by Denwal Press Ltd
www.denwalpress.co.uk

*Front Cover: An ink sketch of Ockwells Manor House,
by Jack Widgery, Chairman, Maidenhead Civic Society 1981-85*

Contents

Foreword

By The Rt Hon Theresa May MP

As we go about our everyday lives it is all too easy to ignore the history that stands around us. Yet the gates we drive or walk past can sometimes hide a fascinating picture of our country's history if only someone is willing to uncover it. That is the story of this book. Ockwells Manor House was built by John Norreys Esquire over 550 years ago and has survived because it has been changed to meet the needs of successive owners. That we are able to read the story of this house is thanks to the vision and determination of the author – Ann Darracott – who has dedicated her time and efforts to uncovering the rich story of this remarkable building.

Ockwells is basically still a medieval manor house, but its Great Hall hides a great treasure of rare domestic armorial glass. The survival of this glass over the centuries is nothing short of a miracle. Clarifying who is represented by their armorial achievements has unveiled the themes Norreys devised and gives us a glimpse of the world in which his King and Queen, lords, abbots and bishops, courtiers and other men Norreys was close to, moved. The glass has been dated to between 1450 and 1454 when the country was in uproar, as England had lost Normandy. It was this unrest that led to the start of the Wars of the Roses in 1455.

As well as describing those who are represented in the armorial glass the book describes the history of the house over the centuries, including the addition and removal of extensions, the owners who, if they lived there, tended to alter it and their tenants who didn't. Sadly, it also records periods of deterioration when the house was left uncared for. Against this backdrop the preservation of the treasures in the Great Hall is remarkable. But just as there have been periods in the past when its future was uncertain so there are concerns today about the future of Ockwells. The author hopes that the book, by documenting the past of this important house, will help preserve its future.

Patron, Maidenhead Civic Society

Preface

This book is the culmination of over thirty years of study of the fifteenth century Ockwells Manor house near Maidenhead, Berkshire, described by the eminent architectural historian Sir Nikolaus Pevsner as the *most refined and the most sophisticated timber framed mansion in England.* It began by accident. In 1988, in my role as secretary of Maidenhead Civic Society, I was asked to see if the new owners, Mr and Mrs Brian Stein, would agree to the Society holding a fund-raising concert in the tithe barn. They had recently moved, with their family, into the house which they had had restored – very necessary as it had been empty for around fifteen years with consequent deterioration. After the concert as a "thank-you" I presented Mr Stein with a copy of the 1892 sale catalogue dating from when the house was being sold after the Victorian restoration. He had an interest in the history of Ockwells, commissioning Mr Harvey Van Sickle to write an account, completed in 1987 but which remains unpublished. The 1892 sale catalogue is held by Berkshire Record Office (BRO) and I was asked by Mr Stein to see what additional material was in the archive there. It transpired that the estate papers of Lord Desborough, William Henry Grenfell, a past owner of Ockwells, had been deposited at the BRO by his daughter Viscountess Gage.

Thus began a search for Ockwells-related material that on the way led to the creation of an exhibition on the history of the house, several information leaflets – including one on the armorial glass prepared for a conference on the fifteenth century at Reading University in 1998 – and PowerPoint presentations on the armorial glass of Ockwells Manor and another that is a virtual tour. Some valuable information has come from people attending such talks or visits to the house.

Ockwells Manor house was built by John Norreys Esquire between 1450 and 1454. It has always been a private house, occupied by owners or their tenants and so has always been inaccessible to the public except when special visits can be organised. Throughout its history owners have striven to ensure the survival of the house's principal attraction – the magnificent armorial glass in the great hall – and thereby the house. Charles Pascoe Grenfell, Lord Desborough's grandfather, had the glass temporarily removed in the mid-nineteenth century because there were fears that the roof of the great hall would fall as the house was nearly derelict. Sir Edward Barry similarly removed the glass for safe keeping during World War II.

The full architectural and historic significance of Ockwells Manor only becomes apparent when seen in the context of the life and times of its builder – John Norreys. A significant portion of this book is therefore devoted to exploring and documenting his relationships, both professional and personal, with those he chose to honour in the glass. This has led to some re-identification of the personalities represented in the glass, updating the previous work of the Lysons brothers and Everard Green, and thus enabling the scheme John Norreys devised to be fully understood – a scheme that illuminates mid fifteenth-century history including the loss of English-held lands in France that led to the Wars of the Roses. Records held in the Bodleian Library, Oxford, have been of great value in both dating the glass and identifying the personalities, so it is intriguing and gratifying to note that it was the purchase by Sir Thomas Bodley, in 1608, of Hindons Farm and water mills in Cookham and lands in Maidenhead from Sir Francis, second Lord Norreys of Rycote, a descendent of John Norreys Esquire, that helped create the endowment for the Library that Bodley founded.

Other buildings linked to the people represented in the great hall glass demonstrate the growing use of brick for building at this period and the examination of the similarities of contemporary construction techniques and styles helps inform the understanding of the architectural developments at Ockwells. Similarly, insight into the lives and interests of the subsequent owners after the Norreys family allows us to chart how the house has been altered by them over the years and why it is the way it is today.

During its history Ockwells Manor house has survived several threats to its existence. Constructed of brick and timber, its location on land subject to waterlogging, means its timber foundation has in the past rotted causing problems with structural stability. The fear that Ockwells would be destroyed was expressed by William Morris in 1880, and the house was one of the first projects of the recently founded Society for the Protection of Ancient Buildings. This public pressure led to a major restoration of the house in the Victorian era. Research for this present book has led to the discovery of photographs, held in private archives, of the house in the process of restoration. The restored house was purchased at the end of the nineteenth century by Sir Edward Barry who both enhanced and modernised it, laying down covenants with the National Trust in 1945 and 1947 to preserve both the house and its setting. Nearly all subsequent owners adhered to these covenants, albeit with variable success, and continued to modernise the house thereby ensuring its survival as a family home.

Ockwells Manor house came on the market in 2019 and at the time of going to print its future is uncertain. In the past the covenants have been lifted to allow roads and housing estates to be built nearby and threats to its setting continue. Information collected by Maidenhead Civic Society assisted the National Trust in successfully defending the covenant on the field opposite the house in 2012. However, the pressure to build housing on any available space is ongoing and unfortunately a restrictive covenant is not a material consideration in determining any planning application. On the plus side the Royal Borough of Windsor & Maidenhead has bought much of the farmland to the south of the house to create Thrift Wood Park, which links with Ockwells Park, so preserving some of its setting.

Since 1960 Maidenhead Civic Society has been an effective voice in the local community, promoting high standards of planning and architecture in Maidenhead, and working to secure the preservation, protection, development and improvement of features of historic or public interest in the town and surrounding areas. In some cases, the Society has taken the lead and undertaken specific projects documenting particular aspects of Maidenhead's history and historic buildings, including detailed studies of Ockwells Manor, St John the Baptist Church, Shottesbrooke, Bisham Abbey and nearby All Saints Church.

It is hoped that this present work will result in a more widespread appreciation of the historic and aesthetic value of Ockwells Manor House and ensure its continued survival.

Ann Darracott – May 2023

1. Ockwells – A most refined mansion

Ockwells Manor house has been described by Nicholas Pevsner as the *most refined and the most sophisticated timber-framed mansion in England*, a perfection partly due to the restoration of 1889-1891 but also due to its elegant carved bargeboards and panelled gables.[1] Tudor chimneypieces and Jacobean woodwork have also helped gentrify the house and twentieth-century plumbing and central heating have made it liveable in, though the current owners wrap up to avoid too much heat damaging the structure.

The east front of Ockwells Manor house

Ockwells Manor house was built in the mid-fifteenth century by John Norreys, Esquire of the Body of Henry VI, after he had married for a second time and when his career had peaked.[2] The name varies in spelling from Norreys, Norrys, Norys, Norreis, to Norris. In this present book the spelling is standardised to "Norreys" for John and his immediate family and descendants.

---

[1] Pevsner, p187-8, who mistakenly attributes this restoration to the C20th; see Tyack, Bradley & Pevsner p413.
[2] Before building Ockwells, Norreys probably lived at Windsor and Yattendon. By 1445 he owned a house in Windsor (Griffiths, 1981, p303). In 1442, together with chaplains from St Georges Chapel, he was involved in granting a messuage in Peascod St, Windsor, and in 1455 a tenement in the same street (St George's Chapel Archives, SGC XV 45, 140 & 197). Yattendon was brought to him by his first wife.

1

Ockwells Manor house, the outer court and garden viewed from the south

Ockwells Manor house, ca. 1987, viewed from the east, showing its construction around a courtyard

Ockwells Manor house, a mixture of fifteenth century and Victorian construction, viewed from the west

Norreys built the house on land that had been owned by his family for 200 years and which had been cleared from Windsor Forest.[3] It was a farm before the house was built and farming evidently continued. In the mid-fifteenth century the nearest village was Bray.

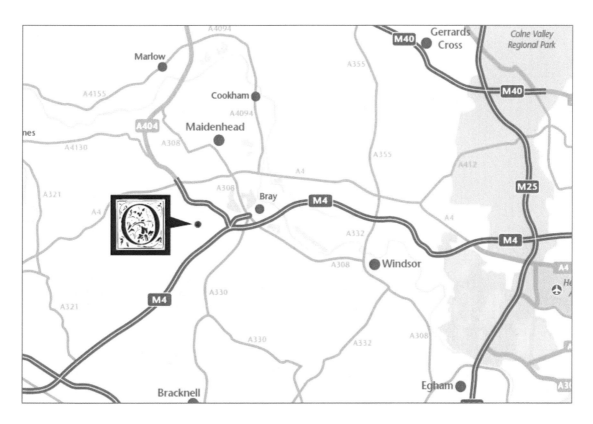

Ockwells Manor today – only a couple of miles to the west of Bray, but nearly encircled by motorways

Over 500 years later the manor house is almost surrounded on its northern side by the urban sprawl of Maidenhead, a town that grew up between the twin villages of Cookham

---

[3] Clearance in the vicinity of Ockwells continued over the centuries so that now only remnants of the original forest on Norreys' land exist today as Great Thrift Wood and Little Thrift Wood.

and Bray because it was possible to cross the River Thames there. The preservation of the setting of Ockwells is an ongoing concern as Maidenhead continues to expand.

Ockwells setting showing urban encroachment to the north of the house (yellow arrow points to the house)
(from Google Earth, April 2020)

Ockwells is famous because of the magnificent armorial glass Norreys put up in his great hall. Its survival is a miracle given that for hundreds of years Ockwells was tenanted, becoming an increasingly decrepit farmhouse until being restored during the reign of Queen Victoria.

In 1899 an account of the personalities represented in the armorial glass was published in *Archaeologia*. Re-identification of some of these armorials, almost all in their original positions, has revealed a coherent scheme that included a commemoration of those involved in attempts to reach a peace agreement with the French in 1445 that had included marrying Henry VI to Margaret of Anjou, the French king's niece, in that year. Their armorials and that of the man who arranged the marriage, William de la Pole, Duke of Suffolk, occur in the great hall. Evidence indicates that the glass was put up between 1450 and 1454, exactly the period when, peace negotiations having failed, England lost, with the exception of Calais, its French possessions, leading to unrest in England – one result of which was the execution of Suffolk, in May 1450 with the Wars of the Roses beginning in 1455.

The story begins with the thirteenth-century acquisition of Okholt (Ockwells) by an earlier member of the Norreys family and then traces the history of Ockwells Manor house, from the mid-fifteenth century when built by John Norreys Esquire, to the present day. Contemporary illustrations and other material show how the house has been altered over the 555 years or so of its existence and something of the men and women who owned or tenanted it.

2. Ockwells in the C13th & C14th

In 1268 Henry III granted "OCHOLT" (oak-wood) to Richard le Norreys and his heirs, Cook (Coci) to Queen Eleanor (of Provence).[1] The king, in 1265, had been victorious over the barons, led by Simon de Montfort, at Evesham, and by 1268 the country was pacified.

Ocholt was described as a purpresture (land cleared for cultivation) in Windsor Forest which Godrey de Lifton, sometime keeper of the king's manors of *Cokham and Braye,* had brought into cultivation.[2] An inquisition had been made by Ebulo de Montibus,[3] constable of the castle of *Windesore,* of the king's right to make the grant for which Norreys and his heirs rendered 40s/year to the keepers of the said manors.

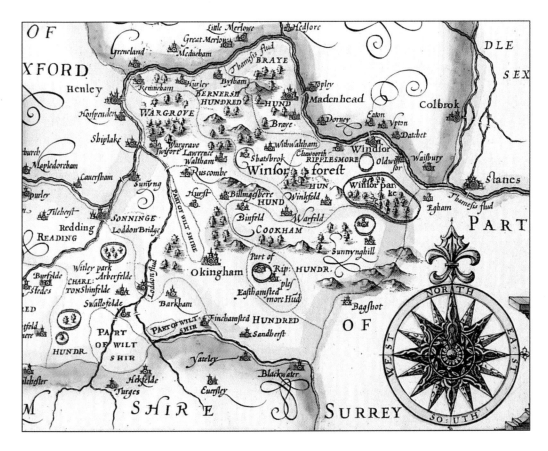

Detail from John Speed's map of Berkshire, 1616 (Original in British Library)

---

[1] Land grant of Ocholt to Richard Norreys in 1268 (see Appendix A, No. 1).

[2] By the C15th these were the Queen's manors. Maidenhead developed on the boundary between them as it was possible to cross the River Thames there; the first known reference to a bridge is in 1254 (CCR 1254-1256, p9). Coincidentally, this also refers to Godrey de Lifton who was mandated to widen the road between the bridge and Henley by clearing the forest between these places to make the road safer.

[3] De Montibus was a Savoyard, a vassal of the Queen's uncle Peter, Count of Savoy. The constable died in 1268 and Queen Eleanor was his executor (Andenmatten B & De Raemy D, p172). Rolle Castle on Lake Geneva was built by him.

In 1270 Richard le Norreys received a long service grant of 4¾d a day[4] and in 1279 a Richard Norreys accompanied Queen Eleanor abroad.[5]

There is no reliable family tree connecting Richard le Norreys in the thirteenth century with John Norreys in the fifteenth century, though members of the Norreys family were certainly present in Bray in the intervening years.[6] In this intervening period, members of a Norreys family, probably kinsmen, also had land in Hurley. Katherine Boteler, widow of John Noreys, granted land in Hurley to Richard de Waleden, prior of Hurley from ca.1299 to 1304 in the reign of Edward I.[7] The prior, in 26 Edward III (1352), undertook to find a chaplain for the chapel of SS Andrew & Mary Magdalene in Maidenhead, the same chapel in which John Norreys Esquire and his kinsmen would in 1451 found a guild. The Norreys connection with Hurley continued. Thomas Ruston (prior 1468-1480) complained of the riotous conduct of William Norreys of Winkfield (brother of John Norreys Esquire) who with others broke the prior's close, destroyed his corn and menaced him before his gate.[8] John Norreys, gent, of Winkfield, probably William's son or grandson (see Appendix C, Tree 1b), exchanged lands with the prior in 1497.[9]

The Norreys of Ockwells Coat (left) and the Norris of Speke coat (right)

The pedigree of the Norris family of Speke in the *Visitation of Lancashire* of 1567 [10] was used by the College of Arms to provide a lineage for Henry Norreys (d.1601), a descendent of John Norreys of Ockwells, who was knighted in 1566 by Elizabeth I, becoming Lord Norreys of Rycote in 1572. However, this supposed descent from the Norris family of Speke, Lancashire, is unlikely. The essential problem is that the Norreys of Rycote

---

[4] CPR 1266-72, p421.
[5] CPR 1272-81, p79. The reason for this visit has not been found but her husband Henry III had died in 1272, her grandson George in 1274 and two of her daughters in 1275 so she may have gone on pilgrimage. She is said to have retired to a convent, probably Amesbury Abbey, Wilts where she died in 1291.
[6] See Bray Court Rolls transcribed in Kerry (p113) reproduced in Appendix A, No. 2. See also volume three (p89-90) of his notes now in the Bodleian Library.
[7] Wethered 1903, p160. Wethered incorrectly dates the charter to the time of Edward II, who did not succeed until 1307.
[8] Ibid, p218.
[9] Ibid, p222. See Wethered 1909, pp68-69 for a list of Hurley priors.
[10] Raines, pp83-85.

pedigree records Sir Henry Norris of Speke (d.1437) as the great-great-grandfather of John Norreys of Ockwells (d.1466) which is clearly impossible (see Appendix B for a fuller explanation). Furthermore, the heraldic coat of John Norreys Esquire of Ockwells (*argent a chevron between three raven's heads erased sable*) is quite different to that of the Norris family of Speke (*quarterly argent & gules in the 2nd & 3rd quarters a fret or overall a fess azure*). Unfortunately, the Norris of Speke coat has been incorrectly used in several locations (see Appendix B). The Norreys of Ockwells coat has been attributed to the family of Ravenscroft. It remains unclear how this coat was acquired.[11]

In the fifteenth century Ocholt (later Ockwells)[12] descended to John Norreys, Esquire.

Ockwells Manor house, Berks, built by John Norreys Esquire in the mid-fifteenth century. It has always been in private hands

Speke Hall, Lancs, built by members of the Norris family in the sixteenth century on the site of an earlier house. They held the house until the eighteenth century. It passed to the National Trust in 1943 after which it was maintained by Liverpool City Corporation and the Merseyside County Council until 1986 when the Trust took over full responsibility

---

[11] Unfortunately, it is the Norris of Speke coat that erroneously graces the Wikipedia entry for Lord Henry Norreys of Rycote (d.1601), rather than the Norreys of Ockwells coat.
[12] A royal grant of 1582 describes the manor of Ockeholte, *alias* Ockholt, *alias* Ocole, *alias* Norrys, *alias* Ffetyplace (Andrews p19).

3. John Norreys Esquire
Builder of Ockwells

John Norreys (1405-1466), Esquire of the Body to Henry VI, was the son of William Norreys of Bray (see Appendix C, Tree 1a).[1] John was one of the inner circle of courtiers around Henry VI and held many important posts, though he was never knighted.[2] A thorough appreciation of this man's career and his many connections is key to understanding the early development of Ockwells Manor house and the importance and meaning of the armorial glass in the great hall.

His principal civic and royal appointments can be summarised as follows:

> Yeoman of the Chamber by 1429
>
> Usher of the Chamber 1437-ca.1441
>
> Esquire of the Body 1437 – end 1455
>
> High Sheriff of Berkshire & Oxfordshire 1437-8, 1442-43, 1457-58
>
> MP Berkshire 1439-40; Oxfordshire 1442; Berkshire 1445-46, 1447, 1449-50,
>
> 1450-51, 1453
>
> Keeper/Clerk of the Great Wardrobe 1444-1446
>
> Chamberlain of the Exchequer 1446-1450
>
> Treasurer of the Chamber & Keeper of the Jewels of Queen Margaret 1445-1452
>
> Keeper of the Queen's Wardrobe 1448-1457
>
> Steward of Cookham and Bray 1447-1461

---

[1] John's grandfather was Roger Norys and great uncle was Thomas Norys. In 1391 they were both witnesses to a grant of land in Maidenhead in Bray by Reginald Jory to Richard Horn of Cookham (St Georges Chapel Archives SGC XV.58.D.43). In 1422 Roger Norys and John Graunger granted lands in Bray to Simon Fazakerley. When this land was re-granted in 1427 and 1435 by others, in both cases William Noreys, Roger's son, was a witness (St Georges Chapel Archives SGC XV.58.D.58). William also witnessed a grant of land in Fifield in Bray in 1431 (St Georges Chapel Archives SGC XV.58.D.65). The Norreys surname is spelt as per the document.

[2] Pevsner, p187 described him as *Sir* John Norreys, for example, but he was never knighted. He describes himself as a *Squyer* (Esquire) in his 1465 will (see Appendix A, No. 2). The revised edition (Tyack, Bradley & Pevsner p413) corrects the error. Both Lysons' 1806 and 1813 named him *Sir John Norris* on page 445; however, this is later corrected in Lysons 1813 on p473 where it is said that *John Norreys Esq was never knighted*. The Visitation of Berkshire of 1532 (Rylands 1907, vol 1, p10) correctly identified him as an Esquire. A later Visitation (Ibid vol II, p185) refers to "Sr John Norris, Knt Banneret," as stated in the erroneous C16th pedigree (E12 f 90-91) in the College of Arms that linked Lord Henry Norreys of Rycote, descendent of John Norreys Esquire, with the Norris of Speke family (see Appendix B).

John Norreys, still in his twenties, was in the court of King Henry VI by 1429 when the latter, still a child, was crowned in London. Although he did attend the king on his expedition to France in 1430 when the king was crowned as king of France in Paris the following year, Norreys seems to have been more civil servant than soldier, dealing with first the king's finances and then the queen's.

Norreys had three wives, two of whom are represented in the Ockwells armorial glass (see Chapter 4, Lights 9 & 14). Evidence indicates that Ockwells was built between 1450 and 1454 by which time his first wife had died and he was married to his second wife.

It is convenient to discuss Norreys' life and his impact on Ockwells in three parts, relating to his three marriages.

Marriage to Alice Merbrooke (by 1439 to ca.1450)

His first wife, Alice Merbrooke, to whom he was married by May 1439, was the daughter of Richard Merbrooke of Yattendon by his wife, Helen (Ellen), a daughter of William Mountfort (Mountford, Montfort) of Lapworth and Codbarrow in Warwickshire.[3]

When Henry IV married Margaret of Anjou in 1445, Alice was made a lady in waiting to the new queen, probably as a consequence of Norreys being close to both the king and William de la Pole, by then Duke of Suffolk, who had negotiated the marriage and brought Margaret to England.

By Alice, John had two sons, William (later knighted) and John (the elder), and two daughters, Margaret and Anne. The elder daughter was almost certainly named for Margaret of Anjou.

Significant Career Events

1429 The coronation of Henry VI in London, when John Norreys' career appears to have begun. His position in court (he was then a yeoman of the chamber) is thought to have brought him to the attention of Richard Beauchamp, Earl of Warwick,[4] the guardian of the young Henry VI. As yeoman of the chamber he was granted 200 acres of wood in Hurst, Berkshire, which Thomas Montacute, Earl of Salisbury, deceased, had held.[5]

1430 Accompanied the young king to France for his coronation there.[6] Also present at the coronation in Paris in 1431 were: Richard Beauchamp, Earl of Warwick, the king's governor and tutor; William de la Pole, Earl of Suffolk; and James Butler, fourth Earl of

---

[3] Dugdale, p581. Codbarrow, now a deserted moated site on the southern edge of Umberslade Park, is to the west of Lapworth. William was son of Richard Mountfort and Rose Brandeston. Rose died ca.1424/5 after which, in 1427, it is thought her manors of Codbarrow in Warwickshire and Yattendon in Berkshire were settled on the Merbrookes, with remainder to the Catesbys. Helen's sister Margaret married John Catesby (Payling 2020a, p773) and inherited Lapworth. Richard Mountfort was one of two illegitimate sons of Peter (Piers) 3rd Lord Mountfort, (d.ca.1369; see Appendix C, Tree 4). Inherited by Alice Merbrooke, Codbarrow remained with the Norreys family until 1534 when Sir John Norreys sold it (VCH Warwickshire, vol 5, pp165-175).
[4] Clark 2020a, p672. (Note: The History of Parliament Trust has standardised on the spelling "Norris" rather than "Norreys" as in this present book (see Chapter 1, page1).
[5] CPR 1429-1436, p37. The earl was wounded at the siege of Orleans in 1428 and died shortly after. He lived at Bisham, Berkshire, where his ancestor, William Montacute, Earl of Salisbury, had founded a priory.
[6] Clark 2020a, p671.

Ormond. Warwick's son, Henry was in France at the time.[7] This is likely as the young king would have needed a playmate.

1437   A grant in 1430 of 6d a day to Norreys *during pleasure* from the issues of Wiltshire was converted by the king to 6d for life.[8]   In this year Henry VI assumed full power and Norreys prospered greatly, being granted various posts – especially in the period 1444-1453.

1438   Norreys purchased the wardship of William Catesby and was a feoffee for Catesby and he for him.[9]   Catesby was the cousin of his wife, Alice.

1439   **April**: Richard Beauchamp, Earl of Warwick, died and his widow Isabel Despenser, included Norreys among those having custody of the Beauchamp estates during the minority of her son Henry, the heir.   **May**: Norreys and Alice his wife were granted two parts of the manors of Wadley & Wicklesham (in Faringdon).[10]   In **December** Isabel died and Norreys together with John Nanfan, Sir William Mountfort (a kinsman of Norreys' wife Alice) and William Menston were executors of her will.   In November/December he received assignments at the Exchequer on behalf of Edmund Beaufort, the Constable, to pay for repairs to the fabric of Windsor castle, and in the early 1440s he was himself allotted 100 marks p.a. for the same purpose.   Presumably, he was expected to oversee the works.   He was still acting for Beaufort in this regard in 1449.[11]

1441   Norreys was a founder member, with Suffolk and others of the Guild of the Holy Cross in Abingdon:

"License for William (Aiscough), *bishop of Salisbury, William* (De la Pole), *earl of Suffolk, Thomas Bekynton, clerk, John Golafre and* **John Noreys, esquire** *and others, for the repair of the road which extends from Abyndon, co. Berks towards Dorchestre, co Oxford, and over the water of the Thames through Burford and Culhamford between the said towns, by which road the King's lieges have had carriage and free passage save when it is flooded so that none can attempt it without peril of his life and loss of his goods - to found a perpetual Gild of themselves and others, both men and women in the parish church of St Helen, Abyndon, for thirteen poor, weak and impotent men and women, to pray for the good estate of the King and of the brethren and sisters of the Gild and their benefactors and for the souls of the King and the brethren, sisters and benefactors aforesaid, after death and of their parents".*[12]

The Guild was the successor to the earlier Fraternity of the Holy Cross who were responsible for building bridges in Abingdon and nearby Culham, the latter bridge, built in 1416, still exists.   The north porch of St Helen's, probably built by the Fraternity or Guild, has an upper room, the Exchequer, which the Guild used for its meetings.   The original entrance was inside the church but was sealed off in 1873.   The adjacent priest's house is thought to have been built at the same time and shared the chimney of the Exchequer room.[13]

---

[7] Monstrelet I, p599.
[8] CPR 1429-1436, p111.
[9] Griffiths 1981, p341.
[10] CPR 1436-41, p309.   In 1440 John & Alice, tenants for life, granted these lands to Oriel College after their deaths (Ibid p396).   In 1441 the College petitioned them for a grant in mortmain (Ibid p540) and in that year the College obtained the manor and lordship of Wadley and Wicklesham from John and Alice (Berkshire Feet of Fines Part II, no. 1355, p55).   The Librarian at Oriel notes that they bought Wadley Manor for £1000 in 1440 and then presumably sorted out tenancies (pers. comm. in 1993).
[11] Clark 2020a, p672.
[12] CPR 1441-6, p36.   See Appendix A, No. 1 for full transcript.
[13] Cox, p80.

St Helen's Church, Abingdon

The Exchequer Room over the porch where the Guild of the Holy Cross met and adjacent priest's house, St Helen's Church, Abingdon

Long Alley Almshouses, built in 1446/47 by the Guild of the Holy Cross based at St Helen's Church (lantern and porches are later additions). It still functions as a retirement home, managed since 1553 by Christ's Hospital of Abingdon

1442   Purchased the overlordship of Yattendon from Edward Langford.[14] With Henry Beauchamp, then Earl of Warwick, and John Nanfan had the keeping of the lands in Cornwall of Sir William Bodrugan during the minority of his heir.[15] Norreys together with chaplains from St George's College in Windsor Castle, and others, granted a messuage in Peascod Street, Windsor, to John Seriaunt of Dorney.[16] Three years earlier an Inquisition had found that Windsor was far from prosperous with many burgages, messuages and tenements ruinous, empty or destroyed. A new charter granted in May 1439 included giving burgesses exemption from several payments.[17] Townsmen (Burgesses), and members of the College, appear to have mixed well together, the first guildhall being opposite the castle gates and forming part of the college's original setting.[18] Norreys seems to have had a long-standing link with Windsor[19] and may have been a member of the Trinity guild.[20] He continued an involvement with Windsor and St Georges Chapel into the next decade.

---

[14] CCR 1441-47, p59; Clark 2020a, p673. In 1442 and 1444 he bought out the rights of other heirs of Hugh Brandeston, Alice's ancestor, to the manor of Yattendon and advowson of the church there (VCH Berkshire, vol IV p127; Berkshire Feet of Fines Part II nos. 1362, 1366, pages 57 & 59).

[15] CPR 1441-46, p83.

[16] St George's Chapel Archive SGC XV 45. 140. One of the chaplains, Robert Chamberlain, was clerk of the king's chapel in 1453 (SGC XV 45. 21.78). In the C16th four tenements in Peascod Street were held by the college to accommodate minor canons, vicars and chantry priests (Lewis 2010, p60, SGC XV.58.C.29).

[17] VCH Berkshire, vol 3, p59.

[18] Lewis 2010, p56. In 1493 Oliver King, the king's secretary, John Morgan, Dean of the College of SS Mary & George in Windsor Castle and the Mayor, John Todde, had a licence to found a fraternity or gild of the Holy Trinity in the parish church of St John the Baptist, New Windsor, They also had licence to elect from amongst themselves two wardens or masters from the burgesses of the town (CPR 1485-1494 p457).This was probably a re-foundation as Edward I in 1277 had granted the town a borough charter with burgesses and a merchant guild (see Astill p7). New Windsor had the right to return MPs from 1302 but often failed to send them including the period from 1340 to 1447 (Ibid p8). In the Parliament of 1447 one of the two MPs was a waterman (Wedgwood p76).

[19] In 1455 three men named in the 1442 grant, one of the chaplains, Robert Cherbury and two other men, Robert Chamberlain and John Bythewode, are again associated with Norreys, this time in a grant of a tenement in Peascod Street to Richard Walgraue of Clewer (SGC XV 45, p197).

[20] Guild members were commoners of substance and wisdom but any gentleman or learned man not dwelling in the town could become a member if invited by the mayor or aldermen (defined as earlier mayors; VCH Berkshire, vol 3 p60). Unfortunately, Windsor's entire medieval archive was destroyed in the late C17th. The only surviving contemporary records are those held in the archive of St George's Chapel (Lewis 2010, p59).

1443 Norreys received from John Somerset, Chancellor of the Exchequer, 100 marks yearly for the repair of Windsor Castle and the Lodge.[21] Norreys founded with others a chantry in All Saints Church, Wokingham: *License to Master Adam Moleyns, dean of the cathedral church of Salisbury,* **John Noreys esquire** *and John Westende, chaplain to found a perpetual chantry for one chaplain to celebrate divine service daily in honour of the Virgin Mary at the altar of the Virgin within the church of Wokingham in the diocese of Salisbury for the good estates of the King, Adam, John and John ...... to be called the chantry of St Mary of Wokyngham.*[22]

1444 In 1440 Henry VI had founded Eton College as *"Kynge's College of Our Ladye of Eton besyde Windesore"* to provide free education to 70 poor boys who would then go on to King's College, Cambridge, which he founded 1441. In 1444 the king granted to the college the manor called "Le Mote" together with all the lands and tenements, the property of the king, lately acquired by the gift and grant of William Marquis of Suffolk, John Norreys, John Pury, and other esquires, situated in New Windsor, Old Windsor and Clewer.[23]

1444-53 The peak of Norreys' career when he held posts including MP for Berkshire (1439 then 1445-53); Keeper of the Great Wardrobe (1444-46); Office of Receipt and Exchequer (1446-1449) and Chief Steward of the lands of the Spensers (1446-c.1449) after the death of Henry Beauchamp, Earl of Warwick; Treasurer of the Chamber and Keeper of the Jewels of Queen Margaret (1445-1452); Keeper of her Wardrobe (1448-57).

1445 On 6th April John Norreys, Keeper of the Great Wardrobe, was ordered to deliver eight yards of *scarlet* to John Lord Dudley,[24] possibly needed for the marriage of Henry VI and Margaret of Anjou which took place on 22nd April. Alice Merbrooke, his wife, was made one of Margaret of Anjou's ladies in waiting as soon as she arrived in England.[25] In 1445 Norreys leased "John of Brayes Place" (afterwards "Heuyndyns"), in the manor of Bray, from Humphrey, Duke of Gloucester, for a rent of £3 9s 2d a year, which was reduced in September after the Duke's death to a mere 6d.[26]

1446 **May**: Norreys pays £1000 to the Queen, at the command of Henry VI, for the daily expenses of her chamber and to cover her expenses from the feast of the Circumcision.[27] **September**: Norreys with William Aiscough, Bishop of Salisbury, who married Henry VI to Margaret of Anjou in 1445, founded the chantry of St Mary in the parish church of Bray (St Michael's): *License for William, bishop of Salisbury,* **John Norys, esquire** *and Thomas Lude , vicar of the parish church of Bray, to found a chantry within the said church*

[21] CPR 1441-46, pp150-1.
[22] Ibid, p190.
[23] Tighe & Davis vol1, p341, Eton College Records, vol 63, pp196-197. John Norden's map of 1607 shows *Moate Park* south of the castle, separated by a road from *Norris his Lodge* at the northwest corner of the *Greate Park.*
[24] Ry.F, p674.
[25] Clark 2020a, p672, citing: E101/409/13 John Norreys' account as Keeper of the Great Wardrobe 23-24 Hen.VI (1444-5); Alice is one of the queen's damsels: E101/409/14; Norreys' account as Treasurer of the Chamber and Keeper of the Jewels of the queen, 24-25 Hen.VI (1445-6) when Alice as *capital damsel Regine* received a gold gown: E101/409/17. Norreys account as Treasurer and Keeper of the Jewels of the queen 25-26 Hen.VI (1446-7) lists Alice Norreys as one of six women attending the Queen (pers. comm. Linda Clark).
[26] Ibid 2020a, p673, CPR 1441-46, p372. It is said that Heuyndyns (Hyndens, Hindons) in *Bray* extended into the manor of Cookham (Kerry, p122; Darby 1899, p42). Hindons farm in *Cookham* together with land in Maidenhead, watermills in Cookham and a close called Berry (also in Cookham) was sold by Francis, 2nd Lord Norreys of Rycote, to Sir Thomas Bodley in April 1608 for £960 (Darby Notebook vol 6, p109). This agreement and the royal confirmation of the sale (Bodleian Library MS ch. Berks. 215 & 220 recto) can be downloaded from Digital Bodleian. Bodley bequeathed these assets in 1612 to the University of Oxford for the support of the "public" library he had founded.
[27] Hookham, p428, citing Issue Roll 24 Henry VI.

of one chaplain to celebrate divine service daily in honour of the Virgin Mary at the altar of the said virgin within the said church, in the diocese of Salisbury for the good estate of the King, the said founders and all others who endow the chantry and for their soules after death; to be called the chantry of St Mary, Bray.[28]

In 1436, the previous vicar of Bray, William Dyer, had granted a house he had inherited in East St Helen's Street, Abingdon, to the Fraternity of the Holy Cross to which both he and his father, Richard, a successful dyer, belonged. This was used as their Brotherhood House.[29] Norreys may have already been a member of this Fraternity.

St Michael's Church, Bray

Bishop Aiscough was murdered in the unrest of 1450 – a major incident in a series of provincial revolts that followed the Kentish rising of Jack Cade.[30]

1446 In the court of Humphrey, Duke of Gloucester, before the Steward of Cookham, Norreys' right to a messuage, mills and land assets in Cookham was acknowledged and the same were released to the complainants as heirs of the said John Norreys.[31] Long Alley almshouses next to St Helen's Church, Abingdon, was built by the Guild of the Holy Cross as provided for in the patent of 1441. Norreys and Suffolk were members of the Guild. Norreys was in a group that included Edward Langford concerning the grant of the manor

---

[28] CPR 1446-52, p2.

[29] Cox, p83.

[30] Kekewich, 2004a.

[31] The complainants include Edmund Brudenell, Sir Edmund Hungerford, John Leyntlo (St Lo) Esq and Thomas Lanyingtone (Lavington), a prominent member of the merchant guild in Reading. The mills are Ray Mills. In 1392 Thomas Noreys, probably a great uncle (see Appendix B), was a grantor of lands and mills called Reyemills in Cookham to Thomas Lillebrooke (Darby Notebook vol 6, p103).

of Earley White Knights.[32] Suffolk, Norreys and Langford with others, obtained the manors of Elington (Elyngtones) and Spencers;[33] today these manors are within the boundary of Maidenhead.

1447   Steward of the manors of Cookham and Bray (1447-1461), replacing Humphrey, Duke of Gloucester, who died in this year; these manors were part of the queen's jointure.

1448   January: Norreys had a licence to crenellate the manor house and empark 600 acres at Yattendon.[34] Recorded in a long list of executors of the will of Henry VI where he is listed with other esquires. Suffolk also was an executor.[35] Norreys and the other feoffees had been given the estates of the duchy of Lancaster, for the purposes of Henry VI's Will.[36] He and Sir Walter Devereux had the keeping of the manor of Leominster, Herefordshire with the assent of the Abbot of Reading (probably Light 7a – see Chapter 4) as certain monks, the previous wardens, had incurred debts.[37] Alice, as a lady in waiting to the Queen, is among those given robes for the Garter Feast.[38] In **September** Henry VI on a tour of England, presumably to show off his new bride, visited Durham where he was entertained by the Bishop of Durham, Robert Neville.[39] John and Alice probably went with them.   In the same month Norreys, his heirs plus others gain Hampstead Ferrers, northwest of Yattendon.[40]

In the Galilee Chapel of Durham Cathedral (left) is extant medieval armorial glass for Margaret of Anjou and for Norreys and his wife Alice Merbrooke[41]

---

[32] CPR 1446-52, p24. In 1443 Norreys and Langford were among those granted successive remainders to the manor. The group then included Edmund Brudenell (Berkshire Feet of Fines Part II no 1365 p58).

[33] Berkshire Feet of Fines Part II no 1375, p61.

[34] Wedgwood and Holt, p638 citing the Calendar of Charter Rolls. He appears to have been using bricks for his works there (see Clark 2020a, p677).

[35] Nicolas 182,6 p21-24. His will is dated 12th March 1447/8, regnal year 26 Henry VI. In those days the calendar year started on 25th March, Lady Day. As the calendar year now starts on 1st January, the modern equivalent is 12th March 1448.

[36] Ibid, p22. Norreys between 1437 and 1441 had been a feudal tenant of the Leicester Honor of the Duchy (Somerville p569).

[37] CPR 1446-52, p142. See also Hillaby, p236.

[38] In 1448 she was the only untitled lady granted robes to attend the feast of St George at Windsor Castle with the Queen (Beltz pccxxiv); E101/409/18 Thomas Tuddenham's Account of Keeper of the Great Wardrobe 25-27 Henry VI (1446-1448). Robes were issued to the Queen, Lady Anne Moleyns, Lord Say, Lord Beauchamp and Alice Norreys, providing an indication of her status at court (pers. comm. Linda Clark).

[39] Wolffe, p367; Pollard 2004. The bishop was brother of Richard Neville, Earl of Salisbury in right of his wife, Alice Montacute. Salisbury was well known to Norreys through their joint involvement with the Beauchamp estates and the proximity of Salisbury's estate at Bisham to Ockwells.

[40] CPR 1446-1452, pp277-8. The group includes Norreys' kinsmen, William Catesby Esq, his wife's cousin, Richard Merbrooke, his father-in-law, William Norreys, his brother, Edmund Brudenell, kinsman of his brother-in-law, and Norreys close associates John Pury Esq, Thomas Lavington, and Thomas Babham.

[41] Probably part of a scheme put up by Bishop Robert Neville in the Exchequer Building near the cathedral that Neville built or altered (Darracott 2018).

1449   **March**: Norreys and John Wenlock in a group enfeoffed with the manor and warren of Fenelsgrove, Bedfordshire. **November**: More details of the grant of Hampstead Ferrers, acquired from William Lord Ferrers, is recorded in the Feet of Fines. It was eventually renamed Hampstead Norris.[42]   In the same month Charles VII of France accompanied by René of Anjou and his brother Charles of Maine, took Rouen. The loss of English held lands resulted in public unrest. John Norreys was one of those against whom public and parliament's anger was vented.[43]

1450   His biographer thought that Norreys was lucky to emerge from the events of 1450 with his life, in view of what had befallen the Duke of Suffolk and Bishop Aiscough.[44]   In this year also, due to the death of Cicely Neville, the wife of Henry Beauchamp, Duke of Warwick, custody of Warwick's lands came to an end and Norreys was among others pardoned all arrears of accounts as guardians.[45]

ca.1450   Alice Merbrooke, Norreys' first wife died.

Marriage to Eleanor Clitheroe (by ca.1450 to ca.1456)

John Norreys was married to his second wife, Eleanor Clitheroe, before 1453-54 by which time she had a son by him.[46]   Eleanor was the daughter of Roger Clitheroe of Ash-by-Sandwich, Kent, by Maud Oldcastle, daughter of Sir John Oldcastle (Appendix C, Tree 3).[47] The latter, a Herefordshire knight had, by marriage to Joan, Lady Cobham, become a landowner in Kent.   Oldcastle became a leader of the Lollards, a religious movement. Henry V protected him but eventually he was executed in 1417.   Shakespeare's *Henry IV Part I* originally featured a Sir John Oldcastle but this was later changed to Sir John Falstaff.

The armorial glass at Ockwells was put up between 1450 and 1454 around the time of political unrest in England following the loss of Normandy in 1449 and Guyenne in 1451. Eleanor Clitheroe's family was based in Kent, a county which bore the brunt of unruly soldiers returning from France contributing to disaffection with the way England was being run.   It was from Kent that John Mortimer (later called Jack Cade) led the largest popular uprising of the fifteenth century, in June 1450, though no Clitheroes are mentioned in the long list of people, mostly from Kent, granted pardons afterwards.[48]

The son Norreys had with Eleanor, John the younger, would later marry Isabel Wyfold, the daughter of Margaret Chedworth, Norreys' third wife, by her first husband, Nicholas Wyfold (see Appendix C, Tree 1a).

---

[42] Berkshire Feet of Fines Pt II no 1398, p67. These were: friends John Pury*, Thomas Lavington, Thomas Bapham; and relatives William Catesby, Richard Merbrooke, William Norreys (his brother), Edmund Brudenell* (those represented at Ockwells are starred).

[43] For example, the poem *On The Popular Discontent At The Disasters In France* includes the line *"The Coundite (Norreys) rennyth not, as I wene"* (Wright vol 2, pp221-223).

[44] Clark 2020a, p674.

[45] Wedgwood and Holt, p622. See John Nanfan's biography for more detail of their business dealings with the Beauchamp family.

[46] See the section on the dating of the glass on page 105.

[47] Eleanor's parents are buried in St Nicholas' Church, Ash by Sandwich, Kent. The church guide mistakenly calls Maud's husband Richard. Richard Clitheroe, who in 1415 played a major part in transporting Henry V's army across the channel, was father of Roger, and Eleanor's other grandfather. In 1414 he, with Thomas Brooke, Lady Cobham's son-in-law, had control of those estates forfeited by Sir John Oldcastle that he held in right of his wife Joan, Lady Cobham. He held these until more than a year after Oldcastle's condemnation to death in 1417 (Woodger in Roskell et al, 1993).

[48] See CPR 1446-52, pp338-374.

Significant Career Events

1450 Collector of tunnage & poundage with John Pury. He continued to hold posts after 1450, when Suffolk was murdered, but hardly any after 1460 when Henry VI came under the control of the Yorkists.[49]

1451 John Norreys Esquire, with William and Roger Norreys (his brothers) and John Pury were founding members of the Guild of St. Andrew and St. Mary Magdalene, one purpose of which was the repair and maintenance of the bridge over the Thames: *"Thomas Mettyngham, chaplain of the said chantry , has now made petition that, as well for the establishment of the chantry and the maintenance of the bridge of Maydenhith over the Thames, whereby divers lieges of the king cannot pass without peril at certain times of the year through floods and the weakness of the bridge, the king should confirm the said writing and grant others to the said Thomas and to* **John Norys, esquire for the bod***y, John Pury, esquire, William Norys, Roger Norys, Thomas Babham and Henry Fraunceys:- the king hereby confirms the writing and grants license to the aforesaid to found a gild for themselves and others, men and women, in the said chapel, to find wax lights and other divine necessaries for the daily celebration of the masses of the chaplain; and grant that the members of the gild may elect wardens from year to year, and that the said chaplain and his successors be surveyors of the gild; and that the surveyor, wardens and members be capable of acquiring possessions and of pleading and being impleaded in any court, having a common seal and able to meet to make statutes; grant also that they may acquire lands, rents and possessions not held in chief to the value of 10 marks a year for the repair and maintenance of the bridge and other premises; grant also to them of pontage for ever, and of the whole water under the bridge and for 50 feet on either side thereof on either bank with the soil and fishery thereof."* (See Appendix A, No.1, p236)

The establishment of this Guild is regarded as initiating civic life in the town. Henry Fraunceys, another founder, had been one of Windsor's two MPs in the Parliament of 1449-50.[50] The Maidenhead Guild was founded the following year. Around this time one of Windsor's MPs had usually been a waterman and grants of pontage (tolls for the repair of bridges) had been collected by the bailiffs there since the fourteenth century.[51] Franceys' Windsor experience probably helped in the setting up the Guild.

The Maidenhead Guild was dissolved in 1547, as were similar fraternities, in the year the son of Henry VIII, Edward VI succeeded to the throne. In 1577, in the reign of Elizabeth I, the patent for establishing the Guild was exemplified by an Inspeximus, and in 1582 Maidenhead was granted its first Charter of Incorporation by the Queen.[52] The Borough's coat (above) shows a bridge flanked by SS Andrew & Mary Magdalene with the spurious crest of a maiden's head.

---

[49] It is said he was a man who successfully transferred his allegiance to Edward IV who rewarded him with posts but the John Norris who was esquire to that king and carried his corpse at his funeral was his son John the elder (see Wedgwood and Holt, p639).

[50] He was described as being *of Maidenhead* (Wedgwood, p133).

[51] VCH Berkshire, vol 3, p58.

[52] Gorham, p45. Both the 1577 Inspeximus and 1582 Charter are in Berkshire Record Office (M/IC1&M/IC2).

Until 2005 town councillors processed from the Guild (Town) Hall in Maidenhead to the present Borough Church for a service when the new Mayor was made. Traditionally leaders of the procession carried the bridge-master's staves, part of Maidenhead's civic regalia. A procession for the same reason once also took place in Abingdon. A plaque marks the location of the original church of SS Andrew & Mary Magdalene that was in the road, west of Chapel Arches Bridge in Maidenhead.

Impression of the Guild Chapel in the sixteenth century with Chapel Arches Bridge in the background (drawn by the late Michael Bayley)

Plaque marking the site of the former Chapel of SS Andrew & Mary Magdalene

The procession of councillors from the Town Hall (earlier the Guildhall) to the Borough Church took place for the mayor making ceremony until 2005 – note the use of the bridge master's staves

1453   Henry VI suffered a mental breakdown and although Norreys was kept on as a squire of the body he seems to have lost his privileged position in 1455 or 1456.[53] By this time Norreys was already married to Eleanor Clitheroe, his second wife. Ashmole recorded inscriptions in Yattendon Church that said Norreys rebuilt the church in "32 Henry VI" (i.e. 1453-54), putting up armorial achievements in its windows similar to those at Ockwells, viz: impaled coats for Norreys and his first wife Alice Merbrooke and second wife Eleanor Clitheroe. Figures representing Norreys, his two wives together with three sons and two daughters were once represented at the base of the east window (see Appendix A, No. 3).[54] The windows were glazed after the church was rebuilt and after Eleanor had given birth to a son.

1454   March: Norreys negotiated a marriage contract for his daughter Margaret to marry the son and heir of Robert Rademylde but the latter had changed his mind by March 1457 – either because Margaret had died or due to the lessening of Norreys' influence at court.[55] Margaret is not mentioned in her father's 1465 will so had probably died.

1455   Together with chaplains of St George's Chapel Windsor, Norreys granted a tenement in Peascod Street, Windsor to Richard Walgraue of Clewer; witnesses include the

[53] Clark 2020a, p675.

[54] Ashmole 850, f173.

[55] Clark 2020a, p673, & Clark 2020f, p296. Norreys only mentions daughters Anne and Lettice in his will of 1465 (see Appendix A, No. 2). College of Arms pedigrees make Anne a daughter of Alice Merbrooke and Lettice a daughter of Margaret Chedworth his third wife (Coll, Arms MS E12 f90 v & E8 f51). The only daughters mentioned in Margaret's will of 1490 are Katherine, married to John Bourchier, Lord Berners, her daughter by John Howard, Duke of Norfolk, and "Marney", who was left a chain of water flowers by her mother. Nicolas 1826 p404 note 2, suggests Marney may have also been her daughter by Howard. However, "Marney" was actually Margaret's daughter by her earlier marriage to Sir Nicholas Wyfold, Mayor of London. Named Elizabeth (Isabel), she married Sir Henry Marney KG as his second wife (Wedgwood and Holt, p575). Elizabeth's first husband was the son of John Norreys Esquire by his wife Eleanor. Interestingly, Margaret's will requests priests in the church at Stoke by Nayland to pray for John Norreys Esquire but not for Howard.

Mayor of Windsor, two bailiffs and others including Edmund Pury, probably a kinsman of John Pury.[56]

ca.1456/7 Eleanor Clitheroe is thought to have died by October 1457 as she is not mentioned in the will of her mother of that date.[57]

Marriage to Margaret Chedworth (by 1459 to 1466)

1458 Norreys' lordships of Cookham & Bray were granted to Henry Beaufort, third Duke of Somerset.

1459 Norreys was by now married to his third wife, Margaret Chedworth. They had a son, William.

ca.1459 John Norreys of Bray purchased the manor of Mapledurham Chazey from Robert Stanshawe. In 1460 Norreys, as lord of this manor, was fined for non-attendance at court. After Norreys died in 1466 he was succeeded at Chazey by John, second son of his first wife Alice Merbrooke.[58]

1459 On a Commission of Array in Berkshire with among others, Edward Langford, John Pury and Edmund Brudenell, to resist the rebellion of Richard, Duke of York, Richard Neville, Earl of Warwick, Richard Neville, Earl of Salisbury and Edmund Neville, Earl of Rutland. In 1459 Norreys, was appointed with others, including William Laken, whose armorial also occurs at Ockwells, to decide the fate of prisoners in the gaol at Windsor Castle indicating an involvement in Windsor affairs.[59]

1461 Edward IV seized the throne. Despite the new regime, in September Norreys won back his lease of the lordships of Cookham & Bray a month after his eldest son, Sir William, had been given the stewardship by Edward IV, but both were removed two months later by the new king. It is suggested this reversal may have been due to their links with John de Vere, Earl of Oxford, executed for treason in February 1462. William may have already been married to his daughter Jane.[60] Jane's mother was Elizabeth Howard who had inherited the bulk of the Howard estates from her grandfather, Sir John Howard (d.1436). Jane's kinsman, also John Howard, descended from Sir John's second wife, inherited little but administered these estates after the earls' execution.[61] This John Howard was knighted in 1461 by Edward, the future king, after the battle of Towton, and remained close to the new monarch. It has been suggested that Sir William gained acceptance at Edward IV's court perhaps by offering his services in a military capacity for the king's 'jorny' into Scotland at the close of 1462, and thereafter his rise in Edward's estimation was remarkable.[62] Both Sir William Norreys and Sir John Howard went with the king to Scotland[63] which would reinforce any relationship. Perhaps Howard's link to the Norreys

[56] St Georges Chapel Archives SGC XV.45.197. Chaplain Robert Cherbury, Robert Chamberlain (clerk of the chapel in 1453) and John Bythewode had also been involved with Norreys in a 1442 grant of a messuage in Peascod Street to John Seriaunt of Dorney (SGC XV.45.140).
[57] Clark 2020a, p673.
[58] Cooke, pp59, 76-77.
[59] CPR 1452-1461, p493 and p557.
[60] Clark 2020a, p675.
[61] Robinson, pp4-5.
[62] Clark 2020b, p680.
[63] Gairdner, p157 lists those who accompanied Edward IV. One of the two dukes who led the list was John 2nd Duke of Suffolk, son of William de la Pole, 1st Duke executed in 1450, whose armorial is at Ockwells.

family protected them and also helped ensure the armorial glass at Ockwells representing the previous king and queen, and Edmund Beaufort (a prominent Lancastrian killed at St Albans in 1455) was not destroyed. In May 1465 Howard sent his daughter Margaret to stay with Sir William and Jane.[64] At some point he would have met Margaret (née Chedworth), Sir William's stepmother, who by January 1467 would be his second wife.

1462 A Feet of Fines document shows that Norreys made provision for his young son William, by his third wife Margaret Chedworth. Most of the assets, including Ockholt manor, were held by John and Margaret and *their male heirs* with successive remainders to John's other male heirs. Only in the case of the manor of Purley and land in Purley and Theale was their son William listed after his earlier sons, with, in this case, John, his second son by his first wife, Alice Merbrooke to inherit after the death of John and Margaret.[65] William is not mentioned in the 1490 will of his mother[66] so was probably dead by then; after she died in 1494, Norreys' eldest son, Sir William inherited.

1465 Norreys wrote his will where he describes himself as *John Norreys, squyer of the parish of Bray*.[67] Whilst his executors were to have priests pray for him in the Yattendon parish church which he had rebuilt in 1453-4, his main provision for his soul was in St Michael's Church in Bray. His body was to be buried in the north aisle of St Michael's, called St Nicholas Chapel, leaving a bequest for the *newe making and edefying* of the chapel and for the making of a tomb and for a marble stone to immediately be laid over his body in the said chapel.[68]

Apart from many bequests for prayers for his soul, and the souls of his parents and wives, he also left money to make and gravel the road between Acroste Gate and Freith Lane (the latter, now Thrift Lane, is to the west of Ockwells); for the repair of Maidenhead Bridge, the responsibility of the guild he had helped found in 1451; and for the *full bilding and making up of the chapel with the chambres ajoynyng with'n my manoir of Okholt in the p'issh of Bray not yet finished*. His eldest son and heir, Sir William Norreys, inherited all his household effects in the manor house at Yattendon[69] and his other children, another William, two Johns, and two daughters Anne (*my eldest daughter*) and Lettice (*my youngest daughter*) also received bequests. He left his third wife Margaret Chedworth the residue of his estate if she lived alone; however, if she married again she would receive goods and chattels to the value of one thousand marks, terms that do not appear to have been adhered to.[70] His executors

---

[64] Clark 2020b, p681.

[65] Berkshire Feet of Fines Part II no 1440, pp78-79.

[66] Nicolas 1826, pp404-5. Lettice, her daughter by Norreys (see pedigree Coll of Arms E8 f51 & E12 f90 v) who was alive when he made his will in 1465 is also not mentioned in her 1490 will. Both William and Lettice are said to have died young (Ibid E12 f90 v).

[67] See Appendix A, No. 2, which includes a transcription of the will from Kerry.

[68] His tomb is long gone. However, the edification, including two stone plaques of the Norreys coat with supporters built into the east wall of what is now called the Norreys Chapel, as well as stone corbels bearing the impaled coats of his second and third wives are extant. Probably the first wife's coat was originally also there. Recent moving of the organ into the chapel has somewhat obscured the impaled coat of the third wife, Margaret Chedworth.

[69] It is suggested that his late mother's inheritance at Yattendon, Berkshire along with her lands at Codbarrow in Warwickshire, had already been transferred to him (Clark 2020b, p680). Certainly, neither Yattendon nor Codbarrow are listed in 1462 among the assets of his father, John Norreys and Margaret his third wife (Berkshire Feet of Fines Part II no 1440, pp78-79), nor are they mentioned in the Inquisition Post Mortem of John Norreys Esquire (see Appendix A, No.7, p253).

[70] Within four months of Norreys' death his wife was remarried and living in Bray and, despite Norreys' will, appears to have held onto many of his estates. By 1473 his eldest son, Sir William Norreys, by then married to his second wife, Isabel Ingoldisthorpe, widow of John Neville, Marquis Montacute, was in financial trouble and had to appeal to Isabel's mother, Joan (née Tiptoft), to enable them to pay their debts (Clarke K L, p355). In later life he was more financially secure. Isabel's inheritance, after her death in 1476, was held by Sir William until his own death in 1507 (CPR 1494-1509, p553).

were his wife Margaret, his brother William Norreys, Richard Bulstrode, his nephew, son of William Bulstrode, and Thomas Babham. The supervisor of his will was John, Lord Wenlock, who was given for his labour a gilt cup called *the housewif.*

The Norreys Chapel of St Michael's Church, Bray

1466 Norreys died in September. His estates included holdings from William Wayneflete, Bishop of Winchester; the Abbots of Abingdon and Reading; and Elizabeth Woodville, queen of Edward IV.[71] By 22nd January 1467 his third wife, Margaret Chedworth had already been married to Sir John Howard (later Duke of Norfolk). On this date a long list was drawn up that detailed what must have been wedding gifts to Howard's new wife including jewels, furs, gowns and many other items including a gold collar with thirty-four roses and suns (the Yorkist badges). They lived in Bray, probably at Ockwells, for the list says *"Item, my master left at London (at his departing for Bray) in his place in Bath Row, the 20th day of February, two broad cloths of blue. Item, the seventh year of King Edward IV and the 16th day of March, my master sent to my Lady to Bray a long cushion of crimson velvet and three short cushions of crimson velvet".*[72]

Margaret, Countess of Norfolk, in her will made in May 1490 and proved in December 1494, left a bequest for priests to sing in the church of Stoke for three years for her soul and that of her husband John Norreys Esquire.[73] John Howard, Duke of Norfolk, was not mentioned.

1507 Sir William Norreys, eldest son of John Norreys Esquire, died seized of Ockwells.[74]

A later section gives more details of what happened to the Norreys Family after the death of John Norreys Esquire.

---

[71] See Appendix A, No. 7.
[72] Paston Letters (ed. Warrington) 1924, revised 1956, pp37-38.
[73] Darby 1909, pp246-7, Nicolas 1826 p404.
[74] Kerry, p114.

4. Ockwells in the C15th

John Norreys built the manor house and put up the spectacular armorial glass in the period between 1450 and 1454. This was during his marriage to his second wife, Eleanor Clitheroe, whose fortune is said to have helped pay for it.[1] The land was still farmed and a tithe barn was provided to store the harvested crops. He built what is regarded as one of the best-preserved and least-altered houses of mid fifteenth-century England.[2]

The east front of Ockwells Manor house in Elizabethan times as depicted by Joseph Nash in 1839 (but note that the window over the porch was blocked by 1815 and the gable and wing on the right were lost by 1832)

The manor house was built of brick and timber and probably used bricks from the brickworks, said to be in Slough, established by 1442, to make bricks for building Eton College, founded by Henry VI.[3] The man who played a leading role in building the college

[1] Emery p124.

[2] Emery p20, who also gives a good description of the structure of the house (Ibid p124-130, and Long pp28-36).

[3] Between 1442 and 1444 one and a half million bricks were delivered to the college (Goodall 2002 p250). Emery p21 considers the extensive use of brick at Eton between 1441 and 1449 informed the development of Ockwells and the Hospital of the Guild of the Holy Cross at Abingdon, all in association with timber framing. Norreys and William de la Pole, then Earl of Suffolk, were both members of the Guild of the Holy

was William de la Pole, then Earl of Suffolk, whose family in Kingston upon Hull had, in the fourteenth century, owned a tilery for the manufacture of bricks there.[4] Eton was still being built when in March 1448 the king decided on a new set of collegiate buildings[5] – plans that gradually went awry, undoubtedly affected by Suffolk's murder in May 1450. In 1450 Norreys' main seat was at Yattendon. Perhaps the hiatus of building at Eton encouraged Norreys to use the available bricks and workmen to build Ockwells, easily accessible from Windsor, which may have functioned as a hunting lodge for entertaining friends and patrons. Eton is also thought to have given him the idea for his house, built around a small courtyard with corridors connecting the rooms on two storeys.[6]

Ockwells is most famous for its armorial glass. Its quality suggests it was made by John Prudde, appointed King's Glazier to Henry VI in 1440.[7] Prudde billed for glazing Eton College windows in 1445-6 and 1450[8] and his indenture for glazing the memorial chapel of Richard Beauchamp, Earl of Warwick, in St Mary's Church, Warwick, was dated 1447.[9] Norreys was involved in managing the estates of the dead earl on behalf of Warwick's wife, Isabel Despencer, during the minority of Henry, their son & heir. He was also a donor to Eton College with a close relationship with Suffolk. He would have been well placed to liaise with Prudde regarding the glazing of his great hall in between 1450 and 1454. Norreys would appear to have had some experience in managing building projects as in 1443, as John *Norys of Bray Esq*, he was paid 100 marks yearly for the repair of *Wyndesor* Castle and the lodge in *Wyndesor* Park.[10]

By 1450 his career was at a peak but the recent loss of Normandy had caused him and others to be blamed by both the public and parliament. His friend William de la Pole, by then Duke of Suffolk, had paid for the loss with his life in May of that year. Ockwells, built 1450-1454, would give him a base closer to the court in Windsor and to the king and queen.

The armorial scheme he put up represented his patrons, friends and relatives still living and commemorated his first wife Alice Merbrooke; Henry Beauchamp, Duke of Warwick; and also Suffolk, his friend and colleague. Themes in the scheme will be described later but the most important theme relates to the marriage of Henry VI and Margaret of Anjou, the French king's niece. Suffolk's armorial, placed between those of the king and queen, acknowledges his role in arranging the marriage that was supposed to lead to peace with France but which ended in disaster for England. Perhaps Norreys also wanted to commemorate Suffolk's sacrifice in the aid of peace.

Cross that built the Long Alley Almshouses in Abingdon in 1446/7. More similar to Ockwells are the Ewelme almshouses founded by Suffolk and his wife, a building that features brick, timber framing, and foliated bargeboards. Its statutes were written ca.1448-50 (Goodall 2001 pxiv).

[4] VCH History of York East Riding p233. In 1324 his great grandfather, also William, and brother Richard, as Chamberlains, claimed expenses relating to either a new brickyard or an extension to an existing one (Brooks p156). In 1327 a charter authorised burgesses to build the town walls with brick and work probably began on the gates (the brick foundations of Beverley Gate are extant). In 1331 William (d.1366) became the first mayor of Hull and in 1341 work began on replacing its timber walls with bricks (see Taylor, 2017). The brickworks established in Hull ca.1303 are among the earliest recorded (Los & Los p82).

[5] Goodall 2002 p252, who notes that the western range of the college quadrangle (of brick) was not completed until the early C16th (Ibid p254)

[6] Hussey, III, p136, and Emery p129.

[7] Myers, p201, and Marks 2004, who note the presence of *jewelling*, insertion of small pieces of glass to resemble jewels, a technique requiring expertise. The moue on the mouth of the boy that forms the crest of Edward Langford is also characteristic of Prudde (pers. comm. Richard Marks).

[8] Marks, p49.

[9] Britton, p11; Marks 2004. Extant stained-glass figures in St Mary's, Warwick, show extensive use of *jewelling*.

[10] CPR 1441-1446, p151.

This is what Norreys built:

The Outer Court

The outer court originally consisted of:

- East side: the tithe barn (the dovecote is a later addition).
- South side: the chapel (now ruined) and a gateway[11] with a room above, thought to be the priest's room[12] and stables.
- North side: farm buildings (now lost) and a brick curtain wall with loop holes.
- West side: the manor house built round a small courtyard.

The Manor house and Outer Court as it is in the twenty-first century (from Google Earth, March 2017); buildings east of the outer court are later

The east (dovecote and tithe barn) and south (stables) sides of the outer court

---

[11] It is unclear how the gateway was accessed. The earliest maps such Rocque's of 1761 and Thomas Pride's of 1790 show the road system as now, with Ockwells Road (formerly Kimbers Lane) to the north of the house and Thrift Road to the west.
[12] VCH Berkshire, vol 3, p96.

The roof timbers of the tithe barn seem to be original as does the timber of the roofs of the two doorways on the west front of the barn. However, the doors have been replaced in the recent past and the windows at each end of the barn were put in by Sir Edward Barry (according to drawings in his sketchbook)

The chapel wall – all that remains of the chapel – is of brick and stone in contrast to the brick and timber of the manor house with stone used for windows and doorways.[13] When Norreys wrote his will in 1465, the chapel that projects from the southeast corner of the house was *not yet finished*.[14] The Norreys armorials carved into the spandrels of both doorways into the chapel suggest it was eventually completed. The presence of dressed stone and the diamond pattern of dark brick headers point to a slightly later date of construction.[15]

---

[13] The windows vary in size and are now largely blocked with brick; the window with two lights is said to be identical to similar windows in the cloister at Eton (Hussey, I, p58). The Eton window is more elaborate and much better preserved.

[14] See will, Appendix A, No. 2.

[15] Emery, p127.

Top: Remains of the chapel wall on south side of outer court.
Above left: priest's room above gateway
Above right: east doorway of stone and brick, with beaver supporters in spandrels

Bottom right: detail in spandrel over west door at the far end of the wall showing a beaver supporter and Norreys coat impaling a blank coat presumably planned for his third wife Margaret Chedworth

The remains of a fortified wall on the north side of the outer court are thought to be part of a curtain wall that shut in the forecourt immediately before the house.[16] On the 1875 O.S. plan this wall is shown connecting with a wall running north south from Ockwells Road to the gatehouse on the south side of the outer court.[17] The 1889 Sale Catalogue refers to stout brick walls on the north east side and partly on the north side that enclosed the forecourt of the house.

Fortified wall – all that remains of the original north side of the outer court with a close up of one of the loop holes/arrow slits. Soot can be seen around the rim, perhaps from the fire reported in the eighteenth century

Most of this wall seems to have been taken down when the current driveway from Ockwells Road was built by Sir Edward Barry.[18] A remnant of it survives in front of the east side of the manor house. It seems likely that the west end of the *loop-holed* fortified wall connected with a wing or range that projected from the north eastern corner of the house attached to a two-storey gable, though it has also been suggested that it was the outer wall of the range.[19] The gable and wing, presumably part of the original construction, were taken down by 1832.[20] This may have been due to fire damage as a fire was reported in the eighteenth century.[21] Farm buildings, which also formed part of the north side of the outer court, were lost in the twentieth century.

---

[16] Hussey, I, pp52 & 56.
[17] See Appendix D.
[18] Ibid.
[19] Emery, p127 says that the ground plan suggests a lodgings range. Unlikely as the wall is fortified.
[20] See Appendix F for drawings and discussion of this missing gable and wing.
[21] *Gentleman's Magazine* 1798 vol LXVIII pt II, p1008. Wooden slats at the east end of the wing suggest fire damage; see Appendix F.

The Manor House

The main entrance to the house is, as originally, through an entrance porch on the east front. Within the porch, on the left, is a door leading to the porter's lodge, whilst on the right there was once a seat, perhaps for people to wait who had business there.

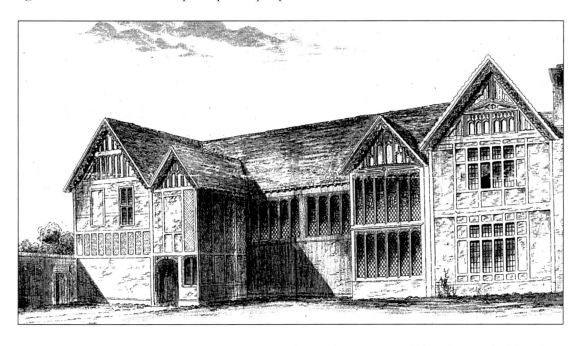

Lysons' view of the east front, 1806, showing the house almost as it would have been in the fifteenth century. Original features include foliated bargeboards, panelled gables, and herringbone brickwork on the side of the porch. The porch entrance was widened in the nineteenth century. The windows of the great hall between the gables are original, but probably not many of the other main windows

Early photo (ca.1885) of porch taken prior to the Victorian restoration (copyright: HEA)

The seat and adjacent side wall were lost during the nineteenth century "restoration". Both the porch doorway and the door into the house have carvings in the spandrels.

Norreys showed his allegiance to his king by depicting the supporter of Henry VI, *the heraldic antelope – collared & chained* – in the left spandrel over the porch entrance with *a wyvern* in the right one. Any significance of the *wyvern* or the *dragon* and *winged lion* badge of St Mark, found over the doorway into the house has yet to be discovered.

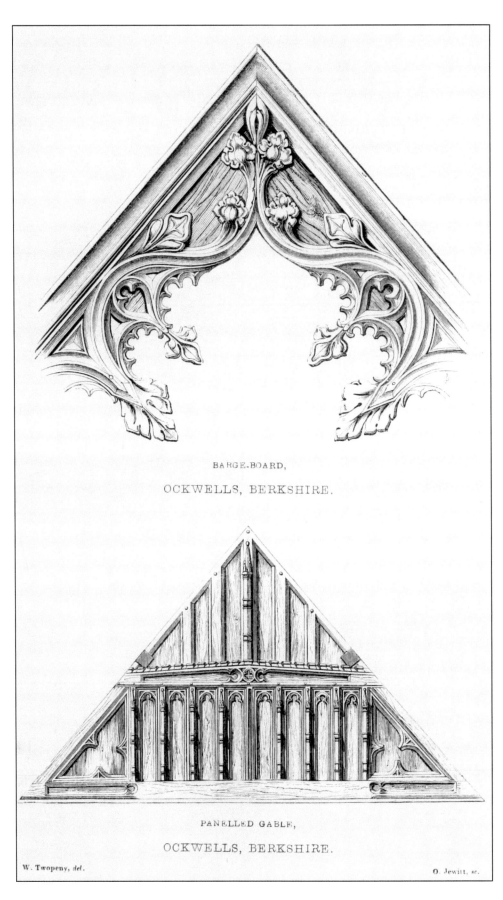

BARGE-BOARD,

OCKWELLS, BERKSHIRE.

PANELLED GABLE,

OCKWELLS, BERKSHIRE.

W. Twopeny, del.

O. Jewitt, sc.

The bargeboards and panelled gables at Ockwells drawn by William Twopeny
and published by Parker in 1859

A romanticised view of the porch and south corridor in Elizabethan times as depicted by Joseph Nash in his 1839 publication. It is unclear whether he actually saw the house. Photos in the Country Life edition of 1924 show there were once tiles on the floor, as shown in Nash's drawing. However, the courtyard lights here are shown as unglazed though they were reported as glazed in 1880 by which time Ockwells had been tenanted for many years. Tenants do not usually pay for alterations, so the lights may have been glazed originally

31

Carvings over the porch entrance. Left: heraldic antelope – collared & chained (a supporter of Henry IV & Henry V, though the collar is usually a crown); right, a dragon

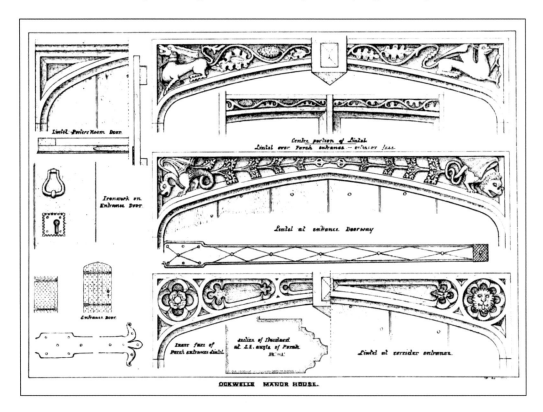

Drawings of the carvings over the porch and door into the house showing on the lintel of the porch entrance; heraldic antelope and dragon; and in the entrance doorway: wyvern and winged lion of St Mark (W. Peart 1879; copyright: RIBA Drawings Collection)

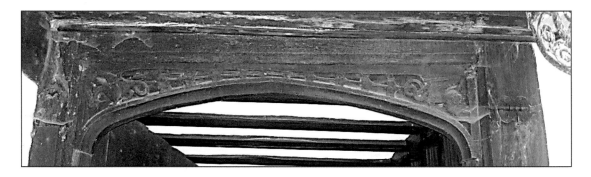

Carvings in spandrels over door entrance. Left: wyvern; right: winged lion badge of St Mark

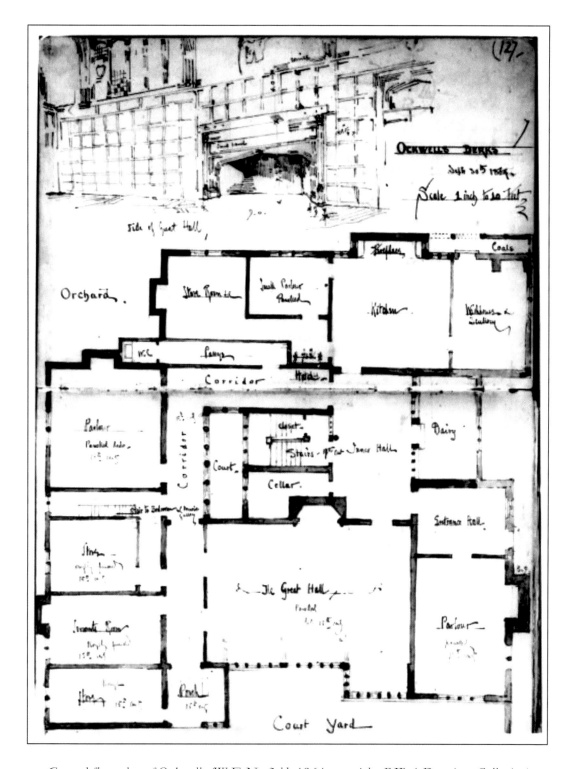

Ground floor plan of Ockwells (W E Nesfield, 1864; copyright: RIBA Drawings Collection)

This is the earliest known floor plan (above) and gives the best indication of the original distribution of the ground floor rooms and the great hall around the inner courtyard, with corridors connecting the ground floor rooms. The rough finish on walls of rooms near to the porch suggest these were originally for use by the porter and other servants whilst other rooms, with later panelling, would be used by the family. However, the plans shows that there had already been alterations including a stair being inserted into most of the inner courtyard, and the north side of the house (to the right) altered to make an entrance hall with the addition of a lean-to dairy. On the west side (top) where, next to the kitchen, the pantry & buttery were originally, walls had been realigned to create a passage to a water closet, with others forming a store-room and a small parlour.

The main entrance leads into a south corridor with the great hall on the right. The house then, as now, was built round a small courtyard with a corridor on both floors connecting rooms on three sides with the great hall on the fourth and east side. An original straight flight of steps connects the floors on the south front, and it is thought a similar stair was once on the north front.[22] The magnificent key to the door is still fixed to its inner side.

Left: The doorway into the house, leading to the screen passage. The stone flags on the floor postdate 1924 when photos published in Country Life showed tiles

Below left: The lock of the heavy oak door

Below right: The key fixed to the back of the door

[22] Hussey, III, p137.

A second massive door at the end of the screen passage could close off access from the great hall to the rest of the house. This would be useful as it would prevent retainers who were accessing the great hall, whether for business or pleasure, from wandering into any of the other rooms.

Entrance into the south corridor: at the left, the inner door; at the extreme right the second entrance through the screen to the great hall. Note the windows overlooking the inner courtyard behind the seating

Stairs to the upper storey. (nb: There is no evidence of a similar stair on the north side of the house on the 1864 floor plan above)

35

The domestic services, kitchen, pantry & buttery were on the west side of the inner court from where servants could go northwards to deliver food to the high table on a dais in the great hall[23] and southwards, through the opened inner door, to serve those *below the salt* at the extant refectory table. The original buttery hatch from which food was collected is still there. Many of the chimneypieces have been replaced, only the hall chimneypiece is definitely original.[24]

Corridor on the west side of the quad with buttery hatch up and down; the pantry & buttery, were once on this side of the corridor. Originally two rooms, now a single room, the ceiling of which has needed the recent support of a Samson pillar

The north side of the house has been much modified. This side had the kitchen and also the withdrawing room where Norreys and his family would have retired to, away from the hustle and bustle of the great hall. Despite the modifications that occurred at different times over the centuries, the north corridor with access to the courtyard is still recognisable as are these two rooms.

Also accessed from the north corridor is the cellar which appears, from the floor plan above, to run underneath the inner courtyard though how it was entered is unclear. In modern times, a trap door in the floor of the corridor allowed entry.

---

[23] It is difficult to believe that the kitchen was formerly the whole height of the house (eg VCH Berkshire, vol 3, p95) as there seems always to have been a bedroom over it, its fireplace sharing the kitchen's chimney stack (see floor plans in Appendix G). Evidence for a dais, now lost, is the raised floor in the bay and difference in floor level between hall and north front (see VCH Berkshire, vol 3, p94).

[24] Many appear to have been replaced in the C16th. The brick fireplace of the old kitchen, possibly original, is topped with a massive polished wooden mantelpiece of unknown age. When owned by Sir Edward Barry the old kitchen had a vast stone fireplace (Wentworth Day, p238).

The north corridor with door to the courtyard, the flanking windows are probably later. The door on the right led to the kitchen

The timber courtyard showing the uncusped arched lights of the windows

Given the age of the house, unsurprisingly, major changes have been made over the years, including a nineteenth century extension projecting from the west front, now demolished, and another in the twentieth century from the north front, still extant. The Jacobean staircase, put in the central courtyard when the main entrance was created in the north front, has been moved twice; and the little lean-to room on the southwest corner originally began life as a means of providing an internal lavatory. Subsequent chapters will tell the story of these changes and the owners who made them happen.

The Great Hall

The great hall has been described as one of the finest domestic interiors of its date in England.[25] It is a resplendent medieval hall with many original features including a plain screen with minstrels' gallery above; an oak braced collar roof with curved wind braces; a stone chimneypiece and an oak table thought to be as old as the house.

The great hall in Elizabethan times as depicted by Joseph Nash in 1839. Nash drew non-existent armorial glass in the lower lights in the oriel and omitted the ceiling then in place in the great hall

[25] Tyack, Bradley & Pevsner, p414.

The great hall is the jewel in the crown of Ockwells. It is easy to imagine Norreys and his family dining at a table, possibly on a dais, at the north end of the hall, whilst his retainers sit at the long refectory table in the body of the hall that is still there.

The great hall, looking north, with the original refectory table and fireplace and later wood panelling

The great hall looking south, showing the screen and minstrels' gallery above

The arched collar braced oak timbers in the great hall

The timber roof is one of the glories of Ockwells – as well as being its potential sword of Damocles. It is very heavy, the weight being taken by the timber supports in the walls. In Victorian times it was feared its weight would bring down the walls and so destroy the magnificent armorial glass.

The stone chimneypiece is of the mid-fifteenth century with a brick fireplace. In earlier centuries the fireplace would be in the centre of the hall with all the problems associated with that location such as smoke. A modern development, when Ockwells was built, saw the fireplace moved to the side of the hall with a chimney to take smoke away. It would be interesting to find out where the stone for the chimneypiece came from. With Norreys' contacts abroad the stone could have come from France.

A later addition, scratched in the spandrels, is said to be the *rose en soleil* badge of Edward IV who seized the throne in 1461. Sir John Howard married Margaret, Norreys' third wife, by 1467 and owed much to Edward IV. This badge occurs on the font he installed at St Mary's Church, Stoke by Nayland, which he completed. Perhaps he added it at Ockwells.

Fifteenth-century Chimneypiece with, inset, the rose en soleil badge, of Edward IV

The oak refectory table has always been in the hall. Because of its great length, well over half the length of the hall, it cannot be removed or for that matter brought in. It has been suggested the table was put together in the hall[26] and may have been part of the original scaffolding when the house was built. The top consists of two very large planks about two inches thick, side by side, supported on a framed trestle with eight pairs of turned legs and rectangular stretchers; the bun feet have been renewed. Its dimensions are: length 23ft 8 ins; width 23 ins; height 32 ins.[27] The hall is 41ft long and 24ft wide.[28] It is very likely that the oak for the table came from Windsor Forest, as did, many centuries later, the present floor. Benches similar to those in the great hall today would have been in use in the fifteenth century for retainers to sit on when they feasted in the hall.

---

[26] Wentworth Day, p227.
[27] Mann 1939, Inventory, p5, now in the Royal Armouries Record 6850.
[28] VCH Berkshire, vol 3, p94; Hussey, II, p92 has 40ft.

The refectory dining table in the great hall

HALL AT OCKWELLS, BERKSHIRE.

1847 Sketch of the interior of the great hall, published by Charles Knight

Above all, however, Ockwells is mostly famous for a magnificent set of armorial glass.

The Armorial Glass

The survival of the Ockwells armorial glass is a testament to the care taken by past owners. The achievements are still mostly in their original position in the windows of the great hall, despite being taken out in the Victorian period. The illustration of the great hall published by Charles Knight before their removal (see above), where the achievements are recognisable, presumably helped when the glass was replaced. Only those in the side of the oriel became mixed up.

The oriel features the armorial achievements of Henry VI and his queen, Margaret of Anjou, together with lords temporal & spiritual, whilst the east wall has achievements for John Norreys Esquire and his first two wives and their associates – making a total of nineteen lights though the armorial achievement in one light has been lost.

Panoramic view of the armorial glass in the great hall

Most of the shields at Ockwells are slightly bowed with a curved notch on the dexter (left as viewed) side to represent where the lance would pass through, thus *á bouche*. However, the shields of the king and queen and those of the ecclesiastics are heater shaped, named for the resemblance to a flat iron, the latter shape being better able to bear crests of crown and mitre. These latter shields do not have mantling. Only the achievements of Henry VI, Margaret of Anjou, and the two for Norreys and his wives have supporters. Norreys' motto *Ffeythfully serve* occurs in all lights except those of Henry VI and Margaret of Anjou which have their own mottos – *Dieu et mon droit* for the king and *Humble et loiall* for the queen. Quarries in all lights have the Norreys badge of three golden distaffs.[29]

---

[29] Hussey, II, p94 suggests it is also the badge of the Wardrobe. Norreys was Keeper of the King's Wardrobe in 1444-1446. He also suggests the motto *Feythfully serve* has the same origin.

The Individual Lights

The sketch below shows the layout of the armorial glass and is followed by a list of those represented in the various lights.

Sketch showing the position of individual armorial achievements in the Great Hall

1. HENRY BEAUCHAMP (1425-1446)	Duke of Warwick 1445 impaled with coat of his wife Cicely Neville.
2. EDMUND BEAUFORT (1406-1455)	Duke of Somerset 1448. Constable of England 1450.
3. MARGARET OF ANJOU (1429-1482)	Queen of England from 1445-1461 & 1470-1471.
4. WILLIAM DE LA POLE (1396-1450)	Duke of Suffolk 1448. Quartered with the coat of his wife, Alice Chaucer.
5. HENRY VI (1421-1471)	King of England 1422-1461 & 1470-1471.
6. JAMES BUTLER (ca.1390-1452)	4th Earl of Ormond in Ireland.
7. ABBEY OF ABINGDON	Abbot William Ashendon 1435- 1467. Originally light no.8.
7a. Missing - probably the ABBEY OF READING	Abbot Thomas Henley 1430-1445. Abbot John Thorne 1446-1486.
8. RICHARD BEAUCHAMP (d.1481)	Bishop of Salisbury 1450. Chaplain of the Order of the Garter 1452, then Chancellor 1475.
9. JOHN NORREYS (1405-1466)	Impaled with coat of his 2nd wife, Eleanor Clitheroe
10. JOHN WENLOCK (1400-1471)	Of Someries, Bedfordshire; Lord Wenlock 1461.
11. WILLIAM LAKEN (d. 1475)	Justice of the King's Bench.
12. HUGH MORTIMER (d.1460)	Of Cure Wyard & Martley, Worcs.; and Tedstone Wafre, Herefordshire; Esquire in 1434; Knight by 1449.
13. JOHN NANFAN (1400-1462)	Of Birtsmorton, Worcs., and Trethewall, Cornwall. Esquire of the Body 1447-54, 1457-?
14. JOHN NORREYS (1405-1466)	Impaled with coat of his 1st wife, Alice Merbrooke.
15. EDWARD LANGFORD (1417-1474)	Of Bradfield, Berks; Esquire of the Body 1443-1452
16. EDMUND BRUDENELL (d.1469)	Of Amersham, Bucks; half-brother of William Bulstrode, who was brother-in-law of John Norreys.
17. JOHN PURY (1415-1484)	Of Chamberhouse in Thatcham, Berks; Esquire by 1448.
18. WILLIAM BULSTRODE (d. after 1479)	Of Upton, Bucks; brother-in-law of John Norreys.

The Armorial Glass Scheme and its Inspiration

Even before the fifteenth century wealthy men put up displays of armorial glass to record those they wished to commemorate. Norreys would have been familiar with such a display put up by Sir William Trussell in the collegiate church he founded in 1337 at Shottesbrooke, not far from Ockwells, commemorating his king, Edward III, and lords who fought with him in Scotland.[30]

Norreys may have been inspired by the scheme put up by the Anglo-Irish Lord, James Butler, fourth Earl of Ormond, in what seems to have been a hospitium associated with the nearby Greyfriars Priory in Aylesbury (now called the King's Head, a National Trust property). The battered remnant of this armorial glass includes the coat of Margaret of Anjou and probably others that also occur in the oriel window at Ockwells and was most likely put up ca.1445-1449 when Butler was in England.[31]

Norreys knew him since both attended the coronation of Henry VI in Paris in 1430 and would have met him again at court when Butler was in England. The earl's armorial occurs in the oriel at Ockwells.

Evidence indicates that the great hall was glazed between 1450 and 1454 when certain of those represented were already dead. John Norreys Esquire had a clear scheme for glazing his great hall. In the main oriel window he placed armorials for his patrons, the king and queen, together with certain lords. Ecclesiastics he knew are represented in the side window. On the east wall of the great hall he put up two sets of lights: one set begins with his armorial impaled with that of his second wife together with armorials for men who were not local, some with links to this wife; and the second set begins with his armorial impaled with that of his first wife and includes armorials for local men including relatives based in Berkshire and Buckinghamshire.

The Main Oriel Window – Patrons & Lords (*Lights 1-6*)

As will be explained below, an important element of the armorial scheme that Norreys put up, commemorates those involved in the diplomacy related to the marriage of Henry VI, King of England, to Margaret of Anjou, niece of Charles VII, King of France – a marriage that was supposed to lead to a peace agreement and bring to an end the long running Hundred Years War between England and France. The failure of subsequent peace negotiations and loss, beginning in 1449, of English held lands in France, led to unrest in England that resulted in 1450 in the head of the English Embassy, William de la Pole, Duke of Suffolk, paying with his life. As a memorial to the duke, Norreys purposely placed his armorial achievement between those of the king and queen symbolising his role in negotiating the marriage including acting a proxy for the king in the 1444 betrothal ceremony in Tours, France.

Also represented in the oriel window of the great hall are Henry Beauchamp, Duke of Warwick, Edmund Beaufort (then Marquess of Dorset) and James Butler, fourth Earl of Ormond, who, with other lords and in addition to Suffolk, greeted the French embassy that arrived in England in July 1445.[32]

Another theme demonstrated in the oriel is the Beauchamp connection. Norreys had been involved in managing the estates Henry's father, Richard Beauchamp, Earl of Warwick

---

[30] Darracott 2014, p3.
[31] More details of the Aylesbury scheme are given in Butler's biography (Light 6).
[32] See Stevenson I, pp153-159.

(d.1439), on behalf of his wife Isabel Despenser, during the minority of Henry, his son & heir. In 1450 custody of Warwick's lands came to an end and Norreys was among others pardoned all arrears of accounts as guardians.

The oriel has armorials for Henry Beauchamp (Light 1) and in the side window Richard Beauchamp, Bishop of Salisbury (Light 8), a distant relative; in addition, the wives of both Beaufort (Light 2) and Butler (Light 6) were Beauchamps. Norreys, in the glazing of the oriel, may also have been commemorating his association with the family which had come to an end in 1450.

Side of the Oriel Bay – Ecclesiastics (*Lights 7, 7a & 8*)

One of the three original armorials is missing. The missing one is probably for the Abbey of Reading; extant is the coat of the Abbey of Abingdon. Norreys had held land from both Abbeys and was involved in local guilds at both places. Bishop Richard Beauchamp's armorial was originally in position 7 (see sketch). He was King's chaplain by 1448, Bishop of Salisbury in 1450 and from 1452 chaplain of the Order of the Garter based in St George's Chapel, Windsor Castle. Ockwells fell within the diocese of this bishop. Norreys would have met

him at court, in connection with his business with the chapel and probably through his involvement with the Beauchamp of Warwick's affairs.

East Wall of Great Hall (*Lights 9 to 13*)
Closest to the oriel is the impaled coat of Norreys and his second wife, Eleanor Clitheroe (Light 9). Her family was based in Kent but through her grandfather, Sir John Oldcastle (ex.1417), she had connections with Herefordshire where offspring from his first wife lived. Eleanor's uncle, Henry Oldcastle, lived not far from where Sir Hugh Mortimer (Light 12) had a base. Norreys would have included John Nanfan (Light 13) in his scheme because, like Norreys, he was a retainer of the Earl of Warwick. However, Nanfan also had a link with Eleanor's family, having purchased Birtsmorton Court, Worcestershire, in 1424-5 from the widow of Richard Oldcastle, a cousin of Sir John.

Mortimer also had land in Worcestershire. William Laken (Light 11) was from Shropshire but worked in Kent as a lawyer before moving to Clewer, Berkshire by 1455. Apart from the armorial for John Wenlock, included because of his involvement in the 1444 betrothal of Margaret of Anjou and the escort to England the following year, all the other men represented had some link to the Clitheroe family.

(*Lights 14-18*)
The impaled coat of Norreys and his first wife Alice Merbrooke (Light 14) is followed by armorials for local men from Berkshire and Buckinghamshire. Edward Langford (Light 15) and John Pury (Light 17) were both based in West Berkshire not far from Yattendon held by Norreys from his marriage to Alice. William Bulstrode (Light 18) was Norreys brother-in-law, being married to his sister Agnes. Edmund Brudenell (Light 16) was Bulstrode's half-brother. Both lived in Buckinghamshire.

Summary of Norreys' scheme - four themes:

1) **A commemoration of the marriage of Henry VI & Margaret of Anjou** – a failed attempt to reach peace with France - recording some of those:
    - who were involved in the negotiations which culminated in the betrothal (May 1444) and marriage(April 1445);
    - who helped escort Margaret to England in 1445;
    - and who greeted the French embassy which came over in July 1445.
2) **A Beauchamp connection** – members of the Beauchamp family, their relatives and retainers; Norreys helped manage the estates of Richard Beauchamp, Earl of Warwick (d.1439), Beauchamp's wife Isabel Despenser (d.1439) and their son Henry, Duke of Warwick (d.1446).
3) **Abingdon connection** – Norreys had dealings with the Abbey and St Helen's Church, Abingdon, also probably a **Reading connection** with the Abbey there.
4) **Local Men** from **Berks** and **Bucks**, including his brother-in-law, linked with his first wife: and men from **Kent, Herefordshire & Worcestershire,** with his second wife.

Heraldic Description and Brief Biographies of those Represented in the Glass

The nineteen lights in the armorial glass of the great hall depict the armorial bearings of prominent people who all had some connection with John Norreys. This section describes in more detail their armorial bearings, key aspects of their lives and the nature of their connection with John Norreys. An understanding of this is desirable in order to fully appreciate the reasoning behind the layout of the glass and what inspired it. The following sources provide further biographic detail for some of the personalities represented in the armorial glass: the *Oxford Dictionary of Biography (ODNB)*; the *Complete Peerage (GEC);* and the *History of Parliament – Biographies of the members of the Commons House 1439-1509* published in 2020 by the History of Parliament Trust.

1. HENRY BEAUCHAMP (1425-1446)
6th Earl of Warwick 1439; Premier Earl of England 1444; Duke of Warwick 1445.

Son of Richard Beauchamp, Earl of Warwick (d.1439), and his second wife, Isabel Despenser. (d.1439). Married to Cicely Neville, daughter of Richard Neville, Earl of Salisbury, and his wife, Alice Montacute, who lived at Bisham Abbey not far from Ockwells.[33]

Armorial Achievement

Crest
Five columbines erect azure leaved and slipped or the personal crest of the Duke of Warwick.[34]

Blazon
Quarterly:
> 1. *Gules, a fess between 6 cross crosslets or*; for Beauchamp.
> 2. *Or, three chevrons gules*; for Clare.
> 3. *Checky or and azure, a chevron ermine*; for Newburgh.
> 4. *Quarterly argent and gules, a bend sable between two frets or*; for Despenser.

Impaling Quarterly:
> 1 & 4: *Argent, three fusils conjoined in fess gules*; for Montacute.
> 2 & 3: *Or, an eagle displayed vert*; for Monthermer.

Overall an ineschutcheon:
> *Gules, a saltire argent*; for Neville (missing the label *gobony argent and azure*).

The armorial achievement bears the impalement and an escutcheon for his wife, Cicely Neville.[35] When the armorial glass was put up Henry was dead, bringing the Beauchamp earls of Warwick line to an end. Cicely died in 1450 so this achievement probably commemorates both of them.

---

[33] Alice was the daughter and heir of the famous Thomas Montacute, Earl of Salisbury, by his first wife Eleanor Holland. He was shot in the face at the siege of Orleans in 1428, dying shortly after. The Montacutes had held the manor of Bisham since the C14th, founding a priory there in 1337. Bisham Abbey, currently owned by Sport England, still has in the manor house armorial glass for the founder of the priory, William Montacute, Earl of Salisbury (d.1344) and his wife Katherine Grandison and another for Richard Neville, Earl of Salisbury (d.1460), in right of his wife Alice Montacute – her coat taking precedence (illustrated in Darracott 2015, pp17-18).

[34] Everard Green, p326.

[35] Everard Green, p325 says the shield is much broken and that the impalement is modern but gives no source. See Appendix E on the authenticity of the armorial glass.

Norreys link

John Norreys was a yeoman of the chamber by 1429 and would have known Henry Beauchamp since the latter was a favoured companion of the young king, Henry VI. Both accompanied the king to France in 1430 and attended the king's coronation there in 1431. In April 1439 Richard Beauchamp, Earl of Warwick, died and his widow, Isabel Despenser, included Norreys among those having custody of the Beauchamp estates during the minority of her son, Henry. In December Isabel died and Norreys together with John Nanfan and others were executors of her will. In 1442 Norreys, with Henry and John Nanfan, had custody of Sir Henry Bodrugan's lands in Cornwall. From 1446 to ca.1449 Norreys was Chief Steward of the lands of the Spensers. After the death of Henry Beauchamp Norreys took over the latter's post of Office of Receipt and Exchequer. Following the death in 1450 of Beauchamp's wife, Cicely Neville, custody of his lands came to an end and Norreys was among others pardoned all arrears of accounts as guardians.

Henry Beauchamp is said to have been made Duke of Warwick is recognition of his father Richards' worth. He died young and was buried near his mother in the chancel of Tewkesbury Abbey where it is said his tomb was found in the 1870s when alterations were being made. Isabel had chosen to be buried with her first husband, the earl of Worcester, also confusingly called Richard Beauchamp. There is no memorial for Henry at Tewkesbury, though on his fathers' tomb in St Mary's Warwick, are enamelled shields for him and another impaling that of his wife, Cicely Neville.

Coats on the tomb of Richard Beauchamp, Earl of Warwick, in St Mary's Warwick. Left: the coat of his son Henry Beauchamp, Duke of Warwick. Right: Henry's coat impaling that of his wife Cicely Neville, (Montacute quartering Neville with the Neville coat being in the subordinate position)

2. EDMUND BEAUFORT (1406-1455)

Earl of Dorset 1441; Marquess of Dorset 1442; Earl of Somerset 1448; Duke of Somerset 1448; Constable of England 1450.

Edmund Beaufort was a younger son of John Beaufort, Earl of Somerset, by Margaret Holland, sister of Joan *Fair Maid of Kent*. Edmund was married to Eleanor, second daughter of Richard Beauchamp, Earl of Warwick (d.1439), by his first wife Elizabeth, daughter of Thomas, Lord Berkeley and Lisle. He was therefore step-brother-in-law of Henry Beauchamp.[36]

Armorial Achievement

Crest

A *chapeau gules* turned up *ermine. A lion statant quardanet or, gorged with a collar gobony* of the Beaufort livery colours *argent & azure*.

Blazon

Quarterly:

1 & 4: *Azure, three fleur de lis or;* for France (modern).
2 & 3: *three lions passant guardant in pale or;* for England.
All within a bordure gobony argent and azure; for Beaufort.

The coat at Ockwells has no charge in the bordure although Edmund was a younger son. No charge is shown on his coat on the tomb of Richard Beauchamp in St Mary's Warwick.

Beaufort was a successful soldier who in 1438 waged war in Maine and at the end of the campaign made an agreement with John, Duke of Alençon and Charles, Count of Maine

---

[36] His father John was one of the children born in adultery to John of Gaunt and Katherine Swynford née Roet. They were surnamed Beaufort and legitimised in 1397 by Richard II. Edmund's uncle, Henry Beaufort, was Bishop of Winchester and Cardinal of England and helped bankroll English armies in France. His aunt, Joan Beaufort, married to Ralph Neville, Earl of Westmoreland, was mother of Richard Neville, Earl of Salisbury in right of his wife Alice Montacute, who held Bisham.

(brother of René of Anjou) to put their possessions under the protection of appatis[37] when he is styled as Captain General & Governor of the King in Anjou & Maine. He was given land rights in Maine in 1442. When Maine was to be given up to obtain a truce for 20 years with René and his brother Charles, he wanted compensation, and for a year he bargained with the government until he obtained it (10,000 livres tournois a year from taxation in Normandy, which was fully paid until the outbreak of war in 1449). Only when Beaufort had secured this could the cession of Maine go ahead and only then would he agree to undertake to be lieutenant-general in France, and governor of Normandy.[38]

Norreys link

Norreys would have known Beaufort, when the latter was, from 1438 to 1455, Constable of Windsor Castle, though evidently not always resident. Norreys was his lieutenant, responsible for receiving money to pay for repairs to the fabric of the castle and probably to oversee the work. In 1446 Beaufort was appointed King's Lieutenant in Normandy & France but didn't go until 1448. The French invaded the following year and the entire duchy was overrun. Richard Duke of York's chief complaint against him concerned the inadequacy of his defence of Normandy. The breach led to the start of the Wars of the Roses in 1455.

Edmund Beaufort was killed at St Albans during the first battle of the Wars of the Roses in 1455. He and others killed at the battle were reportedly buried with their armour under the floor of the Lady Chapel of St Albans Abbey. There is no memorial for him in the abbey, but Edmund's coat does occur on an enamelled shield on the tomb of his father-in-law, Richard Beauchamp, Earl of Warwick, at St Mary's Warwick together with a shield that impales the coat of his wife, Eleanor, Warwick's daughter, by his first wife, Elizabeth Berkeley.

Coats on the tomb of Richard Beauchamp, Earl of Warwick, in St Mary's Warwick.
Left: the coat of his son-in-law Edmund Beaufort, Duke of Somerset.
Right: Edmund's coat impaling that of his wife Eleanor Beauchamp

---

[37] Wolffe, pp163-4. Appatis: an agreement between the local citizenry (or the lord) of a defeated region and the occupying soldiery, essentially a payment system that under the laws of war forbade theft and mistreatment of the locals so long as the appatised country paid the ransom.
[38] Jones 2004.

3.   MARGARET OF ANJOU (1430-1482)
Queen of England from 1445-1461 & 1470-71.

Margaret was born in 1430 at Pont-à-Mousson in Lorraine and was the younger daughter of René of Anjou by Isabella, daughter and heir of Charles II, Duke of Lorraine.

Armorial Achievement

Crest
A triple arched and jewelled royal crown.

Blazon
Quarterly:
1 & 4: *Azure, three fleur de lis or;* for France (modern).
2 & 3: *Gules, three lions passant quadrant in pale;* for England.
Impaling quarterly of six:
1. *Barry of six argent and gules;* for Hungary.
2. *Azure, semy fleur de lis or, a label gules;* for Naples (only remnant of label remains).
3. *Argent, a cross potent between four crosses potent or;* for Jerusalem.
4. *Azure, semy of fleur de lis or, a bordure gules;* for Anjou.
5. *Azure, semy of cross-crosslets fitchy two barbels or;* for Bar.
6. *Or, on a bend gules three allerions argent;* for Lorraine.

Supporters
Dexter: *an heraldic white antelope, armed, unguled, maned and spotted or* supporter of her husband Henry VI.
Sinister: golden eagle of Lorraine[39] supporter of her father René though without the cross of Lorraine.

Motto
"Humble et Loiall" in the glass quarries.

René's mother, Margaret's grandmother, was Yolande of Aragon whose husband Louis II, Count of Anjou, inherited the Anjou claim to the titular throne of Hungary & Jerusalem and the kingdom of Sicily & Naples – a claim that was to have an influence on Margaret's life when it descended in 1434 to her father, René, at the time a prisoner of the Duke of Burgundy. In 1437 he agreed to pay an enormous ransom of 400,000 gold crowns to

---

[39] The eagle occurs as a supporter on the seal of Charles II, Duke of Lorraine. Seals of René from 1435 to 1453, when king of Sicily, had two eagle supporters and an eagle bearing the cross of Lorraine together with a painting of René praying are depicted in *Le Livre d'heures du roi René* (Paris. Bibl.Nat.Ms lat 1156 A, f.81v) (Merindol, pp114-115, pl XXXI-XXXII). Everard Green (p328) identifies the supporter as the golden eagle of Hungary, but this is the double headed eagle.

obtain his release to go to Naples.[40] However, in 1442, losing his kingdom to Alphonso V of Aragon (his second cousin), he returned to France unable to pay the remainder of his ransom. Plans for Margaret's marriage to King Henry VI seem to have begun then. Aged fourteen when she was betrothed by proxy to Henry VI in 1444 in Tours, she was escorted to England in March 1445 and in April 1445 was married to the king at Titchfield Abbey, being crowned at Westminster Abbey at the end of May. Also in May, Isabel, Duchess of Burgundy, arrived in Chalons to discuss various grievances, including René's ransom, with Charles VII. The treaty that was concluded included acquitting René of paying the rest of the ransom. Among the other ladies present at Chalons was René's wife, Isabella of Lorraine, termed Queen of Sicily. An eyewitness account of a meeting between these two noted that *"neither of them was likely to damage their knee caps curtsying to each other."*[41]

By the time the armorial glass was put up at Ockwells, ca.1453-54, there was unrest in England due to the loss of English held lands in France, a loss that Margaret's father, René played an active part in, disregarding the impact it would have on his daughter. The Wars of the Roses began in 1455. At the battle of Tewkesbury in 1471 her son Edward was killed and she was captured. A prisoner, sometimes living with Alice, Duchess of Suffolk, at Ewelme, she was ransomed by her cousin, Louis XI, in 1475. She had to renounce all her English assets in favour of Edward IV and, when she got to France, had to renounce all rights to inheritance from her mother and father to her cousin, Louis XI, who gave her a pension to live on. However, Queen's College (also of brick), that she founded, next to her husband's foundation of King's College in Cambridge, survives as a memorial to her.

Norreys link

In 1445 Margaret arrived in England and Norreys then wife, Alice Merbrooke, was made a Lady in Waiting to the Queen. From 1445 to 1452 Norreys was Treasurer of the Chamber and Keeper of the Jewels of Queen Margaret, becoming Keeper of her Wardrobe in 1452-3. The presence of Margaret's armorial coat in the Galilee Chapel of Durham Cathedral together with that of Norreys impaled with Alice's coat suggests they accompanied Henry VI when he visited Durham in September 1448; this is possibly the remnants of a scheme put up in the Exchequer built by Robert Neville, then Bishop or Durham, on Palace Green, near the Cathedral.[42]

Armorial glass in the west window of the Galilee Chapel in Durham Cathedral for, left: Henry VI (damaged) and Margaret of Anjou; and right: John Norreys and Alice Merbrooke

[40] Villeneuve Bargemont vol 1, pp228-229, claims that in secret clauses, he agreed to be neutral in any conflict between France, Burgundy and England and to cement the peace to marry his second daughter, Margaret, to Henry VI of England. The1437 treaty for René's release from captivity does not mention these clauses (see Lecoy de la Marche vol 2, pp224-233).
[41] Vaughan, pp119-20.
[42] Darracott, in *MCS News* Feb 2018, pp13-14; Darracott 2018, available on MCS website.

Margaret died in 1482 in Chateau Souzay, near to the village of Dampierre, on the banks of the Loire and was buried in the family tomb in the church of St Maurice, Angers.

Chateau Souzay on the bank of the Loire where Margaret of Anjou died in 1482

Plaque outside Chateau Souzay commemorating the place where Margaret of Anjou died

4.   WILLIAM DE LA POLE (1396-1450)
4th Earl of Suffolk 1415; Knight of the Garter 1421; Marquess of Suffolk 1444; Earl of Pembroke 1447; Duke of Suffolk 1448.

He was the second son of Michael de la Pole, second Earl of Suffolk (d.1415), and Katherine Stafford (d.1419).

Armorial Achievement

Crest

Lost. It would have been a *Saracen's head in profile gules, crined and bearded sable, couped at the neck with a gold chain, and with a jewelled circlet around the temples.*[43]

Blazon
Quarterly:
1 & 4: *Azure a fess between three leopards' faces or.* De la Pole.
2 & 3: *Argent a chief gules over all a lion rampant double queued or,* Burghersh for Chaucer.[44]

Everard Green identifies this coat as for Suffolk's son John de la Pole (d.1491) but as he was not born until 1442, had no connection to John Norreys and was too young to be involved in the mid fifteenth-century diplomacy around the marriage of the king, it must represent his father, William.

---

[43] The piece of purple red glass once in its place has also gone. See Everard Green p329. The crest occurs on extant stall plates for William and his son John in St George's Chapel, Windsor and also on and above John's monument at Wingfield. William was made a Garter knight in 1421, prior to his marriage, so the plate quarters De la Pole with Wingfield for Katherine Wingfield of Suffolk, an heiress, who had married his grandfather, Sir Michael de la Pole (d.1389). After William's marriage in 1430 (Watts 2004a) to Alice Chaucer, also an heiress, he quartered his coat with Burghersh (her mother's coat). This coat occurs on the tomb of Alice's parents and her own tomb in St Mary's Church, Ewelme, and in the east window of St Mary's Church, Kidlington, the nave of which was raised and clerestory windows added in the mid-C15th (church guide). Goodall 2001 (p306 note 45) states there was once every variation of the de la Pole and Chaucer arms in the glass of the nave and that as William and Alice owned the manor of Kidlington they probably made a bequest to the church.
[44] His wife evidently preferred the coat of Matilda Burghersh (d.1437), her mother, to that of her father, Thomas Chaucer (d.1434), son of Geoffrey Chaucer.

William served in Henry V's campaign of 1415, during which his father died of a fever at the siege of Harfleur, where he himself was wounded and repatriated. A few weeks later, his elder brother, now the new earl, fell at the battle of Agincourt, making William, Earl of Suffolk. He continued fighting in France, first for Henry V, who made him a Knight of the Garter, and after his death for the Regent, Henry's brother, John, Duke of Bedford. In 1428 he took command at the siege of Orleans when Thomas Montacute, Earl of Salisbury, was killed, marrying his widow Alice Chaucer in 1430. In 1429 when Joan of Arc raised the siege at Orleans he fell back to Jargeau where shortly after he surrendered. Suffolk was taken into the custody of Jean, the Bastard of Orleans (later Count of Dunois), half-brother of Charles, Duke of Orleans, a captive of the English since Agincourt in 1415 and John, Count of Angouleme, a captive since 1412. Suffolk was soon set at liberty – sometime between 28 February and 15 March 1430, but, as a condition of his freedom had to pay a ransom of £20,000, and it appears to have been part of the arrangement for his release that the earl would do everything he could to obtain Angoulême's release.[45] It seems the Bastard of Orleans befriended Suffolk using him to obtain the release of his two half-brothers. Charles was released in 1440 supposedly to assist in peace negotiations and John was freed by Suffolk in Rouen in March 1445[46] as the latter began to escort Margaret of Anjou to England to marry Henry VI.

By 1444 Suffolk was the leading figure in the planning and conduct of English diplomacy for Henry VI. He evidently had concerns when tasked with arranging the king's marriage, for the King said *on account of the fears of William de la Pole, Earl of Suffolk, that his conduct as ambassador in France will be called into question, orders him to execute his instructions concerning peace and the King's marriage* giving him a letter exonerating him and his heirs for ever from any consequences. In April Suffolk and the embassy travelled to France and in May Suffolk acted as proxy for the king when he was betrothed to Margaret of Anjou at a ceremony in Tours Cathedral; for a contemporary account see Appendix A, No. 4. He returned in November 1444 to escort Margaret of Anjou to England, arriving back in April 1445. The French Embassy that arrived in July was greeted by Suffolk and others represented at Ockwells and resulted in a truce. In 1449 after the truce was broken in March, Charles VII attacked English held towns with the help of the Bastard of Orleans. On 11th November the king entered Rouen in triumph flanked by Margaret of Anjou's father René and his brother Charles who both disavowed the 20-year truce they had made with the English when Maine was handed back in 1448.[47]

The resulting public unrest led to Suffolk being impeached by Parliament and sent into exile. The poignant letter he wrote to his son John stresses the need "to obey your sovereign" (see Appendix A, No. 6). In 1450 while en route to exile he was captured in the channel *And in the sight of all his men he was drawn out of the great ship into a boat and one of the lewdest of the ship bade him lay down his head and took a rusty sword and smote off his head within a half a dozen strokes, and laid his body on the sands of Dover and some say his head was set on a pole by it.*[48]

Norreys Link
Norreys accompanied the king to France in 1430 and would have met Suffolk as in 1431 the latter assisted at the coronation of Henry VI in Paris in December. By then Suffolk

---

[45] Watts, 2004a. Sackville West p221 cites sources indicating either he surrendered to a squire after knighting him, or to the "bravest woman in the world" Joan of Arc.

[46] McLeod, p275. Suffolk being proxy for the king was in 1444 not 1445.

[47] Villeneuve de Bargemont vol 2, p77; Monstrelet vol 2, p171. For 20-year truce see Stevenson II, ii, pp710-711.

[48] Paston Letters (ed. Archer-Hind) 1924, vol 1, p25-26. Robert Wennington, Vice Admiral of England and in command of the Fleet, is thought to be the "pirate" of the ship *Nicholas of the Tower* who oversaw Suffolk's murder (Wedgwood and Holt, 1936, pp932-3).

was married to Alice Chaucer, widow of Thomas Montacute, the Earl of Salisbury, who had died at the siege of Orleans in 1428. The Montacutes for many generations had held Bisham not far from Ockwells. The Chaucers held land in Ewelme, Oxon, again not too far away. In 1441 both Norreys and Suffolk were among the founder members of Guild of the Holy Cross based in St Helen's Church, Abingdon and both were feoffees for the king's will of 1448 funded by Duchy of Lancaster assets.[49]

When Norreys was planning to build Ockwells he would have sought advice from Suffolk who from 1440 had been supervising the building of Eton College where there was extensive use of brick. Suffolk was descended from successful merchants in Hull whose assets included a brickworks from which the walls surrounding Hull were built. Suffolk had helped rebuild St Mary's Church in Hull ca.1425 using bricks.[50] Brick also features in the Long Alley Almshouses built in 1446/7 by the Guild of the Holy Cross and in the almshouses and school at Ewelme founded by Suffolk and his wife, Alice Chaucer in 1437.

Suffolk (d.1450) was buried in the Charterhouse monastery in Hull, founded by his great-grandfather William de la Pole in 1384. The monastic church was destroyed in 1538 during the dissolution of the monasteries but the Charterhouse still functions in an eighteenth-century building, providing sheltered independent living and run by a board of trustees including five appointed by Hull City Council. The complex includes an eighteenth-century chapel.

It is almost certain that Suffolk was dead when the armorial glass went up in Ockwells. Norreys placed Suffolk's achievement between that of the king and queen thereby acknowledging his role both in achieving the marriage and the price he had paid.

Ewelme, Oxfordshire. Left to right: school; almshouses; and St Mary's Church. This complex still functions with the aid of the trust founded by Suffolk and his wife Alice Chaucer in 1437

---

[49] Nicolas 1826, p22. From 1437 to 1443 Suffolk had been Chief Steward of Duchy lands in the north and then jointly from 1443 to 1451 with Sir Thomas Tuddenham (Somerville, pp420-421).

[50] He put up armorial glass in the church for himself (de la Pole quartering Wingfield), his king, and another northern magnate, Richard Neville, Earl of Salisbury, in right of his wife, Alice, daughter of Sir Thomas Montacute (*MCS News*, Nov 2017, pp20-21).

Ewelme School, built of mainly brick. The armorial coats on the windows are replacements

Ewelme almshouses – like Ockwells built around a courtyard and with barge boards over the porches similar to those at Ockwells but with unglazed corridors

5.   HENRY VI (1421-1471)
King of England 1422-1461 & 1470-1471.

Henry VI, King of England, Lord of Ireland, and Duke of Aquitaine, was born at Windsor Castle on 6 December 1421, the only child of Henry V (1386–1422) and Catherine, daughter of the French king Charles VI (1401–1437).[51] Henry V never saw his only son, and his 21-year-old queen, Catherine of Valois, joined her husband in France five months after the birth. When she next saw her son, he was king of England, as Henry V died at Vincennes, near Paris, on 31 August 1422, leaving as his heir the nine-month-old baby. As a child he was crowned king of England in 1429 and king of France in 1431. He is credited with losing all lands his father gained. However, his educational foundations of Eton College and King's College, Cambridge
survive to this day.

Armorial Achievement

Crest
A triple arched and jewelled royal crown.

Blazon
Quarterly:
1 & 4: *Azure, three fleurs de lis or*, for France (modern).
2 & 3: *Gules, three lions passant guardant in pale or;* for England.

Supporters
Two heraldic white antelopes, *armed, unguled, maned and spotted or.*

Motto
"Dieu et mon droit" in the glass quarries.

---

[51] His parents were married in June 1420. In May the Treaty of Troyes between Henry V and Charles VI had made Henry V his heir. See Griffiths 2004 for the biography of Henry VI.

His marriage in 1445 to Margaret of Anjou, niece of the king of France, was supposed to lead to peace with France. When the embassy from France arrived in July they reported that the king met them in a great hall (probably Westminster) dressed in a robe of cloth of gold and seated on a chair covered in cloth of gold. At his right hand stood many ecclesiastics whilst on his left stood dukes and lords including the Duke of Warwick (Henry Beauchamp), the Marquis of Dorset (Edmund Beaufort), the Marquis of Suffolk (William de la Pole), and the Earl of Ormond (James Butler)[52] all of whom are represented by their achievements in the oriel at Ockwells. Also present were ambassadors from René of Anjou.[53] They may then have handed over the copy of the document that Henry referred to in December 1445 that said Charles VII had given permission for René, King of Sicily, and his brother Charles, Count of Maine, to make a truce with the English for 20 years, evidently in return for the handover of Le Mans and Maine.[54] The agreement to deliver Le Mans and Maine was signed in March 1448, with the Bastard of Orleans, (now count of Dunois) being the leading French ambassador.[55] This 20-year truce was repudiated by René and his brother in 1449 and led to the loss of all of Henry VI's kingdom of France except Calais; the Wars of the Roses; the ruin of his kingship and eventually the loss of his life.

Norreys Link

Henry would have known John Norreys from boyhood as the latter was already a yeoman of the chamber by 1429 when the king was seven and Norreys was twenty-four. He served the king over many years, being Esquire of the Body from 1437 to the end of 1455[56], Keeper/Clerk of the Great Wardrobe 1444-1446 and Chamberlain of the Exchequer 1446-1450. In 1440 Henry founded Eton College and four years later Norreys, together with Suffolk and John Pury, granted the manor of "Le Mote" and other lands in New & Old Windsor and Clewer to the king for the benefit of the college. In 1447 Henry made his Will; John Norreys Esquire is among the executors.[57] In 1471 Henry VI was imprisoned in the Tower and then murdered there after his son and heir, Edward Prince of Wales, was killed at the battle of Tewkesbury. An account in Warkworth suggests Richard, Duke of Gloucester, was responsible as the principal man in the Tower at the time.[58]

Statue of Henry VI in a quadrangle of Eton College, the college he founded in 1441. Built mostly of brick its construction was overseen by William de la Pole, then Earl of Suffolk, whose family in Hull had owned brickworks. (Photo by Man Vyi on Wikipedia Commons)

[52] Stevenson I, pp157-158.
[53] Ibid I, p155.
[54] Ibid II, ii, pp639-642. Henry requested the original letters that granted permission (p641), probably unsuccessfully.
[55] Ibid II, ii, pp710-718.
[56] Clark 2020a, p675.
[57] Nicolas 1826, p21.
[58] Wolffe, p347, who notes the account was written soon after July 1482.

6. JAMES BUTLER (BOTELER) (ca.1390-1452)

4th Earl of Ormond (known as "The White Earl"); Lord Lieutenant of Ireland 1420-22, 1425-26 & 1442-43.

The earls of Ormond were one of Ireland's leading families. The "White Earl" was the elder son of James Butler, third Earl of Ormond (ca.1360–1405), and his wife, Anne Welles. His first marriage (before 28 August 1413) to Joan (d.1430), daughter of William Beauchamp, Lord Bergavenny, significantly extended his English connections, but at the cost of weakening Butler power in Ireland in the next generation. Through his own second marriage, in 1432, to Elizabeth (1398?–1452), widow of John, Lord Grey of Codnor, and only legitimate child of Gerald FitzMaurice Fitzgerald, fifth Earl of Kildare (d.1432), Ormond acquired the bulk of the Kildare lands for life and also the animosity of the collateral heirs.[59]

Armorial Achievement

Crest
A garb and eagle rising therein, both *or.*

Blazon
Per fess dancetty azure and or.

Everard Green has identified this coat as representing this man's son, the fifth earl, also James Butler,[60] but it could not represent the fifth earl before August 1452, when the fourth earl died, as it is undifferenced. If the glass was put up after 1452, it could still represent the fourth earl, as two other personalities (Henry Beauchamp & Alice Merbrooke, Norreys first wife are commemorated after their death in this armorial scheme.

---

[59] Matthew 2004. See also Kirwan, pp21-24.
[60] Everard Green, p330.

Norreys Link

John Norreys would have known Ormond, the fourth earl, as both men accompanied Henry VI to France in 1430 for his coronation in Paris the following year. He probably met Norreys at court as in 1442, when Lieutenant in Ireland, his disputes with English officials in Ireland led to him being summoned to London. Whilst it appears that it was the fourth earl's son who was part of the escort that brought Margaret to England in 1445, it was the fourth earl who greeted the French Embassy later that year.

It is probable that after the marriage of Henry VI and Margaret of Anjou the earl built in Aylesbury (between 1445 and 1449) a hospitium attached to the nearby friary built by his father. In what is now the King's Head pub (owned by the National Trust) he put up armorial glass including the coats and badges of Henry VI and Margaret of Anjou.[61] His own badge, the covered cup, remains as does that for Richard, Duke of York – a plume of feather out of a crown. Ormond returned to Ireland with York in 1449. Possibly this scheme inspired Norreys when it came to glazing Ockwells. It has not fared as well. The fourth earl died in August 1452 at Atherdee, County Louth, and is buried in the church of the Abbey of St Mary in Dublin.

The hospitium built by the fourth earl in Aylesbury, now the King's Head pub. Above: main entrance and adjacent salon. Below: inside the salon showing the extant armorial glass

---

[61] Gibbs, p80, p406 – the first known attempt to identify the coats and badges. In 1429 the earl was granted a plot of land used for a pound called *Kyngespynfold* in Aylesbury (Birmingham Collection NRA 28607, vol 1, p156), possibly where the hospitium was built.

The coat of Margaret of Anjou in the King's Head pub, Aylesbury,
- the former hospitium founded by James Butler, fourth Earl of Ormond

Badges: top: Henry VI (the Bohun swan, collared and chained or, for his grandmother, Mary Bohun);
Richard Duke of York (panache of feathers in a crown);
bottom: Margaret of Anjou (the daisy) and James Butler, fourth Earl of Ormond (the covered cup)

7.   ABBEY OF ABINGDON
Abbot William Ashendon 1435- 1467.

Abingdon Abbey was one of the largest and wealthiest in England and the greatest medieval landowner in Berkshire.[62] Some of the many manors it held in that county[63] could be granted to others, presumably for a price.   In turn the Abbey could receive grants in mortmain of lands, which appears to have been a tax avoidance scheme.

In medieval times the other major religious organisation in Abingdon was St Helen's Church. Members of the Fraternity of the Holy Cross based in that church had, in 1416, bought land from the Abbot to build bridges at Culham and Burford and a connecting causeway.[64] In 1441, re-founded as a Gild (Guild), it was licensed to collect assets *for the repair of the road which extends from Abyndon, co. Berks towards Dorchestre, co Oxford, and over the water of the Thames through Burford and Culhamford between the said towns, by which road the King's lieges have had carriage and free passage save when it is flooded so that none can attempt it without peril of his life and loss of his goods.*[65]

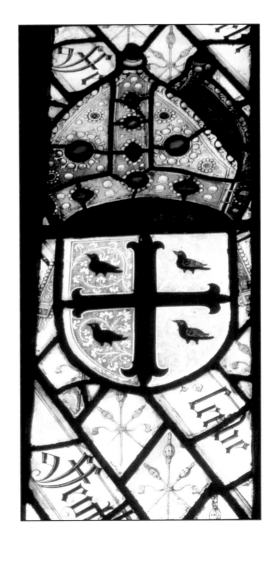

Armorial Achievement

Crest
A gold jewelled mitre.

Blazon
Argent a cross patonce between four martlets sable.

The armorial achievement was originally in Light 8.[66]

---

[62] Allen, p1. It was rebuilt in the perpendicular style from 1427-1495 (information board erected by Friends of Abingdon Civic Society in the Long Gallery, a remaining building of the Abbey).

[63] See map in VCH Berkshire, vol 1, p322 which shows their holdings in the Domesday survey. Its early history is obscure but its history is well documented from AD 953 when re-founded by Aethelwold (Allen p4).

[64] Lysons & Lysons 1806, pp221-222.

[65] CPR 1441-46, p36. The 1416 bridge at Culham is extant. The Culham and Abingdon bridges were built with stone from the quarries of Sir Peter Bessils (d.1424) whose great-granddaughter Elizabeth married Richard Fettiplace (Preston pp36-37). Richard Fettiplace was brother of Sir Thomas Fettiplace who married Elizabeth Norreys and held *Ocolt* (Ockwells) according to his will of 1523 (see Appendix C, Tree 6). Sir Peter Bessils is regarded as a donor to the fraternity of the Holy Cross. His portrait, thought to have been done ca.1580-1610, still hangs in the hall of the Long Alley Almshouses, built by the guild co-founded by Elizabeth Norreys' grandfather, John Norreys Esquire.

[66] *Gentleman's Magazine* 1798 vol LXVIII pt II, p762. An unpublished 1987 history of Ockwells by Harvey Van Sickle noted the original order.

Norreys Link

St Helens Church had on occasion a fraught relationship with the Abbey. In 1327 the church organised a group (including one *Thomas Noreys (sic)*) to rebel against the Abbey, forcing the prior to sign a charter in which the abbot granted the men of Abingdon the right to elect their own reeve and bailiffs.[67] This suggests the Norreys family had a longstanding association with St Helen's Church. In 1441 Norreys was a founder member of the Guild of the Holy Cross in the church. However, he also in 1452 granted land to the Abbey and when he died in 1466 was holding land from them (see Appendix A, No. 7).

Above: Abingdon Abbey gatehouse flanked by St Nicolas Church (to the left) and what was St John's Hospital (to the right). Below: detail of the gatehouse showing the royal coat and the Abbey coat in the spandrels of the main entrance

---

[67] Lambrick and Slade, pp326-329.

7A.   LOST - PROBABLY THE ABBEY OF READING
Abbot Thomas II (Henley) 1430-1445; John II (Thorne I) 1446-1486.

The Abbey of Reading, founded by Henry I in 1121, was one of the main pilgrimage centres of medieval England and one of the richest and most important of the religious houses.[68] In 1126 the king gave the Abbey a gift of an important relic, the hand of St James the Apostle.[69] St James was the patron saint of pilgrims who still, in the twenty-first century, walk the Camino to Santiago de Compostella in Spain carrying a scallop shell, the badge of St James. This gift led to the Abbey's coat bearing scallop shells. [70]

Armorial Achievement

Crest
A jewelled mitre.

Blazon
Would have been *Azure three scallops or*.

Norreys Link
The Abbey, a Benedictine monastery, is likely to be the missing coat as John Norreys held lands (in Reading, Twyford and Hurst) from this Abbey[71] as he had from Abingdon Abbey. These two monasteries dominated the ecclesiastical map of Berkshire.[72]

As with Abingdon, there was also a guild (the Merchant Gild) in Reading which seems to have had a similar occasionally acrimonious relationship with the Abbey.[73] Norreys may

---

[68] Reading Abbey Cartularies of charters in Berkshire and elsewhere are given in Kemp I & II.

[69] Cram, p24. The charter is transcribed in Kemp I, p39-40 who discusses its validity. It is thought all the abbey's relics were destroyed after the Dissolution; however, a withered left hand was found in a wall at the east end of the Abbey Church by workmen digging foundations for the new gaol in 1786. The relic, once claimed to be the hand of St James, is held by the Catholic church of St Peter in Marlow (Durrant & Painter, p17).

[70] The coat reproduced here is from Hurry.

[71] See Appendix A, No 7. Less likely is William Aiscough, Bishop of Salisbury (d1450), who married Henry VI and Margaret of Anjou in England, and, together with John Norreys, established a guild in St Helen's Church, Abingdon and a chantry in St Michael's Church, Bray (CPR 1441-46, p36; CPR 1446-52, p2). Aiscough was murdered in 1450 by soldiers angry at the loss of Normandy. Norreys was an executor of his will (Clark 2020a, p674).

[72] See map of 1535 in VCH Berkshire, vol 2, opp. p47.

[73] Though there was no question of a popular rising against the abbey (Slade 1964, p49).

have been a member of the Gild as he was with the guild at Abingdon; the accounts of the Reading Gild show that in the mid-fifteenth century Norreys received a gift of wine from them and rented from them a garden in Castle Street, Reading.[74] Norreys was certainly close to a prominent member of the Gild, Thomas Lavington, who visited Maidenhead in 1431-2 when Mayor of Reading and had business dealings with Norreys.[75] If Norreys was not a member of the Reading Merchant Gild he was closely involved with a member of it.

By 1448 Norreys, by now an influential courtier, acted as one of the wardens for the Abbey estates at Leominster, Herefordshire. In 1465 priests, it seems, from the Abbey (*religious*) and parish church (*seculers*) are mentioned by Norreys in his will in which he required his executors to find thirty devout priests in *Redyng and nigh ther aboute* to do his obit in the parish church of Yattendon.[76]

Abbey Ruins – restored and opened to the public in 2018

An angel holding the coat of Reading Abbey occurs on a corbel on the west front of St Laurence's Church, one of the heavily restored extant buildings linked to Reading Abbey. The other restored buildings, St John's Hospitium and the Abbey Gatehouse, have had various uses

---

[74] Slade 2002 Part II, pp31, 39, 43 and 49.
[75] Slade 2002 Part I, page xci; Berkshire Feet of Fines Pt II, no 1375, p61; 1380, p62; 1384, p63; 1398, p67; 1399, pp67-68.
[76] Appendix A, No. 2 reproduces his will.

8.   RICHARD BEAUCHAMP (1450-1481)

Bishop of Hereford 1448; Bishop of Salisbury 1450; Chaplain from 1452 and then in 1475 the first Chancellor of the Order of the Garter; 1473 builder and surveyor of St George's Chapel for Edward IV; 1477 Dean of Windsor.

Younger son of Sir Walter Beauchamp (d.1430) of Bromham, Wiltshire (by wife Elizabeth, d.1447, daughter of Sir John Roche), of a cadet line of the Beauchamps, distantly related to the earls of Warwick. His elder brother, Sir William Beauchamp, created Lord St Amand in 1449, has also been identified as being represented by this coat. It can be ascribed to the bishop as the coat bears doctor's caps in the bordure.[77] As the two extant coats, in the side of the oriel, are heater shaped bearing a mitre crest, it is assumed all three represented ecclesiastics.

Armorial Achievement

Blazon

Quarterly:

1 & 4: *Gules a fess between six martlets or* for Beauchamp of Powick.

2. *Gules two lions passant in pale argent* for De La Mare.

3. *Azure three roach naiant argent* for Roche.

All within a *bordure of argent semy of tonsure caps sable.*

In 1798 this achievement was in Light 7 and its mitre was in Light 7a. It is possible they were put together after the Victorian restoration.[78]

---

[77] See identical coat in Harl. Mss 14581 f100 R. Glover Somerset Herald 1580-1588 *de Origine Antiquitate et differentii armorum fine insigni* identified as Richard Beauchamp, Bishop of Salisbury.

[78] *Gentleman's Magazine* 1798 vol LXVIII pt II, p762, which gives the original order. See also Appendix E.

Norreys Link

In December 1448, as the king's chaplain, he was appointed Bishop of Hereford,[79] being consecrated at Lambeth in February 1449. As chaplain he would have known John Norreys. Around this time the quire of Great Malvern Priory was being rebuilt, in part as a memorial to the bishop's kinsman, Richard Beauchamp, Earl of Warwick[80] whose estates Norreys helped manage. In August 1450 he was appointed Bishop of Salisbury after the murder of William Aiscough in June. Beauchamp found himself often called to Windsor by the king: *"Forasmuch as your being about our person is to us full agreeable and your service at such times as you are with us full good and notable"*, ran one such open-ended summons to join Henry, issued on 15 August 1452.[81] This is around the time (1450-1454) that Ockwells was being built and the armorial glass erected. Norreys' contact with the bishop may well have increased when he was appointed chaplain of the Order of the Garter in 1452, as Norreys had dealings with St George's Chapel. In his will of 1465 John Norreys left six shillings and eight pence to Salisbury Cathedral for prayers for his soul.

In 1473 the bishop initiated the building of a new St George's Chapel for Edward IV, who appointed him master and surveyor of the chapel. A patent in 1475 authorised him to clear ground for the building of the new chapel,[82] and in October he was appointed the first Chancellor of the Order of the Garter, then Dean of Windsor in 1477. He died in 1481 and was buried in the chantry chapel he had built on the south side of the Lady Chapel of Salisbury Cathedral. His chapel was demolished by James Wyatt ca.1790.

The new St Georges Chapel built for Edward IV by Bishop Richard Beauchamp, located at the west end of the original chapel of the Order of the Garter, founded by Edward III in 1348

---

[79] CPR 1446-52, p223.

[80] Darracott 2005 p11. The bishop later built a memorial recess in St Georges Chapel with, in the lower part, his coat showing his descent from the Beauchamps of Powick, flanked by the coats of the Beauchamps of Warwick and Holt, both by then extinct in the male line (Darracott 2019, p4).

[81] Davies, 2004.

[82] Begent & Chesshyre, p127. The chapel was intended as a dynastic mausoleum for the House of York (Lewis 2015, p32).

a)

b)

c)

Desk fronts in the choir of St George's Chapel bear the armorial coats of Bishop Richard Beauchamp, as seen in the quartered coat at Ockwells: a) Roche b) De la Mare c) Beauchamp of Powick (vandalised). Each is encircled with the garter (as he was the first Chancellor of the Order) with adjacent snails (his badge) and mitres in the spandrels give his status

9. JOHN NORREYS Esquire of Bray, Berkshire (1405-1466)

(See also Light 14, below)

Builder of Ockwells c.1450-54; Yeoman of the Chamber by 1429; Usher of the Chamber 1437-ca.1441; Esquire of the Body 1437 to end-1455; High Sheriff of Berkshire & Oxfordshire 1437-38, 1442-43, 1457-58; MP Berkshire 1439-40; MP Oxfordshire 1442; Berkshire 1445-46, 1447, 1449-50, 1450-51, 1453; Keeper/Clerk of the Great Wardrobe 1444-1446; Chamberlain of the Exchequer 1446-1450; Treasurer of the Chamber & Keeper of the Jewels of Queen Margaret 1445-1452; Keeper of the Queen's Wardrobe 1448-1457; Steward of Cookham and Bray 1447-1461.

Chapter 3 sets out full the biography of John Norreys Esquire.

He had three wives, two of whom are represented in the Ockwells armorial glass (see also Light 14, below). Here, his coat (said to be of Ravenscroft for Norreys) is impaled with that of his second wife, Eleanor Clitheroe.

Armorial Achievement

Crest
A raven rising proper

Blazon
Argent, a chevron between three ravens' heads erased sable (Ravenscroft for Norreys).
Impaling quarterly:
1 & 4: *Argent three covered cups sable* for Clitheroe.
2 & 3: *Argent, a castle triple towered with the portcullis raised sable* for Oldcastle.

Supporters
Two beavers collared and chained or, each with a fish in mouth.

Motto
"Ffeythfully serve"
This motto is present in the quarries of all the lights except Lights 3 and 5 for the queen and king. However, Norreys' badge – three golden distaffs – is present in all lights.

Everard Green (p332) describes the supporters as sea otters. Lysons correctly describes them as beavers. The beaver identification is based on the feet and the tails. Otters have four webbed feet, beavers only have two (the back ones) and this is usually reflected in heraldry, as at Ockwells. Otters have furry tails, beavers have scaly ones, and the scaly tails seem quite clear at Ockwells.[83]

In Norreys' will of 1465 he specified that his body was to be buried in the north aisle of St Michael's, Bray, called St Nicholas Chapel, leaving a bequest for the *newe making and edefying of the chapel a*nd for the making of a tomb. The tomb is long gone but much of the edification survives including stone plaques bearing the Norreys coat with beaver supporters and corbels of the Norreys coat impaling the coats of his second and third wives. Such a coat for his first wife was also probably once there.

The Norreys coat with beaver supporters each with a fish in mouth – one of two plaques located on the east wall of the Norreys Chapel in St Michael's, Bray – part of the "neue making and edefying" of the former Saint Nicholas Chapel, specified in John Norreys' will

The coat of John Norreys impaled with that of his second wife, Eleanor Clitheroe, on a corbel in the Norreys Chapel

---

[83] Lysons 1813, p449. I am grateful to David Ford for clarification on the supporters.

10. JOHN WENLOCK of Someries, Bedfordshire (1400-1471)

Usher of the Queen's Chamber by May 1445; Chamberlain to the Queen by 1448; MP Bedfordshire from 1433; Sheriff of Bedfordshire and Buckinghamshire 1444-45; Constable of Cardiff Castle & Stewardship of Glamorgan and Morgannok 1446; Esquire by 1444; Knighted 1447/8; from 1460 to 1469 Chief Butler of England; Knight of the Garter 1461; Lord Wenlock 1461; Chamberlain of the Duchy of Lancaster for Life 1461.

Son of William Wenlock (d.ca.1415), a Bedfordshire landowner, and Margaret Breton (Briton). His family, while retaining property in their native Shropshire, had settled in Bedfordshire in the fourteenth century.[84] John was a younger son whose elder brother, Thomas (d.1429), fought at Agincourt; John was his heir. He married twice: firstly (by 1435) Elizabeth, daughter and co-heir of Sir John Drayton of Nuneham, Oxfordshire. She was dead by March 1466, and in 1468 Wenlock married Agnes Danvers,[85] daughter of Sir John Danvers of Cothorpe, Oxfordshire.[86] She outlived Wenlock. He had no children from either marriage.

Armorial Achievement

Crest

A Saracen's head couped proper, and wreathed around the temples argent.

Blazon

Argent a chevron sable between three Saracen's heads erased proper, wreathed around the temples argent.

Norreys Link

An experienced soldier, in 1430 Wenlock was back in France, perhaps as a member of Henry VI's coronation expedition. If so, this may be when he first met John Norreys who was a member of the expedition as were the Earls of Suffolk and Ormond. By 1441

---

[84] Roskell 1958, p12; Moreton 2020, p418.

[85] Roskell 1958, p15 says her brother was William Danvers, Justice of the Common Pleas. He married Anne, daughter of John Pury of Chamberhouse, Berkshire. A tree in MacNamara (facing p171) records Agnes as a daughter of Sir John Danvers by his first wife, Alice Verney, whilst William was son of Sir John by his second wife Joan Bruley (see MacNamara, p202 for her lineage). Agnes had four husbands, Wenlock being the third (see Darracott 2021 for her link to Holy Trinity, Long Melford, where John Howard, later Duke of Norfolk, who married Norreys' widow Margaret Chedworth, was a benefactor.)

[86] Kekewich, 2004b.

Wenlock had entered the king's household and in June he began to be involved with English diplomatic activities in France designed to bring an end to the war; being closely identified with the peace policy of the Earl of Suffolk.[87] In 1444 the English Embassy including Wenlock was at Tours by 16th April. On 24th May Margaret of Anjou was betrothed to Henry VI with Suffolk acting as king's proxy. In April 1445 Wenlock was part of the escort that brought Margaret of Anjou to England to be married to Henry VI. By the time Margaret landed at Portsmouth he may already have secured the position of an usher of her chamber, an office he certainly held at her coronation on the following 30 May.[88] At the same time Norreys was treasurer of her chamber and keeper of her jewels. In March 1449 Norreys and John Wenlock were in a group were enfeoffed with the manor and warren of Fenelsgrove, Bedfordshire and in 1454 Wenlock, described as lately Chamberlain to the Queen, was in the group that granted lands, tenements etc in Staines to another group that included John Norreys Esquire and Edmund Brudenell.[89] On 1st July 1463 Wenlock and his wife Elizabeth were *deforciants* with John Norreys Esquire, one of the *querents,* concerning the sale of the manor of West Wittenham, plus part of the manor of Burghfield, Berkshire, and part of the manor of Kempston in Bedfordshire.[90] These manors, of his wife's inheritance, were conveyed away to Wenlock and his heirs shortly before her death, after 1 July.[91] In 1465 Wenlock was charged in the will of John Norreys with "assisting his executors" for which he was to receive a gilt cup. His buildings include Someries Castle, another early use of brick, and a chapel he had built in 1461 onto the north side of St Mary's Church, Luton, evidently as a chantry chapel for himself and his first wife, Elizabeth Drayton, though there are now no monuments to either of them.[92]

He changed sides during the Wars of the Roses but eventually, in 1471, at the battle of Tewkesbury, he died fighting on the side of Margaret of Anjou and her son who also died at the battle. His king, Henry VI, was by then in the Tower and did not long survive him.

It is not known whether Sir John was eventually buried in the chapel be built but certainly his helmet and gauntlets from Tewkesbury were once displayed on its north wall.

A fifteenth-century jug bearing the words "My Lord Wenlok" is thought to refer to John Wenlock or his great uncle, William, (whose extant tomb does occur in the chapel Sir John built in St Mary's, Luton). In 2005 funds were raised by public subscription, to which Maidenhead Civic Society contributed, to ensure it stayed in this country. It was unveiled in 2006, stolen in 2012, found later that year and reinstated the following year at the Stockwood Discovery Centre, Luton, with better security.

---

[87] Ibid.

[88] Moreton 2020, p421.

[89] St George's Chapel Archives SGC XV 21, 83 & 84.

[90] Berkshire Feet of Fines Pt II no 1443, pp79-80.

[91] As it happened, Wenlock did not retain either Long Wittenham or Burghfield Regis, both of which he formally quitclaimed to Alice, Dowager Duchess of Suffolk in March 1466, presumably after she had purchased them from him (Moreton 2020, p428).

[92] In the east window of the chapel there were once eight lines of prayer that began *Jesu Christ, most of myght, have mercy on John le Wenlock, Knight, and of his wife, Elizabeth,* but already lost when transcribed in C19th by Cobbe, p345-6. In the same window Cobbe recorded Sir John's kneeling figure bearing his arms on the surcoat and a Yorkist collar.

Someries Castle (a fortified manor house) Bedfordshire.
Ruined remains of the chapel which, with the gatehouse, are said to be an early example
of brick building; built by Sir John Wenlock in the mid-fifteenth century.

The Wenlock Chapel in Luton Parish Church (two windows on left)

a)   *b)*

c)   *d)*

Armorials on the screen separating the chapel Wenlock built from the chancel in St Mary's Church, Luton

a) The quartered coat of Sir John Wenlock – Wenlock quartering Breton (Briton) the coat of his mother – at the apex of the screen (facing chapel). The achievement has a different crest (of feathers) to that seen at Ockwells.
b) The coat of Sir John Wenlock impaling that of his first wife, Elizabeth Drayton at the apex of the screen (facing chancel).
c) The quartered coat of Sir John Wenlock on the wall of the screen.
d) The coat of Sir John Wenlock encircled by the garter on the top of the screen.

Wenlock's badge, a lance rest with the word "Hola" inscribed on it, probably his war cry, is also carved into the screen and on the spandrels of the piscina in the chapel

11.   WILLIAM LAKEN (d.1475)
Justice of the King's Bench.

William Laken (Lacon) (d.1475) of Betton Alkmere, Shropshire and Stone, Kent was the illegitimate son of Sir Richard Laken (d.ca.1446) of Laken and Willey in Shropshire. By his first wife Maud he had three sons and three daughters. By October 1460 William had married secondly Sybil, daughter and coheir of John Siferwast (Syferwast) of Clewer, Berkshire.[93] The eldest son of his father, he was a rising young lawyer but the main estates of his family passed to the legitimate sons, firstly to Richard and after his childless death in 1451 to another William.[94] William and Sybil had two sons, William, George and a daughter Elizabeth who married a Mortimer.[95]   This is interesting as a Mortimer coat occurs in the next light at Ockwells.

Armorial Achievement

Crest
Seven bullrushes sable, slipped and leaved or.

Blazon
Azure five fleurs de lis or.

This attribution, made by Everard Green, appears to be based on canting arms as yellow flags (fleurs de lis) and bullrushes grown on a lake, (are Lake-on) though he notes that no such arms are on record, suggesting that Laken abandoned the canting arms and bore what was the coat of the main line, *Quarterly, per fess dancetty ermine and azure* on the tomb for him and his wife in St Michael's Bray:. His brass effigy and shield are extant though the *azure* now looks black. His wife's effigy was stolen about 1841.[96]

---

[93] Payling 2020b, p145.
[94] Ibid, p146. Confusingly, Richard Laken, the father, had two Williams, two Richards and a Thomas.
[95] Ibid, p151.
[96] Ibid, p152.

Norreys Link

Laken was a lawyer and although his family was based in Shropshire, he evidently also worked in Kent for several landowners including, in the mid-fifteenth century, Edward Brooke, Lord Cobham. His work in Kent may be how he originally came in contact with John Norreys as the family of Norreys' second wife, Eleanor Clitheroe, was based in Kent. Her grandfather, Sir John Oldcastle, had been Lord Cobham in right of his wife. Laken was illegitimate so Norreys may have used canting arms at Ockwells, rather than the main Laken coat. In 1454 Laken was a King's Justice in the Welsh lordship of the duchy of Lancaster. John Norreys Esquire was a feoffee of the estates of the duchy around this time[97] so may have dealt with him regarding these estates. The following year Laken became Norreys' neighbour as by 1455 he married to Sybil Sifrewast, the youngest of three daughters of John Sifrewast, whose main property was the manor of Clewer, near Windsor. This probably brought him into this area of Berkshire. Via this marriage he extended his property. By 1464 he was given a life interest in her inheritance, holding in her right a moiety of the manor together with 400 acres and £4 of annual rent in Hurst, Cookham, Bray and Binfield.[98] John Norreys also held assets in those manors at his death in 1466 (see Appendix A, No. 7). In 1459 Laken was appointed with others including John Norreys (Norys) to examine prisoners in the gaol at Windsor Castle, in effect to decide on their guilt and either release them or if their offences warranted it to send them to the court of King's Bench at Westminster.[99]

William Laken died in 1475 and was buried in St Michael's Church Bray by his widow, his executrix, who probably chose to use the coat of the legitimate Laken line on their joint tomb rather than the Ockwells coat.

Left: monument to William Laken (d.1475) in St Michael's Bray. Right: Ashmole's drawing of Laken's tomb showing the lost brasses (Ashmole 850 f298. Copyright: Bodleian Library)

---

[97] Norreys remained a feoffee of the duchy in 1458 (Clark 2020a, p673).
[98] Payling 2020b, p149.
[99] CPR 1452-1461, p493.

12.   HUGH MORTIMER (d.by 1460)
Esquire of the Body; Knight by 1449.

Hugh Mortimer, of Cure Wyard & Martley, Worcestershire, and Tedstone Wafre, Herefordshire, was the son of Sir John Mortimer who died at Agincourt in 1415.

Armorial Achievement

Crest
A panache of feathers argent issuing out of a coronet or.

Blazon
Azure, three bars or, on a chief of the second, a pale between two gyrons of the first, over all an inescutcheon ermine.

In 1838 a watercolour drawing by Thomas Willement, Queen Victoria's glazier (*left; copyright: BL*) made before the armorial glass was removed to Taplow Court shows that the feathers of the crest were *per pale sable and argent*, identifying it as Mortimer.[100] The sable colour of the dexter half of panache of feathers is no longer apparent. Everard Green in 1899, described the glass after it was re-instated, noting that the dexter half of the panache of feathers was missing. Evidently it was later repaired but the sable colouration was not reproduced.

---

[100] See BL Add MSS 34868, p198. Habington, vol 2, p186, identifies the panache of feathers as the Mortimer crest.

Apart from his lands in Herefordshire and Worcestershire Hugh Mortimer seems to have had a local base, being also of Mortimer's Hall, possibly located in Mortimer West End on the Berkshire/Hampshire border.[101] He was of the cadet line of this family, distinguished by an ermine difference mark on the inescutcheon of the Mortimer coat that descended from Roger, first Lord Mortimer of Chirk (d.1426). Lord Mortimer was imprisoned in the Tower with his nephew, the famous Roger Mortimer, after they joined the rebellion against Edward II in 1422. The nephew escaped and with Isabella, wife of Edward II, returned in 1426 to overthrow the king and become Earl of March. His uncle died in the Tower apparently from his wounds. The nephew claimed that his uncle had made him his heir thereby effectively disinheriting his uncle's actual descendants. The cadet line seems to have survived by retaining the lands of Roger Mortimer of Chirk's wife, Lucy de Wafre, and subsequent judicious marriages.

Hugh married Eleanor Cornwall in 1454, daughter of Sir Edmund Cornwall, Baron of Burford and had a son John and two daughters, Elizabeth and Alice.[102] Son John was knighted by Henry VII at the battle of Bosworth after Richard III was slain and was a banneret at the battle of Stoke in 1487.[103] John married Margaret Neville, third daughter of John Neville, Marquess Montagu (d.1471) by his wife Isabel Ingoldisthorpe, but had no issue. Isabel subsequently married Sir William Norreys, eldest son of John Norreys Esquire.

Norreys Link
Mortimer is likely to have known Eleanor Clitheroe, the second wife of John Norreys, as her uncle, Henry Oldcastle Esquire, son and heir of Sir John Oldcastle by his first wife Katherine, lived at Tillington, northwest of Hereford,[104] separated by approximately fifteen miles from Tedstone Wafre. In 1434 both took the oath in Hereford not to maintain peace breakers. There is evidence that Mortimer was a donor in the rebuilding of the quire of Great Malvern Priory where his coat once occurred in a window of St Anne's Chapel. The rebuilding appears to have been a memorial to Richard Beauchamp, Earl of Warwick and his wife, Isabel Despenser,[105] so he probably knew John Norreys who was one of those managing the earl's estates during the minority of the heir, Henry Beauchamp. After the latter's death in 1446, Mortimer was a member of the jury concerned with the Inquisition Post Mortem of his estates in Herefordshire and the adjacent March of Wales. He died reputedly in 1460 at the battle of Wakefield fighting for Richard Duke of York though there is some evidence he died before the battle.[106]

---

[101] Mortimers Hall is described as being in Hampshire (Wedgwood and Holt, p613). At one time Mortimer West End was part of the cross-county parish of Stratfield Mortimer which is mostly in Berkshire and was held by Richard, Duke of York, in the mid C15th. Stratfield Mortimer was already part of the Mortimer estates at the start of the C12th when Hugh Mortimer (d.1180/1) gave it to his son of the same name who gave it to Reading Abbey (Kemp II, pp232-3). St Marys Church in Stratfield Mortimer was rebuilt in 1869 but retains in the organ loft medieval stained glass including the Yorkist symbols, falcon in fetterlock, white roses, the sun of York and feathers issuing out of a crown dating evidently from when Richard, Duke of York, rebuilt the north aisle. Ashmole recorded his armorials in the east window of this aisle plus the Yorkist symbols (Ashmole 850 f.no 27 Bodleian). York apparently allowed his kinsman to live in the manor. Our Hugh was probably a kinsman of the Hugh *Mortemer,* who in 1416 with others, obtained a reversion of the castle and manor of Donnington and other manors, messuages, lands etc in West Berkshire from Thomas Chaucer, which would have become effective after the death of his daughter, Alice, the document noting that *Alice who was the wife of John Philipp chivaler holds for her life from the inheritance of Thomas on the day the agreement was made* (Berkshire Feet of Fines Part II no 1232, pp23-24). Alice's first husband Sir John Philipp had died in 1415.

[102] Draft genealogy of the Mortimers given to the Mortimer Society by, Ian Mortimer 2013.

[103] Darracott 2005, pp11-13, citing Metcalfe, pp10, 14. See also Shaw vol II, pp22, 24.

[104] Wedgwood and Holt, pp646-7.

[105] Darracott 2005, p11, note 79.

[106] See Hampton, p207; Darracott 2005, p12, note 91. Wedgwood and Holt, p613 give ca.1455.

Reconstruction of armorial achievement for Sir Hugh Mortimer once in a window of St Anne's Chapel, Great Malvern Priory, described by Habington as "Mortimer's arms with an inescutcheon ermine quartering chevrons defaced and I suppose misplaced; on his helmet a bunch or plume of feathers party per pale argent and sable out of a Duke's or Earl's crown"

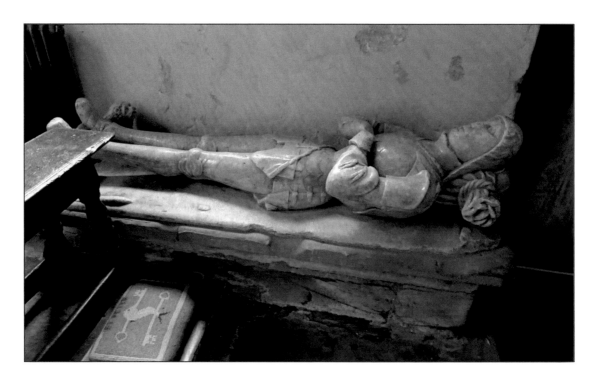

An effigy believed to be of Sir Hugh Mortimer, (with the Yorkist collar of suns and roses and a crest of feathers), in St Peter's Church, Martley, Worcestershire, whose tower he is said to have built ca. 1450[107]

---

[107] Grant p53; Hampton 1979, p207.

13.   JOHN NANFAN (1400-ca.1462)

Constable of Glamorgan 1423; Sheriff of Cornwall 1428-30, 1439-40, 1450-1 & 1456-7; Chamberlain of the Exchequer 1445-46; Esquire of the Body 1447-54, 1557-?; Governor of Jersey 1452-till death.

John Nanfan, of Birtsmorton, Worcestershire, and of Trethewell, Cornwall, was perhaps the son of James Nanfan and Geta Penneck. He married Jane, widow of Sir Remfry Arundell, and daughter and heir of Sir John Coleshill, by whom he had a son Sir Richard Nanfan MP (1445-1507), a second son and a daughter. The marriage of his ancestor Thomas Nanfan, probably his grandfather, to Johanna Penpons, led to him quartering her coat.[108]

Armorial Achievement

Crest
A wolf statant azure.

Blazon
Quarterly:

1 & 4: *Sable on a chevron between three dexter falcon's wings argent, a cross between four ermine spots sable* – Nanfan.

2 & 3: *Argent, three wolves passant in pale azure* – Penpons.

Left: copy by Charles Kerry of a drawing by Sir Thomas Reeve of Hendon's House, Holyport, made in 1765 which indicates that some damage has occurred to quarters 1 & 4 – the chevron and lower falcon wing being lost. It seems they were replaced probably while the windows were at Taplow Court in the nineteenth century. The falcon's wings have been replaced in a different orientation. No identity was given for this coat (from Kerry's notebook Vol II p118, Bodleian Library; copyrighted).

---

[108] See family tree in Maclean, p218 who gives Jas (James) Nanfan? as son of Thomas, and the latter's grandson as John. This tree gives John a son, also John, who was Governor of Jersey & Guernsey. His recent biographer considers the details of his career to indicate that of a single man of that name (see Kleineke, p600, note 17).

Norreys Link

Everard Green[109] identifies this coat as for John Nanfan's son Richard but he was not born until 1445. Richard's father John certainly knew John Norreys through their joint responsibilities regarding the estate of Richard Beauchamp, Earl of Warwick, and dealings with his son Henry and wife Isabel Despenser. Nanfan with Norreys and others had been granted the manor of Tewkesbury in November 1439 to fulfil the will of Isabel Despenser, Countess of Warwick (d.1439), who had been buried in Tewkesbury Abbey with her first husband in the Beauchamp chantry chapel.[110] Nanfan is also likely to have known the Oldcastle family of John Norreys' second wife, Eleanor Clitheroe, through his purchase of Birtsmorton Court, Worcestershire in 1424-5 from the widow of Richard Oldcastle, a cousin of Sir John Oldcastle, Eleanor's grandfather.[111] It is suggested Nanfan rebuilt the manor house adding crenelations some of which survive.[112]

In 1442 wardship of Henry, son of Sir William Bodrugan, was granted to Henry Earl of Warwick, John Nanfan and John Norreys,[113] and in 1445 to 1446 Nanfan was appointed Chamberlain of the Exchequer,[114] being succeeded by John Norreys. In 1450 Cicely Neville, Henry Beauchamp's wife, died and so custody of Warwick's lands came to an end and Nanfan and Norreys were among others pardoned all arrears of accounts as guardians. By then, Henry and Cicely's daughter, Anne, had died so her assets descended to Henry's sister, Anne, wife of Richard Neville, Earl of Warwick, in right of his wife.

Nanfan was appointed warden and governor of the Channel Islands in 1452 for five years, a post renewed in 1457 while in England. He was back in Jersey at Mont Orgueil Castle when it was easily captured in an invasion ordered by Charles VII in May 1461, leading to a suggestion that Margaret of Anjou had sent Nanfan secret orders to surrender the islands to the French,[115] the queen seeing the islands as a refuge for Lancastrian hopes after the defeat at Towton (in March 1461).[116] It is thought Nanfan died in French captivity before May 1463. At the time he was said to die intestate, but it appears he had made a will in 1446 asking to be buried in Tewkesbury Abbey, leaving charitable bequests for the salvation of his soul to the Abbey, the priory at St Michael's Mount in Cornwall and elsewhere.[117]

In a final tenuous link to the Norreys family, Katherine Norreys, the great-great granddaughter of John Norreys Esquire. lived at Mont Orgueil, from 1583, with her husband, Sir Anthony Paulet (d.1600), who was lieutenant governor, and in 1590, governor of Jersey. Their impaled coat can still be seen over the Queen Elizabeth Gate to the castle, the blazon unfortunately being erroneously for the Norris family of Speke (see Appendix B & Tree 1a iv).

---

[109] Everard Green, p238.
[110] CPR 1436-41, p359. Nanfan had been in the retinue of her first husband in 1417 and 1421 when en route to the battlefields of France and may have been with him when he died at the siege of Meux. He remained in the service of his late master's widow (Kleineke p596).
[110] Kleineke, p596.
[111] VCH Worcestershire, vol 4, p120.
[112] Kleineke, p596.
[113] CPR 1441-46, p83.
[114] Wedgwood & Holt, p622.
[115] Kleineke, p600, who finds this suggestion hard to reconcile with Nanfan's ties to the Yorkist, Richard Neville, the Earl of Warwick.
[116] Marr, p79.
[117] Kleineke, p600; Habington vol 1, p121. There does not appear to be a memorial to Nanfan in the Abbey.

The crenellated entrance to Birtsmorton Court.
Nanfan probably reconstructed the manor house though this may be all that remains of his work

Birtsmorton Court - now a wedding venue. The venue website notes the house was remodelled for a
descendent Giles Nanfan ca.1572 and restored in 1871-72, with the east range rebuilt in 1929-30 after a
fire in the eighteenth century

Birtsmorton Church next to the manor house

Left: tomb of Jane née Coleshill, wife of John Nanfan. The south side has the kneeling figure of John Nanfan, her second husband, flanked by their daughter and two sons. Traces of paint survive.

Right: figure of John Nanfan on the tomb of his wife

14.   JOHN NORREYS Esquire of Bray, Berkshire (1405-1466)
(See also Light 9, above)
Builder of Ockwells c.1450-54; Yeoman of the Chamber by 1429; Usher of the Chamber 1437-ca.1441; Esquire of the Body from 1437to end-1455; High Sheriff of Berkshire & Oxfordshire 1437-38, 1442-43, 1457-58; MP Berkshire 1439-40; MP Oxfordshire 1442; Berkshire 1445-46, 1447, 1449-50, 1450-51, 1453; Keeper/Clerk of the Great Wardrobe 1444-1446; Chamberlain of the Exchequer 1446-1450; Treasurer of the Chamber & Keeper of the Jewels of Queen Margaret 1445-1452; Keeper of the Queen's Wardrobe 1448-1457; Steward of Cookham and Bray 1447-1461.

Chapter 3 sets out full the biography of John Norreys Esquire.

He had three wives, two of whom are represented in the Ockwells armorial glass (see also Light 9 above). Here his coat (said to be of Ravenscroft for Norreys) is impaled with the quartered coat of his first wife, Alice Merbrooke.

Armorial Achievement

Crest
A raven rising proper

Blazon
Argent, a chevron between three ravens heads erased sable – Ravenscroft for Norreys impaling quarterly Mountfort coats assumed by Richard Merbrooke:
1 & 4: *Bendy or and azure, a bordure gules* Mountfort (Warwickshire).[118]
2 & 3: *Or two bars gules, a bend azure* Brandeston.

Supporters
Two beavers collared and chained or, each with a fish in mouth.

The crest and supporters are the same as in Light 9.

---

[118] Everard Green (p334) identifies this coat as Merbrooke, citing College of Arms MSS. It is clearly the Mountfort coat (see Foster, p142) with a bordure indicating illegitimate descent (see Cole 1950, p22).

Alice Merbrooke, Norreys' first wife, was a daughter of Richard Merbrooke of Yattendon by his wife, Helen (Ellen), a daughter of William Mountfort (Mountford, Montfort) of Lapworth and Codbarrow in Warwickshire (see Appendix C, Tree 4). Alice brought Yattendon, west Berkshire, to her marriage as dowry.

Yattendon Church, west Berkshire, near to the Yattendon Estate

Head stops on each side of the door were described to Everard Green in 1899 as representing John and Alice. These were put up when the church including the south doorway was vigorously restored in 1858-60 (VCH Berkshire, vol 4, pp125-130)

St Mary the Virgin, Lapworth. The Mountfort Chantry Chapel (west chapel) founded by Richard Mountfort and Rose Brandeston, great-grandparents of Alice Merbrooke, projects over the footway

Mountfort impaling Brandeston, in west window of St Mary the Virgin, Lapworth; this is the coat of Alice Merbrooke's great-grandparents seen at Ockwells as a quartered coat. (The photo has been reversed as the armorial was installed incorrectly, as noted in an information leaflet in the church)

15. EDWARD LANGFORD of Bradfield, Berkshire (1417-1474)

Sheriff Berks and Oxon 1446-49 & in 1471; MP Berkshire 1449-51, 1459; JP Oxfordshire 1452-1455; JP Berkshire1452-1458, 1471; Esquire 1443-52 and probably longer.

Son and heir of Sir Robert Langford (d.1419) of Bradfield by Elizabeth, daughter Sir John Cheyne of Beckford, Gloucester, and married before May 1445 to Sancha, daughter of Sir Thomas Blount (d.1456). Edward was the grandson of Sir William Langford (d.1411) whose estates included holdings in Devon and the Isle of Wight but had at their core eight manors in Berkshire inherited from the De La Beche family.[119]

Armorial Achievement

Crest
A naked boy erect argent, crined or, holding with both hands a club across his waist barwise of the first.

Blazon
Paly of six argent and gules, on a chief azure a lion passant or.

Everard Green wrongly identified this coat as representing Sir John Langford who married Katherine, granddaughter of John Norreys Esquire, and daughter of Sir William Norreys, John's eldest son

Copy (left) by Charles Kerry of a drawing by Sir Thomas Reeve of Hendon's House, Holyport, made in 1765. The colour of the chief has changed from gules to azure. No identity was given for this coat. (From Kerry's notebook Vol II p119 Bodleian Library; copyrighted)

---

[119] Clark 2020d, p163. Much of the details of Langford's biography is from this source except when otherwise indicated.

Norreys Link

Edward Langford remained loyal to the house of Lancaster in the later 1450s, doubtless encouraged by his close links to John Norreys Esquire with whom he remained on friendly terms right up to the end of the reign of Henry IV.[120] They had similar careers including both being MPs for Berkshire in 1449-50 and 1450-51. Their manors in West Berkshire (Bradfield and Yattendon) are not far apart. Following the death of Langford's grandmother in 1420, Bradfield was committed to two highly influential members of the local gentry – Thomas Chaucer and John Golafre. Both were leading members of the Fraternity of the Holy Cross in Abingdon attached to St Helen's church.[121] Norreys and the then Earl of Suffolk would later be involved in licensing this fraternity as a guild. In 1442 Langford relinquished the overlordship of the manor of Yattendon to Norreys.[122]

In 1445 Langford acted as a feoffee for Norreys together with Suffolk and Sir Edmund Hungerford in connection with the purchase by Norreys of the manors of Elington and Spencers in Cookham. In 1446, together with Norreys, Edmund Brudenell and others he was involved in the grant of the manor of Erlegh White Knygtes.[123] He was also appointed Sheriff of Oxfordshire and Berkshire – a thankless task which Norreys may have persuaded him to take on.[124] Again in 1447 he acted for Norreys in the acquisition of the manor of Frilsham.[125] From 1449 to 1451, at a time of crisis with garrisons in Normandy capitulating to the French, Langford was appointed MP for Berkshire, together with Norreys.[126] These parliaments saw the impeachment of William de la Pole, Duke of Suffolk. Suffolk was murdered in 1450 whilst en route to exile. Another casualty was William Aiscough, Bishop of Salisbury, who had married Henry VI and Margaret of Anjou in 1445, murdered by local people while at mass in Edington, Wilts. Langford was commissioned to take charge of the bishop's movable goods and deliver them to the treasurer. In 1452, with Norreys and others, he obtained a royal licence to grant in mortmain to Abingdon Abbey various landed holdings in Sugworth, Radley, Sonnyngwell and Kennyngton,[127] and in 1455 was on commission to raise money in Berkshire with Norreys, the Abbot of Reading and others.[128] In 1459 he represented Berkshire in Parliament for the third and last time, and was on a Commission of Array in Berkshire with among others, John Norreys, John Pury and Edmund Brudenell to resist the rebellion of Richard, Duke of York, and the Nevilles.[129] He was the steward of estates forfeited by the Richard Neville, Earl of Salisbury, and Alice (Montacute) his wife in Devon and Cornwall, and escheator of estates ("Denbigh landes" in Wales) forfeited by Richard, Duke of York. Finally, in 1463 the burgesses of Reading made him a member of their guild,[130] almost certainly the Merchant Gild of Reading. From this same guild, from 1457 for three years, John Norreys had rented a garden in Castle Street, Reading, and may have been a member.[131] In 1474 August Langford died, and though it is unclear where he was buried, it was possibly in St Andrew's Church, Bradfield, rebuilt in the mid-nineteenth century. His grandson John would later marry Katherine, daughter of Sir William Norreys and Anne Horne (see Appendix C, Tree 1a iii).

---

[120] Ibid, p165.
[121] Preston, p21. Thomas Chaucer was the father of Alice, who married Suffolk after the death at the siege of Orleans of her husband, Thomas Montacute, Earl of Salisbury.
[122] CCR 1441-47, p59.
[123] CPR 1446-52, p24.
[124] Clark 2020d, p165.
[125] CCR 1441-7, p496.
[126] Wedgwood, p615.
[127] CPR 1446-52, p549.
[128] Nicolas 1837, p240.
[129] CPR 1452-61, p557.
[130] Clark 2020d, p168, note 1.
[131] Slade 2002, Pt I, pp39, 43, 49.

16.   EDMUND BRUDENELL of Amersham (d.1469)

Lord of manors of Raans, Colshill, Chalfont, Burleys in Stoke and patron of Missenden Abbey; JP Buckinghamshire (1441-1449).

Son of William Brudenell by Agnes Bulstrode who brought Bulstrode's manor in the parish of Chalfont St Peter to the marriage (Appendix C, Tree 5a).[132] He inherited Raans from his uncle, Edmund Brudenell, and the manor of Stoke from his uncle Henry.[133] Edmund was a half-brother of William Bulstrode by the second marriage of their mother, Agnes, to John Shobbington/Chopinden who took his wife's name (Appendix C, Tree 5a). He seems to have been close to his half-brother describing him as his "brother" and giving him remainder rights in his will dated 1457. Edmund married twice, firstly to Agnes Depden[134] having one daughter Alice (b.1438). He married secondly Philippa Englefield, daughter of Philip Englefield Esquire of Finchingfield, Essex, and had four sons (Drew/Drue, John, Edmund and Robert) and two daughters, Joan and Elizabeth (Appendix C, Tree 5b).

Armorial Achievement

Crest

Lost by 1899. *A Swan standing with open wings.*[135]

The original swan crest can be seen in the drawing of Ockwells Hall in Knight's Olde England, published in 1847 (*below*).[136]

Blazon

Quarterly:

1 & 4: *Argent a bend gules.*

2 & 3: *Barry of six gules and argent, on a chief of the last a lion passant azure.*

---

[132] VCH Buckinghamshire, vol 3, pp193-198.

[133] Lipscomb vol 2, pp446-447.

[134] Collins & Brydges, pp489-491.

[135] The crest and possibly the upper part of the coat may have been damaged when the armorial glass was taken out by Charles Pascoe Grenfell and stored at Taplow Court.

[136] The *swan standing with open wings over a lotus flower* is the Brudenell crest on a seal dated 32 Henry VI (1 Sept 1453 to 31 Aug 1454); see Ellis vol 1, p11.

The present Brudenell crest of a sea horse was chosen in 1559 by a later Sir Edmund Brudenell (d. 1585).[137] Everard Green states that this armorial had been renewed. Quarters 1 and 2 of the present blazon are spurious. In 1765 this shield was among the drawings made by Sir Thomas Reeve of Hendons House, Holyport, and subsequently copied by Charles Kerry.[138]

At that date, the blazon Reeve drew can be described as:

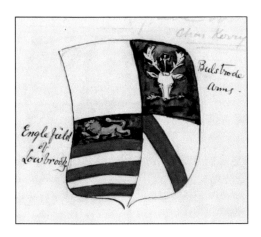

Quarterly:
> 1: Lost – probably *Argent a chevron gules between three hats azure* - Brudenell.[139]
> 2: *Sable, a buck's head caboshed argent, attired and ensigned with a cross or, pierced through the nose with an arrow barwise of the last* – Bulstrode.
> 3: *Barry of six gules and argent, on a chief sable a lion passant azure* – Englefield "of Lowbrook."[140]
> 4: *Argent a bend gules* – possibly Depden.

The colour of the field in chief in the Englefield coat has been changed from sable to argent. It is possible that when Sir Thomas Reeve in 1765 drew this coat he used silver (argent) paint for the field in chief, which, by the time it was seen by Charles Kerry in the nineteenth century, had tarnished accounting for the sable colour in Kerry's copy.

Although quarter 1 was lost by 1765 this identification seems reliable. Edmund Brudenell is suggested because his mother was a Bulstrode and his second wife was Philippa Englefield, daughter of Philip, younger son of son of Sir Philip Englefield (d.1380).[141] Furthermore, he was a Buckinghamshire man who had documented links to John Norreys Esquire. The Bulstrode coat is reflected in the dexter supporter used in their arms by the later Brudenell earls of Cardigan: a *stag argent attired or; between the attires a cross pate of the last; in his mouth an arrow in bend sinister or.*[142]

The current identification as Edmund Brudenell is supported by armorials for his father and mother at each end of the tomb of their son, Sir Robert Brudenell, in St Peter's Church, Deene, Northamptonshire.

---

[137] Wake, p68.

[138] Kerry's Notebook vol II, copyright: Bodleian Library.

[139] Based on the Brudenell coat on his son Robert's tomb in St Peter's Church, Deene, Northants which bears the crescent for a second son as two of his elder brothers (John and Edmund) had died (Wake, p10).

[140] So labelled by Kerry. The manor of Lowbrook is to the west of Ockwells. However, the Englefields did not acquire Lowbrook until the mid-C16th so *of Lowbrook* is misleading. In 1541 Robert, grandson of Christopher Martyn, sold Lowbrook to John Yate and Thomas Elyott, trustees for Elizabeth, widow of Sir Thomas Englefield (Kerry, p107). Sir William Martyn (d.1504), Robert's great-grandfather and Sir Thomas Englefield (d.1514), Elizabeth's father-in-law, were both made Knights of the Bath at the marriage of Arthur, Prince of Wales, on 14th Nov 1501 (Shaw vol, 1 p146). Probably the families knew each other.

[141] Appendix C, No. 7 shows the descent of the Englefields who later would own Ockwells.

[142] Collins & Brydges, p487 & p500.

Left: St Peter's Church, Deene, Northamptonshire. Right: armorial on the tomb of Edmund's son Sir Robert Brudenell: Quarter 1 Brudenell; 2 Bulstrode; 3-5 other coats impaling Englefield (where the field in chief is or (gold) not argent (silver))

Norreys Link

In January 1446 an agreement was made in the court of *Humfrey,* Duke of Gloucester, wherein Edmund with John Norreys Esquire and others appear as complainants before the Steward of Cookham concerning a messuage, mills and various land assets in Cookham. The right of John Norreys is acknowledged and the same were released to the complainants as heirs of the said John Norreys.[143] Also in this year Edmund, together with John Norreys and Edward Langford among others, were involved in a grant of Erlegh White Knyghtes (Knights) and the chapel thereof.[144] Again in 1446 Edmund was described as late escheator in Buckinghamshire[145] and late escheator in Bedfordshire when he and John Wenlock held separate inquisitions concerning the inheritance of the same Bedfordshire manor.[146]

In 1448 Edmund was among a group that included John Norreys Esquire, John Pury Esquire, William Norreys (brother of John), Richard Merbrooke (father of Alice Merbrooke, first wife of Norreys), and William Catesby Esquire, (cousin of Alice), which was granted the manor of Hampstede Ferrers (alias Hampstede Cyfrewast), Berkshire, by Sir William Ferrers of Chartley.[147] This manor became Hampstead Norreys and is still known as such today. Later, in 1452, Edmund with the Abbot of Abingdon, John Norreys, Edward Langford and others served on a commission *de kidellis* (inspection of weirs and dams) for the Thames from Abingdon to New Windsor.[148] In December that year, Edmund, together with the attorney of the Dean and Chapter of St Peter's, Exeter, attended an inquisition at *Thurverton* (Thorverton) regarding the rights of the Dean and

---

[143] Darby Notebook vol 6, p107 (unpub ms in Maidenhead Library); transcribing information from the Bodleian Library. The other complainants were Sir Edmund Hungerford, John Leyntlo (St Lo) Esq and Thomas Lanyingtone (Lavington), a prominent member of the merchant guild in Reading. The mills are Ray Mills.

[144] CPR 1446-52, p24. It seems likely that the 1443 record relating to Earley Whiteknights, giving Norreys, Langford, Brudenell and the others remainder rights (Berkshire Feet of Fines vol II no 1365, p62) is in error in naming him *Edward* Brudenell.

[145] CPR 1441-6, pp 434-5.

[146] CCR 1441-47, p328.

[147] CPR1446-52, pp277-8. In 1449 Thomas Babham was included in the group (Berkshire Feet of Fines Part II no 1398 p67). Two years later he, with the Norreys family, founded a guild in Maidenhead to maintain the bridge over the Thames.

[148] Ibid 1446-52, p578.

Chapter to the parish church there. The findings of the jury were reported to another attorney of the Dean & Chapter, a Thomas Norreys.[149]

During 1454 and 1456 Edmund served on Commissions of the Peace in Berkshire together with John Norreys, Edward Langford and John Pury but more often on the same commission in Buckinghamshire (from 1453 to 1459).[150] In 1459 the Coventry Parliament attainted Richard, Duke of York, Edward, Earl of March, Richard, Earl of Warwick, Richard, Earl of Salisbury, and Edmund, Earl of Rutland of high treason. The Berkshire contingent of the Commission of Array to resist their rebellion included Edmund Brudenell, John Norreys, Edward Langford and John Pury.[151]

On 7 October 1457 he wrote his will, describing himself as Edmund Brudenell of Amersham. His body was to be buried in Amersham church with bequests to the church for a new bell and lights before the great cross and St Katherine's cross; he left money for the poor; goods were to be sold and the money used to repair the highway to Aylesbury and Wendover; and there were substantial bequests to his children Joan, Alice, John, Edmund, Drue & Sir Robert, though not Elizabeth. His wife Philippa was left for life his manor of Hugeley (Hedgerly Bulstrode) and all his lands in Burnham, Ashburnham, Dorney, Taplow, Heckam and Farnham. The executors were Philippa his wife, Richard Bulstrode, John Cheney and Richard Parsons.[152] In December he served on a commission to assign how many archers be supplied by Buckingham and to assess goods and chattels etc for the support of 205 archers. The same commission involved other Ockwells men: William Laken the elder (Shropshire); John Wenlock (Bedford) and the Abbots of Reading and Abingdon together with John Norreys, Edward Langford and John Pury (Berkshire).[153] Edmund died 1469, some years after making his will.

St Mary's Church Amersham. The memorial brasses for Edmund Brudenell and his wife Philippa née Englefield were once in the north aisle of the church

---

[149] CPR 1452-1461, p41. Thought to be a cadet of the family of Norreys of Bray (Wedgwood & Holt p639).
[150] Ibid 1452-1461, pp660-1.
[151] CPR 1452-1461, p557.
[152] Nicolas 1826, pp282-4, Collins & Brydges, p490-91. Richard Bulstrode was the son of Edmund's half-brother, William Bulstrode (18). William (Edmund refers to him as his brother) occurs in the entail of lands bequeathed by Edmund to sons Drue (Drew), John and Edmund. Richard Bulstrode, one of Edmund's executors was also an executor of the 1465 will of John Norreys Esq (Appendix A, No. 2; Kerry, p116-120).
[153] CPR 1452-1461, pp406-408.

17.   JOHN PURY of Chamberhouse in Thatcham, Berkshire (1415-1484)

"Of the Household" 1442-55; Esquire by 1448; MP Bridport 1447; Oxfordshire 1449; Berkshire 1472-75; JP Berkshire 1448-49 & 1452-63.[154]

Son and heir of Thomas Pury, a servant of Henry IV, and Maud Atmore, daughter of William Atte More of Cookham and Bray, Berkshire. He married by April 1439 firstly Elizabeth, daughter of Sir John Isle (or de l'Isle), whose son, also Sir John, in 1439 settled on them the Little Park at Crookham and the nearby manor of Chamberhouse in Thatcham. Their daughter Mary died without issue. By October 1442 he had married Isabel, daughter of Waurne (Wawne) of Beverley, with whom he had a daughter Anne. He also had an illegitimate daughter Susan.[155] Anne married Sir William Danvers and had three sons, Thomas, John and William.[156]

Armorial Achievement

Crest

A peacock's head argent between two eagle's wings erect sable.

Blazon

Quarterly:

1 & 4: *Argent on a fess sable, between three martlets, as many mullets, all countercharged* – Pury.

2 & 3: *Argent, a chevron engrailed between three moor-cocks sable* – Ate More of Cookham.

Norreys Link

From the early 1440s, Pury's recorded association with William de la Pole, Earl of Suffolk, steward of the Household, became more frequent. He also became closely linked with an influential neighbour, John Norreys Esquire. In 1444, together with, Suffolk, John Norreys and others, Pury donated the manor of "le Mote" in Windsor to the king, who in turn granted it to Eton College.[157] In 1448, described as an Esquire, he was again with Norreys and the latter's kinsmen, including Edmund Brudenell, and business associates, in a group granted Hampstead Ferrers and other lands by Sir William Ferrers.[158] The Brudenell armorial occurs in the next light to Pury's. During the period 1448-52, together with John Norreys he served on Commissions of the Peace in Berkshire, and also with Edward

---

[154] Wedgwood & Holt, pp702-3.

[155] Clark 2020e, pp260- 264, Everard Green, p335.

[156] See pedigree in Barfield II, opp p241.

[157] Tighe & Davis, v1, p341; Clark 2020e, p261, who notes that Pury acquired 300 acres of land from Suffolk in 1447 to expand the Chamberhouse estate. Suffolk's wife, Alice, was the widow of Thomas Montacute, Earl of Salisbury (d.1428) whose family had held land there for generations (Barfield v1, pp276-277).

[158] CPR 1446-52, pp277-8; Berkshire Feet of Fines vol 2, p61.

Langford in 1452.[159] In January of 1449 Pury and Norreys were granted an office of collector of tunnage and poundage in the port of London,[160] and in June Pury joined John Norreys, Edward Langford and others to conduct an inquisition in Berkshire regarding the construction of a mill on Lambourn water by the Prior of Poughley that had diverted the water.[161] In September Pury, with Norreys, Langford, the Abbots of Abingdon and Reading plus others, raised a loan in Berkshire for the war in Normandy and elsewhere.[162]

In April 1450 Pury executed a deed granting of all his goods and chattels to John Norreys, and Anne and Susan Pury among others by delivering a gold ring[163] - this being one month before the death of William de la Pole then Duke of Suffolk.[164] In 1451 a commitment was made to John Norreys Esquire, his brothers William and Roger and eldest son William, by mainprise of John Pury of Thatcham and Richard Bulstrode of Bray, *gentilman* (son of William), of the keeping of the lordship of Cookham & Bray for twenty years.[165] In December 1451 Pury was associated with John Norreys and his brothers in founding the Guild of SS Andrew & Mary Magdalene, one purpose of which was to repair Maidenhead bridge. In 1452, Pury with John Norreys, Sir John Lisle (probably his brother-in-law) and others served on a commission of *de kidellis* on the Thames.[166]

By a charter dated 1453 Pury obtained for four acres of meadow in the parish of *Cokeham* (Cookham); this was witnessed by John Norreys, steward of Bray, William Norreys and Roger Norreys and two others.[167] In 1459 Pury served on the Commission of Array in Berkshire with among others, John Norreys, and Edmund Brudenell, to resist the rebellion of Richard, Duke of York. In 1476 Pury came to court in Cookham with others including William Bulstrode, brother-in-law of John Norreys, and John, Lord Howard, married to John Norreys' widow, Margaret Chedworth. Roger Norreys, John's half-brother, and William Bulstrode were among those elected to the office of Receiver of the Queen's rents.[168] Pury died in 1484 and was buried in St Mary's church, Thatcham, leaving as sole heiress the issue of his second marriage, Anne, who subsequently married Sir William Danvers (d.1509), one of the Justices of the Common Bench.[169] In 1530 Anne in her will wrote *I give my body to be buried in the church at Thatcham in a chapel newly made by me in a vault of fayer bricke; where an honest priest is to pray for my dear friends, for me, and for my children.*[170]

St Mary's Church, Thatcham. The Chamberhouse Chapel, at the east end of the south aisle, was built by John Pury's daughter Anne, of "fayer bricke". It was faced in stone and flint during the Victorian restoration (from information in the church)

[159] CPR 1446-52, p586.
[160] Ibid, p206.
[161] CPR 1446-52, p271.
[162] Ibid, p279.
[163] Barfield v1, pp109, 279-280; II, pp163-164.
[164] Barfield v1, p280.
[165] CFR 1445-52, p229.
[166] CPR 1448-52, p578.
[167] CCR 1447-54, p47.
[168] Darby Notebook vol 11, p29.
[169] Barfield v1, p280.
[170] McNamara, pp183-189.

18.   WILLIAM BULSTRODE of Upton, Buckinghamshire (d. after 1479)
Brother-in-law of John Norreys Esquire.

Son of Agnes Bulstrode and John Shobington/Chopinden, her second husband. William took his mother's name quartering his father's coat with his mother's but keeping his father's crest. He married Agnes Norreys, sister of John Norreys Esquire. They had nine sons and two daughters (Appendix C, Tree 5a). He was the half-brother of Edmund Brudenell, son of Agnes by her first husband, William Brudenell (Appendix C, Tree 5a).

Armorial Achievement

Crest

A squirrel sejeant gules, holding in his dexter paw a bunch of nuts or – the crest of the Shopington/Chopinden family.

Blazon
Quarterly:
1 & 4: *Sable, a buck's head caboshed argent, attired and ensigned with a cross or, pierced through the nose with an arrow barwise of the last* – Bulstrode.
2 & 3: *Argent, a chevron gules. Between three squirrels sejeant sable –* Shobington/Chopinden.

Everard Green identified this armorial as for Richard Bulstrode (d.1502), his eldest son, but it can be identified as the father for the following reasons:
a) William Bulstrode was alive in 1479, long after the armorial glass at Ockwells was put up.
b) There are no difference marks on the armorial to indicate an eldest son.
c) William was the brother-in-law of John Norreys and the half-brother of Edmund Brudenell whose armorial is also at Ockwells.

Norreys Link
Little information has been found on this man's career. He is glimpsed through the records left by his children and his half-brother, Edmund Brudenell. It appears that the main asset of his mother, Agnes Bulstrode – i.e. Bulstrode Manor, in the parish of Chalfont St Peter – remained with her children from her first marriage to William

Brudenell.[171] This may account for the low profile of William Bulstrode, son of her second marriage to John Shobington. It appears William's only asset was the manor of Upton, presumably held from Merton Priory who owned it from the twelfth century until the Dissolution.[172] It is suggested that the family connection with his wife's brother, John Norreys Esquire, an influential courtier, benefitted William's son Richard, who entered the service of Queen Margaret of Anjou when Norreys became Treasurer of the Chamber and Keeper of the Jewels of the Queen (1445-52).[173] Richard's career seems to have improved the family fortunes, as on his death he held a lot of land in Buckinghamshire, land including holdings in Upton, Hugeley and Chalvey.[174]

In 1447 Richard, *gentilman,* together with another of his Norreys kinfolk, received from a London skinner custody of his goods & chattels. It is suggested Richard was attached to Norreys' retinue, possibly living with his uncle.[175] Records also show an Easter 1448 commitment to John Norreys Esquire, William his son, William and Roger Norreys (his brothers) by mainprise of Richard Bulstrode of Cokeham, *gentilman* and Thomas Crychefeld of Bray, *gentilman*, of the keeping of the lordship of Cookham & Bray for twenty years.[176] In 1451 this was renewed by mainprise of Richard Bulstrode, now of Bray, and John Pury of Thatcham who had replaced Crychefeld.[177]

Throughout the 1450s, William Bulstrode's son Richard continued to be close to John Norreys, assisting him in the acquisition of property. Norreys is regarded as his most important associate.[178] In January 1453 Richard was paid for materials and wages for a *disgisynge* at the royal manor of Pleasaunce. Evidently, he had been responsible for organising the Christmas revels. In the same month he paid for silks and cloth of gold purchased for the Queen.[179] Norreys was then Keeper of her Wardrobe. Together with John Norreys Esquire, he was granted Fulscot manor in South Moreton.[180] In 1463 Richard Bulstrode was involved in a deed of entail involving properties in Mapledurham owned by John Norreys Esquire.[181] Richard was also named as executor in the will of John Norreys dated 1465. Ca.1455 Richard married Alice Knyffe, daughter and heir of Richard Knyffe of Chalvey. Chalvey is adjacent to the Bulstrode holding of Upton.[182]

In 1457 William, half-brother of Edmund Brudenell, is mentioned in the latter's will, proved 1469.[183] William's son Richard Bulstrode was an executor. Agnes his wife died in April 1472 and was buried in St Laurence's Church, Upton. In 1860 a slab showed matrices of William Bulstrode (her husband) and also a brass of their children with an inscription, both now lost, reading (original in Latin): *Pray for the souls of William Bulstrode and Agnes his wife, daughter of William Norrys of Bray and for the souls of Richard, Robert, Isabella, John,*

---

[171] Hugeley Bulstrode was alienated to Edmund Brudenell in 1449 (VCH Buckinghamshire, vol 3, p278-281) perhaps indicating it was also part of Agnes's assets. It is thought William Brudenell (his father) is buried in the church at Hugeley (Hedgerley) Bulstrode that once had the arms he bore in its windows i.e. Brudenell impaling Bulstrode (Collins & Brydges p489). Edward Bulstrode, grandson of Agnes and William Bulstrode is said to have been of Hugeley Bulstrode (Visitation of Buckinghamshire in 1634, 1909, p13) so the Bulstrodes may have regained the manor.
[172] VCH Buckinghamshire, vol 3, pp314-318).
[173] Clark 2020c, p633.
[174] See *CIPM* Henry VII, Vol 2, 1915, no. 627, pp395-6.
[175] Clark 2020c, p633.
[176] CFR 1445-1452, p110.
[177] CFR 1445-1452, p229.
[178] Clark 2020c, p634.
[179] Clark 2020c, p634.
[180] Berkshire Feet of Fines Part II no 1416, p71.
[181] Cooke, p78.
[182] Clark 2020c, pp633-634.
[183] Nicolas 1826, pp282-284.

William, Edmund, Agnes, Thomas, Roger, Henry and George children of the aforesaid William Bulstrode and Agnes which Agnes, the mother died April 12 A.D. 1472 and in the 11th year of the reign of King Edward IV. And the aforesaid William Bulstrode, the father, in the year of his life (not filled in).[184] All that remains of their monument is a brass of a woman kneeling, enveloped in a shroud (see photo below).

During 1472-75 Richard (d.1502) was the MP for Bucks. He was appointed Sheriff in 1473, described as "Richard Bulstrode Esq of Hedgerley".[185] But it was William who in October 1476 came to the manor court in Cookham with others including John, Lord Howard Knt, by then married to John Norreys widow, Margaret Chedworth, and John Pury Esq, regarding a land issue when the tenants of the manor elected to the office of Receiver of the Queen's rents that year several men including William, Roger Norreys, possibly the half-brother of John Norreys Esquire and Thomas *Batham* (sic), who was elected Bedell.[186] Also in 1476 he was appointed as a justice with others including his cousin, William Norreys Knt (eldest son of John Norreys Esquire), *Drugo* (sic) Brudenell (his kinsman) and William Danvers, (son-in-law of John Pury) to survey the River Thames and determine offences concerning the erection of weirs, mills etc.[187]

Another son, William, a citizen and draper of London, wrote his will on 28 December 1478 naming his brother Robert and wife Joan as executors and his father William and brother Richard as supervisors.[188] He wished to be buried at Beaconsfield, almost certainly in the church of St Mary's & All Saints where his brother, Robert's, tomb is extant.

William the father was still alive in 1479 as he was mentioned in his son William's Inquisition Post Mortem. Before William's death William Norreys Knt and Roger Bulstrode, gentleman, had enfeoffed William Bulstrode senior, Richard Bulstrode and William Bulstrode, citizen and draper, with Bradley (Bradwells) in the manor of Cookham held of Elizabeth, queen of Edward IV.[189] William senior and his son Richard still held Bradley after William junior's death. Agnes Norreys and her husband, William Bulstrode, were buried in St Laurence's Church, Upton by Chalvey, as were several of their descendants. Extant brasses occur for Edward Bulstrode (d.1517) and Edward Bulstrode (d.1598) together with a stone monument for Henry Bulstrode (d.1632); see below.[190]

---

[184] See Records of Buckinghamshire vol 7 1892, p78 and vol 9 1909, p248; and Baker J H, 2004, p103. The date should be April 11 Edward IV is 1471 not 1472 – probably an accidental error. His son William's name was omitted from the transcribed inscription but that there were nine sons and two daughters is evident from the rubbing of the children's brass as well as the inscription (both lost). Browne Willis in 1733 recorded the figure of Agnes and inscription in 1733 together with arms of Bulstrode quartered with Shobington on a surviving shield, (also lost - see Baker J H, 2004, pp102-103); this is the same as the Ockwells coat.

[185] Cooke, p78.

[186] Darby's Notebook vol 11, p29. Bapham with Norreys, his brothers and John Pury, had founded the Guild of SS Andrew & Mary Magdalene in Maidenhead in 1451.

[187] CPR 1476-1485, p23 (Commission of *de kidellis*).

[188] Clark 2020c, p634.

[189] Darby's Notebook vol 18, pp135-6 that transcribes the Inquisition Post Mortem (IPM) of William Bulstrode citizen & draper (d.1478). The IPM also notes that William Norreys Knt and Roger Bulstrode had enfeoffed William Bulstrode & Richard Bulstrode Esq, William Noreys (sic) of the Inner Temple & Richard Batt citizen & draper of London with the manor of Pynkneys and other lands & tenements. This manor is remembered by the National Trust common of Pinkneys Green near Maidenhead.

[190] Bulstrode memorials are found at St Mary & All Saints Church, Beaconsfield: the tomb of William's son Robert Bulstrode bearing crescent of 2nd son; and at St Mary's Ewelme: brasses for Thomas Broke (d.1518) and Anne Bulstrode, his wife, William's granddaughter (alive 1535) (Napier pp204, 338-9). See Tree 5a, page 294.

St Laurence's Church, Upton by Chalvey

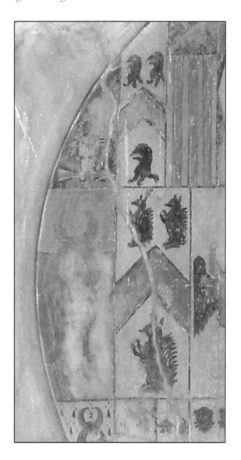

Left: brass of Agnes Bulstrode née Norreys, sister of John Norreys and wife of William Bulstrode
Right: coats of Bulstrode, Norreys and Shobington on the monument of a descendent, Henry Bulstrode (d.1632), in St Laurence's Church, Upton

Early Attempts to Identify Personalities Represented in the Glass

The identification of the personalities represented by their armorial achievements, detailed above, is based on heraldic and biographical research and represents current thinking. There have been two previous published attempts to do this, the first by Lysons in 1813 (his page 449) and the second by Everard Green in 1899. Later authors repeated these identifications. The table on page 104 shows where the identities have changed and where they have stayed the same.

In 1765 the first known drawings of this unique armorial glass were made by Sir Thomas Reeve who mostly drew the coat rather than the whole achievement. In the nineteenth century these were copied by Charles Kerry but not included in his 1861 book on the history of Bray. Kerry's notebook containing his copied drawings is in the Bodleian Library, Oxford.[191] Unfortunately, Reeve's original drawings have not so far been located, so the author of the labels in unclear. An example of Kerry's drawings is shown below, and all are reproduced in Appendix A, No. 10.

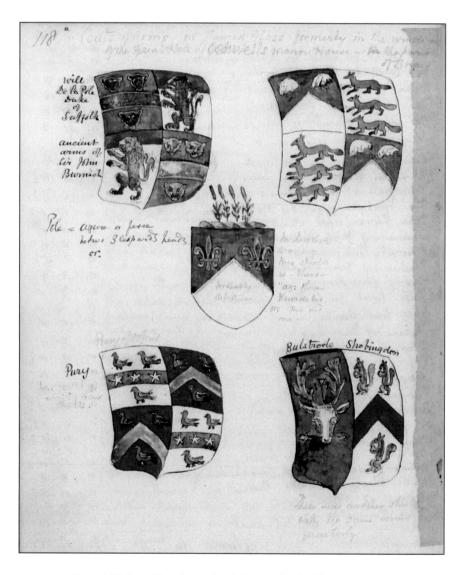

Page 118 from Kerry's notebook (copyright: Bodleian Library)

---

[191] Kerry's notebook Vol II, pp118-121. This cites additional information on the glass in vol IV of his notebooks but unfortunately this is not possessed by the Bodleian.

In 1798 the *Gentleman's Magazine* published comments about the armorial glass indicating some damage. The authenticity of the glass, including remarks on possible damage and alterations, is assessed in more detail in Appendix E.

In 1899 Everard Green, in describing the stained glass, said *"What the scheme of the heraldic glass was at Ockwells it is now difficult to say"*. His conclusion was based on the idea that there was once additional heraldic glass in the hall windows *"so that a considerable part of the story is lost"*. He added *"the other difficulty is that the glass having been removed to Taplow Court, the original order of the shields is now lost"*.[192]

Lysons' drawing of 1806, the earliest known drawing of the east front of the house, shows a single row of shields, as now.[193] There is no evidence that there was once additional heraldic glass in this front or elsewhere in the great hall.

Everard Green's second difficulty can be overcome by the realisation that although the armorial glass was removed for safe-keeping to Taplow Court in the mid-nineteenth century, because there were fears that the roof would fall, a coloured illustration of the hall windows was made before removal and published by Knight in 1847.[194] Particular individual armorial

Detail from Lysons' drawing of the east front, showing a single row of armorials in the oriel window

achievements are identifiable from the illustration and show that the achievements were put back in the original order. The only armorials not in the original order are the ones in the side window of the oriel that were not visible in the illustration.[195] Green's other actual difficulty was that he had not identified correctly all the personalities represented by the armorial glass. The identification of the shields described above shows that Norreys had a clear scheme for the armorial glass he put up, involving his relatives and colleagues, which portrays a set of people contemporary with each other rather than an *"apparently haphazard assembly"* as previously assumed.[196]

---

[192] Everard Green, p324.
[193] In his drawing the royal achievements, today in lights 3 & 5, are shown in lights 2 & 4, but this is a drafting error as in 1798 they were in the same lights as now (see *Gentleman's Magazine* vol LXVIII Part II, p762).
[194] Knight's *Olde England*, 1847 vol II opposite page 108. Charles Knight, a publisher in Windsor, invented by 1839 a way of printing colour plates at a low price for the mass market. Vol I was published in 1845. See http://www.historyofinformation.com/expanded.php?id=3645 for more on Charles Knight's printing.
[195] The *Gentleman's Magazine* of 1798 (Pt II, p762) describes the original order of coats in the side of the oriel that can be identified as, from left to right: Richard Beauchamp, Bishop of Salisbury; defaced coat with mitre; Abbey of Abingdon (see Appendix E, p306).
[196] See Hussey, II, p97.

Comparison of the Identification of the Armorial Achievements in the Windows of the Great Hall of Ockwells Manor House

No	Present Work	Everard Green 1899	Lysons 1813
1	HENRY BEAUCHAMP 1425-1446	HENRY BEAUCHAMP	HENRY Duke of Warwick
2	EDMUND BEAUFORT 1406-1455	EDMUND BEAUFORT	BEAUFORT Duke of Somerset
3	MARGARET OF ANJOU 1429-1482	MARGARET OF ANJOU	MARGARET OF ANJOU
4	WILLIAM DE LA POLE 1396-1450	John de la Pole William's son	DE LA POLE Duke of Suffolk
5	HENRY VI 1421-1471	HENRY VI	HENRY VI
6	JAMES BUTLER 4th Earl of Ormond c.1390-1452	James Butler 5th Earl of Ormond	
7	ABBEY OF ABINGDON	ABBEY OF ABINGDON	Abbey of Westminster
7a	Missing - probably the ABBEY OF READING		
8	RICHARD BEAUCHAMP d.1481	RICHARD BEAUCHAMP	William Beauchamp, Richard's brother
9	JOHN NORREYS 1405-1466	JOHN NORREYS	JOHN NORREYS
10	JOHN WENLOCK 1400-1471	JOHN WENLOCK	My lord WENLOCK
11	WILLIAM LAKEN[197] d.1475	WILLIAM LACON	WILLIAM LACON
12	HUGH MORTIMER d.1460	Mortimer of Chirk	Edmund, last earl of March
13	JOHN NANFAN 1400-ca.1462	Richard Nanfan	Richard Nanfan, John's son
14	JOHN NORREYS 1405-1466	JOHN NORREYS	JOHN NORREYS
15	EDWARD LANGFORD 1417-1474	John Langford – Edward's grandson	
16	EDMUND BRUDENELL d.1469	De la Beche family	
17	JOHN PURY 1415-1484	JOHN PURY	JOHN PURY
18	WILLIAM BULSTRODE d. after 1479	Richard Bulstrode William's son	Bulstrode quartering Shobington

(NAMES in capitals are regarded as correct)

In 1798 a heraldic description of the armorial glass was published but the only identities given were the Abbey of Abingdon and the arms of Mortimer and also England.[198]

---

[197] Name changed from Lacon to Laken based on his memorial brass in St Michael's Church, Bray.
[198] *Gentleman's Magazine* 1798 vol LXVIII Pt II, p762. See Appendix E (page 306).

Dating the Armorial Glass

The glass can be dated to between 1450 and 1454 for the following reasons:

- It was put up when Norreys was married to his second wife as only the armorials of his first and second wives (he had three altogether) occur in the great hall. As his first wife, Alice Merbrooke, was still alive in ca.1449[199] the glazing cannot date from earlier than 1450. By 1450 Henry Beauchamp, Duke of Warwick, was already dead; during 1450 Henry's wife, Cicely Neville died, and William de la Pole, Duke of Suffolk, was executed. They are all represented in the armorial glass.
- Similar armorials for Norreys and his first two wives, Alice Merbrooke and Eleanor Clitheroe, once occurred in the windows of Yattendon Church and can be securely dated because Elias Ashmole in the mid-seventeenth century recorded an inscription that said Norreys had rebuilt it in the year 32 Henry VI (Sept 1453-Aug 1454) (see Appendix A, No. 3). Norreys' first wife, Alice, had brought Yattendon, West Berkshire, to her husband and when he rebuilt the church there he put up the armorial glass.

Detail from Ashmole 850 of armorials at Yattendon for John Norreys and his second wife Eleanor Clitheroe (from left 2ⁿᵈ and 4ᵗʰ) and his first wife Alice Merbrooke (5ᵗʰ)

- At Yattendon, as well as the armorials, Ashmole recorded figures for Norreys, his two wives and five children, three sons and two daughters. Alice had only two sons so the third must be Eleanor's. Assuming Alice, his first wife, died in 1450, the earliest the glazing at Ockwells could have been put up would be a couple of years later, giving time for his marriage to Eleanor and the birth of a son – so probably in the period 1453-1454.
- The roof of the Yattendon church and the hall at Ockwells are thought to be by the same architect.[200]
- Eleanor is thought to have died by October 1457.
- The glazing at Yattendon and Ockwells must have been done before he married a third time, to Margaret Chedworth, ca.1459.

In the years 1450-1454 there was tumult in England. In 1450 Normandy was lost resulting in the Duke of Suffolk being blamed and executed. Gascony was finally lost in July 1453 and shortly after this Henry VI suffered a mental collapse resulting in Richard, Duke of York, being appointed Protector. York's struggle with the Duke of Somerset then led to the start of the Wars of the Roses in 1455. From 1453 Norreys' career began to decline.

---

[199] In TNA E101/410/2 an account of John Norreys as treasurer of the chamber and custodian of the jewels of the Queen 27-28 Hen.VI (1448-9) records Alice receiving a gift from the queen of a silver-gilt cup showing she was still alive at some point in this accounting year i.e. after September 1448 (pers.comm Linda Clark).
[200] Everard Green, p334, note d.

The Norreys Family after the Death of John Norreys Esquire

The 1465 will of John Norreys, apart from leaving money for the *full bilding and making uppe of the Chapell with the Chambres ajoyning with'n my manoir of Okholt*, has no other mention of Ockwells.

John Norreys died in 1466 so was alive when Richard, Duke of York's son, Edward, seized the throne in 1461 as Edward IV. On the chimneypiece in the great hall, this king's badge, the rose en soleil, is crudely carved, perhaps as a placatory gesture in a room containing the armorials of Henry VI, the king Edward replaced.

Within four months of Norreys' death, his widow Margaret had married Sir John Howard (later 1st Howard Duke of Norfolk), as his second wife and, despite Norreys' will, which gave her a reasonable part of his goods and chattels to the value of 1,000 marks (ca. £667) if she remarried, Margaret held for life a very substantial part of the inheritance of Sir William Norreys, John's eldest son.[201] Probably Edward IV facilitated the marriage of Howard to the now rich widow, as he had had the king's patronage since the battle of Towton (1461) when Edward seized the throne.[202] In January 1467 Margaret was living in Bray, almost certainly at *Okholt*, when her new husband sent her wedding gifts from his house in London.[203] It appears that she retained control of the manor of *Okholt*, which was returned to Sir William after her death in 1494.

Also, by 1467, the church of Holy Trinity in Long Melford, Suffolk, was being rebuilt with help from Sir John Howard,[204] whose figure in stained glass together with his relatives was still in its windows in 1637.[205] In that year it was seen and drawn by Henry Lilly, Rouge Dragon, who noted that when the figure was put up he was not yet Duke of Norfolk. Sir John's figure is now lost, but fortunately, that of his wife, Margaret, is extant as is the figure of Elizabeth Mowbray, Duchess of Norfolk, née Talbot and other relatives.[206] Perhaps Norreys' assets helped Howard contribute to the rebuilding at Long Melford; the nearby Stoke by Nayland church where he completed the work of his grandfather; and his own chapel at Tendring Hall.[207]

As the senior co-heir Howard could expect to inherit the Mowbray estates. However, by 1481 Howard's prospects had already dimmed. Edward IV had married his younger son, Richard, Duke of York, to Lady Anne Mowbray, heiress of the fourth Mowbray Duke of Norfolk, an Act of Parliament ensuring that the prince would enjoy the Mowbray estates for life even if she predeceased him. She died in 1481 leaving Richard as Duke of Norfolk in right of his wife, so that Howard found his inheritance blocked, considered to be reason enough for Howard to support the king's brother, Richard Duke of Gloucester, after Edward's death in 1483.[208]

---

[201] Clark 2020b, p681, who suggests that resentment against his stepmother's husband, Lord Howard, now elevated to the dukedom of Norfolk, and still in possession of his paternal inheritance may have played a part in William's rebellion in September 1483 after the throne was seized by Richard III.

[202] Eavis, p100.

[203] Paston Letters 1924, revised 1956, pp37-39.

[204] Eavis, p83.

[205] The glazing is dated to 1481-2 as the clerestory was not finished until 1481 (Eavis, p101).

[206] For a comparison of figures of the Howards seen by Henry Lilly in 1637 and extant in 2019 (see Darracott 2022). Lilly's magnificent work is in the archives of Arundel Castle, seat of the Dukes of Norfolk.

[207] See Eavis, pp101-102 for his building activities and career.

[208] Robinson, p6.

*Figures of Elizabeth Mowbray (née Talbot) and Margaret Howard (née Chedworth)
in Long Melford Church*

*The family tree of the Howards showing the two marriages of John Howard, Duke of Norfolk KG,
illustrated by the impaled coats. In Henry Lilly's 1637 tome "The Genealogie of the Princelie familie of
the Howards" (reproduced courtesy of the Duke of Norfolk)*

William and John, John Norreys' sons by Alice, had prospered under King Edward IV. William was a king's knight and John an esquire of the body.[209] When Edward unexpectedly died, John, on 17th April 1483, helped carry Edward's corpse to the Abbey. Later, the cortege, led by John, Lord Howard, as King's Bannerer, progressed from Westminster Abbey to St George's Chapel, Windsor, for the funeral – a chapel, then incomplete, that the king had built.[210] His son and heir, Edward V, had ridden into London in May with an escort that included John Norreys.[211] In the power struggle that followed Howard was as one of the lords who induced the queen, who had taken sanctuary in Westminster Abbey, to allow her younger son, Richard, Duke of York and Norfolk, to leave sanctuary and join his brother Edward V in the Tower. It is thought her son was surrendered on 16th June, as on that date Howard's Household Book accounts record *8 botes uppe and down from Westminster.*[212] On 22nd June, Edwards' sons were declared bastards; on 26th June Gloucester was hailed king as Richard III and on 28th June Howard was created Duke of Norfolk.[213]

Although William Norreys took part in Richard's coronation[214] and his brother was promoted by the new king,[215] they both rebelled, with William leading the Berkshire contingent during the Duke of Buckingham's rebellion in Sept 1483 together with their brother-in-law John Harcourt Esquire.[216] It is said that the original plan was to put Edward V on the throne and this only became a bid to replace Richard with Henry Tudor when it became clear that the princes were dead;[217] they were dead by early to mid-July.[218] Both brothers were to be attainted; however, John secured a pardon[219] and avoided attainder, being taken to the king by the Duke of Norfolk, in Feb 1484,[220] who seems to have had his custody.[221] Perhaps Margaret, the brothers' stepmother, persuaded her husband to help. The pardon was perhaps a favour to Howard from Richard III. It would also have helped that the second cousin of the Norreys brothers was William Catesby, regarded as one of the closest allies of the king.[222]

William may have joined Henry Tudor in Brittany and appears to have fought against Richard III and the Duke of Norfolk at Bosworth in 1485. The new king, Henry VII, reversed his attainder and rewarded him, but not his brother John who had obtained a pardon from Richard III. William and his son Edward supported Henry against the pretender Lambert Simnel in 1487, Edward being knighted at the battle of Stoke. Also knighted was a William *Norrys.*[223] Somehow this has created the myth that Sir William Norreys (John Norreys Esquire's son) was a banneret at the battle of Stoke. This Sir

[209] Gill, p33.

[210] Tighe & Davis, vol 1, p392. Howard also carried the kings' banner to the Abbey at the head of the cortege (an eyewitness account in Ibid pp391-394).

[211] Gill, p60.

[212] Note by Armstrong in Mancini p124 note 74.

[213] Kendall, p227.

[214] Clark 2020b, p682.

[215] Gill, p62.

[216] Both were attainted (Ibid p179). Harcourt died in exile in June 1484 (Ibid p98).

[217] Ibid, p93.

[218] Ibid, p63.

[219] His pardon describes him as *late of Yatenden co Berks, Esquire, alias late of London* (CPR 1476-1485, p458).

[220] Gill, pp97, 107, and 179. Their brother-in-law, John Harcourt Esq, was also attainted, dying in exile in 1484 (Ibid, p108, pp176, 179). He left Stanton Harcourt to his widow Anne (Norreys) (Baggs et al, p7).

[221] Clark 2020b, p683.

[222] Horrox 1993, p59. See also Appendix C, Tree 4.

[223] Shaw vol II, p25; Metcalfe, p17; Herald's report of ca.1488-90 transcribed in Bennett, p129.

William was knighted by Henry VI at the battle of Northampton in 1460.[224] The William knighted at Stoke has been identified as one of the Norris family of Speke.[225]

When William finally inherited the bulk of his father's estates in Bray and elsewhere on the Duchess of Norfolk's death in 1494, he became a very wealthy man.[226] The duchess appears to have been active in managing her estates for in 1489 when Roger Norreys was elected Beadle, she came to court in Cookham with others including the Prior of Bisham over a tenancy dispute.[227] This suggests she still resided at Ockwells on occasion as it would be convenient for attending court at Windsor Castle.

William evidently had some resources as in 1493, the year before Margaret, his stepmother, died, he purchased messuages, land, meadow, pasture and rents in Cookham from Thomas and Richard Bullok.[228] William died in 1507 having had, like his father, three wives.[229] His third wife, Anne Horne, was closely related to Sir Thomas Fettiplace who married Williams' daughter Elizabeth and inherited Ockwells.[230]

Today this family is best known for the unfortunate Henry Norreys Esquire, great-grandson of John Norreys Esquire, who was beheaded in 1536 having been accused of adultery with Anne Boleyn. It is said that the Norreys family in the sixteenth century obtained the head of Henry Norreys and buried it in their private chapel at Ockwells. It is suggested that Elizabeth I ennobled his son Henry, Lord of Rycote (see Appendix C, Tree 1a), because his father had protested Anne's innocence.[231] Anne was descended from another lord represented by armorial glass at Ockwells, James Butler, fourth Earl of Ormond (see Appendix C, Tree 2).

It is unclear who lived at Ockwells after Margaret, Duchess of Norfolk, stepmother of Sir William Norreys, died in 1494. The main residence of the Norreys family seems to have been in Yattendon but Ockwells, as noted above, would have been convenient for the court in Windsor.

---

[224] Shaw vol II, p12.

[225] Lumby, page vi. Metcalf, p17 does not give arms for this Sir William Norrys (sic).

[226] Clark 2020b, p684.

[227] Darby's Notebook vol 10, p16 (unpub ms in Maidenhead Library). Thomas Bulstrode and Thomas Langford also involved in the dispute are probably descendants of men represented at Ockwells.

[228] Berkshire Feet of Fines II no 1501 p98. This has been identified as a second manor in Cookham. He bequeathed it in 1507 to his son William with remainder in moieties to sons Lionel and Richard; the other manor was White Place, extant until 2018 as a farm (VCH Berkshire, vol 3, p128).

[229] See Appendix C, Tree 1a.

[230] See Appendix C, Tree 6. In 1490 Sir William Norys (sic) together with William Fetyplace (Fettiplace), Thomas's brother and William Besels, father-in-law of Richard, another brother, were gifted lands in Shinfield, Whitley and Reading (Berkshire Feet of Fines II no 1496, p96). By 1490 he must already have been married to Anne Horne half-sister of the Fetyplace brothers.

[231] It is said that Henry VIII offered Henry Norreys his life if he would confess his guilt. This he nobly rejected saying *"That in his conscience he thought the queen innocent; and that he would die a thousand times rather than ruin an innocent person* (Burke 1883, p403). Napier, pp343-346 also transcribes the legal proceedings leading to the execution of Lord Rochford, (Anne's brother), Henry Norreys, Mark Smeaton, William Bryerton (Brereton), Sir Francis Weston and the queen, Anne Boleyn). Among the list of lords & knights summoned in April 1536 for the trial of these men and the queen was Sir Thomas Englefield, father of Sir Francis, who would later marry Katherine Fettiplace, daughter of Elizabeth Norreys, and cousin of Henry Norreys. Francis and Katherine would live for a time at Ockwells.

5. Ockwells in the C16th

The Fettiplaces/Ffetyplaces

Sir William Norreys died in 1507 and, as his son Edward was already dead, his grandson John was his heir, the elder of Edward's two sons. Sir John Norreys who held Yattendon in 1517 and 1539, and entertained Henry VIII in 1520, married Elizabeth, sister to Edmund, Lord Bray, and died in 1564 without issue.[1] In 1517 John had been pardoned for the murder of a Nettlebed man on payment of a 1000-marks fine and the surrender of his lands to a value of £40 yearly to his younger brother Henry for life. John's property in Maidenhead, Bray and elsewhere was accordingly granted to trustees for Henry's use for life with all lands to revert back to John after Henry's death.[2] Unfortunately Henry Norreys was executed in 1536 by Henry VIII accused of adultery with Anne Boleyn.

Fettiplace coat of arms

By 1536 Sir Thomas Fettiplace, one of the trustees was dead.[3] Instead of reverting to John, Okholt was inherited by Elizabeth Norreys, daughter of Sir William Norreys[4] and wife of Sir Thomas, as specified in his will of December 1523 which mentions Ocolt (Okholt).[5]

---

[1] VCH Berkshire, vol 4, p127. The Cookham Court Rolls of Feb 1562, state *Presentment of the death of William Norris who held diverse lands and tenement in Cookham of the Queen in ancient demesne within the manor of Cookham. John Norris son of Edward Norres son of William Norres next heir, idiot heriot* (Darby Notebook vol 3, p23 - unpublished ms in Maidenhead Library). This might mean that Sir John was mentally incapacitated near the end of his life. Nolan (p9) states that he died in 1563, citing Yattendon Parish Records 1558-1914 (BRO MF 341 1/1/).

[2] VCH Berkshire, vol 3, p103.

[3] Ibid, p103 states it passed to Sir Thomas Fettiplace and he was holding it when he died in 1524.

[4] The families had a close relationship as Sir William had married as his third wife, a stepsister of Thomas Fettiplace (see Appendix C, Tree 6).

[5] Proved May 1524 (TNA PROB 11/21/315). Hussey, III, p130 states Elizabeth carried Ockwells to her husband as her dower.

In this will Thomas described his wife as being *great with child* and was evidently hoping for a son *if God send me any* and if not another daughter. *Ocolt* was only one of his estates; others included Compton (Beauchamp) and Stanford. *Ocolt* is mentioned twice in the will detailing how the manor and all the lands and tenements in Bray would descend to Elizabeth his wife, the heirs of their body lawfully begotten, and if the line should be extinguished, to his nephew John *Ffetyplace*. In 1523 Katherine, their young daughter, was unwed and the will specified the money she would have on her marriage. Thomas had died by May 1524, when his will was proved. His widow Elizabeth bore a son Nicholas who died in March 1525, Elizabeth dying two months later; so Katherine, aged four, again became her father's sole heir.[6]

By 1541 Katherine had married Sir Francis Englefield and lived at Ockwells. In 1909 it was reported that when the ruins of the chapel at Ockwells were cleared away a man's head was found in a tin box under the church.[7] Perhaps Katherine obtained the head of her cousin, Henry Norreys, beheaded in 1536, and buried it in the family chapel.[8]

Katherine and her husband are thought to have installed the plain and decorated Tudor arch stone chimneypieces that still exist in the house. Chimneypieces located in the withdrawing room, and in the solar above, are decorated with Tudor roses and the former has been described as a late form of the Tudor Arch.[9] A similar chimneypiece is found in a bedroom in Hever Castle said to be where Anne Boleyn slept.

Left: Tudor arch chimneypiece in the withdrawing room

Above: Detail of the Tudor rose and lozenge decoration from the right-hand corner

---

[6] VCH Berkshire, vol 4, p528.
[7] O'Reilly, p15.
[8] Support for this comes from an account that says after execution on Tower Hill, Lord Rochford's body *with the head* was buried in the chapel of the Tower; the other four (including Henry Norreys) in the churchyard (Napier, p345).
[9] Shuffrey, p83.

The Englefields

Katherine Fettiplace married Francis Englefield, eldest son of Sir Thomas Englefield, and is thought to have lived at Ockwells with her husband.[10] One of Francis' biographers[11] notes that early in his career he was not an unbending catholic, indeed he was only fifteen in 1537 by which time Henry VIII had completed his reformation of the nation's religion. This was also the year that his father Sir Thomas died having settled the manor of Englefield on his wife Elizabeth (née Throckmorton) who survived him.[12]

Englefield coat of arms

Francis inherited his father's estate in 1543 on the death of his mother. It has been suggested that at a similar date he married Katherine Fettiplace (d.1579/80), daughter of Sir Thomas Fettiplace and heir of Compton Beauchamp, Berkshire, as his father had requested him to do before his death in 1537.[13] Most probably they were married by 1541 and living at Ockwells, for in that year trustees for Francis's widowed mother, Lady Elizabeth Englefield, had acquired the manor of Lowbrook, immediately to the west of Ockwells. In 1543 she died leaving the manor to her younger son John and the custody thereof to her elder son Francis[14] who had obtained his inheritance in November of that year.[15]

In 1547 Henry VIII's only son succeeded as Edward VI and Francis Englefield was knighted at his coronation and became part of Princess Mary's household. Soon after, in November 1547, he followed in his father's footsteps as sheriff of Oxfordshire and Berkshire. One biographer says *he may have been planted in Mary's household by the government, for his relapse was apparently unexpected*. In 1551 he was one of three men committed to the Tower for their refusal to make their mistress forbid the mass.[16] It is tempting to speculate that the concealed opening reported to be on the north side of the fireplace in the great hall at Ockwells (according to a note on a nineteenth century photo) and the subterranean

---

[10] Hussey, III, p131.

[11] Baker T F T 1982a.

[12] VCH Berkshire, vol 3, p103. A Thomas Englefield is mentioned in the difficult to decipher will of Sir William Norreys (d.1507) (TNA E/150/784/11) indicating the families had known each other for many years.

[13] Loomie 2013.

[14] VCH Berkshire, vol 3, p104; see Appendix C, Tree 7 which traces the Englefields from the C14th to the C17th.

[15] Baker T F T 1982a.

[16] Ibid.

passage said to have been discovered in the orchard adjoining the manor house at Lowbrook,[17] if they exist, date from the period when Sir Francis lived at Ockwells.

However, when Mary succeeded in 1553 his career bloomed.[18] In 1554 he became an MP for Berkshire. By 1555 he had already moved to Englefield when the queen granted him the manor of Wootton Bassett with remainder to his brother John.[19] He is credited with building the northeast range of Englefield House including the Long Gallery. Builders repairing the gallery in 1838 apparently found the date 1558 on one of the roof timbers.[20]

When Elizabeth I succeeded in November 1558 his career collapsed and in April 1559 he obtained a licence to travel abroad for his health for two years, on condition that he avoid the queen's enemies and return when summoned. After assigning his wife's revenues on 8 May 1559, he left England for Flanders[21] (then part of the Spanish Netherlands). In 1562 when summoned to return he stayed in Flanders and the queen ordered a survey of his properties under lease from the crown for later distribution to others. He travelled to Madrid to ask Philip II, former husband of the now deceased Mary, to intercede with Elizabeth, but the queen politely refused to change her mind. Therefore, as a favour, Philip wrote on 30 October 1568 to the Duke of Alva (Alba) that Englefield had been appointed one of the duke's advisers at 1000 florins a year until he recovered his property.[22] The duke, Fernando Alvarez de Toledo, had been sent to the Spanish Netherlands in 1567 to punish the rioting Dutch. Englefield returned to Flanders (where he lost his sight) but was back in Madrid by 1580 when, following the death of his wife in England, he had his pension as an adviser on English affairs transferred to Madrid. Philip's failure to consult him and the other exiles prior to the 1588 Armada debacle is regarded as a grave omission.[23]

He seems to have been involved in the 1583 Throckmorton Plot (named for Sir Francis Throckmorton, whose father John was Englefield's first cousin) for in 1584 he was indicted for treason and outlawed; in 1587 he was attainted which had to be supplemented by an act in 1593 directed at his 'golden ring' conveyance.[24] In a last effort to preserve his lands, he had, in 1575-6, settled the bulk of his property, including the manor of Englefield, on his nephew, Francis, to be returned to him on his tender of a ring. Legal wrangling led to Elizabeth passing a special statute to confirm the attainder and her agents presented a ring to the nephew so that the property was lost.[25] Thus the manor of Englefield passed from the family.

Ironically the legacy of Sir Francis may be the English College (also known as St Alban's College) in Valladolid in Spain that still exists. In 1589 he was anxious to secure approval for the college, the first English seminary in Castile[26] which was founded in that year.[27] He

---

[17] Kerry, p108. Brayley, p373 said the opening led, between the walls, to the upper storey of Ockwells.
[18] She appointed him Keeper of Reading Abbey (Durrant & Painter, p65). The Abbey's armorial is probably the one missing from the oriel in the great hall.
[19] Dunning et al, p24.
[20] http://www.berkshirehistory.com/castles/englefield_house.html.
[21] Loomie 2013.
[22] Ibid.
[23] Ibid.
[24] Ibid.
[25] VCH Berkshire, vol 3, p407; http://www.berkshirehistory.com/bios/fenglefield.html.
[26] Loomie 2013.
[27] He was a close friend of Cardinal William Allen and provided genealogical information to Robert Persons regarding the succession after Elizabeth (Ibid). Allen and the Jesuit Robert Persons are regarded as founders of the English College http://www.sanalbano.org/a-living-history/. The Throckmorton Plot of 1583 to

died on 13th September 1596, while at the college where he wrote his will, and is buried there.[28] The college, founded to train catholic priests to send as missionaries to England, has in its entrance hall a list of its students martyred in the seventeenth century, mostly at Tyburn.

Nephew Francis does not appear to have held on to any of his uncle's lands as in 1601 he was "of Lowbrooks" inherited from his mother.[29] The Tudor manor house at Lowbrook (now called Lillibrooke Manor) was probably built by John, with help from Francis, after 1543. It has sixteenth century wood panelling on its walls and Tudor arch chimneypieces. Similar panelling and chimneypieces (of whiter stone) are found at Ockwells. Lowbrook also has a garden enclosed by a brick wall with a central gate. This is also to be seen at Ockwells though the wall is said to be of the same age as the house,[30] in which case the feature has been copied at Lowbrook.

The Royal English College of St Alban, Valladolid, Spain

Tudor Lowbrook House with brick wall enclosing garden

---

overthrow Elizabeth and place Mary, Queen of Scots, on the throne planned to include a revolt of English Catholics in which Allen and the Jesuits were involved.

[28] Loomie 2013.

[29] Kerry, p107. However, he did inherit Vastern Manor from his father John and became baronet in 1612 (http://www.berkshirehistory.com/bios/fenglefield.html).

[30] Hussey, I, p59.

Tudor arch chimneypieces at Ockwells. Left: decorated with Tudor roses in the solar above the withdrawing room. Right: undecorated in another bedroom

It seems that Francis redecorated the withdrawing room at Ockwells with panelling and the stone chimneypiece ca.1550.[31] A similar carved chimneypiece occurs in the bedroom (solar) above with a plain one in another bedroom, all presumably replacing earlier ones. We do not know what was there originally. There is a fifteenth-century stone chimneypiece in the great hall and the more important other rooms may have had original stone chimneypieces. Both the plain Tudor chimneypiece in the downstairs room and later overmantel were moved in the twentieth century by Sir Edward Barry from what was his drawing room to his study (the porters lodge) and are now lost.

The drawing room at Ockwells (in 1904) with a plain Tudor arch chimneypiece and later Jacobean overmantel, both removed by Sir Edward Barry and placed in his study (photo from Latham 1904)

---

[31] Hussey, III, p133.

It is unclear where Katherine, Sir Francis's wife, lived after the departure of her husband in 1559. At some point Ockwells was let to a tenant – James Winch (Wynch). Katherine died in 1579, before her husband's lands were seized. However, Ockwells was part of her dowry so, as they had no children, it was returned to the Fettiplaces (see Tables 1 and 2) and as specified in her father's will, her cousin Sir John Fettiplace inherited in October 1580, and a short time later, on the 9th December, surrendered Ockholt to the Crown on payment of the sum of £200. Within a month he was dead.[32] In February 1581 his son Basil (Bessel, Besils) was granted a 21-year lease by Elizabeth I[33] and in May *Besils Fetyplace* of *Compton Beauchamp, Berks Esq*, made an indenture with *William Day, Provost of Eaton,* to lease Ockwells to trustees acting for the provost and his son. After a royal grant was obtained in 1582, Ockwells was sold to the Days in 1583 with a sitting tenant, James Winch (Wynch).[34]

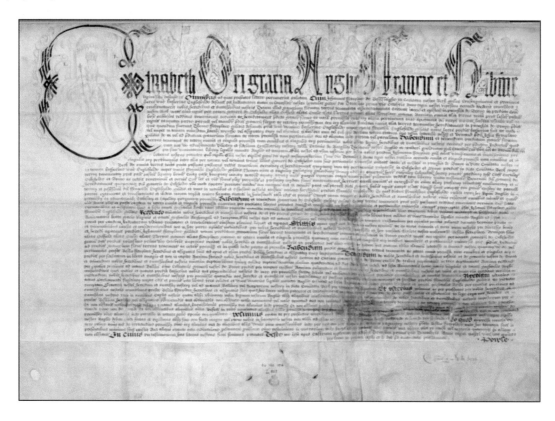

The 1582 Royal Grant of Ockwells to Basil Fettiplace (copyright: Victoria & Albert Museum)
(See Appendix A, No. 9 for a translation of the Latin text)

Thus Ockwells, though changing owners, continued to be occupied by a tenant – James Winch – who remained in residence when the next owners – the Days – took over.

---

[32] Andrews, p23. In his will he left £10 for the repair of Abingdon Bridge (Baker T F T, 1982b). This suggests he was a member of the Guild of the Holy Cross in St Helen's Church, Abingdon, that was responsible for maintaining the bridge.

[33] Andrews, p23. The documents described by Andrews were purchased by Berkshire Record Office via eBay in 1994 (BPRO D/EZ97/1-4). They were described by Andrews when in the possession of Colonel C. Du Pre Penton Powney, and complement other documents already in the Record Office relating to the Day, Baldwin and Powney ownership donated by the estate of William Henry Grenfell, Lord Desborough.

[34] Andrews, p24, who thinks Winch was the same James Winch, alive in 1560, who headed the pedigree of that family in Kerry (opp p126). The royal grant to Basil Fettiplace was presented to the Victoria & Albert Museum by Colonel C. Du Pre Penton Powney. *James Wynch*, the tenant, is mentioned in the grant. Winch held manor lands including Altwoodriding (a large close opposite the house) and many others (see Andrews, p26) which he presumably farmed. The remaining field of Altwoodriding, immediately north of the manor house, has been subject to repeated attempts to have the covenant protecting it lifted.

6. Ockwells in the C17th & C18th

The Days

In 1583 when Basil Fettiplace sold Ockwells to trustees acting for William Day, Provost of Eton, they in turn enfeoffed it to trustees for his wife Ann and William, their son, not yet of age. William Day's election as Provost in 1561 had been influenced by William Cecil, the same man who had helped Sir Philip Hoby acquire nearby Bisham Abbey in 1532. Day remained Provost until 1595 when he was elected Bishop of Winchester, again, according to Day himself, with help from William Cecil, then Lord Burghley, and his son Robert.[1] Day died in 1596, the year after becoming bishop and, as James Winch[2] the tenant occupied Ockwells until he himself died, ca.1590-1600,[3] it is assumed that William, the provost's son, did not move into Ockwells with his family until then.

The Rt Rev William Day (d.1596), Provost of Eton, and later Bishop of Winchester.
(Portrait in King's College, Cambridge)

---

[1] Usher, 2004. Day is reported to have been as rigid a Protestant as his elder brother George (Provost of Kings College) had been a Papist, both brothers managing colleges founded by Henry VI.

[2] The Winch family appear in Bray Court Rolls from the C13th. A pedigree of the Winch family records that in 1602 Richard Winch (grandson of James) purchased a messuage and 45 acres from William Day or Day gent (Winch pedigree in Kerry opp p126). By 1600 the Winch family occupied the nearby manor of Shoppenhangers (VCH Berkshire, vol 3, p106) probably moving there when James died and William Day, the provost's son, and his family moved into Ockwells. The memorial stone of Richard Winch and his brother Robert is located in the floor of the porch in St Michael's Bray next to that of the Days.

[3] Hussey III, p132. In 1639 witnesses claimed he died 40 or 50 years before (Andrews, p24).

James Winch seems to have been the first tenant in Ockwells' history, and as tenants tend not to alter the property they live in, it is likely that by 1600 Ockwells manor house needed some work. William Day junior and his family lived there until 1625 and he is credited with many major changes, including:

a new entrance hall on the north front and an oak staircase put in the northwest corner of the courtyard.[4] This was roofed over and was, at least in 1889, lit by a leaded casement.[5] The staircase was accessed via a contemporary and similarly massive oak screen; and

a new main entrance of the house to access the new entrance hall.[6] The carriage sweep created to serve the new entrance lasted until the early twentieth century when Sir Edward Barry altered the entrance again.

A drawing of the massive oak staircase in the courtyard, accessed by an oak screen, put in by the Days
(From the 1889 Sale Catalogue)

Oak overmantels were inserted in the solar (Queen Elizabeth's Room[7]) and in another bedroom, with one of a more typical Jacobean appearance occurring in a south sitting

---

[4] Probably this was when windows were put in the north front, on either side of the main entrance and also on the floor above, possibly to admit light. Windows are shown in these positions in the 1864 floor plans. See Appendix G, 1864 floor plan b.
[5] 1889 Sale Catalogue.
[6] In the C16th there was a further gable and wing on the east end of the north front, lost between 1815 and 1832; see Appendix F.

room and in the room immediately below the solar, the withdrawing room. The latter overmantel had a matching carved oak chimneypiece that covered the earlier stone one. The overmantel is still in situ in the withdrawing room though the oak chimneypiece was removed during the restoration of the house by Sir Stephen Leech in the nineteenth century and sold.

Overmantels installed by the Days. Left: an overmantel and matching oak chimneypiece in the withdrawing room; right: an overmantel in the solar above the withdrawing room (The drawing is from the 1889 Sale Catalogue)

The oak overmantels at Ockwells are similar to wall panelling and doors at Montacute House (built between 1598 and 1601). Even though the overmantels are of two different designs they were probably put up at the same time as both designs occur in the same lower room at Montacute.

William Day junior appears to have lived at Ockwells until 1625 when he settled Ockholt manor on Michael Poultney, his son-in-law, and Thomas Baldwin. From 1625 the Baldwins and then, by marriage, the Finches of Redheath, Hertfordshire, owned Ockwells.[8] During this period it was leased to other members of the Day family (see Tables 1 and 2). Ralph Day (senior, d.1701), resided there in 1661, as did his son Thomas.[9]

Thomas Day is reputed to have been knighted by Queen Anne for riding ahead to open gates and tear down hedges for her when she was hunting. He lived to be over eighty and is said to have drunk every morning at 5am a bottle of his home brewed seven-year- old beer.[10] It was during this later tenancy of the Days that, in 1765, Sir Thomas Reeve visited Ockwells and made the drawings of the armorial glass, later copied by Charles Kerry.

---

[7] See the 1889 (p6) and 1892 (p14) Sale Catalogues. There is no evidence that the Queen ever stayed at Ockwells.

[8] Charles Finch (d.1675) married Mary, the last surviving daughter of Henry Baldwin of Redheath and Ockwells, Berks (Burke 1871, p435). His son John inherited after the death of two elder brothers.

[9] Kerry p115; Andrews, p25; Wrathall, p140. In 1679, Ralph Day the elder, gent., of *Ocalls* (sic), Bray, and John Ray of Cookham sold land in Cookham to William Cherry Esq of Maidenhead (Darby's Notebook vol 3, p210).

[10] *Gentleman's Magazine* 1798 vol LXVIII Pt III, p1008.

119

Thomas had a son, Ralph (junior), and five daughters. Ralph (d.1772) was a lawyer in Clifford's Inn in London. He visited Ockwells occasionally when his three unmarried sisters Joan, Elizabeth and Amy, lived there. In 1762 he retired from Clifford's Inn – a year after his wife Mary died – to live permanently at Ockwells until he died. As Ralph and Mary had no surviving children the sisters inherited their assets. The sisters moved out when Ockwells was sold to the Powneys in 1786, though evidently continued to live in the area as all are buried in St Michaels' Church, Bray.[11] Their family vault is said to be located under the porch of St Michael's Church, Bray;[12] a memorial stone located on the floor of the porch lists their names, beginning with Thomas Day, gent. (d.1749) and ending with Amy Day (d.1801).

Here lies interred the Bodies

of THOMAS DAY Gent who died
the 4th of July 1749 Age 81 Years

Also SARAH his wife who dyed
the 21st of Feb 1759 Aged 80 Years

Also KATHERINE HILLY their
Daughter
who dyed the 29th of May 1761
Aged 50 years

Also MARY the Wife of
RALPH DAY Gent who dyed
the 26th of February 1765
Aged 48 years

RALPH DAY
Died Sept ye 28th 1772
Aged 65

Also JOANA DAY
died March the 12th 1794
Aged 80 Years

Also ELIZABETH DAY
died Decr the 31st 1796:
Aged 81 Years

AMY DAY
died April 1st 1804
Aged 82 Years

Memorial stone of the Days in the porch of St Michael's Church, Bray, and the author's transcription

[11] Wrathall, pp143-144, pp156-157.
[12] Wentworth Day, p230, though in 2018 the church warden (Jim Tucker) was unaware of any vault.

120

During the tenancy of the Days it is said that a beggar started a fire by knocking out the ashes of his pipe in the straw of the farm yard and a "considerable portion of Ockwells burnt down". It is unclear where the fire was, but it seems the ruins were still standing ca. 1780 although by 1798 had been removed.[13] Certainly today the loop holes in the wall on the north side of the outer court contain soot, perhaps evidence of a fire, and it seems likely that in the past this wall connected with a wing projecting from the northeast corner of the house, now lost. Fire damage may have led to the gable and wing being demolished.

The Powneys

On 28th September 1786, John Finch, Anne, his wife, and Thomas Day (not the Thomas mentioned above) leased the Ockwells estate to Penyston Portlock Powney for a year and then the following day sold it to him.[14]

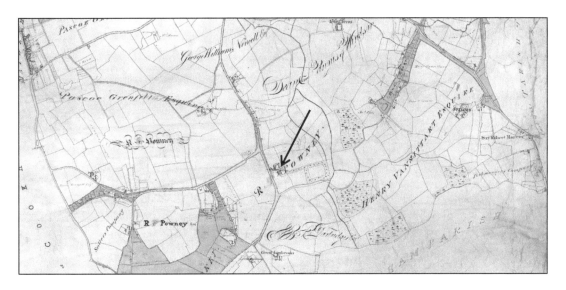

1817 Enclosure Map showing Powney ownership of Ockwells (copyright: BRO);
red arrow shows location of the house

Penyston Portlock Powney was MP for Old Windsor; he evidently sold his assets in Old and New Windsor to buy the manor and farm of Ockwells and also St Ives House, Maidenhead, where he and his wife may have lived.[15] On 30th September Powney re-leased the estate to Messrs Powis and Dayton (Hayton). William Payn, the attorney of Maidenhead, was employed in the sale of the Old Windsor and Ockwells estates.[16] The Powneys appear to have continued the practice of leasing the Ockwells estate to middlemen and the Payn family seem to have continued as Stewards.

Powney wrote his will in 1787 and in the same year acquired land via the Bray Enclosure Award, with Powney representing both himself and John Finch, the previous owner.[17]

---

[13] *Gentleman's Magazine* 1798 vol LXVIII Pt III p 1008.

[14] BRO D/EG/T6.

[15] In 1800 the St Ives Mansion house was described as until lately leased by Elizabeth Powney. It was also described as being in a ruinous state (Act in Chancery 40 Geo III 1800, pp8-9 – Maidenhead Library 90458 B.M. 92).

[16] *Gentleman's Magazine*, cited in Gomme, p119. William Payn signed the sale document as Steward (BRO D/EG/T6).

[17] 1787 Enclosure Award, pp5-7. The award (p7) indicates that Penyston Portlock Powney paid the highest amount for expenses of the enclosure in Bray (£163 6s 2d), indicating he enclosed the most land.

This must have greatly increased the acreage of Ockwells Farm and is probably when the map labelled "Ockwells Farm" now in Berkshire Record Office was drawn.[18]

Powney died in 1794 and, as his eldest son Penyston died intestate three years later, his second son, Richard became his heir. When the enclosure awards were mapped in 1817, Richard Powney is named as owner of Ockwells. The extract from the award of June 1817 notes that he purchased over 13 acres of land in Maidenhead Thicket, plus other bits of land including 1 rood (!) between Ockwells Lane and Ockwells Farm,[19] further increasing the Ockwells Estate.

Thus from 1625, when owned by the Days, began the period when Ockwells Manor house was again tenanted and eventually farmers replaced gentleman farmers, leading to it being used as a farm house in the nineteenth century. This may be why the Powneys evidently had possession of earlier documents relating to Ockwells. As noted above, a descendent, Colonel C. Du Pre Penton Powney, had donated the 1582 Royal Grant of Ockwells (to Basil Fettiplace), to the Victoria & Albert Museum and at the time he held other documents relating to Ockwells. In 2003 local historian Elias Kupfermann spotted that a number of sixteenth- and seventeenth-century Ockwells documents had been offered for sale on ebay.com; these proved to be documents once held by Col Powney that had at some stage been purchased by private collectors. The present author was alerted and contacted Berkshire Record Office (BRO) who agreed to acquire the eleven documents, ten of which concerned Ockwells. The deeds date from the ownership of the Fettiplace family including a lease to trustees acting for William Day, Provost of Eton, and trace the ownership and growth of the manor estate from 1581 to 1777, forming a valuable addition to existing Ockwells material at the Record Office.

Pat Curtis (Maidenhead Library), Theresa May MP, Mark Stevens (BRO) and Ann Darracott looking at a sixteenth-century lease of Ockwells Manor (Photo: Sue Hourigan of Berkshire Record Office)

---

http://ww2.berkshirenclosure.org.uk/CalmView/getimage.ashx?app=Archive&db=Catalog&fname=Q_R_D_C_76A\007.jpg.

[18] A map of ca.1800 lists the fields, noting the total acreage as 305 acres, 3 chains and 29 perches (BRO D/EG/P8). The northern border of Ockwells Farm on the map is approximately where the main rail line is today.

[19] BRO D/EG/T6.

7. Ockwells in the C19th

During the nineteenth century the house continued to be tenanted and to deteriorate. A gable and wing on the north-eastern corner was pulled down between 1827 and 1832, probably due to a fire. Early in this century, despite being tenanted, an increase in interest was being shown in the house, with drawings being made and published, and later on concerns about its future appeared in the press.

In 1800 an Act in Chancery to implement Powney's will suggests Ockwells was in bad repair. It was also specified that it was not to be sold without the consent of his wife Elizabeth and his trustees.[1]

Joan Day (a descendant of Thomas Day)[2] was the tenant ca.1786 but by 1800 the tenants were Ann and Robert Lucas. The Lucases leased, for £315, a farm house (the manor house), barns, stables and other outbuildings plus about 306 acres of arable, meadow and pasture land and coppices.[3] Other tenants are mentioned in later deeds (see Table 1).

Richard Powney, a soldier, was an absentee landlord, appointing trustees to manage his estate. In 1815 he mortgaged Ockwells to James Payn probably the son of Powney's father's attorney, William Pay.[4] In 1818 the trustees put up for auction about 75 acres of Ockwells Farm, the advert noting that Richard Powney Esq was then in the East Indies.[5] On 28th November 1823 William Payn, son of James, then deceased, his sisters and brothers-in-law, leased Ockwells Farm for a year to James Bayley Esq and the following day assigned the mortgage to him. In 1823 Ockwells Farm was still in the tenure of Robert Lucas, or his under-tenant Thomas Young, whilst the house and grounds, including dovecote, barns, stables etc, was occupied by James William Pile (Pyle)[6] – evidently a tenant. Pile was resident in 1820 when Ockwells was visited by the astronomer Sir J F W Herschel FRS.[7] By 1832 the manor house was back in use as the farm house as Thomas Shackel, described as a farmer in the 1841 census, was living at Ockwells.[8]

The house, however, continued to attract interest. Thomas Willement, "Artist in Stained Glass" to Queen Victoria, visited in 1838, drawing three of the armorials identifying them as for Richard Beauchamp, Bishop of Salisbury; Mortimer and one unidentified (actually

---

[1] Act in Chancery 40 Geo III 1800, p9.

[2] See Table 2.

[3] Act in Chancery 40 Geo III 1800, p20.

[4] BRO D/EG/T6. James Payn was Recorder of Maidenhead, dying on 22nd January 1822 (Kerry p137).

[5] The Times 1818 Oct 22nd p2, issue 10494.

[6] BRO D/EG/T6.

[7] Wentworth Day, pp231-232. Herschel in his diary noted that Ockwells was *a very strange old place, a farmhouse, formerly the residence of the Norris family which remains in the same state almost precisely in which it was in in the reign of Henry VI* and proposed to take the painter Sir David Wilkie there. Coincidentally Herschel is buried in St Laurence's Church, Upton by Chalvey, together with several Bulstrodes, including Agnes Bulstrode, née Norreys, sister of John Norreys Esquire.

[8] UK Poll Books & Electoral Register 1538-1893 London Metropolitan Archives.

for John Pury). He also drew the name "Langford", thereby supporting evidence that each light once had at its lower margin identification of the armorial (see Appendix E, p311).[9]

In 1839 the trustees of James Bayley Esq, then deceased, re-conveyed the mortgage to Richard Powney Esq.[10] Thus continued Ockwells' use as a tenanted house with consequent deterioration though happily without the alterations owners often inflict on their properties.

Growth in Public Interest: the northern gable and wing is taken down and deterioration continues

As Ockwells continued to deteriorate, public interest in it developed, leading to the publication of many drawings and articles. In 1806 Lysons *Magna Britannia of Berkshire* had published drawings of the east front and of four achievements from the armorial glass, two of which were of Henry VI and his queen, Margaret of Anjou. In 1813, the Lysons brothers also published the first list of who might be represented in the glass (see page 104).

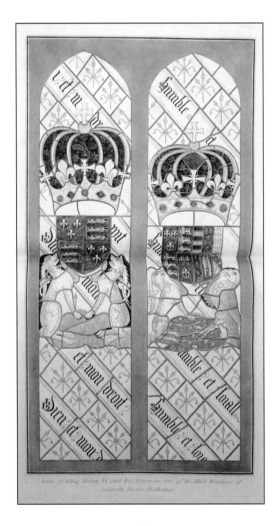

Lysons original caption: "Arms of King Henry VI and his queen in one of the hall windows of Ockwells House, Berkshire"

[9] BL Add. MSS 34868. Willement's drawings of the three armorials were copied by Charles Winston (www.cvma.ac.uk/jsp/location.do?locationKey=450&mode=COUNTY).
[10] BRO D/EG/T6.

The earliest drawing of the gable and wing on the north-eastern corner of the house was that made in 1815 when John Buckler came to Ockwells. They are apparent in the original drawing of the east front, now in the British Library.[11] The drawing he reproduced for sale almost completely omitted the gable and wing, presumably for artistic purposes; this is perhaps why the earlier Lysons drawing of 1806 also omitted it. Further drawings indicate the gable and wing were still up in 1827 (see Appendix F).

Buckler's original 1815 drawing of the east front of Ockwells showing gable and wing (to the right)
(Copyright: British Library)

The watercolour drawing of Ockwells manor house sold by Buckler which omits the gable and wing

---

[11] BL Add Mss 36356 f 220-221.

By 1832 a drawing of the east front by W A Delamotte shows that the wing and gable had been taken down by then.

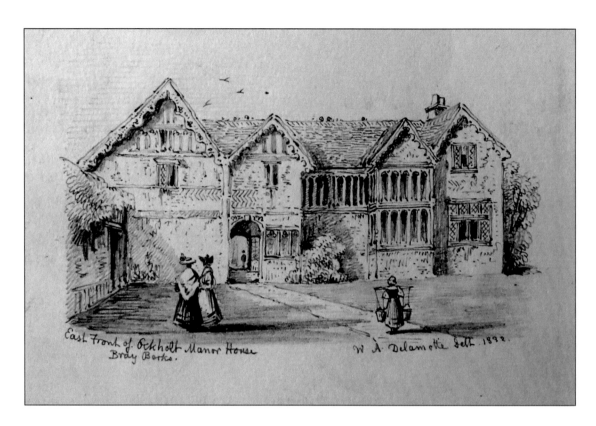

Ockwells by the painter and printmaker W A Delamotte, 1832.
Delamotte's woodcuts were used by E W Brayley for his own book published in 1834[12]

However, this did not stop drawings of the east front, together with the gable and wing, being published. Both were drawn in one of the several prints of Ockwells published in 1839 by Joseph Nash (see Chapter 4), whilst Parker, in 1859, used Twopeny's drawing of the east front (see Appendix F) and his drawings of the bargeboards and panelled gable, describing Ockwells House as now converted into a farm house and in a dilapidated state.

By the nineteenth century the gable and wing had lost,[13] or never had, the carved bargeboards and panelling present in the gables of the rest of the east front. It is likely that this part of the house was for domestic or farm use and was part of the original build.

The windows now on the northern face of the withdrawing room and the solar above must date from after the gable was taken down.

The 1834 publication by Brayley also contains an illustration showing a ceiling in the great hall probably put in at some point to provide support and also gives an idea of the decrepit state of the great hall. As noted earlier, Nash, when he published a drawing of the great hall in 1839, omitted the ceiling instead depicting the roof timbers which by 1839 were covered over (see drawing by Nash in Chapter 4).

---

[12] Brayley, p372. Delamotte's drawing is in the Slocock Collection of Reading Public Library.
[13] Emery, p127.

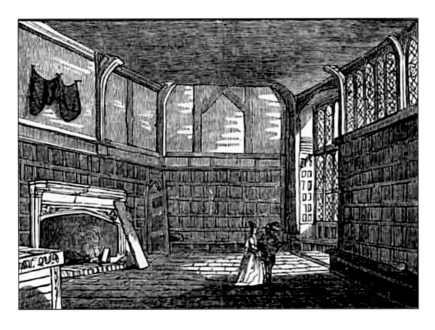

The great hall at Ockwells, by Brayley, showing the ceiling

Brayley notes that in the windows are various coats of arms, (repeating the Lysons 1813 identifications), and that also in the hall are a pair of large iron boots, some swords of peculiar shape, and the remains of a chain jacket. Not all are shown in his illustration. He further describes the flooring as being of red tiles with traces of figures on them, whilst the left side of the chimneypiece concealed an opening large enough to admit a person that led, between the walls, to the upper storey. It is not known whether there are any tiles under the wooden floor put down by Sir Edward Barry and the concealed opening seems to have been plastered over.

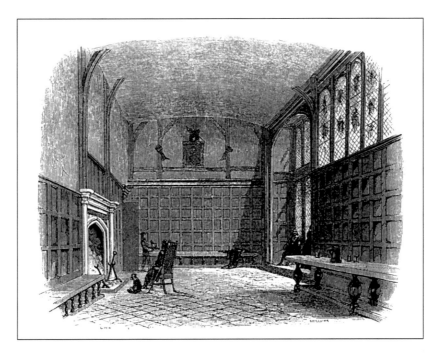

The great hall at Ockwells by Jesse, showing ceiling, jack boots and armorial glass

A similar drawing was made by Edward Jesse, published in his book of 1847.[14] He commented on the *very old and curious stained glass*, and again used the Lysons 1813

[14] Jesse, p174.

identifications and noted that there are still a few specimens of old armour in the hall. Although his illustration shows the boots (known locally as "Cromwell's Boots"), suspended on the north wall of the hall, he does not mention them. Later still, huge jack boots and an ancient shirt of mail were reportedly seen carelessly lying about in one room.[15] A local tradition claims that Cromwell stayed at Lowbrook farm (next to Ockwells) before bringing his guns to Cannon Hill to shell the tower of Bray Church. The boots would remain in the house until sold by Sotheby's in 1965.

Hughes in 1890 described Ockwells as a crumbling shell of a once important mansion that is now fast perishing, with a window frame hanging only by a rusty nail, a door fallen off its hinges and vines growing through the unglazed casements.[16] Furthermore, a poem of the time read:[17]

On Ockwells rich and feudal halls / Its storied roofs and turrets gay,
See Times relentless power falls / But spares the vicar's house of Bray.

That interest in Ockwells was shown by the popular press of the time is evidenced by an article in the *Saturday Magazine* of March 1840. The edition used a re-drawn version Nash's 1839 drawing of the great hall on the cover (with permission of the publisher!) Nash's book – *The Mansions of England in the Olden Time* – is referred to as a "splendid work". The magazine quotes Nash as saying "*Altogether this house is well deserving the attention of the architect as well as the antiquary; for it offers features that might be adapted to the present style of building country residences of moderate dimensions*". See Chapter 4 for Nash's original drawing

Richard Powney (d.1865) is mentioned on the 1843 tithe map but sold Ockwells to Charles Pascoe Grenfell in 1847. It must therefore have been when Ockwells was in Powney's ownership that Charles Knight, the Windsor based writer and publisher, using his own patented "illuminated printing", published in his book *Olde England,* a painting of the great hall that showed the glass in situ (see Chapter 4).[18] The armorials are recognisable and confirm that after the restoration of the great hall many years later, they were replaced correctly except for those in the side windows of the oriel.

---

[15] Hughes G M, p376.
[16] Hughes G M, p374. It is unclear when Hughes visited Ockwells but it was long before his description was published in 1890 since by then the process of restoration had begun.
[17] Anon in Jesse, p175.
[18] Knight began issuing *Olde England: A Pictorial Museum* in parts during 1844 and 1845 (Jeremy Norman's History of Information).

The Grenfells

Charles Pascoe Grenfell

The Grenfells had made their money from copper. Pascoe Grenfell (d.1810) had a tin and copper business in Cornwall. His son, also Pascoe (d.1838), had joined another "copper king", Thomas Williams of Llanidan, as his principal manager. Williams's purchase of Temple Mills at Bisham in 1788, to smelt copper, evidently brought them to the area. Williams built a mansion, Temple House near Bisham (now demolished), and was MP for Great Marlow from 1790. After Williams died in 1820, Pascoe Grenfell (d.1838) succeeded him as a Marlow MP.

The 1817 enclosure map that showed Richard Powney as owner of Ockwells (see page 121) also shows that Pascoe Grenfell had already bought land in the Maidenhead area. Land acquisition was continued by his son, Charles Pascoe Grenfell (b. 4 April 1790; d. 21 March 1867) – a businessman and Liberal Party politician – who on 29th September 1847 purchased Ockwells.[19] A day later Grenfell mortgaged the manor and estate of Ockwells to John Arkwright Esq, an arrangement that was endorsed in 1860.

Charles Pascoe Grenfell

The house continued to be tenanted and continued to deteriorate so that by 1849 Grenfell had the armorial glass taken out and moved to his home at Taplow Court.[20] In 1861 Grenfell's son, Charles William, died. His son's death may have triggered his financing of the repair to the roof of the Norreys Chapel in St Michael's Church, Bray in the following year. Charles Pascoe put up a stone corbel bearing the coat of himself and his wife Georgiana Molyneux, daughter of the Earl of Sefton, together with another of Grenfell

---

[19] See 1892 Sale Catalogue, p30. In addition, he purchased Kimbers (1846); Taplow Court from Lord Orkney (1852); Lowbrooks (1856); Cresswells (1860); Philberts (1863) and Foxley (1864), forming the Taplow Court Estate (see BRO Grenfell Catalogue D/EG). Bucks Record Office in Aylesbury has the Buckinghamshire records of the Grenfell estate.

[20] Nash had first published in 1839 several drawings of Ockwells in his book on medieval mansions. This proved popular so was published again in 1840, 1841 and 1849. A description of the Ockwells plates noted that *Until recently stained glass of a date coeval with the building, adorned the hall windows. These interesting relics, we believe, are now at Taplow Court, the residence of Pascal Greenfell* (sic), *owner of Ockwells* also noting that the music gallery *has now sunk into the degraded condition of a lumber room* (Nash 1839; edition 1849, pp3-4).

impaling St Leger in memory of his father Pascoe, and Pascoe's second wife Georgiana St Leger.[21] He also placed brass memorial plaques in the chapel, one for his father and his two wives and another in memory of his wife and son. Perhaps, as he owned Ockwells, he felt a particular link with the Norreys Chapel in St Michael's, choosing it to house memorials to his family. When he himself died his daughter placed a similar brass in the chancel of the church.[22]

Heraldic corbels in the Norreys Chapel, St Michaels, Bray. Left: for Charles Pascoe Grenfell and his wife; right: for Pascoe Grenfell, his father, and his second wife

Taplow Court, Buckinghamshire

---

[21] His mother, Charlotte Granville, his father's first wife, died in 1790, probably due to giving birth to him, so he would have only known the second wife.
[22] In 1818 Pascoe Grenfell built a family vault in the old churchyard next to Taplow Court in which he, Charles Pascoe and many other Grenfells are buried.

In 1864 the architect William Eden Nesfield[23] visited Ockwells and drew the first known floor plans of the house, now part of the RIBA drawings collection (see Appendix G). He was evidently interested in this type of architecture having published his *Specimens of Medieval Architecture* two years before. These plans are of interest as they show that the manor house was already in use as the farm house because a lean-to dairy, described as modern, had been added and a large bedroom was used for farm labourers (retainers). The addition of the dairy on the north front of the house seems to have blocked the entrance created in the seventeenth century and necessitated the formation of a new entrance hall in the withdrawing room/parlour. The floor plans also show:

- The seventeenth-century staircase occupying part of the inner courtyard
- The single-storey washhouse and scullery demolished in the early part of the nineteenth-century restoration.
- The original buttery and pantry room, modified to include a passage to a WC contained in a small lean-to added to the southwest corner of the house.[24]
- Various dates for the panelling: great hall late-fifteenth century; withdrawing room seventeenth century; and south front parlour eighteenth century.

In 1866 John Arkwright Esq conveyed the Ockwells estate back to Charles Pascoe Grenfell, who died the following year.[25]

Mortgage (1847) and eventual re-conveyance (1866) of Ockwells (copyright: BRO)

---

[23] His father was the landscape architect and painter William Andrews Nesfield.

[24] A larger version of the lean-to was later constructed though removed by 1892 and then reinstated by Barry (see floor plans in Appendix G). At some point a connecting door was put in allowing movement between the two rooms that avoided the corridor.

[25] BRO D/EG/T6.

William Henry Grenfell

As Charles Pascoe's son, Charles William, had died in 1861 Charles Pascoe's eldest grandson, William Henry Grenfell, became his heir. Because the heir was a minor, trustees managed his estates including Ockwells until 1876 when he came of age.[26]

William Henry Grenfell, 1st Baron Desborough, KG, GCVO, DL (30 October 1855 – 9 January 1945) was a British athlete, sportsman, public servant and politician. He sat in the House of Commons first for the Liberal Party and then for the Conservatives between 1880 and 1905, when he was raised to the peerage. He also was President of the Thames Conservancy Board for thirty-two years.

William Henry Grenfell, 1st Baron Desborough, in 1921

In 1872 Ockwells farm and cottages were leased to Mr Robert Parrott for a term of 14 years (1871-1885). The lease is interesting as it describes the house when in use as the farm house (see Appendix A, No. 11) including a *Mens Room*, a *Mens Bedroom* as well as a *Dairy* (as seen in the 1864 floor plans). In 1876 Parrott assigned the lease for the residue of the term to Mr Allport Wilkerson, a farmer of Barley, near Royston in Hertfordshire who moved to Ockwells with his family.[27]

1877 is the date of an enormous map *Plan of the Taplow Court Estate the property of W H Grenfell* – the estates covering Berkshire and Buckinghamshire – that is extant at Taplow Court, now the home of SGI UK, a Buddhist organisation from Japan. It seems a section of the estate map, with added pencilled notes, probably for the use of the farm manager, was kept in the former porter's lodge at Ockwells, where the author saw it at the end of 2004. The 1881 Census records Wilkerson as farming 347 acres with 8 labourers and 3 boys, an increase from the 306 acres of Ockwells farm in 1800.

---

[26] Trustees were Henry Riversdale Grenfell of 15 St James Place; Pascoe St Leger Grenfell of Swansea; Pascoe Du Pre Grenfell of Springfields House, Taplow; and Charles Seymour Grenfell of Elibank House, Taplow. The inscription "PG 1870" on a pump with associated trough is extant in the outer court and can be associated with two of the trustees.

[27] BRO D/EG/T14.

Around this time, William Henry Grenfell may have begun to take an interest in the manor house for in 1877 the *Building News* featured a lithograph drawn by G R Webster of the east front of Ockholt manor.

"The Building News" Oct 1877 shows the original appearance of the porch doorway, growth of vegetation especially in the area around the porch – the window above the porch appears to be blocked-up

In 1879 Walter Peart (1854-1893), who assisted a number of architects in the restoration of medieval buildings, came to Ockwells and made various drawings. These included drawings of the lintels and spandrels of the porch and entrance doorway (see Peart's drawing in Chapter 4). The drawing of the porch lintel shows its original appearance and another shows carvings on a part of the porch lost when it was widened during the nineteenth-century restoration.

In the 27th December 1884 edition of *The Reading Mercury* newspaper there was printed an article entitled *The Ancient Manor of Ockwells near Bray*, written with the help of Mr James Rutland and drawing on Kerry's *History of Bray*, Lysons' *Magna Britannia* and other sources. The article noted the flat ceiling in the great hall, the boots and sword, said to have belonged to Cromwell, and that the stained glass was taken out thirty years previously, restored and taken to Taplow Court and that *it appears to be in nearly as complete a state as when the house was first erected*. The article ended with *At the present time this grand old mansion is in a very dilapidated condition, and unless some steps are taken to arrest this much to be regretted decay, the interesting features of the building will be entirely lost*.

James Rutland, a resident of Taplow, was a builder by trade who specialised in the restoration of ancient buildings; he was also a keen antiquary, famous for his involvement in the excavation of a Saxon burial mound Taeppa's Tump, at Taplow (mound immediately next to Taplow Court, the Grenfells' home). He would soon become involved in the restoration of Ockwells.

133

The Victorian Restoration

Deterioration was such that at the end of the nineteenth century a campaign was begun to restore the house.

This photo ca.1880 shows the increasingly decrepit state of the house as vegetation grows through walls, brickwork crumbles. Broken plaster covers the window over the porch

*The decrepit state of brickwork in the south and west fronts, ca. 1880.
No windows in south face of west front; compare with page 154*

The Society for the Protection of Ancient Buildings (SPAB) had been founded by William Morris in 1877 and the preservation of Ockwells was one of its early cases. In 1880 the SPAB contacted W H Grenfell by letter, (dated 9th November) asking to visit the house to "*ascertain its state and condition.*" Grenfell replied two days later offering them every facility for viewing it and seeing what repairs are requisite. He mentioned that it had been shown to some distinguished architects and that their opinion was that it would require a good deal both of money and care to restore it.

William Morris (1834-96)
founder of the SPAB

What seem to be notes for the report dated 20th November 1880 stated: "*Roof repair is wanting as the entrance of rain is very marked particularly at the entrance porch and in the big chamber (great hall) so the loft above and over bay window of hall, another bad place on fire place. At all these points the mischief is of old standing. Offer to supply a clerk of works and a few labourers under him to [...] repair under proper direction. Floor of hall is [...] to let it remain in foresaid broken condition. Hall is non-ceiled: should not one bay of the ceiling be opened to admit air flight, to allow antiquarians to see it and also that repair and care of it might be more easy. Roof timbers in fine state of preservation very big [...], tiling only small repair; do not remove the main timbers of present ceiling of Great Hall. Ivy* over front of building near porch. Tiling in many parts is very good ought not to be removed.*" (*A diagram locates the ivy and identifies a glazed corridor).

The final report written by George Wardle and Philip Webb said "*They have the pleasure of reporting that in spite of the neglect under which it has evidently suffered for many years the natural strength of its materials has resisted decay to a surprising extent & but very modest amount of absolute repair is needed to put the building in a condition to withstand decay for many years to come.*" Ironically in view of what was to come they also said "*The entrance porch & hall are practically perfect & the gables of the oriel & cross buildings are also original and unmodernised.*" They went on to suggest that "*such an important example of domestic architecture should not be allowed to remain unmeasured and carefully drawn & hereby beg leave to propose that accurate and complete drawings be made by order of the Society as soon as permission of owner & tenant & weather permits*" (see Appendix A, No. 12 for full report). It seems permission was delayed until the tenant left the house, as it was 1887 before drawings were made.

In 1885 the lease on Ockwells Farm, then held by Allport Wilkerson expired. William Henry Grenfell decided to build a farm house for the farmer (giving rise to rumours that he planned to demolish Ockwells and build labourers dwellings with the materials). A new farm house and labourer's cottage, the latter located near the road, was built in 1887.[28] Wilkerson moved into the farmhouse with his family and must have continued to farm the estate as he is recorded there in the 1891 Census.

In February and November 1887 Roland Paul visited Ockwells making many sketches, (some including measurements) now held by the Society of Antiquaries. Two of these were published in *The Builder* magazine of January 1888, the one of the east front showing the growth of vegetation and a window over the porch that appears to have been plastered over, as in the early photos. Paul also drew a floor plan showing minor changes to the 1864 Nesfield plan. An unpublished sketch (see below) of the north front shows the

---

[28] *Pall Mall Gazette* 27 August 1887, p6; 1892 Sale Catalogue, pp18-19.

single-storey washhouse and scullery and adjoining brick curtain wall. Appendix G demonstrates how the ground floor plan changed in the nineteenth and twentieth centuries.

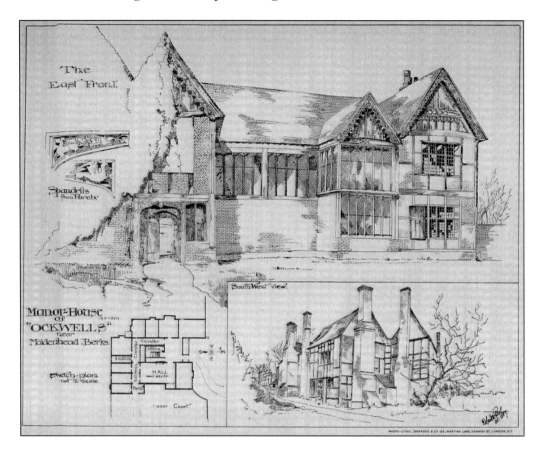

"The Builder" Jan 1888; note overgrowth of vegetation & blocked up window over porch.
The floor plan appears to indicate that the north entrance was no longer part of the withdrawing room
(see 1864 plan on page 33)

1887 unpublished sketch by Roland Paul of the north front showing single storey washhouse and scullery
still in place and a brick wall with attached outbuilding (copyright: Society of Antiquaries)

Paul also made a sketch of the farm buildings in the outer court. The tithe barn seems to have additional structure to its front not seen now. Buildings on the north side of the outer court were later taken down by Sir Edward Barry (compare Plan 1 with Plan 2 in Appendix D); probably he also modified the tithe barn.

When Paul visited in 1887 these farm buildings would still be in use though the tenant farmer had moved to a new farmhouse and the manor house was empty.

Farm buildings in outer court in November 1887 (copyright: Society of Antiquaries)

Also in 1887, the artist C R B Barrett MA visited Ockwells and made sketches. Many would later be used in the 1889 Sale Catalogue and six would be published by Catty & Dobson.[29] His introductory note to the published sketches described the state of the great hall and noted that until the winter of 1886 it had contained armour, antlers etc. He said:

The great hall, a fine room, with an oriel and a ruined screen was once entered by a door in the screen near the porch. The open roof, alas! is hidden by plaster, the fireplace is in disrepair and the general condition of the room is ruinous. Until the winter of 1886 armour, antlers etc remained in their old places on the wall, but these were torn down, damaged and partly stolen by persons who obtained entrance to the then unguarded premises. A very old saddle, in green velvet and gold lace, is however yet at Ockwells.

The armour, antlers etc must date from before it became the farmhouse. Possibly when his lease expired in 1885 Allport Wilkerson found other accommodation, leaving the house temporarily unoccupied, leading to items being stolen.

The process of "restoration" now began, involving both Tom Columbus Smith and Sir Stephen Leech. Their activities would cause vocal opposition from the SPAB.

---

[29] *Six Etchings of Ockwells Manor House.* A copy of the set of six signed prints is in the Slocock Collection vol 1 ff77-79, Reading Public Library.

Tom Columbus Smith

In August 1887 the Pall Mall Gazette published a sketch of the east front of Ockwells by John Seymour Lucas ARA with the headline *"Is Ockwells to be destroyed"?*[30] Two days later in the same paper, William Morris wrote *"It must not"*, and W H Grenfell wrote *"I hope not."*

IS OCKWELLS TO BE DESTROYED?

If local reports can be credited, Ockwells is to be pulled down, in order that labourers' dwellings may be built on the site, with the old materials. But the large estate on which Ockwells stands belongs to one proprietor, and the surrounding grounds, indeed the whole neighbourhood, is equally available for the purpose of building dwellings; so that the demolition of this unique fifteenth-century hall is a piece of wanton destruction. This report has created no little excitement and indignation among the artistic community, who, as usual, have got early wind of it. Ockwells, of which Nash gives no less than three plates in his monumental work, was built by Sir John Norreys in 1466, on the site, it is said, of the manor house originally granted to Richard de Norreys, Queen Eleanor's cook, in 1267. The large building is quaintly gabled with extraordinarily fine foliated barge-boards. It contains a large oak-wainscoted hall, with a musicians' gallery at the end, and a deep square-bayed window extending almost from the ground to the roof. This at one time contained much stained glass, on which appeared the arms of Henry VI, with antelopes as supporters; of Queen Margaret, with the antelope and the eagle; of Norreys, with the beaver and the motto, " Feythfully serve "; as well as those of the Abbeys of Westminster and Abingdon; the Beauforts of Somerset; the Earl of March; Henry, Duke of Warwick; the De la Poles, Dukes of Sussex, and others. But all this was removed some fifteen years ago. Mr. Elliot Stock deals with the place in his " County History of Berks."

The speciality of Ockwells is that it is an almost unique specimen of mediæval *domestic* architecture of the period, that it was all built at one and the same time, that stone hardly, if at all, enters into its composition, and that sacrilege on the part of the "restorer" has never yet been perpetrated. Compton Wynyate in Warwickshire, Athelhampton in Dorsetshire, and Penshurst in Hertfordshire, with several more celebrated mansions, are all fine examples of architecture of the same period, but they are mostly of stone, and we doubt if one of them can boast the same purity of style and beauty of carved gable-boards as picturesque Ockwells, down in East Berkshire.

The old house remained in the Norreys family till 1786, and is now the property of Mr. Grenfell, of Taplow Court. We are sure that Mr. Grenfell cannot be aware of the artistic value of the fine old place, but it is to be hoped that now that we have called attention to the subject he will stay his hand. It is true that, owing to neglect, Ockwells has fallen into a state of disrepair, consequent on its having been given over to the uses of a barn during the past few years. But a little attention and intelligent repair will bring it back to perfect soundness at a very moderate cost, and we have no doubt but that many a willing tenant would be forthcoming who would gladly undertake the duty of 'godfather. It would be well if Mr. Grenfell would pause before it is too late; for the number of our manor houses is thinning all too rapidly. But it would be better still if he would place it in such a condition as to render it not only habitable but an object of permanent value to the artist, the antiquarian, and to every lover of the beautiful.

Pall Mall Gazette of 25th August 1887

Two days later Grenfell advertised for a tenant prepared to restore the manor house, noting that the glass had been taken out by his grandfather because, due to serious settlement, it was not safe where it was. He said: *if anyone can restore Ockwells as it should be restored I should be most happy to hand it over to be put back in the windows of the old hall where it came from – I should be most happy to meet with anyone who thinks he can do it justice.* He further observed that the chief problem was that the roof was too heavy for the walls supporting it and also that he had had copies made in oak of the barge boards.[31]

In June 1886 Grenfell's land agent met local resident, Tom Columbus Smith, to agree terms for the latter to hold a 99-year lease on Ockwells.[32] Smith, a currier by trade, was born 1852 in Shepton Mallet, Somerset, the fifth child and second son of William Smith and his wife Amelia. William Smith was by 1861 a successful currier and leather dresser, employing five men. By 1871 Smith himself was working as a currier and tanner in Bradford, Wiltshire – possibly for his father – though by 1876 he was working in Merthyr, Glamorgan, where he was declared a bankrupt.[33] In October 1880 he married Elizabeth

---

[30] *Pall Mall Gazette* 25 August 1887, p5. Lucas had a later connection during Barry's ownership.
[31] *Pall Mall Gazette* 27 August 1887, p6.
[32] *M.Ad* 9 November 1887, p3.
[33] *London Gazette* 19 December 1879, p7051.

Jane Taylor, the daughter of James Taylor, also a tanner. Soon after this he operated as a currier in partnership with John Johnstone in Queen Street, Maidenhead – though the partnership was subsequently dissolved in January 1882 and Smith continued on his own account. Berkshire electoral registers for the period show the family home was at 4 Sydenham Villas, Grenfell Road, Maidenhead, and in 1889 also at Ockwells Manor for a short period. By 1892 the family had removed to Kidderminster, Worcestershire, where Smith continued as a currier. No doubt typical of most businessmen of his generation, Smith was a long-time member of the freemasons, in this case the Ellington Lodge at Maidenhead. Whatever the later details of his business life, he was a wealthy man when he died at Kidderminster in November 1917, leaving an estate to his widow valued at nearly £28,000.[34]

In September 1887 Smith's solicitor wrote to the local newspaper complaining about Grenfell's statement that *he would be glad to meet with anyone who thinks he can do it justice* whilst a court case was pending over ownership of glass. In the court case – Smith v Grenfell – the phrase *"The lessee to have the stained glass which have been removed to Taplow Court"* was said by Grenfell's representative to mean that he (Smith) should have the glass in the character of lessee and not to have absolute ownership and a right to sell it; the court adjourned for a compromise to be reached,[35] and a lease with Smith was eventually signed on 30th December 1887.[36]

A condition of the lease was that Smith had to spend £400 on the restoration of the house within the year.[37] The lease was for the manor house standing in about two and a half acres. The next year in January an article in the Illustrated London News[38] pointed out that Ockwells is one of the few "timber" halls still remaining in the south of England and referring to the armorial glass, commented that *"The owner was wise enough to remove this glass to his own residence, ... and this was a wise course of action, judging from the present smashed condition of the white panes of glass that had taken the place of those beautiful relics."* Referring to the rumour that the house was to be pulled down, the article continued: *"We cannot but hope that this report is without foundation; but if any measures are to be taken they must be taken at once, for the place is fast falling into ruin and decay".*[39]

Correspondence held at the Society for the Protection of Ancient Buildings (SPAB) in 1888 February shows that the future of Ockwells was still a cause for concern.[40] Conscious of previous articles about Ockwells in the *Pall Mall Gazette*, the Secretary of the SPAB requested that journal to re-publish a statement from *The Builder* which read: *"The proposed alterations to the interior would destroy all its antiquarian and architectural value. The hall (represented in Nash's Mansions) would be divided into two storeys containing three rooms and a staircase. An entrance-door would stand where the lovely bay window now is, and the porch would be removed. The owner of the property is very reluctant to do anything which will destroy the interesting character of the house, and would, I believe, surrender it to any antiquarian society, provided they would undertake to properly restore and maintain it."*

---

[34] Biographical details of Thomas Columbus Smith from relevant censuses, electoral registers, the *London Gazette*, the United Grand Lodge of England Freemason Membership Registers, 1751-1921, and the National Probate Calendar.

[35] *M.Ad* 21 September 1887, p2, *M.Ad* 9 November 1887, p3.

[36] *M.Ad* 9 November 1887, p3. 1889 Sale Catalogue, p9.

[37] Letter from Ernest Law to the Society for the Protection of Ancient Buildings, 1st Feb 1888.

[38] *Illustrated London News* 14 January 1888, pp40-41.

[39] The article noted that the room next to the porch was a fowl house and in the great hall the panelling was bleached and cracked, the floor was smashed, and a creeper had found its way through the broken panes of the bay window (Ibid p 40).

[40] This correspondence is still held by the Society.

Illustrations accompanying the article in the Illustrated London News of 14 January 1888 showing views of Ockwells manor house. Note the view of the porch (centre right) showing its seat with, in the distance, the tithe barn behind a brick wall

A letter to SPAB from Ernest Law, who was interested in buying the lease, said "*I feel pretty sure that all his threats of destroying its archaeological character are therefor made in order to induce some enthusiasts to step forward and make him an extravagant offer in order to save it - He is working the newspapers with this object; and has put an advertisement in the Morning Post saying he is ready to treat for sale; or lease of it. His terms however are preposterous - asking thousands where 3 or 4 hundred would be more than a fair price.*"

The letter gives an idea of the conditions of the lease imposed by Grenfell:

He is under strict covenants in his lease from Mr Grenfell not to interfere with the old part of the house, or to remove or destroy any of the oak panelling, staircase or the fireplaces - but this he does not allow to be known - but plays a game of brag as to what he will do and can do. I am still in hopes he may come round at least to taking £400 or £500 for his lease – whereby he will be relieved from the covenants of having to spend £400 on the premises within the year.

Also in February, Allan Fea, the historian and antiquary, wrote to the *Standard* newspaper:

"Surely one of the many existing antiquarian societies cannot allow this venerable perhaps unique house to be destroyed, when but a comparatively small sum carefully expended would rescue it, for the property has recently changed hands and I understand the present owner, wishing to utilise the house and make it habitable (for it is now very decrepit) so as to suit his own requirements, will have to modernise it and make very considerable alterations which will completely destroy all its ancient characteristics but before commencing these 'improvements' he has generously offered to hand over the interesting part of the house to any antiquarian society that will undertake the restoration in which case he would simply re-build a portion for his own domestic use leaving the ancient part unimpaired.

I will not trespass upon your valuable space by pointing out the numerous architectural features of this picturesque old pile but will simply state the fact that King George IV was so much struck with its beauty that he wished to become a purchaser of it, and that a portion of it subsequently furnished the designs of the Kings' Cottage in Windsor Great Park.

The east front remains now as it is represented in Lysons Berkshire and Nash's Ancient Mansions, though fast falling to decay and ruin. I may here state that all the heraldic painted glass of the hall exists and could be placed in its original position. But if some steps are not taken immediately to preserve it, it will be too late for I believe workmen are now on the spot ready to pull down and destroy what can never be replaced."

On 29th February 1888, Fea's letter was reprinted in the *Maidenhead Advertiser* which commented that *"as is well known Ockwells, which is one of the most perfect specimens of fifteenth century manor house in England, is the property of W H Grenfell of Taplow Court who has recently leased it to Mr T C Smith, currier, for 99 years. Mr Smith is converting the old house into a habitation for himself and his family, but his present plans will leave untouched the parts of chief antiquarian interest; and it is hoped their restoration will be undertaken by archaeologists."* [41]

Fea, in his book *Picturesque Old Houses* described the great hall as being in a state of dilapidation with oak panelling crumbling off the walls and heavy festoons of ivy growing through the windows and the great bay. He credited his letter to the *Standard* newspaper with prompting other papers to take up the cause of conserving Ockwells. [42]

On 25th February 1888 the Secretary of Berkshire Archaeological Society was reported to be prepared to open a fund to repair Ockwells if there was any prospect of the work being realised, giving an estimate of around £500 for the restoration. [43] Nothing further has been found about this fund.

---

[41] *M.Ad* 29 February 1888, p3.
[42] He also described the following as being present on the walls above the panelling in the Great Hall: a pair of Cromwellian jack boots; a dilapidated Elizabethan saddle of green velvet; a fragment of chain mail; a rusty sword or two; and some iron hoops which once served as stirrups (Fea pp115-116).
[43] *Reading Observer* 25 February 1888, p5. The actual cost was £1500.

In June 1888 Smith wrote to the *Maidenhead Advertiser* saying the house is open to visitors for a small charge, with tickets available at the library or the house (see below).[44]

Correspondence.

[Letters intended for publication must contain the name and address of the sender, as a guarantee of good faith. We do not hold ourselves responsible for, or necessarily endorse, the opinions expressed by our Correspondents.]

OCKWELL'S MANOR HOUSE.
To the Editor.

DEAR SIR,—As the above historical place continues to attract so many visitors, it may interest your readers to know that, at the request of many antiquarians and others, I have decided to open it for a few weeks—on Mondays, Thursdays, and Saturdays, when I shall be pleased to point out all that is interesting. A small charge will be made, not for profit but to meet the expenses (see advertisement). If you will kindly insert this in your next issue you will favour

Yours truly,
T. COLUMBUS SMITH.

Ockwell's Manor House, Maidenhead.

In May 1889 an article in the *Maidenhead Advertiser* noted that Smith has *"for the past two years been judiciously and thoughtfully repairing the grand old place including making the roof weatherproof and underpinning the walls which showed a disinclination to support the heavy roof"*, evidently with professional advice from Mr J Rutland, a Taplow architect. The article further noted that *"there still remains a great deal that the tender-hearted antiquary (with money to command) can do, taking care that the ancient features and characteristics of the place shall be: Preserved with pious care, but not restored / By rude presumptuous hand; nor modernised / To suit convenience."*[45]

The article concluded with: *"Ockwells is a 'pearl of great price' and it is earnestly to be hoped that some lover of the antique and the artistic will step in to buy – and to preserve it."* Views evidently not held by certain subsequent owners!

It seems unlikely Smith did much work on the hall as, when he sold the remainder of the lease, the hall ceiling, put in sometime in the past to help stabilise the roof, was still in place and he did not get back the armorial glass. Work carried out by Smith included:

- Putting a new window over the porch on the east front.
- Removing the single storey washhouse/scullery on the north front.
- Putting French windows in the now exposed north wall of the kitchen. Coloured glass in these windows probably the *stained glass horrors* referred to in the press.
- Many of the principal apartments said to be restored.
- Erecting by the west entrance gate a brick building of three floors for use for his business (stretching and finishing tanned hides).[46] See site plan below. This building and gate no longer exist.

---

[44] *M.Ad* 27 June 1888, pp2-3.
[45] *M.Ad* 22 May 1889, p3.
[46] 1889 Sale Catalogue, p7.

Ockwell Manor House, Near Maidenhead.

Above: Ockwells east front in May 1889. By then Tom Columbus Smith had inserted a new window over the porch. Since 1880 brickwork on this front has been repaired

Left: a similar view of Ockwells later featured in a series of postcards produced by Shurey's Publications

The great hall looking north (above) and south (below), ca.1889. The ceiling is still in with broken tiles on the floor and some form of support equipment in the fireplace. The refectory table can also be clearly seen. The view above shows the original position of a door, further north than now

The north front of the house: this shows the remains of the roof line of the single storey wash house/scullery Smith removed plus the French windows he placed in the now exposed north wall of kitchen. Stained glass panels in said windows probably the stained glass horrors referred to in the press. The small window to the left of the porch would be blocked later when this front was extended (copyright: HEA)

In June 1889 Smith put the remainder of the term of the lease on the market.[47] The Sale Catalogue stated: *"for some time prior to 1887 Ockwells was unoccupied and grievously neglected. Since then it has been in the possession of the present occupier* [Smith] *and the work of restoration then commenced under the direction of J. Rutland, architect of Taplow – many of principal apartments (including dining, drawing and breakfast room, library and six bedroom) have been carefully and artistically restored."* It also claims the Elizabeth I slept in the solar (Queen Elizabeth's Room), a view repeated in the 1892 sale catalogue. No evidence of such a visit has been found

---

[47] *"The property is held for a term of 99 years from the 24th December 1887, at the low ground rent of £35"* (1889 Sale Catalogue, p8; note that p9 quotes a date of 30th December 1887).

The catalogue includes a centre double page of illustrations comprising many of the 1887 sketches by C R B Barrett and also a scale plan of the house and grounds.

Barrett's 1887 drawings of Ockwells in the 1889 Sale Catalogue

The drawing of the great hall shows that the armorial glass was still absent, and the ceiling in the hall was still in situ. The drawing of the fireplace in *one of the lower rooms* (the withdrawing room) is of interest at it shows the chimneypiece and matching overmantel still in position (see Chapter 6). The chimneypiece would later be removed by the architect for the subsequent purchaser of the lease (Stephen Leech) and sold. Also to be noted is that the ancient saddle was at that time hanging on a wall in an attic.

Detail from the above illustration. Left: decorative sixteenth century wall panel probably part of the Day "modernisation", now lost. Right: a velvet saddle hung on the wall, identified as both Elizabethan and seventeenth century. The saddle and "Cromwell's Boots" had long been in the house

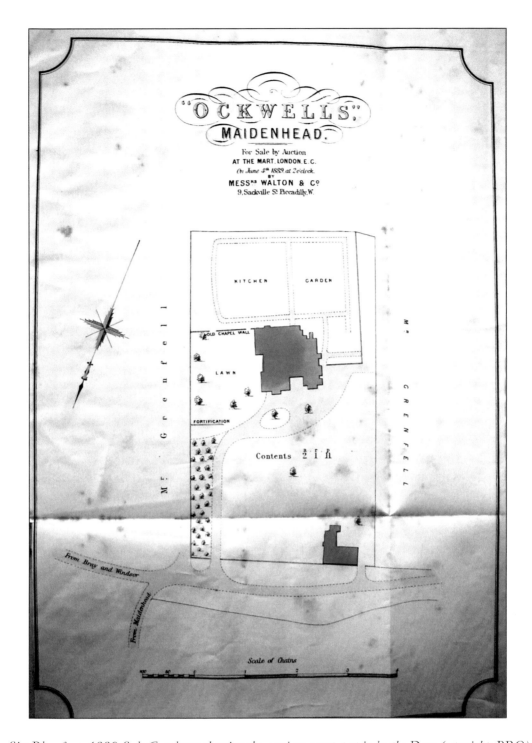

Site Plan from 1889 Sale Catalogue showing the carriage sweep put in by the Days (copyright: BRO)

The sale catalogue site plan shows that the area that Smith leased was 2 acres 1 rood and 11 perches and was surrounded by land owned by Grenfell. The plan also shows two openings in the wall to the north of the house; the west gate to Smith's new building; and the drive to the entrance on the north front created by the Days in the seventeenth century. Another opening is shown to the east of the wall to give access to the farm buildings. Unfortunately, there is no extant original floor plan so the 1889 plan in Appendix G should be regarded as tentative.

In the 1891 census the manor house was recorded as uninhabited though Charles Williams, described as an agricultural servant, lived on the site with his family – probably as caretakers. By then the remainder of the lease had been purchased by Stephen Leech and his restoration must have already started.

147

Sir Stephen Leech KCMG

In June 1889, Stephen Leech purchased the remainder of the term of the lease on Ockwells for £2,500[48] and commissioned Felix Wade to restore the manor house. Leech was a career diplomat, and at this time he had only recently in April been appointed attaché to Berlin 1889 remaining there until transferred to Brussels in April 1892.[49]

Stephen Leech (copyright: National Portrait Gallery)

Stephen Leech was born on 8 July 1864, the son of John Leech of Gorse Hall, Dukinfield, Cheshire, and his wife Eliza. By 1871 Eliza was a widow and the young family were living in the household of her wealthy father, Henry Ashcroft, at Turton, Lancashire. Ashcroft was a cotton manufacturer, employing some 800 workers. One of Stephen Leech's aunts was Helen Leech, the mother of the famous author Beatrix Potter. His older sister, Ethel, was married to the Rev Sir William Hyde Parker, 10th Bt, of Melford Hall, Long Melford, Suffolk.[50] Leech went on to be educated at Eton and Magdalen College, Oxford, entering the diplomatic service in 1888, and continued to serve until his retirement in 1920. He was knighted (KCMG) in 1919. In July 1902 Leech married the Hon. Alice Florence Murray, the daughter of the 10th Baron and later 1st Viscount Elibank, of Scotland, at St James Church, Westminster. However, the marriage was subsequently annulled in 1909 and Leech did not re-marry or have any children. He died in May 1925.

1889 painting by Samuel Evans of Ockwells Manor house before restoration at the end of the nineteenth century

---

[48] *M.Ad* 19 June 1889, p2. He seems also to have bought adjacent land from Grenfell.
[49] The Foreign Office List 1921, p422. It is thought he was not in the UK for any length of time during the Berlin posting (pers. comm. FO archivist Carole Edwards 1990).
[50] In the C15th Long Melford had an earlier connection with Ockwells when Sir John Howard, having lived at Ockwells, paid for figures in stained glass for himself, Margaret, his second wife and widow of John Norreys, and other Howards to be put up in Holy Trinity Church, Long Melford (Darracott 2022).

It is said that Leech, when a scholar at Eton, was taken to see Ockwells by his drawing master (Samuel Evans) *to sketch the decayed and forlorn old manor house, overgrown with ivy and muddied about by carts and geese.* It is claimed his boyhood dream of buying the ancient house led to him making it structurally safe and sound.[51] He certainly commissioned Evans to draw Ockwells before restoration began. The painting, now in the possession of Brian Stein, the current owner of Ockwells, has a note on the back stating *"This drawing was done by Samuel Evans of Eton College (my old drawing master) in 1889 before I began the repairing of the house. I paid eight pounds for it. Stephen Leech."*

A letter from SPAB dated 18th November 1889 to Mr P Boyce stated: *"My committee is much frightened at the idea of Mr Wade having the building".* On 25th November Mr G P Boyce replied: *"I'm afraid that little can be done in the way of influencing Mr L [i.e. Leech] and his architect as regards the proper treatment of the old building."*

In 1890, after meeting with Felix Wade at Ockwells in mid-July, the SPAB sent him a six-page letter, principally pointing out that:

"The Committee is glad to find that the complete stripping of the building showed it to be in a far sounder condition than had been expected, but it is at a loss to understand why you should have removed [indecipherable] *in the way of covering the floor boards.*

Respecting your proposal to put back the [indecipherable] *of the porch as you suppose it was at one time, as it probably was, the Committee would suggest that such an alteration would be a mistake because you cannot be certain that it was as you propose and also because the alteration necessitates the discarding of the existing ancient post on the right as you enter.*

Your suggestion that the staircase should be removed from the internal court is in the Committee's opinion unfortunate. The staircase is a fine piece of oak work obviously made for its present position. If placed anywhere else most of its interest would be lost, whereas in its present position it is part of the history of the building.

The Committee cannot sympathise with your proposal to jack up the timbers of the big hall so as to bring the wall plates level for it believes such a course will result in straining the ancient work without any corresponding advantage. Neither can the Committee sympathise with the proposal to add a bay window to the right end of the main front or the removal of the brick filling under the hall windows.

The Committee would not advocate any action which would render the house unfit for habitation but it fails to see how the alterations above named in any way render the building more fit for habitation except perhaps in the case of the proposed new bay window and such an addition would not be objectionable from the Society's point of view, provided no attempt was made to imitate the ancient work. This addition or any other addition made should be substantial, [...] and not directly imitative in design.

It appears that you consider no harm is done if no actual ancient work in taken away. The Committee considers that the value of the ancient work may be seriously diminished by being overpowered by the large quantity of modern work surrounding it. There is no reason whatsoever why the fine old front should not have been so carefully repaired as to alter its appearance but little. Even now it is not too late but if the enclosed extracts from Prof. Ruskin's work do not seem to you reasonable it is of course foolish to hope that you should do otherwise than you are doing."

Leech replied that:

---

[51] Wentworth Day, pp232-233. However, Leech may have been influenced by Sir William Parker (d.1891), his brother-in-law's father, who had helped restore Holy Trinity Church, Long Melford.

"As Mr Wade will himself answer it I will only say that I regret very much that the Society should disapprove of so many of my proposed alterations. I feel that I am doing as little as possible to the place consistent with keeping it at all and that all additions and alterations will only be carried out where there is sufficient proof to justify me in deciding upon them."

Leech's reconstruction, with its negative and positive aims, included the following:

- Inserting new windows on the east front,[52] and other windows elsewhere.
- Widening the porch entrance by removing the side panel and seat adding wood inserts to make the spandrels fit. This was obviously done to give a central position to the carved wooden moulding, bearing the armorials of himself and his family, under the new porch window above.
- Removing the bricks from under the hall windows and under the porch window, replacing them in a herringbone pattern.
- Moving the door at the north end of the great hall.
- Removing the Jacobean chimneypiece from the withdrawing room, later sold, but leaving the matching overmantel.
- Replacing some panelling.
- Removing the ceiling from the great hall to uncover the roof timbers and reinserting the armorial glass.
- Moving the Jacobean staircase & screen from the courtyard into the old kitchen
- Adding a new extension on the west front accessed through the old kitchen and the relocated staircase (compare Plan 1 with later plans in Appendix G).
- Re-siting the kitchen in the adjacent original buttery and pantry.
- Dividing into two the large room (the Lord's Room) on the southeast corner, used as the men's bedroom when it was the farmhouse.
- Possibly digging a well to supply water to the toilets in his new extension.[53]
- Probably dismantling the single storey lean-to at the junction of south and west fronts.

Sketch of the access to Leech's extension, through the old kitchen, and showing the relocated Jacobean staircase and screen (from the 1892 sale catalogue)

---

[52] Said to be modern reconstructions on old foundations (VCH Berkshire, vol 3, p95). If so, they would have been simpler that their replacements.
[53] A well roughly in line with Leech's extension was located during the ownership of Brian Stein and a grating placed over it (pers. comm. Martin Little, former head gardener at Ockwells, July 2020).

It is said that the village master builder, Benbow Rolls, impressed by the work of the earlier craftsmen, had described the partly dismantled manor house as standing "like a great bird-cage and hardly a rotten timber in it".[54] Four photographs commissioned from J P Starling of High Wycombe show well the works in progress.

Two photos of work on east front showing the new windows being installed

The great hall, showing the armorial glass back in place; the now exposed roof timbers; and the damaged brick floor covered with what seems to be some form of plaster

The Jacobean staircase and screen after re-location to the old kitchen

Views of Leech's extension. Above: looking north, with the extension at the left attached to the west front. Note new windows in south end of west front. Below: looking south; note the large doors to the fuel store. The French windows put in by Tom Columbus Smith on the north front of the old kitchen have been removed and the front repaired

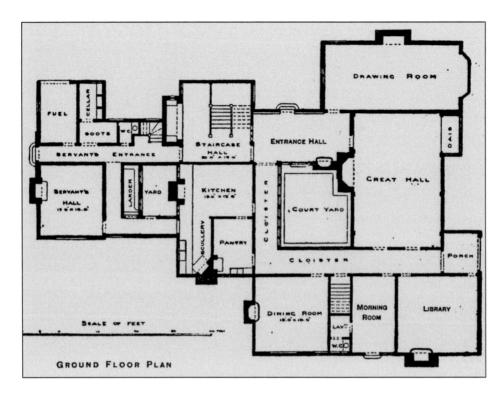

GROUND FLOOR PLAN

The ground floor plan from the 1892 sale catalogue (*see above*) shows the extension added by Stephen Leech, accessed through the old kitchen into which the Jacobean stair had been moved from the courtyard. Also, the lean-to extension housing the WC inserted into the pantry by 1864 has been lost and the interior walls changed with one wall cutting across the fireplace on the south wall (compare with 1864 floor plan). This was done by either Tom Columbus Smith's builder or Felix Wade, Leech's architect. The fireplace on the west wall of the newly located kitchen has since been blocked off (see Appendix G).

Front cover of the 1892 Sale Catalogue – drawing based on the Starling photo (copyright: BRO)

On 12th July 1892 the Ockwells estate was put up for auction by Leech in three lots, consisting of the Ancient Manor House, Ockwells Farm house plus cottages and woodland (Lot 1); land with woodland (Lot 2); and a field plus a cottage (Lot 3). The field in 1979 was purchased by the District Council as playing fields for Cox Green. The 1892 Sale Catalogue noted that the extent of the whole is ca. 366 acres 0 rood and 31.5 perches.

Also to be auctioned, on 15th July 1892, were various items being surplus building materials provided for the restoration; old oak panelling; a massive carved oak mantel twelve feet wide (removed from the withdrawing room) and a quantity of glazed tiles.

Friday, July 15th, 1892.

Ockwell's, Maidenhead.

MR. J. H. HUMFREY is favoured with instructions from Mr. Williams (whose contract has been completed) to Sell by Auction on FRIDAY, July 15th, 1892, at 2 for 3 o'clock in the afternoon, a large quantity of Oak Timber, Scaffold Poles and Boards, Laths, Baulk Timber. old Oak Pannelling, about two tons of Lead, three Wheelbarrows, 6 Ladders, massive carved Oak Mantel 12 feet wide, quantity of glazed Tiles and cut Nails, being the surplus building materials provided for the restoration of the above house.

Catalogues from the Auctioneer, 28, Queen-street, Maidenhead.

Advertisement for the auction of items, including the oak chimneypiece from the withdrawing room, following the 1892 restoration (Maidenhead Advertiser)

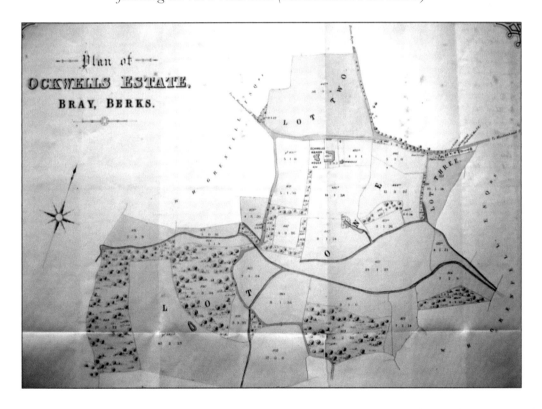

1892 Sale Catalogue map delineating the Lots and also showing the position of the farmhouse, east of the tithe barn. The building to the north, near the road, is probably the labourer's cottage also built by Grenfell. The other building near the road was already there by 1875 (see Appendix D) (copyright: BRO)

As bidding on Lot 1 (which included the manor house restored at a cost of ca. £15,000) only reached £22,500, the Lot was withdrawn as were the other two Lots.[55] The auctioneer said *"but as for the mansion, they could not give an estimate of its value any more than most people could give to a work of art at Christies"* and that he wished somebody had the *"patriotism to purchase the property and present the house to the nation as a specimen of what an English house had been and should be.*[56] Leech was evidently now the owner of Ockwells.

By June 1893 Ockwells was still with Leech as in this month he was summoned to Maidenhead County Bench regarding alleged obstruction of the highway (trees had been planted on the side of the road opposite his entrance). He did not appear personally but his solicitor told the court that the trees were planted on land conveyed to Mr Leech. The bench decided on a nominal fine and that the trees were to be transplanted.[57] It seems that Grenfell's estate manager, Edward Lodge, was managing the house at the time since in April 1893, when the encroaching trees were being discussed, a member asked *"Has any member of the committee been in communication with Mr Lodge, steward of Taplow Court Estate?*[58]

Grenfell evidently wanted to record his family's ownership of Ockwells for he had a replica built at Taplow Court as his Estate Office (*see right*). In the Pall Mall Gazette of 1887, he noted he had had copies made of the barge boards on a small scale. It seems that the bargeboards, together with copies of the carved spandrels of the porch and a replica stone fireplace, were used to build the new Estate Office.[59] The woodwork must have been done by his estate manager, Mr Edward Lodge, who also made beautiful furniture. The estate office is joined on to another building that has been decorated, rather awkwardly, with similar bargeboards.

One can only speculate as to why Stephen Leech would spend so much money restoring a house when he was abroad working as a diplomat. He presumably he got his money back in 1894 from Sir Edward Barry who bought the restored house from him. It has been suggested he was fulfilling his *boyhood dream to restore the house.*[60] Probably he wanted to put his mark on the house, which he did by putting his heraldry on the moulding under the porch window, one of the windows he had inserted on the east front. The porch entrance was widened so the armorials occupied a central position; the wooden inserts to allow this are visible today.

[55] Handwritten note on Grenfell's copy of Sale Catalogue (BRO D/EG/E11/3; also D/EG/E11/4).

[56] *M.Ad* 3 August 1892, "Ockwells under the Hammer", p6.

[57] *M.Ad* 28 June 1893, p8.

[58] *M.Ad* 12 April 1893, p3.

[59] *MCS News* May 2011, p11. For what little is known of the lodge see Buckinghamshire Record Office, D/GR/18/25 – plan of entrance lodge 1887; and D/GR/18/38 – undated plans & elevations.

[60] Wentworth Day, pp233-234.

The porch entrance. Left: the original entrance (part of 1887 drawing by Barrett). Right: the widened entrance (from a photo taken by Cyril Ellis in the 1930s)

Leech armorials under the porch window. Left: the impaled coat for his parents; right probably the impaled coat for his paternal grandparents. Centrally: the coat of Stephen Leech with above the helm his crest (in hand couped at the wrist, a snake) and the family motto Virtus est venerabilis

According to the visitors' book of Sir Edward Barry, Stephen Leech visited Ockwells in 1895. He was by then serving with the British Legation in Lisbon. For someone who presumably never actually lived at Ockwells he played a surprisingly major role in its restoration. Whilst the house was made structurally safe with the magnificent roof timbers exposed and the armorial glass returned from Taplow Court, as promised by W H Grenfell, there was damage to the historical integrity of the manor house, preserved for decades whilst it was tenanted. His restoration was a bit like the curate's egg – good in parts, though to be fair when Pevsner in 1966 described Ockwells manor house as *"the most refined and the most sophisticated timber framed mansion in England"* he did continue to say *"It is true that its perfection is partly due to the C20 (sic) restoration by Felix Wade."*[61]

[61] Pevsner 1988, pp186-187. In the revision of Pevsner's work (Tyack et al 2010), the date of late C19th for the restoration is given (p413).

8. Ockwells in the C20th & C21st

During the twentieth century, the ownership of Ockwells changed hands a number of times. The manor house, after the restoration, was again extended by the new owner who also altered the house, as did some of the subsequent owners. However, by the early 1980s it was in a state of disrepair and neglect and in need of further substantial restorative work. The latter half of the century also saw increasing pressure for additional local housing on the land adjacent to the manor house, leading in turn to growing concerns over the setting of Ockwells Manor – a threat to its architectural and heritage status.

Sir Edward Arthur Barry Bt FSA JP

Having been put on the market in July 1892, but not then sold as the reserve price was not reached, Ockwells was eventually purchased in February 1894 for an undisclosed sum by Edward Arthur Barry who also bought from Leech the other lots of surrounding land listed in the 1892 catalogue.[1] He continued to buy land around Ockwells and lived there with his second wife, Eleanor, and their family.

The Barry family can be traced back to the fifteenth century (the Barrys of Eynsham). However, their recent background was more in commerce than landed gentry, with interests in shipping and trading, and they were modestly prosperous. More particularly, Edward's father, Francis Tress Barry (1825-1907) went to work in Bilbao (Spain), although whether this was in connection with his father's firm or not is unclear. In 1846 he was appointed British Vice-Consul there, and he was later offered the opportunity to become the full-time Consul in Madrid but turned this down to concentrate on his business interests. He formed a partnership (Mason & Barry) with his brother-in-law, James Mason (1824-1903), and took a fifty-year lease on a copper mine in Portugal, which they converted to open-cast mining; there were large profits, and at their deaths, the two partners left a combined total of over £1.5m. This wealth translated into honours and estates. Mason bought and rebuilt Eynsham Hall (Oxon), while Barry became the MP for Windsor in 1890 and was created a baronet in 1899, having previously been ennobled in Portugal as the Baron de Barry.

In 1872 Francis Barry bought St. Leonard's Hill, Windsor, a Georgian house with royal associations and a clear view of Windsor Castle, which he more than doubled in size in an over-the-top and conspicuously expensive French Renaissance style. Together with 230 acres it cost the substantial sum of £59,100. Like most Victorian men of his class Sir Francis bought a castle in Scotland – in his case, Keiss Castle in Caithness, which had recently been rebuilt in the Scots Baronial style for the Duke of Portland. He was also something of a philanthropist, supporting a number of local institutions in the Windsor and Caithness areas.

---

[1] See BRO D/EG/EII/3, p33. In 1950 when Ockwells was sold the conditions of sale refer to a conveyance dated 19th February 1894 made between Stephen Leech and Edward Arthur Barry (1950 Sale Catalogue).

In 1899 Sir Francis Barry was granted these arms:[2]

Coat
Argent, three bars gemel gules between two wolf's head erased in chief sable and a trefoil slipped in base vert
Crest
Issuant from a castle with two towers argent a wolf's head sable holding in the mouth a trefoil slipped vert between four roses, two on either side gules, stalked and leaved proper
Motto
Boutez en avant

The baronetcy and the Portuguese title passed in 1907 to Francis' eldest surviving son Sir Edward Arthur Barry who was born in April 1858.

Edward Barry married twice: firstly, in January 1883 to Kathleen Ellen Bicknell, daughter of Mr Percy Bicknell of Shinrone, Ireland. They had two children – Claude Francis, born in December 1883 and Gerald Tress, born in November 1885. Sadly, Gerald died only a few weeks later, as did Kathleen, probably due to complications with the birth. Barry married again in February 1891 to Eleanor Margaret Scott, daughter of Col Courtenay H S Scott, believed to be a descendant of the old Kentish family of Scotts of Scot's Hall.[3] After honeymooning in the Isle of Wight they then resided with his parents until moving into Ockwells. They had four children – a son (Edward Courtenay Tress, b.1896) and three daughters: Cicely Eleanor ("Kitty") b.1892, Margaret Colquhoun ("Peggy") b.1894, and Rosamonde ("Bunny") b.1901.

Portraits of Sir Edward Barry and his second wife, Eleanor

---

[2] Barry, p26.
[3] Barry, pp26, 31.

Barry was educated at Harrow and Cambridge and was keen on shooting, both as a sport and for purposes of national defence. He also had a great fondness for riding and was one of the members of the local Garth Hunt. He was most interested in archaeological and antiquarian research and became a Fellow of the Society of Antiquaries.

Sir Edward and Lady Barry and their two eldest daughters outside the east front of the house ca.1900

Round about 1902 he was instrumental in starting the Windsor Squadron of the Berkshire Yeomanry, beginning with a sergeant and one trooper, increasing it to a strength of 104 when he handed it over on being appointed as Lieut.-Col in command of the regiment in 1910. Like many of the gentry of that period, Barry served as a Justice of the Peace, and was appointed High Sheriff of Berkshire for the year 1907-8. In later life he was appointed Vice-Lord Lieutenant of Berkshire and also to other honorifics such as Master of the Grocers' Company. During the early years of the First World War, Eleanor had been a regular visitor to the wards at the Canadian Red Cross Hospital at nearby Cliveden. Sadly, she died in February 1916 from a heart seizure whilst travelling on a train back from King's Lynn to London. She had been visiting Sir Edward who had by now retired from the Royal Berkshire Yeomanry Regiment but was currently serving under a temporary commission as a major and was quartered at King Lynn. The visit was to celebrate their silver wedding anniversary. Not long after this, the youngest daughter, Rosamonde, effectively became the "Lady of the House" until her own marriage in 1925 – quite a responsibility for such a young girl.

Barry had sold Keiss Castle in 1913 but retained his father's house at St. Leonard's Hill for his mother's use until her death in 1926, after which he simply pulled it down and sold off the land for building development. Earlier, once he had purchased Ockwells he set about making major structural changes, gentrifying and modernising the house and devoting much of the rest of his life to collecting a fine collection of armour, Tudor and Jacobean furniture which was displayed to great effect in the Great Hall and other rooms.

The manor house as seen during Barry's residence. Above: the east front.
Below: looking north-westwards showing the remaining wall of the chapel and the east front

The restored house was changed by Barry in a number of ways:

- By 1904 a wing, *in absolute harmony of style,* was added on the north-west corner,[4] necessitating the removal of the Jacobean stair to a new position outside the north front and the addition of a side passage from his new extension to the withdrawing room, his dining room.
- Due to the changes to the north front, the main entrance, with its carriage sweep created in the early seventeenth century, was lost, built over by the new wing and relocated staircase.
- By 1918 farm buildings on the north side of the outer court had been demolished.[5] Later a hedge was planted. Additional farm buildings were built behind the tithe barn to replace those lost. The nearby pond was converted into an ornamental fish pond with paved surrounds and stone steps leading down to it.
- A new drive was made over the site of the old farm buildings to reach a lodge on the road. This drive was later closed and a new one created closer to the house, fitted with wrought iron gates and a new brick wall, was built along Ockwells Road. The building near the road became the lodge at the end of the new drive.[6]
- Between 1904 and 1924 the Jacobean overmantel and Tudor chimneypiece in Barry's drawing room were removed.[7] A more decorative chimneypiece from Somerset, dated 1601, replaced the latter. It appears that the Tudor chimneypiece and overmantel were moved to the "porters lodge", with its separate door to the porch, which was Sir Edwards' study.[8] Neither is still there.
- Interior walls between the original pantry and buttery were removed and a decorative chimneypiece dated 1673 inserted. One of these walls had split the original fireplace in two (see floor plan on page 154).
- A single-storey extension was built to connect the west and south fronts – approximately the area originally created by 1864 to house a WC.
- In the great hall *the worn and broken floor* was ripped up and huge planks laid down.[9]
- By 1904 the walls of the drawing room were covered in Spanish leather.[10]
- Outside downpipes and gutters were added with Barry's initials, together with the wolf from his crest and coat and the Catherine wheel from his wife's coat on the hopper heads. The central downpipe on the east front is different, bearing initials and badges (portcullis, Tudor rose & the Garter) for Edward VII (s.1901).
- The priest's house was restored, installing a bay window frame bought at a house-breaker's yard in Windsor.[11]
- Windows were fitted into the tithe barn[12] and its west front altered.

---

[4] Latham, p338.

[5] A survey by Atlas Assurance in March 1918 noted that old farm buildings (farm house, cart shed, dairy and a further shed) had been pulled down by 1897 (see page 300). Any bricks from these buildings may have been used to build houses in Highfield Lane. At that time Atlas valued the house with its two extensions at £16,000 and the windows at £1,800).

[6] In 1918 the lodge at the end of the second drive (valued at £300) was still there but was gone by 1932 (see Appendix D). The lodge at the end of Barry's first drive was built by him rather than being the labourer's cottage built by Grenfell which is located further west (cf. estate map from 1892 sale catalogue on page 155 and the 1897 O.S. map, Plan 2 in Appendix D.

[7] See Latham, p331 and Hussey, III, p134.

[8] 1950 Sale Catalogue; Wentworth Day, p237.

[9] See Wentworth Day, p235. If Leech's architect had spread a form of plaster on the floor some of the brick tiles could have survived under the flooring.

[10] See photo in Latham, p331. The leather, made from fifty skins, is said to have been obtained "from the house of the Spanish ambassador's house in Mexico City, bought from Trollope" (unpub mss Royal Armouries, Leeds - Mann 1939; Wentworth Day, p236). This may refer to F J A Trollope (d.1910), the son of Anthony Trollope (d.1882) the author.

[11] The seller claimed the window came from Ockwells originally (Wentworth Day, p236).

- A new dovecote was created by a London architect[13] and installed before 1923 near the tithe barn.[14]
- By 1936 the extension built by Stephen Leech on the west front was knocked down and the existing Ockwells Home Farm was built with the bricks.[15]
- In his bedroom Barry installed a chimneypiece bearing his coat impaled with that of his wife, Eleanor Scott; this is no longer at Ockwells.
- He put the servants' rooms in the roof.[16]
- He also, during World War II, had the armorial glass removed and stored in a pit in the grounds.[17]

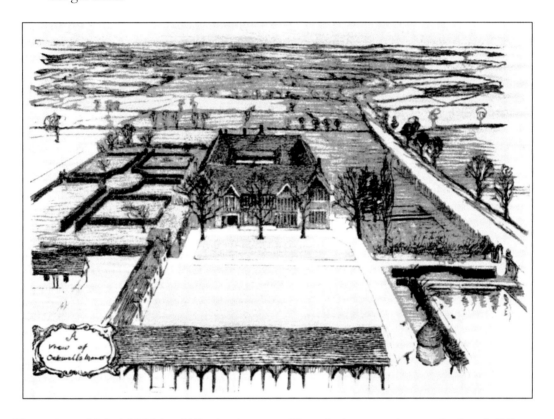

Illustration published 1923 by Aldin showing some of Barry's changes to the grounds: farm buildings on north side of outer court already gone, replaced by dovecote, hedges and fish pond; new drive to north and ornamental yew hedges to south of house added. Barry's 1904 extension on north-west corner of house has been omitted, perhaps for artistic reasons

---

[12] Barry's sketchbook contained drawings of these windows (Muspratt archive, original now lost though the present author has copies).

[13] Pers. comm. David Muspratt, 1995, and Mr M Conboy, 2014, who as a boy was tasked with burning plans for the dovecote, wrought iron gates and heraldic birds for the gate pillars when Mr Barnett moved out of Ockwells. A dovecote is mentioned in the 1892 catalogue (p19), described as being of the same date as the manor house and located near to the Ockwells farm house *erected a few years ago* (p18; erected by Grenfell and later demolished by Barry). An old estate map in the porter's lodge at Ockwells locates *the pigeon house* to behind the tithe barn i.e. near to Grenfell's farmhouse, built in 1887. It is unclear whether Barry's architect re-used any material from the old dovecote which apparently had fine timber work.

[14] A sketch of Ockwells published in 1923 shows the dovecote in its current position between the tithe barn and the hedge (Aldin, p95).

[15] Pers comm Mr Pharo, 1995, whose father had worked for Sir Edward for a time. The extension was still there in 1932 (see Appendix D, Plan 4). The farmhouse erected by Grenfell was set back from the road (1892 sale catalogue p18) and is east of the tithe barn. The farmhouse, cart shed, dairy and another shed were pulled down by Barry by 1918 (surveyor's report for Atlas Assurance Ltd; see Appendix D, Plans 2, 3, & 4).

[16] According to his family (pers. comm. 1995, David Muspratt).

[17] So Jan Golding, gamekeeper, informed the late Peter William Cannon, Estate Manager to Harold Barnett and Patrick Chung. The pit was in clearing in a wood called Home Cover (Beech Fields when owned by William Henry Grenfell).

The 1924 floor plan (Appendix G, Fig 5) shows Barry's new wing on the north front and the relocated staircase and side passage. The west wing added by Leech was still attached. Barry's removal of the wall between the pantry and buttery resulted in the roof sagging in the twenty-first century. At some point after 1924 and before 1984, when purchased by the present owner, the buttery fireplace was blocked off though the chimney stack is still there.

A present-day view of the east front showing Barry's extension at the right-hand side

The western elevation of Barry's extension as it was in 1984 when the house had been empty for some time. The large chimney stack on the left is from the old kitchen and on the right from the old buttery (now blocked)

164

James Excell's water-colour sketch drawn later from rough sketches he made in 1908, showing clearly both Barry's and Leech's extensions existing together[18]

The gatehouse with priest's room over, window put in by Barry. The trough in the foreground is dated 1870 with initials PG, probably one of William Henry Grenfell's trustees

---

[18] Ernest James Excell MBE (1893-1971). Born in Twyford, Berkshire, in his youth he had worked in the garden and house. He later became a teacher of physical training and art at Aberdare Boys Grammar School, Glamorganshire. He presented the picture to Lady (Rosamonde) Muspratt in 1950 (Muspratt archive).

165

Photo of a farm building being taken down; this is thought to be one of those lost by 1918. Compare with the 1887 sketch of farm buildings by Roland Paul above in Chapter 7

"Bunny" (Rosamonde Barry) on horseback beside the stable and garage block (left) and thatched farm stables (right, now lost)

166

In place of the farm buildings a drive was created, young plants for a hedge were planted, and stone steps built that lead down towards Barry's ornamental fish pond

A later photo showing the hedge, the top of the stone steps and the dovecote that Barry had built

Having demolished the farm buildings on the north side of the outer court, Barry constructed a new drive and lodge, constructed further along the road (see below and Appendix D). He later built his extension and extended outwards the north front to accommodate the staircase.

The lodge built by Sir Edward Barry. Left: when he owned Ockwells. Right: today

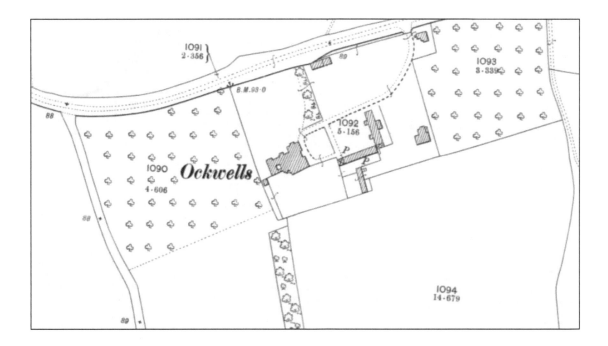

The Ordnance Survey map of 1897 shows Barry's first new drive and lodge. The farmhouse built by Grenfell was still there but the labourer's cottage near the road had gone. The plan also shows that Leech's extension is still there (courtesy: HMSO)

The building near the road to the west of Barry's lodge was evidently in use after the building of the new lodge. In 1918 it was described as "a lodge" in the survey by Atlas Assurance by which time Barry's drive nearer the house was in position.

Subsequent OS maps (see Appendix D) show Barry's extension, the creation of his fish pond, and the loss of Grenfell's farmhouse and Leech's extension. The section of drive he built in place of the farm buildings had gone by 1932.

The south face of the priest's house showing Barry's second drive and lodge next to Ockwells Road

The drive today with the priest's house in the distance and much taller trees lining the drive

The ornamental gates, the design influenced by sketches made by Sir Edward Barry. On the ground to the left are the remains of a stone eagle. A pair may have once been on top of the pillars. A similar design is found in the extant gates to the chapel garden which he must have put in

One of Sir Edward Barry's sketches of gates and gateways

A view of the south front of Ockwells during Barry's ownership showing the yew hedges he planted to his design in what had earlier been the kitchen garden. Photo taken before 1936 as Leech's extension is visible on the left behind the tree

The south front today with more developed yew hedges. The enclosing wall is either Tudor or contemporary with the manor house

Hopperhead showing Barry's wolf crest and his initials and the Catherine wheel from his wife's coat

The north front as extended by Barry, showing his extension (right), the large window behind which is the relocated staircase, and lower down, the single-storey servery that linked the domestic offices in his extension with the withdrawing room, the latter serving as Barry's dining room

Barry's drawing room (now the billiard room) showing the chimneypiece, from Somerset, dated 1601, put in by Barry, and the embossed Spanish leather skins he obtained to cover the walls. Note the hidden door to the right of the chimney piece to connect with his library

Barry's library (now the sitting room) showing the chimneypiece dated 1673 put in by Barry, and the interior of the single storey extension with window he reinstated to connect the two rooms

The staircase and screen relocated by Barry into an extension of the north front. The door on the right leads to the withdrawing room. The extension blocked up a window on the west side of this room
(Copyright: HEA)

The withdrawing room used by Barry as his dining room, ca.1910. A painting of his two older daughters covers the blocked up window. The hidden door to the servery is at the far end on the right
(Copyright: HEA)

The drawing below, another original record kept safe by Peter Cannon, is a puzzle. It appears to be for a planned set of lights for a window at Ockwells as it shows, in the central light, the motto of the Barry family (*boutez en avant*) and the crest for the barony (*out of a castle argent, a wolfs head, gules* (Fairbairn's Crests cites *sable*). The same source identifies the adjacent mottos as for the Smith family. Norman Herbert Smith was Barry's father's executor and also Barry's cousin. However, the armorial coat for Barry is incorrect. If this drawing ever became an actual window, it might have been planned for Sir Edward's bedroom (at the south end of the west front) where the motto and his coat impaled with that of his wife was once displayed on the chimneypiece (*see below*).

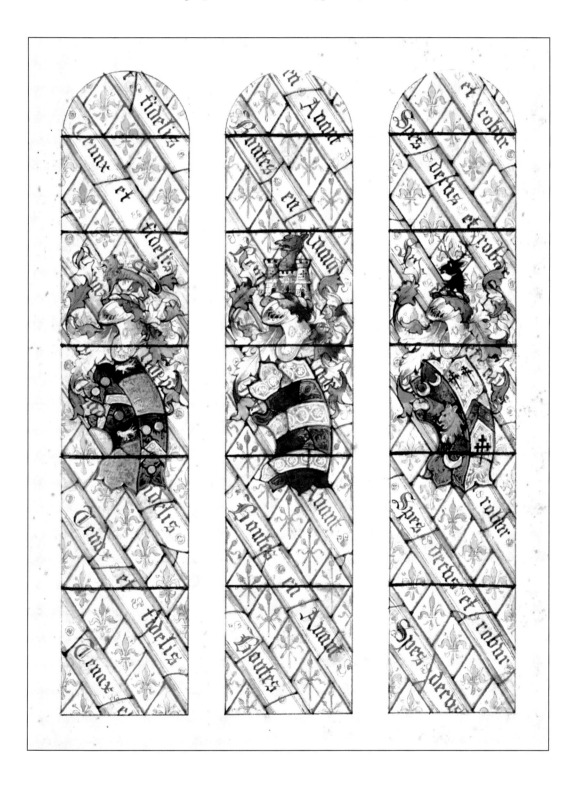

Photos taken at different times showing the chimneypiece bearing Barry's coat impaled with that of his wife with, underneath, the names Edward and Eleanor. This must have been installed in the house at some point as two inventories of Barry's possessions describe the two firedogs (a man holding a sword and an angel holding the coat of France) and a Dutch brass hanging chandelier (seen in the left photo) as being present in Barry's bedroom.[19] The chimneypiece has been removed by a later owner

Sir Edward Barry was a keen collector of armour and furnished the great hall with much of his collection. Along the way he had developed a close association and friendship with James Gow Mann (later to become Sir James) – another armourist – who advised him on suitable acquisitions. In 1924 Mann was appointed Assistant Keeper at the Wallace Collection becoming Director in 1936 after a spell at the Courtauld Institute of Art. He later became Master of the Armouries at the Tower of London (in 1939); President of the Society of Antiquaries (1949-1954); and Surveyor of the Queen's Art from 1952 until his death in 1962. After Barry's death in 1949 Mann, one of his executors, arranged for the most interesting items in the collection to go to the Tower and possibly some other armour collection with

Sir James Gow Mann KCVO FBA FSA (1897-1962)

which he was associated.[20] In 1938 he compiled a catalogue of arms and armour at Ockwells and in 1939 a catalogue of the furniture and pictures in the house. These, together with inventories for probate in 1949 and what was sold to S H Barnett in 1950,

---

[19] Mann's 1939 catalogue in the Royal Armouries, Items 177-8 (firedog) and 179 (chandelier).
[20] Letter from David Muspratt, Sir Edward's grandson, to the author 9 August 1995.

and some private papers and photos given to him by Sir Edward's daughter, Rosamonde (Lady Muspratt), were subsequently deposited with the Royal Armouries (now at Leeds).

A watercolour of the great hall at Ockwells showing some of Barry's collection of armour

Views of the great hall showing some of Barry's collection of armour and furniture. Note that in the upper left-hand corner of the picture on the left the two heralds' trumpets hanging on the wall have banners bearing the differenced coat of the Barrys of Santry Manor in Ireland, granted to Barry's father Sir Francis Tress Barry in 1899. However, in 1926 it was proved that the family was entitled to the coat of the Barrys of Eynsham, Oxfordshire (azure two lions passant guardant or) and the right-hand picture shows that the banners have been changed accordingly (courtesy the Royal Armouries)

177

Barry's collection of arms and armour became famous and was the subject of many articles by noted armourists. One of these, Guy Francis Laking, made the following observation:

"Among the few heirlooms attached to Ockwells we should not forget to mention:
- *a fine green velvet saddle of the time of Charles I*
- *a pair of jackboots sadly destroyed by rats, said to have been worn by Cromwell*
- *a portion of a chain mail hauberk a little of which remains owing to the fact that in former times each tourist, if their gratuities were considered sufficient, received a few links of the shirt in order to carry away a remembrance of Ockwells Manor, Bray.*[21]

These items had been in the house prior to Sir Edward Barry buying it and were in the great hall when the inventory was made in 1950 detailing the contents of the house when it was sold to S H Barnett after Barry's death.[22] The saddle and jackboots (despite the story about rats) were sold by Barnett with his collection of early armour in 1965.

THE SUNDAY TIMES, MAY 18, 1947

[Specially drawn for THE SUNDAY TIMES by Hanslip Fletcher.
The Great Hall at Ockwells, near Maidenhead, an unspoiled 15th century manor-house which is the seat of Sir Edward Barry.

Ockwells, even after World War II, continued to attract the attention of the press. This 1947 drawing of the Great Hall shows some of Barry's armour & furniture collection as well as the fifteenth century chimneypiece, vaulted roof, refectory table and armorial glass

---

[21] Laking 1905, p75. Tom Columbus Smith apparently handed out bits of chain mail to visitors.
[22] Inventory, dated June 1950, of the contents of Ockwells Manor House sold to S H Barnett (Royal Armouries RAL 11470).

Barry's Land and the National Trust

Barry gradually expanded his land holdings in and around Ockwells. Apart from land purchased from Leech with Ockwells in 1894 that included the field to the north of the house, he, in 1903, purchased from Grenfell, land to the south that included Great Thrift Wood and Little Thrift Wood. In 1918 Grenfell, now Lord Desborough, put several nearby farms on the market including Lowbrooks Farm. Barry bought Lowbrooks (Lot 1) and a field north of Ockwells Road (Lot 2) adjacent to land that he already owned.[23]

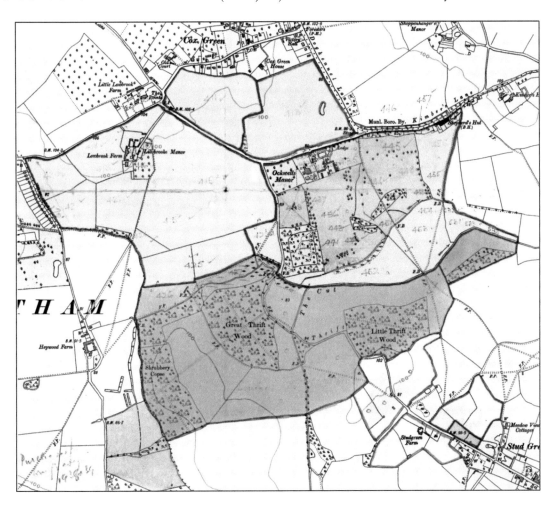

The full extent of Barry's land (delineated by the red lines) around Ockwells Manor. Broadly, the yellow area (except Lowbrooks and the adjacent field to the north) represents the original purchase in 1894; the pink areas purchased from Grenfell in 1903 (but compare map on page 155); and the blue in 1901 from Rush and Aur

Sir Edward was evidently protective of the setting of Ockwells. In 1928, when it was proposed to build the Maidenhead Bypass nearby, the Society for the Protection of Ancient Buildings (SPAB) wrote after being contacted by a member, James Gow Mann (later to become Sir James and a close friend), to offer support in any action he was taking to *save this fine house,* pointing out that the Society had papers about Ockwells dating to 1880. In the same month Sir Edward wrote to Lord Crawford, President of the Council for the Preservation of Rural England saying that he was worried about the future of this interesting ancient Manor house saying *"One of its greatest charms has been the peace and restfulness*

---

[23] See Grenfell's 1918 Sale of Outlying Farms BRO D/EG/E11/29/2. This inaccurate map (not all the area in yellow was part of the original purchase) was in the possession of Barry's solicitor, and was amongst documents retrieved by his great grandson, Sir Edward Barry.

still existing at it. For I have enough land to have been able to hold back the rising tide of bricks and mortar in the immediate neighbourhood of the old Manor House".[24]

A later letter to Lord Crawford in December 1938 describes an attempt by Mr W Thornton Smith, who had created Shoppenhangers Manor (a pastiche of architectural salvage aiming to create a Tudor mansion)[25] to have the agreed route moved away from his house and nearer to Ockwells.[26] In the letter Barry says the alternative route would cross his land, in front of his entrance gates and that he had applied to the Council for the Preservation of Rural England (CPRE) who had given valuable assistance. In January 1939 a letter to Sir Edward from A A Somerville of the House of Commons noted that Austin Hudson, Parliamentary Secretary for the Ministry of Transport, had assured him that the route of the bypass would not be altered and in March 1939 Sir Edward wrote to the Reading *Evening Gazette* saying he had now heard from the Ministry of Transport that the Minister had refused to alter the route of the Maidenhead Bypass from the line agreed two years previously, which would keep the road at a distance of 700 yards from Ockwells.[27]

A further threat to the setting of the manor house arose in 1937 when Maidenhead Corporation proposed to place a sewage pumping station 300yds from the front door. Sir Edward again appealed to the SPAB for help, suggesting an alternative site. This site, that he had professionally surveyed, was a chalk pit in Curls Lane. It was on Lord Desborough's land, who fortunately did not object to it being built there.[28]

It is possible that these threats were what prompted Sir Edward to lay down covenants with the National Trust in 1945, extended in 1947, to protect the house and its setting.

In 1936, James Lees-Milne – then a newly appointed architectural historian working with the National Trust – had visited the house. It seems that six years later in 1942 Sir Edward wanted to sell to the National Trust and had invited Lees-Milne for lunch to progress this desire. A previous offer from Ernest Cook had been turned down as Sir Edward wanted more. The failure to sell may also have been affected by Lees-Milne *not being pleased* by the house. As Lees-Milne noted in his diary entry for Sunday 22nd February 1942:

"From High Wycombe I bussed to Bray Wick (Berkshire) and from there walked to Ockwells Manor. I was last here in 1936. My host, Sir Edward Barry, now eighty-four, is as lively as ever. He has one servant. Sir Edward stokes the boiler every morning. The house is sadly dusty. We had a delicious English roast beef luncheon with Yorkshire pudding, rhubarb tart to follow. A gin and vermouth warmed me first of all, for it is still bitterly cold. Sir Edward wants to sell. He owns 600 acres with a rental value of £1,200 and is asking £75,000 because an American millionaire offered him that figure ten or more years ago. He spurned Cook's offer of £40,000. I fear I cannot help him unless he changes his tune. He took me round the house again. Although it is most important, yet it does not please. Sir E. is 2nd Baronet and Baron du Barry in Portugal, which is strange"[29]

---

[24] Letter in the Ockwells file at the SPAB. This remark is poignant in view of more recent developments.

[25] See the *Evening Standard* 9 September 1937.

[26] In 1937 Sidney Seymour Lucas, (son of Barry's friend John Seymour Lucas) wrote sarcastically to Sir Edward saying *I cannot imagine how it is that Nash in his celebrated work omitted this!!!* (i.e. Shoppenhangers Manor). With a postscript *seriously you must write to the Sunday Times and expose this rotten impudence.*

[27] These letters had been in the possession of the Barry family, though their current whereabouts is unknown; I have copies.

[28] Letters in the SPAB Ockwells file.

[29] Lees-Milne 2007. The millionaire was probably Franklin Seiberling, co-founder of the Goodyear Tire Company (see page 183).

Ernest Cook, a grandson of Thomas Cook of travel fame, was a rich, eccentric recluse and a benefactor of the National Trust and may well have made the offer with a view to passing the house to the Trust (as he had done with Montacute House). However, this did not happen.

The extent of the covenanted areas: red line – 1945; addition pencil line – 1947

Later, in 1973, when Ockwells was owned by Reginald Broadhead, Lees-Milne visited again, this time accompanied by John Cornforth – an architectural historian with the Historic Buildings Committee of the National Trust who was involved in the vetting of many houses that were offered to the Trust – and Christopher Wall another representative of the Trust. They were clearly not impressed, as Lees-Milne records in his diary entry for Thursday 5 April 1973:

"Yesterday I visited Ockwells in Berkshire. The first time I was there was in 1936, the then owner being Sir Edward Barry. The result was covenants over the house and estate, but no gift to the National Trust. Sir Edward wanted to give, but could not afford to do so. He had two married daughters, as I remember, neither of whom was very rich. Even so, their agreement to their father giving the covenants was a generous concession. In those days Ockwells was generally considered a very important house indeed. It was written up in all the architectural textbooks, as a mid-fifteenth century manor house of the earliest non-fortified sort, of much importance. Sir Edward extensively restored it before the First World War with the help and advice of people like Lutyens, Edward Hudson and Avery Tipping. No one disputed its merits. Yesterday however John Cornforth and Christopher Wall, who accompanied me, expressed the view that

Ockwells was an over-restored fake, beastly in every way, and not worthy to be held by the National Trust. Thus I have lived to see taste change. Ockwells was never the sort of house I cared for, yet in the 1930s I did not dream of questioning its importance."[30]

Lees-Milne still worked for the Trust in 1973 when a later owner offered it to them and the fact that Ockwells was not the sort of house he cared for may have influenced their decision to refuse.

One suspects that if these experts had had more understanding of the armorial scheme put up by Norreys at Ockwells in the mid-fifteenth century, they may have taken a different view. The diary entry also shows a lack of knowledge about who actually was responsible for restoring Ockwells. Most of what Sir Edward did was more gentrification than restoration but at least this has meant the house still survives as a family home. There is some evidence that during the last decade of his life management of the estate was not ideal.

Visitors to Ockwells

Sir Edward filled the house with paintings, tapestries, furniture and armour and welcomed visitors. His visitors' book, now in the possession of his descendent, also Sir Edward Barry, lists visits by Stephen Leech (1895), several by William Henry Grenfell (1896-1898; 1902, 1914, 1916), the artist John Seymour Lucas (1895, 1914), and historians such as P H Ditchfield (1896), William F S Dugdale (1898), Allan Fea (1902), Christopher Hussey (1912) and the architect Edwin Lutyens (1916). Another notable visitor was the author James Wentworth Day who stayed there (his family's ancestral home!) in 1945 and 1946 and subsequently wrote about Ockwells. Apart from the Grenfells, descendants of other past owners also visited during this period, including members of the Norris family (1928) and the Finch family (1950). Perhaps the most important visitors were Queen Mary, her son Albert (later George VI) and his wife, Elizabeth, who visited in April 1931 and signed the visitors' book.[31]

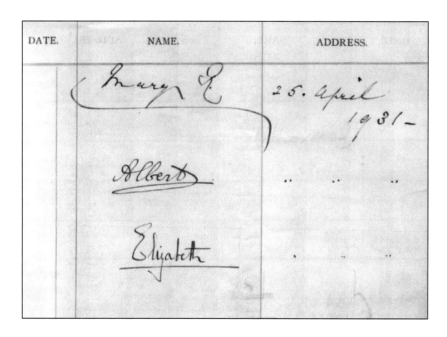

Royal signatures in the Ockwells visitors' book

---

[30] Lees-Milne 2011.
[31] Both King George V and Queen Mary are said to have visited Ockwells four times (Wentworth Day, p254) though this is not recorded in the visitors' book.

Regular visitors to Ockwells were John Seymour Lucas RA (1849-1923), a Victorian English historical and portrait painter, and his artist wife Marian. Lucas was also an accomplished theatrical costume designer and shared with Barry an interest in armour. Apparently, some of the interior scenes of his historical pictures were based on Ockwells.

A signed photograph sent from John Seymour Lucas to Edward Barry in 1915
(Courtesy the Royal Armouries)

Visitors from overseas included Mr and Mrs Franklin A Seiberling from America in 1915. Mr Seiberling (*see left*) was a co-founder of the Goodyear Tire and Rubber Company and on his return home had a stately home built in Akron, Ohio, which he named Stan Hywet. Its architecture reflected that of several English houses including Ockwells. Its great hall is said to be copied from that of Ockwells and the house also has copies of eight of the armorial glass achievements made by Heinigke & Bowen of New York. Apparently the Seiberlings wanted to buy the original armorial glass but Sir Edward didn't want to sell![32]

---

[32] *MCS News*, Feb 2018, pp14-15, has photos and more details of the glass. Stan Hywet House and Gardens is open to the public.

Nineteenth-century Stan Hywet Hall built by Franklin A Seiberling in Akron, Ohio, USA – a replica of some of Ockwells' armorial glass is located in the large lower window of the central rectangular tower

Replicas of eight of the Ockwells armorial achievements seen in the staircase window at the base of the main tower (courtesy of Stan Hywet Hall & Gardens)

The great hall at Stan Hywet – said to be modelled on that at Ockwells

Sir Edward also opened Ockwells to the public in aid of charity in 1935 and 1937.[33]

OCKWELLS MANOR AT BRAY

Famous House and Garden Open to the Public To-morrow

Ockwells Manor, Bray, the residence of Sir Edward Barry, will be open to the public from 11 a.m. to 6.30 p.m. to-morrow and from 2 p.m. to 6.30 p.m. on Sunday, in aid of the Princess Louise Kensington Hospital for Children and the Maidenhead Hospital. Ockwells Manor is one of the few houses left in England that was built in the year of the founding of Eton College, and besides being a private residence in a perfect state of preservation it houses a unique collection of armour and Tudor furniture, and contains some fine stained glass windows of the period of King Henry VI. Sir Edward Barry first opened it to the public in 1935.

[33] *Windsor & Eton Express* 18 June 1937.

Sir Edward Barry lived with his family at Ockwells for over fifty years, probably the longest an owner has actually lived there rather than letting it to tenants. He altered it, continuing the process of gentrification and modernised it. He also maintained the house, took an interest in its history and, most importantly, took steps to protect the setting of the house by giving covernants on the house and grounds to the National Trust.

Sir Edward Barry in later life, wearing the court dress for a High Sheriff of Berkshire
(Courtesy the Royal Armouries)

In 1949 Sir Edward Barry died aged ninety-two, the baronetcy passing to his eldest son, Claude Francis Barry (1883-1970), an artist with a bohemian lifestyle who abandoned his first wife and family and later remarried. The title continues today, although later generations have not been country house owners.

Sidney Harold Barnett

In June 1950, after Barry's death, Ockwells, described as a "historic, residential, agricultural and sporting estate with about 603 acres", was sold, by private treaty prior to the auction, to Sidney H Barnett, together with much of the contents of the house – including the armour – for a total sum of £70,000.[34] As well as Ockwells manor house the sale price included Ockwells manor farm, a period residence Lillibrooke Manor, Lowbrooks Farm and Sturt Green Farm.[35] He later also purchased Foxleys Farm.

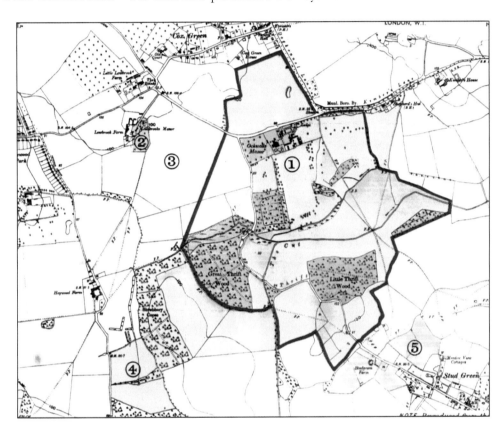

Map from the 1950 sale catalogue highlight the five lots purchased by Sidney Barnett

Sidney Harold Barnett was born in Aston, Warwickshire, in 1892, the youngest of nine children of Samuel George Barnett, an artisan jeweller, and his wife Sarah Ann. In December 1915 he enlisted for duty with the Royal Engineers, and at that time was working as a manager of a furriers' and tailors' business in Bristol. In 1916 he transferred to the Royal Garrison Artillery as a gunner involved in anti-aircraft defence, and also that year married Miss Sarah Ann Elizabeth Cope, in Walsall. He was demobbed in 1919 and by 1926 had a house in Walsall and a flat in Edgbaston.[36] They had two daughters, both born in Lichfield – Ann in early 1932 and Marion in 1933.

Mr Barnett became a founding director of Barnett-Hutton Limited (incorporated in 1945) – a chain of ladies clothing shops that included one next to Selfridges in Oxford Street and with factories in Birmingham and Manchester.[37] The 1939 Register compiled for ID

---

[34] Memorandum at back of Sale Catalogue for auction on 12 July 1950 entered in the copy kept in the Ockwells deed-box once held at Messrs Lovegrove & Eliot, solicitors, Windsor.

[35] 1950 Sale Catalogue – see in "Unpublished Reports and Theses" in Reference List.

[36] Biographical details of Barnett and his family are from censuses, electoral registers, and his military record.

[37] In 1952 Hide & Co Ltd bought a controlling interest in the chain, then headquartered in Nottingham, as well as many other stores. Apparently, the Chairman of Hide's bought the shares on his own account and then sold them to Hide & Co taking a commission leading to an investigation into the affairs of Hide & Co

document purposes just prior to WWII records him as a "company director (clothing)" and his wife Sarah Elizabeth, a "buyer (ladies clothing)" living in a beachside property in Prestatyn, Flintshire together with their two daughters and their nurse/housemaid, Prudence Evans. Mr Peter William Cannon, Barnett's estate manager, recalls him saying that he had moved from North Wales to Ockwells because he wanted a country estate. It is possible that personal reasons also led to the move. His wife, Sarah, did not accompany him to Ockwells, staying in Lichfield with the two children, whilst Prudence Evans came with him as his secretary. Sarah Barnett died in 1956 in Lichfield and Barnett then married Prudence Evans, who was twenty-seven years younger than him, in Manchester in the following year.

The Barnett-Hutton store next to Selfridges in Oxford Street, London

According to the late Peter Cannon, the film star, Diana Dors (who lived in Maidenhead) once visited Ockwells, arriving in a pink Cadillac. She was apparently there to model clothing from the firm

Barnett evidently had work done on the house before moving in and was in trouble from the start. In May 1951 R Romily Fedden of the National Trust (NT) wrote a confidential letter to Mrs Dance of the SPAB saying that the new owner of Ockwells was doing a lot of

Ltd by the Board of Trade (published by HMSO. in 1958). Hide & Co merged with Tootals and eventually was subsumed into the House of Fraser group.

work on the house and that he had been told by Sir James Mann that Barnett was grouting gallons of linseed oil into the beams and using some form of expanding putty on the plaster between them. He expressed fears that if the floors and ceilings would be made too airtight that this may produce dry rot and enquired whether the SPAB could arrange for one of their experts on timber buildings to have a look at the work. If so, he would write to Mr Barnett who he describes as a "well-meaning but somewhat entêté (pig-headed) business man."

The letter must have been sent by the NT as on 18th June 1951 Mr Barnett wrote from Barnett-Hutton Limited, 3 Broadway, Nottingham, to Mr C V Wallace of the NT saying that he had been endeavouring to make the house watertight and draught-proof and was not carrying out any other work though new bathroom fittings had been delivered. He noted that he had only spent a few weekends at Ockwells where he had found the grounds completely overrun and that for the last ten years people had been coming in with barrows, cutting trees down, picnicking and the estate was little more than a public playground. Noting the new Act relating to access to the countryside, which included a survey of footpaths, he expressed the hope that Mr Wallace would help him modify the existing footpaths. He also enquired whether Mr Wallace would visit him on the afternoon of 20th June as he was sailing for South Africa the next morning.

Presumably leaving time for Barnett to return from South Africa, on 7th Sept 1956 Wallace wrote to Barnett in response to his letter expressing dismay that Barnett planned to use linseed oil in infringement of clauses in the deed of covenant, pointing out that the SPAB has advised that linseed oil is useless as a preservative and would turn the timber black. He reiterated his suggestion that an architect from the SPAB visit to advise on preservation methods. On 17th Sept Barnett replied suggesting that if the use of linseed oil was an infringement the Trust should apply for an injunction and that he didn't agree with the Trust that linseed oil is useless as a preservative or that it turns timber black., pointing out that the timber work at Ockwells is black, brown, grey and many other colours, and that if he had the latest card from Bradford Dyers Association he could include a few more shades![38]

The 1950 Sale Catalogue listed two bathrooms, one located next to the solar (above the withdrawing room) and a bath/dressing-room accessed from a part panelled bedroom with a Tudor chimneypiece on the west side of the house. Mr Cannon recalled that when Mr Barnett lived there this bedroom was a dressing and breakfast room, whilst his bedroom, on the southwest corner of the house, was on the opposite side of the bathroom. He did not remember the bedroom having a chimneypiece and the 1984 Sale Catalogue notes a *bricked up fireplace with air vent* in this room. If this was Barry's bedroom with its chimneypiece bearing the impaled coat for Barry and Scott (see page 176), Barnett apparently removed it. He did install a bathroom, for the use of his estate manager (Mr Cannon) and the butler (Nobby Clarke) next to their bedrooms on the north-west corner of the house (in Barry's extension). He added another bathroom in the room next to the bedroom at the southeast corner of the house to create a guest suite, including a corridor to connect the two rooms. Previously access to this bedroom would have been via the Minstrels Gallery and the room over the porch. In addition, he installed a small bathroom on the west front of the ground floor. Some maintenance work was also done, as noted above – oiling timber and replacing the plaster between the roof timbers of the great hall. The Estate Office was in the stable range between the stables proper, used for the calves, and the garage where Mr Barnett kept his Rolls. The "Porters Lodge" next to the porch was the workshop. The water supply was from three pumps: one near the house, used to

---

[38] Letters in the Ockwells file at the SPAB.

fill a tank in the house; one in the outer court; and one between the orchard and the field to the west of the house. The latter may be the unconnected pump and trough now near the back door.

In 1951 Tom L Lucas, the tenant of Ockwells Farm since 1940,[39] won the right to continue to farm there following three notices to quit served on him by Mr Barnett which were disallowed by the Lands Tribunal. Part of Barnett's claim was that he wished to open the house to the public but this was impossible when surrounded by land which was in effect not his. According to his estate manager, Barnett bought Foxleys because he couldn't get the tenure of the Ockwells farmland as the tenant, Lucas, resisted.

When first living at Ockwells, for some years, Mr Barnett arranged for the choir from St Michael's Church, Bray, to sing carols in the Minstrels' Gallery at Christmas. Guests came and afterwards refreshments including mince pies would be served in the Great Hall. Mr Barnett gave the church a donation. He also took an interest in the estate pheasants. A wood called Home Cover (known as Beech Fields in Grenfell's time) had an enclosed lawn where pheasants would be fed. Mr Cannon was told by Jan Golding, the gamekeeper, that the armorial glass was buried in Home Cover during WWII.

During 1953-4 Barnett permitted Ockwells to be used in the filming of the period drama "Beau Brummel." According to a contemporary newspaper account:[40] "...during the filming Elizabeth Taylor was able to nap in a bed once occupied by the first Queen Elizabeth and Stewart Granger was fitted with Oliver Cromwell's boots. The mansion, in whose interiors much of the action of "Beau Brummell" takes place, has seen many strange happenings from its inception in the early 15th century to the present time. One of the strangest of its contents is the "Maiden of Nuremberg," which stands as a mute onlooker to a dramatic scene involving Granger, Miss Taylor and Peter Ustinov. She is but one of the unusual features distinguishing Ockwells Manor, which during its 500-year existence played host to such royalty as Queen Elizabeth, Henry VI, Margaret of Anjou, Edward IV and Henry VIII. Oliver Cromwell's visit there must have been a hurried one, for he left his boots behind! The venerable mansion, situated near Windsor Castle, is still in perfect condition. In the panelled dining room stands the 24-foot long table where Henry VIII pulled apart joints of roast beef. The four-poster bed used by Queen Elizabeth remains undisturbed in her bedroom, with an oil portrait of the Queen hanging above it. It was here the Elizabeth Taylor, waiting for a lighting set-up, took her nap. According to Miss Taylor, the bed was soft and snuggly. Nevertheless, she found it difficult to get to sleep. She felt the Queen's eye on her."

---

[39] M.Ad 2 March 1951, p5. Lucas lived in Ockwells Farm House which Mr Cannon says had been extended. Apparently, Barnett owned cottages along Ockwells Road, except the first red brick one. Lucas used some cottages for his staff, and they were included in the rent he paid for the farm. The rent for the others (£1/two weeks) was collected by Mr Cannon, the estate manager. In the Sotheby's catalogue of 1965 (on page 39) it is claimed that John Seymour Lucas (d.1923) obtained the English Saddle from a local farmer before Ockwells was bought by Sir Stephen Leech and later returned it to Sir Edward Barry. It seems the farmer removed it after Tom Columbus Smith left the house and before the Leech restoration.

[40] The Statesville Record and Landmark, Statesville, North Carolina, USA, Saturday 20 November 1954. Filming commenced on 15 November 1953, and the Royal Premiere was held in London in November 1954. Barnett had bought the "Iron Maiden" referred to.

It is unlikely Grainger wore seventeenth century boots during filming and the bed slept in by Elizabeth Taylor had in fact been brought in by Sir Edward Barry. Nevertheless, the legends about boots and bedroom were good publicity, and no doubt Barnett received a handsome fee.

In 1955, James Mann noted that Ockwells had been advertised in *Country Life* magazine as for sale through the agents Brown & Clifton. Mann also observed that the asking price was £85,000 though "this does not include the contents but B[arnett] might perhaps sell lock, stock and barrel."[41] It is not known what interest was shown at the time.

At some time between 1958 and 1960 the Barnett family moved to Checkenden Court, Oxfordshire, and then after a short time to Claverdon Hall, Warwickshire. Ockwells had been purchased with its contents, so Barry's collection of early armour moved with him. The collection together with Cromwell's Boots, an ancient saddle and mail shirt were sold by Sotheby's in 1965.[42]

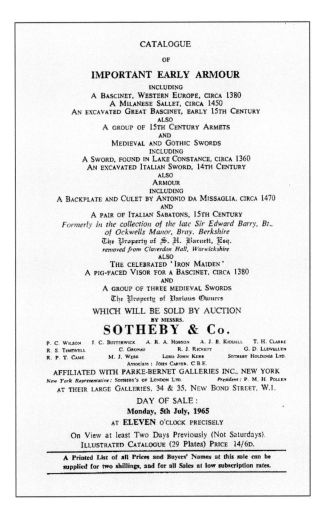

CATALOGUE
OF
IMPORTANT EARLY ARMOUR
INCLUDING
A BASCINET, WESTERN EUROPE, CIRCA 1380
A MILANESE SALLET, CIRCA 1450
AN EXCAVATED GREAT BASCINET, EARLY 15TH CENTURY
ALSO
A GROUP OF 15TH CENTURY ARMETS
AND
MEDIEVAL AND GOTHIC SWORDS
INCLUDING
A SWORD, FOUND IN LAKE CONSTANCE, CIRCA 1360
AN EXCAVATED ITALIAN SWORD, 14TH CENTURY
ALSO
ARMOUR
INCLUDING
A BACKPLATE AND CULET BY ANTONIO DA MISSAGLIA, CIRCA 1470
AND
A PAIR OF ITALIAN SABATONS, 15TH CENTURY
Formerly in the collection of the late Sir Edward Barry, Bt., of Ockwells Manor, Bray, Berkshire
The Property of S. H. Barnett, Esq.
removed from Claverdon Hall, Warwickshire
ALSO
THE CELEBRATED 'IRON MAIDEN'
A PIG-FACED VISOR FOR A BASCINET, CIRCA 1380
AND
A GROUP OF THREE MEDIEVAL SWORDS
The Property of Various Owners
WHICH WILL BE SOLD BY AUCTION
BY MESSRS.
SOTHEBY & Co.
P. C. WILSON   J. C. BUTTERWICK   A. R. A. HOBSON   A. J. B. KIDDELL   T. H. CLARKE
R. S. TIMEWELL   C. GRONAU   R. J. RICKETT   G. D. LLEWELLYN
R. P. T. CAME   M. J. WEBB   LORD JOHN KERR   SOTHEBY HOLDINGS LTD.
Associate : JOHN CARTER, C.B.E.
AFFILIATED WITH PARKE-BERNET GALLERIES INC., NEW YORK
New York Representative: SOTHEBY'S OF LONDON LTD.   *President:* P. M. H. POLLEN
AT THEIR LARGE GALLERIES, 34 & 35, NEW BOND STREET, W.1.
DAY OF SALE :
Monday, 5th July, 1965
AT **ELEVEN** O'CLOCK PRECISELY
On View at least Two Days Previously (Not Saturdays).
ILLUSTRATED CATALOGUE (29 Plates) PRICE 14/6D.
A Printed List of all Prices and Buyers' Names at this sale can be supplied for two shillings, and for all Sales at low subscription rates.

Front cover of Sotheby's 1965 sale catalogue

Sidney Barnett died in May 1974 and left his estate worth nearly £½ million to his wife, Prudence, and his daughters.

---

[41] Personal memo in Box 56, Rec. 573, Mann collection at Royal Armouries, Leeds.

[42] Sotheby & Co *Catalogue of important early armour* July 1965, p39-40. The saddle was sold for £38 to a P C L German and the boots for £22 to a Mr Keefe. Sotheby's seem to have taken Laking's word for the dating of the saddle to the C17th. It has also been said to be Elizabethan (O'Reilly p14). The present whereabouts of saddle and jackboots is unknown.

Patrick Wilkinson Chung

In August 1960 the Ockwells Manor estate was sold for £100,000, sight unseen, to the 54-year-old Patrick Wilkinson Chung, who on the eve of his move to Bray said "*I never like to talk about money. Figures are so vulgar. I love Britain and the British way of life*". He also thought our great men were not conceited; our policemen were wonderful and planned to spend a lot of money in London stores furnishing his new house.[43]

Mr Patrick Chung buys Ockwells (from the Evening Standard 26 July 1960)

Patrick Wilkinson Chung was a self-made man born in Berbice, Demerara-Mahaica, British Guiana (now Guyana) in 1906 of Chinese heritage where he was raised by his grandparents. Beginning as a clerk he trained as an accountant and at the age of 24 began working for himself as an insurance underwriter. He later moved to Kingston to become agency manager for Jamaica for two Canadian insurance companies, eventually from 1940 serving for two terms as President of Crown Life Insurance Company (Underwriters). He entered the real estate business in Jamaica in 1945 expanding into cocoa, sugar, citrus, cocoanuts and cattle,[44] becoming one of the wealthiest men in Jamaica. Newspapers noted that he was married with eight children.[45] His business interests in Jamaica included plantations, real estate, construction, a salt works, a hotel and insurance among other things. He was also the biggest racing owner there with a string of 127 horses and planned to take up

---

[43] *Straits Times* 2 August 1960. This is a syndicated fuller version of a very similar article from the *Daily Mail* 26 July 1960, p12.
[44] Chung, pp3-4.
[45] Mr Chung had five children from his first marriage to Rhoda Letitia Lee and three from the second to Beatrice May Chin. He also had an adopted son (pers. comm. August 2020, Helen Chung Patterson, Mr Chung's granddaughter from his first marriage).

racing here having already brought over several horses.[46] Mr Chung was said to be the owner of 200 suits![47] The *Evening Standard* reported that he planned to stay at Ockwells only during the summer months.

Chung's wife (his second wife, Beatrice May Chung), visited Ockwells a few times during the summer with one of his younger children. An older son, Hugh (a doctor who lived in London) also lived there for a while with his first wife and their young family and was effectively "master of the house" as Mr Chung Snr was away so much of the time.[48] The family apparently used more water than the predecessor, Mr Barnett, and so Chung had the house finally connected to mains water supply. The pipe came in near the lodge gate.

For entertainment Mr Chung used to like going up to London in his Rolls Royce to visit night clubs and also held the occasional partridge and pheasant shooting parties on the Ockwells Estate.[49] He is said to have enjoyed visiting Speakers' Corner in Hyde Park and telling the soapbox orators what he thought of them while claiming to be a West Indian dock worker.[50]

Mr Barnett's Estate Manager, Peter Cannon, continued in that post for Mr Chung. Most of the estate was held by tenants. His family think only about 34 acres was held by Mr Chung.[51] Chung returned to Jamaica as winter approached in 1960, leaving Mr Cannon to manage the estate. The following March Mr Cannon travelled to Jamaica to manage the sugar cane plantations there while Mr Chung returned to Ockwells. However, due to the hot weather and deteriorating security situation Mr Cannon left after three months returning to eventually work again for Barnett who was by then moving to Claverdon Hall. Chung presumably left finally as winter approached in 1961 so he was only at Ockwells a short time; Jamaica achieved independence in July 1962 and this may have influenced his plans. Presumably the farms on the estate continued to be tenanted. He died in Kingston, Jamaica, on 26 April 1988.

Sadly, in the book Patrick Wilkinson Chung wrote some years later, Ockwells is not mentioned. In an interesting chapter on England (described as the "Mother Country") he suggested that for England to make the leap into the future, she must adjust her thinking to the twenty-first century![52]

In 1960 a review of the town map for Maidenhead and Cookham proposed a new road across the covenanted land to the north of Ockwells, separating 10 acres from the remainder – a portent of further future threats to the setting of Ockwells Manor.

---

[46] *Evening Standard* 26 July 1960, p12. Sale arranged by solicitors Barrington & Co, London with estate agents Hampton & Sons handling the purchase (pers. comm. June 2017, Suyen Talken-Sinclair, Mr Chung's niece). Arthur Perrett & Partners in Maidenhead acted for Mr Barnett. These horses were never raced (pers. comm. August 2020 Peter William Cannon).

[47] *Straits Times* 2 August 1960.

[48] Pers. comm. August 2020 Peter William Cannon, and pers. comm. August 2020, Helen Chung Patterson, Hugh's daughter and Mr Chung's granddaughter. Hugh was an ophthalmologist who did part of his training in London at Moorfields and went to medical school in Leeds. He was working at King Edward VIIth hospital in Windsor where he met his second wife, Leonora Goodier, who was a medical secretary there; they married in 1966 and lived in Datchet for some years, as well as in Jamaica.

[49] Pers. comm. July 2020 Peter William Cannon, who also noted that partridges were taken in the mornings on the neighbouring Lowbrook estate whilst pheasants were shot in the Ockwells woods in the afternoon.

[50] *Daily Mail* 26 July 1960, p12.

[51] Pers. comm. June 2017 Suyen Talken-Sinclair, Mr Chung's niece.

[52] Chung, p165, p186.

Reginald Malcolm Broadhead

In 1962 Ockwells was sold to Mr Reginald Malcolm Broadhead, a land and property investor who, then resident at Michelmersh Court, Romsey, Hants, registered Ockwells Manor Estate Ltd with the Land Registry.[53] Around the same time Broadhead seems to have bought out Tom Lucas the tenant farmer[54] and the National Trust (NT) allowed a deed of variation releasing 10 acres of the covenanted land enabling it to be developed for housing and provision for tree planting to the southern border.[55]

Mr Broadhead was born in Nottingham in 1912, son of Albert Broadhead, a successful lace manufacturer in the city, and his wife (née Harrison).[56] In 1942 he married Vera Dobson in Hyde, Cheshire, and had three sons and two daughters, eventually divorcing in 1972.[57]

He was a pilot in his early life, initially as a Pilot Officer in the Auxiliary Air Force and then subsequently he was granted a commission in the 504th (County of Nottingham) Bomber Squadron) on 18th May 1936 with seniority from 18th July 1934.   In early April 1936, just before gaining his commission, he had crashed his plane, a Westland Wallace, biplane bomber, near Heywood, Lancashire, when flying off course from RAF Hucknall.[58] This evidently had not put him off flying, though he did later relinquish his commission on 28th May 1939.[59]

His career after leaving the Royal Air Force seems to have been initially in sales. The 1939 Register lists him as "Sales Manager (Foodstuffs)" living in a flat in Nell Gwyn House in Sloane Avenue, Chelsea, apparently an upmarket residential building complex.[60] He then seems to have become an inventor applying in ca.1947 for a trademark for an antiseptic ointment called *Septilene* when living in Broadstairs, Kent,[61] whilst in 1948 the US Patent Office records show him assigning a patent for a design for a glass bottle with lid to Lifeguard Products Ltd; his address is given as 1, Queen Victoria St, London. In 1950 he attempted to register the trademark *Alka-vescent* (tablets) but not surprisingly this was refused by the High Court as it was opposed by the owners of *Alkaselzer*.[62]

Up to 1946 he and his wife still lived in the north as his first two children were born respectively in Ashton and Sheffield, whilst by 1951 the family was living in London, births being registered in Lambeth and Hammersmith. Electoral registers show him living in 1951 in Hallam Street, W1, moving to Cadogan Lane, SW1, Kensington and Chelsea, by 1956 and then Hans Road SW3 by 1964. By 1964 he had bought Ockwells and moved his

---

[53] *London Gazette* 15 May 1962. Ockwells Manor Estate Ltd, subsequently registered in Guernsey, became Thames Valley Homes Ltd and then finally Thames Valley Holdings Ltd, incorporated in May 1981 – all in Guernsey.

[54] The area Lucas farmed included land north of the manor house.

[55] Unpublished National Trust document prepared for 2012 Land Tribunal case, p4.

[56] General Registry Office Birth Index.

[57] *Evening Post* 10 March 1972, p10.

[58] *Western Morning News and Gazette* 6 April 1936.

[59] *London Gazette* 8 September 1936; 4 April 1939.

[60] The 1939 Register lists him as married though he was the sole occupant of the flat. Details of this marriage have not been found, though he was previously engaged to a Miss Jean Margaret Eardley Simpson in 1935 (*Derby Evening Telegraph*, 29 October 1935).

[61] *Chemist & Druggist Magazine* January 1947.

[62] He continued applying for patents after moving to Ockwells. From 1970 to 1973 patents for various designs of bottles with caps were registered, apparently for whisky and other spirits, as these were assigned to Crown Distillers Ltd and Drum Horse Distillers Ltd (U.S. Patent Office records).

family there[63] but evidently kept the Hans Road address as he appears in the 1963, 1964 and 1965 registers, albeit without his wife.

A 1966 proposal to build the M4 motorway affected covenanted land to the south of the manor house. The NT supported Broadhead in the final scheme which cut off a smaller portion of the covenanted land and left the tree screen (Great Thrift & Little Thrift Woods) intact when the route was determined in 1969. In 1967 a deed with Sunley Homes allowed about 1.5 acres of the restricted land to the north of the manor house to be released from the covenant to allow construction of the new road (Shoppenhangers Road) and the completion of the tree screen.

In 1973 agents for Broadhead applied for planning permission to develop 36 acres of land to the north of the Manor including some 20 acres still subject to covenants. The application was refused by the Local Planning Authority. Broadhead had earlier offered the NT the Manor house, outbuildings and part of the field to the north on condition that the remainder of the field was released from covenants. The NT felt the price of the gift was too high and that the setting of the house would be compromised, the principal factor in the refusal of the offer. Broadhead appealed and planning permission was granted by the Secretary of State, subject to tree screening requirements. The NT objected but was not represented at the appeal.

In 1976 consent was granted to Bovis Homes for building phase I on land northwest of Ockwells Manor and Mr Broadhead sold this covenanted land to Bovis. Subsequently, planning consent was granted in 1979 for phase II, entailing 120 houses on the covenanted land including tree screen. This is the 23-acre field north of the manor house. The NT opposed this, and applications during 1979 to 1981 by Bovis Homes to the Lands Tribunal (LT) to permit 120 houses to be built were dismissed. Ockwells at the time was vacant but still owned by Broadhead. The Cox Green Community Association raised money to contribute to the NT's costs. Bovis had advanced the argument that the covenant was not in the public interest because of the need for housing. The LT found that the proposed development would *be very damaging to Ockwells manor and its setting and make the task of preservation of it more difficult.*

At the tribunal the National Trust representative said that Sir Edward granted the covenants *"in the belief that the Manor and its surrounding land would be protected for all time. Correspondence with Sir Edward at the time makes clear his intention and deep-rooted impression that the terms of the covenants would be respected. So keen was he to ensure that his estate was preserved that he was considering giving the property to the National Trust. He died before any final decision was taken".*[64]

Aware that Ockwells Manor was to be sold and noting that the house had been empty for many years, in 1983 the Cox Green Community Association campaigned to save the manor and surrounds by forming a preservation group to buy it as an amenity for the local community and as a means of opening it to the general public. The Association also pressed the Royal Borough of Windsor & Maidenhead council to buy the 23-acre field for use as a recreational park.[65] Maintenance costs of the Manor were to be financed from rental of the building to local groups, use as a conference centre and entrance charges. The Association noted that if it was not possible for the building to come into community ownership then it would aim to ensure that the building was not left empty and locked up as it had been for so many years. Any commercial use should not be detrimental to the

---

[63] His second son Anthony refers to spending part of his childhood at Ockwells (*M.Ad* 23 March 1984).
[64] Unpublished National Trust document prepared for 2012 Land Tribunal case, p6.
[65] *M.Ad* 14 October 1983, p1 & 5.

careful preservation of the structure. Access would be given to local residents and the general public to view the building and its grounds.

The Association concluded that *permanent wardenship of the building would permit regular access for visitors and it could become as much a tourist attraction as Windsor Castle.*

Front cover of 1983 campaign leaflet

Councillor Eric Brookes, a founder member of Maidenhead Civic Society, campaigned for the local authority to buy the house and a display board featuring photos of the house was created to publicise the attempt which was unsuccessful.

Views of the east front from the chapel garden (above) and the north front (below) in about 1983 showing the effect of being empty for 15 years

Views of the great hall (above) and the withdrawing room (below) from the 1984 Sale Catalogue

Ockwells east front, from the 1984 sale catalogue

It is unclear exactly when Reginald Broadhead left Ockwells and moved to Guernsey; possibly after his divorce in 1972. From 1980 to 1992, when it was dissolved, he was a director and President of Arembie International Incorporated S.A., registered in Panama; two of his sons were also directors, his second son, Anthony, being the Treasurer. He died in Guernsey in 1996.

In March 1984 Anthony Broadhead, on behalf of his father, handed over a gift of 34 acres of land to the east of the Manor adjoining 10 acres previously bought by the Council in 1979 in order to provide playing fields for Cox Green. This became Ockwells Park. The National Trust was requested to relax the covenants to allow a car park, pavilion and play area to be built.[66] Broadhead finally sold Ockwells Manor house and what was then called Home Farm (now Ockwells Home Farm) to separate owners, the latter with a substantial parcel of land.[67] Lillibrooke Farm to the west of Ockwells had already been sold in 1983.

---

[66] *M.Ad* 23 March 1984, p1; 30 March 1984, p1.

[67] David Pearl, the new owner, renamed it Ockwells Home Farm, using the land for his polo team, growing hay and for training racing greyhounds. He put it on the market ca. 1995 in two lots. The farm house found a buyer but he kept the rest of the land naming it Thrift Wood Farm. He applied for planning permission to build houses there several times before selling most of it to the Royal Borough in 2016. He retained ownership of the barns and dog kennels eventually selling the site to a developer (pers. comm. 2018 Martin Little, former head gardener at Ockwells Manor House).

Brian Peter Stein

Having been put on the market in 1984 after being unoccupied for some fifteen years, Ockwells Manor, together with 42.4 acres of surrounding land, was purchased by Mr Brian Stein around October. Born in South Africa in 1943, Mr Stein served in the Israeli army as a paratrooper before coming to London at the age of 21. He now owns the Maxwell's restaurant chain and manages a commercial property portfolio. In 2018 he was appointed as the Chairman of the Guards Polo Club, having been a member since 1987, and is patron of the Ockholt polo team.

Mr Stein has said that his main reasons for acquiring Ockwells were centred around his love for early English architecture. As a young man he always marvelled at the quaintness of early English domestic architecture and identified with its 'hand-made' character. Much later, having lived in a relatively substantial London Jacobean property and then seeking to escape to the country, he discovered Ockwells being offered for sale. Although massive restoration was required, it also offered a unique opportunity to express some of his own personality in bringing the property back to life. He was also very fortunate in having Mr David Mansfield Thomas, a most able "historical buff" architect, who had worked with him on the restoration of his previous property and who was able to give him confidence in this new undertaking.

By the time it was purchased the house had suffered some deterioration, exacerbated by the relatively high water-table. The *Times* property correspondent noted that it needed extensive restoration and was *"surrounded by tat"* – a comment on the nearby housing estates![68]

Local newspaper reports pointed out that the 23-acre field to the north of the manor house was not included in the sale and local residents feared that there may be further attempts by developers to have the protective National Trust covenants set aside to allow building there.[69]

Problems that had to be dealt with included:

- The ground frame of oak had decayed. Due to the rotting, the vertical posts had sunk causing cracks in the surrounding brickwork. The posts were shored up while the ground frame was taken out and restored.
- In the great hall the weight of the roof had caused the vertical posts to bow out. To avoid the straps moving out even further the whole structure, including hammer-beams and wind-braces, was tied together with huge bolts.

---

[68] The *Times* 14 August 1985.
[69] *M.Ad* 26 October 1984, p1 & 2 November 1984, p43.

- Roof tiles were renewed, chimney stacks rebuilt, window frames replaced and leaded light windows refurbished.

In addition, some underfloor heating was installed and seems to have been extended over time and more bathrooms were added. Other changes & repairs included:

- Converting Barry's fish pond into a swimming pool, placing the coat of Stephen Leech on the bottom while retaining Barry's stone surrounds. Wallpaper covered with Leech's heraldry was put up in a ground-floor passage.
- Water damage in the oriel window of the great hall was repaired by McCurdy & Co.
- Sagging of the ceiling in the former pantry/buttery was repaired by Gareth Williams & Associates by inserting a floor beam on the original brick foundation and a Sampson post (with a "pillow beam") to support the weight of the floor beam and joists above.
- The tithe barn was restored and new doors and a drainage scheme implemented.
- The chimneypiece in the room next to the porter's lodge (see Appendix G, Fig 5) has a carved wooden mantel beam of a style typical of the mid-fifteenth century[70] but this was inserted by Mr Stein, replacing a stone open chimneypiece.[71] This was probably the "open Tudor fireplace" moved by Sir Edward Barry from his drawing room to his study.[72]
- When the grass on the west side of the house was removed to create a patio, a well was discovered, perhaps linked to Leech's lost extension. This is now covered with a grating.
- New building constructed on eastern border to accommodate a helicopter.

Aerial view of Ockwells Manor house and outer court. Barry's Italian garden of yew hedges visible in the foreground within an enclosing brick wall that is either mid-fifteenth century or Tudor

---

[70] Shuffrey, pp73-74.
[71] 1983 Sale Catalogue, p4.
[72] See description of Barry's study in the 1950 Sale Catalogue, and Wentworth Day, p237. The Jacobean oak overmantel that Barry also moved was present in 1950 but is not mentioned in the 1983 Sale Catalogue. A subsequent owner, after Barry, evidently removed it.

Aerial view of the 1984 restoration in progress. Note the scaffolding on the chimney stacks

The east front during the 1984 restoration when Maidenhead Civic Society visited

Alterations by Brian Stein include replacing the doors of the tithe barn (above) with new ones (below)

The stables at Ockwells where polo ponies are housed.
The statue reflects Brian Stein's interest in this sport

The gardens at Ockwells were developed by the Steins.
Within parts of Barry's Italian garden a chess board (above) and the coat of Stephen Leech in flowers
(below) were created by former head gardener Martin Little

The Steins converted Barry's fish pond into a swimming pool with the coat of Stephen Leech on the bottom

The Steins created a lily pond and adjacent summer house to the north of the main house

A new chimneypiece in the original porter's lodge used as a study by both
Sir Edward Barry and Brian Stein

Samson post inserted by the Steins to support the sagging floor above.
Originally there was a wall here separating the buttery from the pantry, that had over the centuries been
altered and finally removed by Sir Edward Barry

206

The withdrawing room encapsulates Ockwells history, especially the original chamfered ceiling beams, Tudor arch chimneypiece, Jacobean overmantel, Victorian window frame, and (not visible) on left a secret door to the later servery

The Jacobean staircase and screen originally inserted in the courtyard by the Days, moved into the old kitchen by Leech and to its present position on the north front by Barry

The Solar (also identified as Queen Elizabeth's bedroom) with original vaulted ceiling, Tudor chimneypiece, Jacobean overmantel, and Victorian window frame

The Lord's Chamber with original vaulted ceiling and Victorian window frame put in ca.1890. This room is half of what had been the men's bedroom when Ockwells was the farm house. The chimneypieces therefore had to be placed diagonally; see 1864 (Fig 2b) & 1892 (Fig 4b) first floor plans in Appendix G

The Steins encouraged the use of Ockwells by the local community. In 1988 Maidenhead Civic Society held a fund-raising *Concert of Early Music* in the tithe barn. Afterwards a copy of the 1892 Sale Catalogue was donated to Mr Stein who had by then commissioned a report on the history of the house,[73] and the Society was asked to investigate what other information was available. The following year the Cox Green Community Centre held a *Medieval Celebration* with *entertainment, feasting and libation* in the barn.

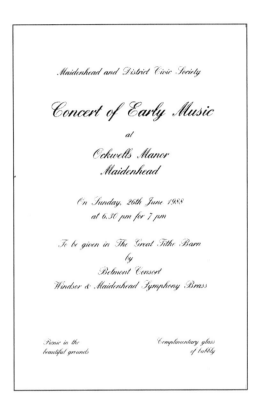

The Steins allowed the use of Ockwells to raise funds for national and local charities

In 1989 Thames Valley Holdings, by now owner of the 23-acre field, approached the National Trust pointing out that:

Ockwells was now occupied and in good repair and that the tree screen to the north of the manor house was well established.

Since the last tribunal in 1981 the local Council's need for land for playing fields has been satisfied.

The demand for housing cannot be met within the local Borough and therefore there is a clear public interest in developing the land.

Then in 1990 Thames Valley Holdings applied to the Land Tribunal (LT) and in 1992 the LT heard an application to permit the 120 houses to be built on the covenanted land. The Cox Green Community Association again took an interest and Mr Stein appeared as a witness for the National Trust. The LT dismissed the appeal saying: *"The setting of a building includes its approach and the northern approach to Ockwells is historically and naturally the principal approach to it."* Referring to the 120 houses scheme, it further stated *"That development would be very damaging to the setting and quite incongruous. Further the setting of the Manor is not to be judged solely in visual terms."*

---

[73] By Harvey Van Sickle 1987.

Later that year Maidenhead Civic Society organised a group visit to Ockwells. An exhibition on the history of the house was put up in the grounds and a supporting leaflet entitled *"Ockwells Manor House – historical notes on the house and grounds"* was produced by the Society.

The Mayor and Mayoress of Windsor and Maidenhead, Cclr. and Mrs. Robin Austin, and Jill and Brian Stein (right), owners of Ockwells Manor since 1984, at the Maidenhead Civic Society exhibition.

The Exhibition at the house (photo from Maidenhead Advertiser 6th July 1990)

The following year the exhibition was re-displayed in Maidenhead Library.

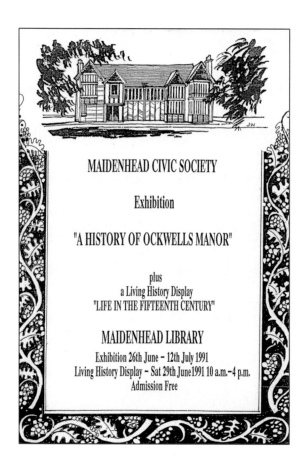

The exhibition included floor plans showing changes to the house over the years, headed by a poem penned by the author:

A north façade that ebbs and flows
A stair which hops from place to place
Extensions to the west and north
A room on the southeast corner that comes and goes

From 1993 to 1997 Mrs Jill Stein opened the gardens at Ockwells as part of the National Garden Scheme. The Civic Society put up their exhibition in the tithe barn and guided visitors round the grounds. The Society produced a leaflet "*A History Trail in the grounds of Ockwells Manor, Berkshire*" in support of this. In 1998 the Society organised a visit to Ockwells for historians attending a conference on the fifteenth century at Reading University for which the Society produced a leaflet "*The armorial glass of Ockwells Manor, Berkshire – a summary*" which was later revised in 2016/17 following further research.

The research into the history of Ockwells had led in 1995 to the author meeting David Muspratt, grandson of Sir Edward Barry, who gave permission for his archival collection to be copied and used. The following year the Steins kindly allowed a visit by the descendants of Sir Edward Barry to the manor house.

The "Barry" group visited in 1996

Back row, l-r: William Colquhoun, Gill Barry, Sir Edward Barry (5th Bt), Angela Bartlett, David Muspratt, Sue Ann Colquhoun, Judy Davies, Miles Lambert, Cllr. Eric Brooks (RBWM)
Front row, l-r: Mrs Daphne Brooks, Armorel Lambert, Ann Darracott, Elizabeth Colquhoun, Sally Gow. Cllr Brooks had campaigned for the Royal Borough to purchase Ockwells when it was on the market in 1983

Contact with David Muspratt arose from Michael Bayley, a founder member of Maidenhead Civic Society, meeting David at a Berkshire Family History Society meeting in 1995. Also, the author had known for some time that the solicitors Lovegrove & Eliot held a deed-box holding a variety of documents relating to the Barry family. So again in 1995, through the good offices of the late John E Handcock, one of Windsor's most prominent citizens and long-time Secretary of the Prince Philip Trust Fund for the Royal Borough, the box was retrieved by the present Sir Edward Barry, great-grandson of Sir Edward, who in November that year shared the contents with the author. Both archives provided a treasure trove of material relating to Ockwells much of which was photocopied

211

– most fortunate as both sets of original papers now seem to be misplaced! In 2016 a further visit by Barry descendants included Judith Rosamonde Poore (a great-granddaughter of Sir Edward), visiting from New Zealand, and this led to contact with her cousin Sara Poore who held the "Poore archive" – a collection of material relating to Sir Edward's time in the house. The material held by his descendants has illuminated the history of Ockwells during Sir Edward Barry's ownership of the house.

Information collected has also been used to update the entry about Ockwells Manor house in the revised *Buildings of England – Berkshire* (Tyack G, Bradley S & Pevsner N, 2010) and in 2004 an article was published in *Cornerstone*, the magazine of the Society for the Protection of Ancient Building (SPAB), that looked back to 1880 when it launched one of its first campaigns involving a private home and revealed for the first time in detail the glory of the stained glass.

The front cover of Cornerstone, v 25 (4) 2004, with detail of the heraldic white antelope (armed, unguled, maned and spotted or), a supporter of the armorial achievement of Henry VI at Ockwells. "Armed" means has fangs and talons; "unguled" means these are a different colour to the rest of the body; "maned and spotted or" means the mane and spots are gold.

For some 550 years Ockwells Manor has been in near continuous occupancy by its owners or their tenants. This period has seen huge transformations in England's social and technical development as well as in the way we live. This evolution is very apparent in the changes made to the house, both inside and out, which largely reflect the needs and fashions of the time. Perhaps nowhere is this demonstrated more vividly than in the observation that at the time when John Norreys built Ockwells, he would have travelled round and about by horse, whereas today the owner of the manor and his guests can arrive and depart by helicopter.

Set away from the house and behind the stables is a modern purpose-built building used as an aircraft hangar, with concrete floor and roller shutter doors

9. Ockwells – threats to its setting

The first twenty years of this century have seen Ockwells Manor house continue to be in good decorative order under the stewardship of Brian Stein. However, there has been renewed and steady pressure on its setting. Although not directly impinging on the integrity of the manor house and immediate outbuildings, this demand for more housing is a threat to the cultural value of this important heritage asset.

The following chronology of key events, mainly relating to planning issues affecting the immediate area, will hopefully provide a record to inform future decision-making in this regard.

Prior to 1999

Commenting on the draft Borough Local Plan, adopted in 1999, the Cox Green Community Association made the following recommendations to the Council:

6.0	(8.0 & 9.0)	Conservation, Recreation and Environment
6.1	(3.2.13 & 9.3.5)	Recommendation 9. In view of the lack of a specific statement on the future use of land north of Ockwells Road, the Community Association will require the council to clearly state its intentions for this area in the Local Plan.
6.2		Recommendation 10. The Community Association reiterates its long term policy of supporting the National Trust in retention of its covenants prohibiting development of land adjacent to Ockwells Manor and consider that they should also be supported by the council by the inclusion of a clear statement to this end in the Local Plan.
6.3	(8.3.4)	Recommendation 11. The Community Association request that the council use its powers to designate Ockwells Manor House and outbuildings, together with all lands covered by the National Trust Covenants, the new recreational areas and the adjacent areas of natural woodland to the south of the Manor House as a Conservation Area within the Local Plan in accordance with its proposal CA2.
6.4	(8.2.14)	Recommendation 12. We request the council to make immediate use of its prescribed powers to enforce the return to good repair of all Listed Buildings on the Ockwells Manor estate in accordance with proposal LB4.

These recommendations were largely ignored as far as the Local Plan was concerned, with the land opposite Ockwells being classified as white land, suitable for development. This enabled the Royal Borough of Windsor & Maidenhead to appear to meet its housing targets, subject to the lifting of the covenant. However, a local planning policy noted: *The Borough Council will have special regard to the preservation of listed buildings and their settings*; and further that it will *ensure that development proposals do not adversely affect the grounds and/or setting of listed buildings.*

2004-2005

An agent from Thames Valley Holdings approached the National Trust expressing a wish to re-open discussions regarding their remaining 23-acre field immediately north of the manor house; the NT's Regional Management team declined the offer to consider any modification of the covenants.

2009

Following an abortive public enquiry regarding the new Borough Local Plan which failed due to inadequate future provision for housing, it became obvious that the bulk of any new housing in the Royal Borough would be in Maidenhead, and that there would especially be development pressure to the west of Maidenhead thereby potentially threating the setting of the manor house. Maidenhead Civic Society approached the Council seeking to have the 23-acre field re-designated as green belt.

2010

Thames Valley Holdings, having applied to have the covenant lifted, the National Trust approached Maidenhead Civic Society for information relevant to any link between Ockwells manor house and the field opposite. Drawing on documents in Berkshire Record Office deposited by the Grenfell family, the Society demonstrated that the 23 acres are all that remains of a field, once known as *All Readings*, spelled variously, that was part of Ockwells Farm as far back as before 1639.[1]

2010 and 2011

The Civic Society organised visits to places linked to Ockwells to raise publicity for the campaign to protect the setting.

2011

Thames Valleys Holdings' case came before the Land Tribunal which subsequently sent it for a hearing in the High Court. Borough councillors representing Cox Green launched a petition:

"We the undersigned petition The Royal Borough of Windsor and Maidenhead to use all its powers to stop development on land adjacent to Ockwells Manor in Cox Green in order to both preserve the setting of Ockwells Manor and to avoid overloading the present Cox Green infrastructure."

The petition was discussed by the main Council in April 2012 when the following recommendation was passed unanimously:

"That Cabinet recommend to the Head of Planning and Development, Lead Member for Planning and Partnerships, the Planning and Housing Overview and Scrutiny Panel and the Borough Local Plan Working Group that planning policy is revised though the Borough Local Plan to protect the land to the north of Ockwells Manor by designating it as Green Belt."

July 2012

An attempt by Thames Valley Holdings to postpone the hearing in the High Court was rejected and they subsequently withdraw their case, paying the National Trust's costs.

2012

A RBWM planning study included several fields near to Ockwells as potential housing sites. In 2014 these were rejected on Green Belt grounds, though it was said that *"The rejection of sites through this study does not necessarily mean that they will not be delivered in the future."*

---

[1] *MCS News* Aug 2010, pp7-9.

2013

The RBWM Preferred Options document proposed that the field opposite Ockwells should be re-designated as green belt. The same document proposed building 200 houses on Fir Tree farm and 10 acres of Ockwells Park owned by the Council, all in the Green Belt.

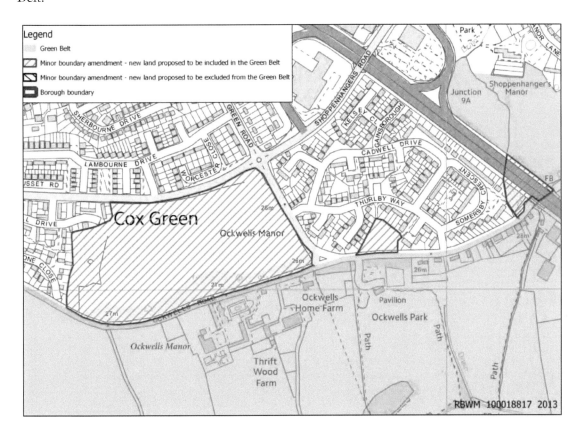

Land proposed for Green Belt shown within the red lines (courtesy RBWM)

2016-2021

Early in 2016 the Royal Borough purchased Thrift Wood farmland, but not the farm buildings, as an extension to Ockwells Park, now called Thrift Wood Park.[2] In December the Borough published for public consultation the draft Borough Local Plan (BLP). No mention was made of the 23-acre field north of Ockwells Manor though it did state that land at Ockwells would be allocated to provide open space to meet the needs of new development within the town centre – presumably a reference to the Thrift Wood Farm purchase.

There have been various planning applications to build housing on the footprint of the barn and stables (kennels) of Thrift Wood Farm (see map below); the latter immediately abuts the stables at Ockwells. As the farm is within the area of the 1945 covenant with the National Trust, they have the right to object. However, permission has been granted by RBWM and the NT for a new dwelling on the 'stables' site and one on the barn site. As at the end of 2022 neither had been built. The future of the site is uncertain as it seems the 'stables' site has now been sold separately though the Trust maintains that only construction of the approved scheme will be permitted.

---

[2] To inform their management of the new Thrift Wood Park, in 2019 the Royal Borough commissioned a study of the setting of Ockwells Manor house and the surrounding landscape including the park. This comprehensive report includes the recommendation that RBWM need to inform the National Trust of planning applications affecting the covenanted area (Rutherford 2019 p50).

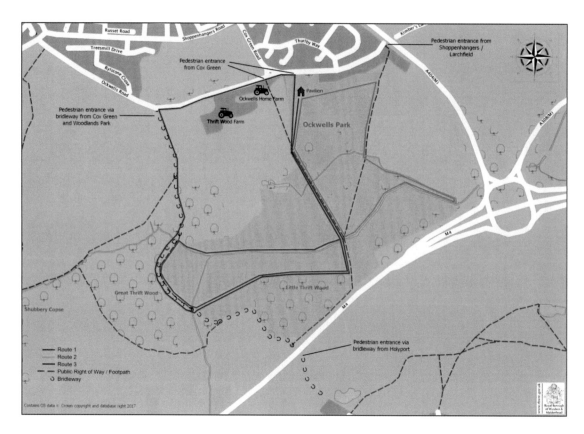

A Map of April 2017 showing Ockwells Park, gifted to the Royal Borough by Reginald Broadbent in 1984 when Ockwells was sold, and the new Thrift Wood Park to the south – land purchased by the Royal Borough in 2016. Three walking routes are shown in different colours (courtesy RBWM)

Inexplicably, in 2018, an application included under the section "Heritage Matters" stated that the *"RBWM consider there is no heritage impact for development on the site, that the site is not within the curtilage of a listed building and the distance and position of the proposal in relation to Ockwells Manor and its associated listed buildings means that there is no impact on the setting of heritage assets."*

The 1945 Deed of Covenant between Sir Edward Barry and the National Trust stated:

No building shall without the previous written consent of the National Trust at any time be erected or allowed to remain on any part of the land.

It also stated that:

Nothing in the foregoing stipulations shall prevent the cultivation of the land or any part thereof in the ordinary course of agriculture, husbandry or forestry in accordance with the custom of the land.

The existing farm buildings would fall into this category but construction of houses would mean change of use.

The Borough Local Plan aims to put the majority of new housing in the Maidenhead area and it is clear that if it were not for the covenant the 23-acre field would have high density housing on it. The 2013 Borough Local Plan Preferred Options proposal to re-designate the field as Green Belt following the unanimous recommendation of the Cabinet in 2012 was not included in the 2016 draft. When the local MP, then Prime Minister, Theresa May, enquired as to why, the reply from the Royal Borough's executive director was that:

216

The National Planning Policy Framework is clear on how and for what purpose a planning authority might designate land as being Green Belt. The purposes of putting land into the Green Belt are fivefold. The purpose to simply protect it from development does not pass the relevant tests. I appreciate that the Cabinet might have a view but plan-making is required to be underpinned by evidence; political view should not dictate otherwise and has not done so in this case.

Apparently the proposal to re-designate the 23-acre field as Green Belt in the Borough Local Plan cannot be implemented because of the 1979 extant planning permission for housing which is still valid, albeit subject to the restrictive covenant being lifted (see previous chapter).

There was a further call for housing sites which, in 2012, resulted in a RBWM planning study that included several fields near to Ockwells to be proposed. It is clear that the area around Ockwells, despite the covenant and the fact that much of it is Green Belt, is exposed to the incremental urban creep of Maidenhead.

The Future

That Ockwells Manor and the surrounding area should be part of a conservation area was suggested to the Council by the Cox Green Community Association prior to the 1999 Local Plan and similar comments have been made by the Civic Society in relation to the Maidenhead & Cox Green Neighbourhood Plan which, in 2019, became the Cox Green Neighbourhood Plan – the Maidenhead part being split off. Such comments were also made in the 2016 draft Borough Local Plan (BLP), adopted in 2022.

Among the conclusions of a study of Ockwells Manor and the surrounding landscape undertaken for the Royal Borough in 2019 was that "*Recent gradual encroachment of development in close proximity to Ockwells Manor, with the expansion of Maidenhead to the north, creation of a modern park to the east, and routing of the motorways (M4 and A404(M)) to the south and east, has heightened the significance of the surviving elements of this setting as the context to this exceptionally important building complex. Thus it is of still greater importance that the surviving historic character and fabric of this setting should be retained intact.*[3]

The National Trust's view is that no further degradation to the setting of the manor house should be permitted, that it is time to draw a line on matters such as incremental urban creep around the house. Furthermore, they note that little weight should be given to the idea of the tree screen/tree belt here, because the principle of bringing development within such close proximity of a listed building is considered to be fundamentally the wrong approach.[4]

It is evident that the combination of ancient woodland with attractive walks and manor houses of great heritage interest (Ockwells and Lillibrooke) would make a unique conservation area/heritage park, especially if combined with occasional public access to Ockwells manor house. The Royal Borough of Windsor & Maidenhead already own land to the south (Thrift Wood Park) and east (Ockwells Park) which will help preserve the setting of the house as well as providing recreation for residents and protection for wildlife.

---

[3] Rutherford, 2019, p8.
[4] Unpublished National Trust document prepared for the 2012 court case, p23.

10. Ockwells and its impact on the wider world

Ockwells has survived because throughout its history successive owners have been prepared to restore the house. While long periods of occupation by tenants led to benign neglect, many of the medieval features of the house have nevertheless been preserved and, though some have been lost either by accident or design, what remains gives visitors lucky enough to see it a good idea of what a medieval house not only looked like but how it functioned. Not the least of Ockwells medieval features still extant is the buttery hatch on which in times past food stuffs would be deposited for transfer to the great hall.

That it is primarily a fifteenth-century house, despite the later gentrification and modernisation, is evident contradicting the sneering comments from Lees-Milne, who worked for the National Trust in 1973 when Reginald Broadhead offered it to them. Pevsner's oft-quoted statement that Ockwells is "*the most refined and the most sophisticated timber framed mansion in England*" is after all followed by "*It is true its perfection is partly due to the restoration by Felix Wade*", Stephen Leech's architect, who at the end of the nineteenth century, put in the attractive east front windows that are still there today.

It is clear that the presence of the relatively undamaged set of armorial glass in the lights of the great hall has facilitated the survival of the house. We must be grateful to past owners such as William Henry Grenfell, Lord Desborough, whose grandfather had removed the glass to Taplow Court for safekeeping when Ockwells was nearly derelict, and for returning it to the great hall after the house was restored. According to an article in *The Times* of 29th April 1920 Desborough said that *his joy in presenting it was somewhat tempered a little later when a dealer said he would be pleased to offer him £24,000 for the stained glass.*

That this stunning and historically important armorial glass has survived in its original setting is a miracle and must be unique in the world.

The Wider World

The account in Chapter 7 details the furore in the press in Victorian times when it was thought that the survival of the house was in danger. What is less well known is that the armorial glass evidently inspired Queen Victoria's glazier, Thomas Willement, who not only visited Ockwells in 1838 to draw some of the coats of arms but made copies in stained glass of at least two of them. His copy of the Henry VI achievement is extant in St James the Great, Radley, whilst that of Margaret of Anjou, formerly in Crockerton Church, Wiltshire, is now on display in the museum of stained glass in Ely Cathedral. The Radley church contains other Royal achievements by Willement and a single mitre similar to those at Ockwells. Perhaps Willement was practising making royal armorials prior to him re-glazing St George's Chapel, Windsor!

The armorial of Henry VI. Left: Ockwells; right Willement's copy in St James the Great, Radley

The armorial of Margaret of Anjou.
Left: Ockwells; right: in the Stained Glass Museum in Ely Cathedral

However, although his inspiration for the window next to the tomb of Henry VI in St George's draws extensively on Ockwells' achievements, they are not exact copies.

219

Window next to the tomb of Henry VI in St Georges Chapel, Windsor Castle: banners bear the Royal Coats of the king and his queen, Margaret of Anjou: beneath are their supporters, the heraldic antelope and the eagle of Lorraine. The king's badge of the red rose of Lancaster is set between the coats of his foundations of Eton College and Kings College, Cambridge, whilst the queen's daisy badge flanks her foundation of Queen's College, Cambridge. Note the monogram for Thomas Willement at bottom right.

Copies of Ockwells' stained glass are also found overseas. In America, in the twentieth century, Franklin Seiberling, a co-founder of Goodyear Tire and Rubber Company, had copies of eight achievements made for the house – Stan Hywet – he built in Akron, Ohio.

The armorial of John Norreys Esquire and his second wife, Eleanor Clitheroe. Left: Ockwells; right: in Stan Hywet, Akron, Ohio, one of eight copies of Ockwells armorial glass in the Tower Room

In Ireland in the nineteenth century Sir Charles Denham Orlando Jephson-Norreys in Mallow Castle put up two achievements. One, a replica of Light 14 (Norreys impaling Merbrooke), is almost certainly copied from the drawing in Lysons. Sir Charles was created a baronet in July 1838 and had added Norreys to his name by royal licence later that month. The other achievement quartered the Norris of Speke coat with that of Norreys of Ockwells, perpetuating the family belief that they were descended from the Norris family of Speke. Sir Charles was a descendent of Sir Thomas Norreys, great-great-great-grandson of John Norreys Esquire and Alice Merbrooke and no doubt put up the glass to celebrate his ancestry.

The armorial of John Norreys Esquire and his first wife, Alice Merbrooke. Left: Ockwells; middle: Mallow Castle, Ireland, ca.1838. The red mantling, ferrety faced supporters and feathers on the raven crest show this was copied from Lysons' 1806 drawing, on right

In 2019 Mallow Castle was being restored by Cork County Council. The Council have improved access to the surrounding gardens and parkland and were proposing to put in new paths and a deer-viewing platform. The white deer there are the descendants of a pair that Elizabeth I gave to Sir Thomas Norreys to celebrate his daughter Elizabeth's baptism. Young Elizabeth would later marry Sir John Jephson. The County Council's laudable aim is to create "a long-life local heritage, amenity, recreational and tourism asset for Mallow and the surrounding area."

Ockwells and Neighbouring Heritage Assets

Just to the west of Ockwells is Lowbrook (Lillibrooke) Manor house, a Tudor mansion with a barn used for weddings. Further west is St John the Baptist Church at Shottesbrooke, founded by Sir William Trussell in 1337, regarded as the finest fourteenth-century church in Berkshire, and which has a remnant of the armorial glass Trussell put up after 1340 which includes the coat of Edward III.

Within a few miles is Bisham Abbey – a thirteenth-century Knights Templar preceptory added to by Sir William Montacute, Earl of Salisbury in the fourteenth century and by Sir Philip and Sir Thomas Hoby in the sixteenth century, with heraldic embellishment by the Vansittarts in the nineteenth century. It is now owned by Sport England. The Abbey contains armorial glass dating from the thirteenth century (for William Montacute, Earl of Salisbury, impaling Katherine Grandison, made earl for helping Edward III overthrow Roger Mortimer, Earl of March); the fifteenth century (for Richard Neville and Alice Montacute, made Earl of Salisbury in right of his wife, contemporaries of John Norreys Esquire); and sixteenth century (for Margaret, Countess of Salisbury, the last Neville to hold Bisham). Bisham also has achievements for Thomas Cecil, Earl of Exeter, and his wife, Dorothy Neville (daughter of Richard Neville, Lord Latimer) and royal heraldry for Elizabeth I and James I. Nearby All Saints Church encompasses the Hoby Chapel, built onto the church to house tombs for Sir Philip and Sir Thomas Hoby, Lady Elizabeth Hoby, the latter's wife, and their daughter-in-law, Margaret. The spectacular armorial glass in its east window includes a prayer for their souls.

Ockwells Manor house in the centre, surrounded by (clockwise from top left) Lowbrook (Lillebrooke) Manor house; St John the Baptist Church at Shottesbrooke; All Saints Church, Bisham; and Bisham Abbey

All these historically important buildings are near to each other, and all have relatively little public access for visitors interested in their history, apart from the very occasional Heritage

Open Day. They have all survived, with variable success, by being adapted to suit the needs of the time.

In 2019 the current owner, Mr Brian Stein, put Ockwells up for sale with an asking price of £10 million, and at present its future is uncertain. In 1946 Wentworth Day suggested it should *become a royal manor* pointing out that *it is within easy reach of Windsor and of a fit dignity and proper history to be the minor residence of a prince*. The auctioneer in 1892, when Ockwells failed to sell for the reserve price, said he wished ***"someone had the patriotism to purchase the property and present the house to the nation as a specimen of what an English house had been and should be"***. On current understanding, the National Trust could not consider taking on the house without a very substantial endowment. Ideally Ockwells should remain a family house rather than a museum, but if it could be open to the public on a regular basis it would be a major cultural and tourist attraction.

In 1890 Hughes said *It has been said that this place [Ockwells] has no history but the place has more reason to say no historian. It has plenty of history if we only knew it*[1]. It is hoped that this present contribution to the understanding of the history of the house, its occupants and its setting will help in finding a long-term solution to ensure its survival.

---

[1] Hughes G M, p376.

223

Table 1: Summary of owners, tenants and changes to Ockwells Manor house

Date	Monarch	Owner	Tenant	Remarks, including Changes
1267-68	Henry III	King grants Ocholt to Richard le Norreys, Cook (Coci) to Queen Eleanor		Ocholt, a purpresture brought under cultivation by Keeper of Cookham & Bray, Godrey de Lifton
1450-54	Henry VI	John Norreys Esq builds Ockholt Manor House putting up armorial glass in its Great Hall		Norreys would have appointed a bailiff to manage the farm
1465	Edward IV	Norreys writes his will noting that the chapel was not yet finished		
1466	Edward IV	Norreys dies. His 3rd wife, Margaret née Chedworth, by Jan 1467, is already married to Sir John Howard and they live in Bray, almost certainly at Ockholt. Howard later made Duke of Norfolk by Richard III		This was probably when the *rose en soleil* badge of Edward IV was scratched into the spandrels of the chimneypiece in the great hall
1494	Henry VII	Margaret, Duchess of Norfolk, dies. The Norreys family regain estates she held		
1507	Henry VII	Sir William Norreys, eldest son of John Norreys Esq, dies seized of Ockholt		

224

Date	Monarch	Event	Tenant	Notes
1517	Henry VIII	Sir John Norreys grants Ocholt to trustees for his brother Henry		
1524	Henry VIII	Sir Thomas Fettiplace, husband of Elizabeth, daughter of Sir William Norreys, dies seized of Ockholt		Elizabeth inherited after Henry's execution in 1536
By 1541-1553	Henry VIII / Edward VI	Katherine Fettiplace, sole heir of Elizabeth and Thomas, marries Sir Francis Englefield and they probably live at Ockholt		Tudor arch stone chimneypieces installed and probably walls panelled
1553-58	Mary I	Sir Francis's career blossoms under Mary and this may be when he & his wife move to Englefield House and put a tenant in Ockholt	?James Winch	It is unclear whether the tenant also managed the farm
1558	Elizabeth I	Sir Francis Englefield goes abroad shortly after the succession; 1584 outlawed; 1593 the Englefield estates were finally attainted	James Winch	
1579	Elizabeth I	Katherine Englefield dies. Ockholt inherited by her kinsman Sir John Fettiplace who surrenders it to the Crown in Oct 1580, dying shortly after	James Winch	
1581	Elizabeth I	Queen grants Ockholt to Sir John's son, Basil Fettiplace, for 21 years. Basil leases it to trustees acting for Provost William Day and his son William	James Winch	

1582-3	Elizabeth I	Queen grants Ockholt to Besils who the following year sells it to the same trustees who enfeoff it to trustees of Anne, wife of the Provost and his son William	James Winch
1583-1590/1600	Elizabeth I	Ockholt continues to be tenanted	James Winch until ca. 1590-1600 when he died
After ca.1600	James I	William Day, the son, and his family live at Ockholt after the death of the tenant	Jacobean stair inserted into courtyard with new entrance made on north front. Jacobean overmantels in the solar, another bedroom, in a south sitting room and the withdrawing room (latter with a matching wooden chimneypiece)
1625-1786	Charles I Commonwealth Charles II James II William and Mary Anne George I, II & III	William Day settles Ockholt on Michael Poultney (his son-in-law) and Thomas Baldwin who back rent it to members of the Day family. Ockholt descends to Mary Baldwin who marries Charles Finch	Ralph Day Thomas Day Ralph, Amy, Elizabeth and Joan Day	It is probably at some time from now on that a ceiling was placed in the great hall
1786	George III	Sold by the Finch family to Penyston Portlock Powney MP who had sold his assets in Old and New Windsor to buy the manor & farm of Ockwells and purchase St Ives Place in Maidenhead		William Payn, attorney in Maidenhead, dealt with the sale as Powney's steward

226

Date	Monarch			
1800	George III	Penyston Portlock Powney d.1794. Inherited by his second son Richard	Robert Lucas and his wife Ann lease 306 acres, lease includes a farm house	1800 Act in Chancery for Powney's will says Ockwells is in bad repair. Manor house probably in use as farm house. By 1864 a WC had been installed in the pantry, perhaps the first
1815	George III	Richard Powney mortgaged Ockwells to James Payn, probably son of William Payn, his father's steward		East front drawn by John Buckler. Original drawing shows additional gable and wing on northeast corner. Both lost by 1832
1823	George IV	William Payn, son of James Payn, now deceased, and his relatives assign the mortgage to James Bayley Esq	Ockwells Farm: Robert Lucas or his under-tenant Thomas Young	James William Pile is resident in the manor house, evidently a tenant
1832	William IV		Thomas Shackel resident at Ockwells	
1839		James Bayley Esq re-conveys the mortgage to Richard Powney		
1841 Census			Thomas Shackel and family living in the manor house	Census shows also four agricultural labourers living at Ockwells
1847-64	Victoria	Sold to Charles Pascoe Grenfell (d.1867), who immediately mortgages Ockwells Manor and estate to John Arkwright Esq. Ockwells was re-conveyed to Grenfell in 1866. Trustees for his grandson, William Henry Grenfell, manage the estate after his grandfather's death	After 1841 Thomas Shackel retires to Stoke Poges and by the 1851 census his son, also Thomas, unmarried, is head of the household at Ockwells	By 1849 Grenfell had removed the armorial glass from the great hall because of fears that the roof would collapse. Glass stored at Taplow Court. Before removal a painting was made showing the glass *in situ* and published 1847 in *Olde England* by Charles Knight. WC installed in an extension to the old pantry. Modern dairy added to north front

Year	Monarch	Event	Person	Notes
1871		Ockwells farm and cottages leased from 1871-1885 to Robert Parrott who assigned remainder of lease to Wilkerson in 1876	Robert Parrott, then Allport Wilkerson whose lease expires in 1885	The inclusion of a *Men's Room* in the manor house shows it was still in use as a farm house in 1872 (see Appendix A, No.11)
1876		William Henry Grenfell, (made Lord Desborough in 1905) inherits		
1880		Society for the Protection of Ancient Building (SPAB) founded by William Morris in 1877 contact Grenfell asking to visit the house to ascertain its state and condition		The SPAB report notes the need for roof repair and the problems caused by rain getting in (see Appendix A, No. 12)
1885			Allport Wilkerson's lease expires	Two years later Wilkerson moves his family into a new farmhouse built on the estate by Grenfell
1886	Victoria	After the lease of Ockwells expired in 1885 Grenfell advertises for a tenant prepared to restore the house. Local currier Tom Columbus Smith agrees terms to hold a 99-year lease on Ockwells during which he agrees to spend £400 per year on restoring the house. In the agreement the phrase *"The lessee to have the stained glass which have been removed to Taplow Court"* is included	Tom Columbus Smith	An article in the *Pall Mall Gazette* 25 August 1887 asks *Is Ockwells to be Destroyed? It must not* –William Morris *I hope not* – W H Grenfell

| 1887-1889 | Victoria | Court case Smith v Grenfell over ownership of glass. The above-mentioned phrase was said by Grenfell's representative to mean that he should have the glass in the character of lessee and not to have absolute ownership and a right to sell it; a compromise is reached | Tom Columbus Smith from date of lease 30th December 1887 until lease offered for sale on 4th June 1889 | Smith puts a new window in room over porch on east front. Remodels the north front by knocking down the washroom on the northwest corner and inserting French windows into the new outside wall. The 1889 Sale Catalogue says the work of restoration was under the direction of J. Rutland, and many of the principal apartments *(including dining, drawing and breakfast room, library and six bedrooms have been carefully and artistically restored)* |
| 1889-1894 | Victoria | Remainder of lease of "about 99 years" plus surrounding land bought by Stephen Leech for £2,500, who commissioned Felix Wade to restore it (at cost of ca. £15,000). Letter from SPAB 18 Nov. 1889 to Mr G P Boyce: *"My committee is much frightened at the idea of Mr Wade having the building"* | Stephen Leech, a diplomat working in Berlin at the time of the restoration | The SPAB after meeting Felix Wade send him a 7-page letter querying some of his plans including; discarding the ancient post on the right of the porch (and also the seat). This widening of the porch entrance required insertion of new wood to make the spandrels fit; adding new windows to the east front,. the new window over the now widened porch bearing Leech's arms underneath; moving the stair from the courtyard into the old kitchen; Wade also removed the carved wooden chimneypiece in the withdrawing room, uncovering the Tudor stone one; removed the ceiling in the great hall; replaced the armorial glass; added a west wing, possibly added a new oak chimneypiece to the old kitchen fireplace and installed the first bathroom |

229

1892		Restored House plus land auctioned, the last bid being £22,500 that did not reach the reserve, so it was withdrawn
1894-1950	Victoria Edward VII George V George VI	Sold to Sir Edward Barry who lives at Ockwells with his family and makes many alterations. He collected early armour. Items already in the house: seventeenth-century "Cromwell's" boots, an "Elizabethan" saddle and sixteenth-century mail shirt. In 1899 *Archaeologia* publish an article on the armorial glass by Everard Green In 1945 and 1947 Sir Edward places restrictive covenants with the National Trust, on Ockwells Manor to protect the buildings and wider landscape of ca 260 acres: *No act or thing shall be done or placed or permitted to remain upon the land which shall injure, prejudice, affect or destroy the natural aspect and condition of the land.*	Moved stair from old kitchen to outside the north front which is pushed out to accommodate it. Extension built on north west corner, a side passage connects the extension to the withdrawing room. By 1904 Spanish leather already added to walls of the drawing room. Between 1904 and 1924 Jacobean overmantel and Tudor arch stone chimneypiece removed from this room to the porter's lodge (his study) and latter replaced. Chimneypiece in former pantry replaced; both replacements imported from elsewhere. Wall between former pantry and buttery removed. Lean-to extension at the southwest corner rebuilt. Farm buildings in outer court demolished to allow creation of drive to new lodge. Fish pond put on site of farm pond. Windows put in tithe barn. Later new main entrance created with wrought iron entrance gates. New dovecote near tithe barn. Guttering and hopper heads bearing Barry's crest added, also one on the east front with the crowned initials of Edward VII and some Royal badges. In 1936 knocks down Leech extension and builds nearby Ockwells Home Farm with the materials. Mains electricity connected but not water

1950	George VI	Sold with its contents to Mr S H Barnett	Added bathrooms and probably removed from Barry's bedroom the chimneypiece bearing Barry's impaled coat of arms
ca.1958-62	Elizabeth II	Mr Barnett moves to Checkenden Court, Oxon, and then Claverdon Hall, Warks. Barry's collection of armour goes with him. Barry's collection of early armour including "Cromwell's Boots", a seventeenth-century saddle and mail shirt was sold by Sotheby's in 1965	
1960-1962		Mr Patrick Chung bought the Ockwells estate for ca. £100,000, but lived at the house only occasionally before it was sold to Reginald Broadhead	Connected Ockwells manor house to mains water. Lodge and cottages on Ockwells Road connected by 1892
1962-1984	Elizabeth II	Sold to Mr Broadhead. 1962 deed of variation releases 10 acres of land from the covenant enabling the land to be developed for housing and a road. 1980, while Ockwells was unoccupied, an unsuccessful attempt was made to lift the covenant on the 23-acre field opposite the house. The Cox Green Community Assoc. raises funds to help pay the National Trust's legal fees	Not known whether this owner altered the house. However, when ca.1983 the house was put on the market the Sale Catalogue described the house as having 6 bathrooms, one in the attic (as now). By 1980 the house had been left unfurnished and unoccupied for some 15 years

			House restored by architect David Mansfield Thomas. Main problems: 1) Ground frame of oak had rotted so vertical posts were subsiding. Ground frame restored. 2) Weight of roof causing vertical posts to bow out. To avoid further movement the whole structure was tied together with huge bolts. Later: Barry's fish pond converted into a swimming pool with Leech's coat on the bottom. Repairs to oriel window in great hall due to water damage. Samson pillar inserted to support ceiling in former pantry/buttery. Tithe barn doors replaced, and drainage scheme installed. Removal of stone chimneypiece from the porter's lodge and replaced with a carved wooden one
1984-present	Elizabeth II	Sold to Mr Brian Stein. In 2012 another attempt to lift the covenant on the 23-acre field was to be heard in the High Court but was withdrawn. The Trust is helped by Maidenhead Civic Society who provide evidence that the field was once part of Ockwells Farm. Also in 2012, a RBWM planning study includes several fields near to Ockwells as potential housing sites. In 2014 these were rejected on green belt grounds, but it was said that *The rejection of sites through this study does not necessarily mean that they will not be delivered in the future.* The 1999 Borough Local Plan (BLP) Policy LB2, 5 says: *Ensure that development proposals do not adversely affect the grounds and/or setting of listed buildings.* The 2022 BLP, Policy HE1, 2) says: *Heritage assets are an irreplaceable resource and works which would cause harm to the significance of a heritage asset, or its setting, will not be permitted without a clear justification in accordance with legislation and national policy*	

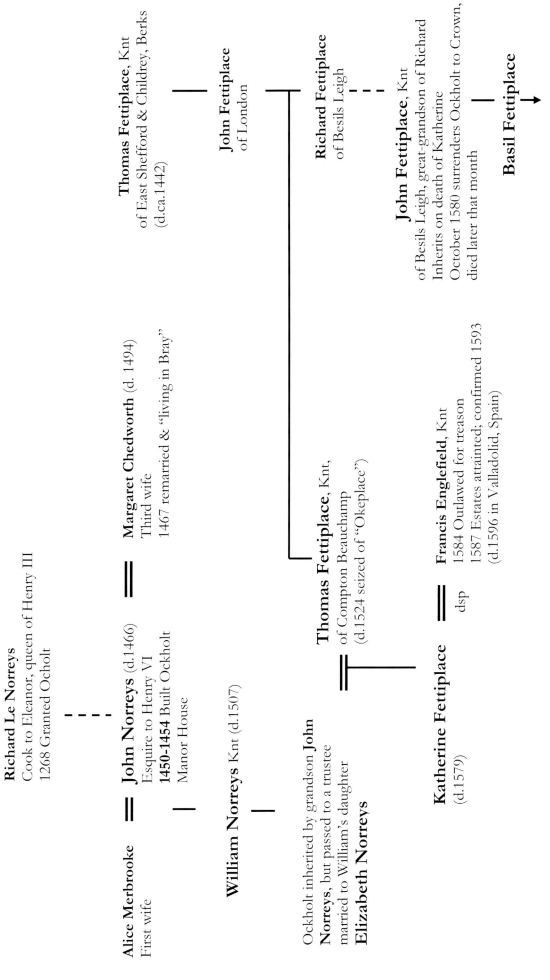

Table 2: Ownership of Ockwells from the 13ᵗʰ to 18ᵗʰ centuries (1)

Richard Le Norreys
Cook to Eleanor, queen of Henry III
1268 Granted Ocholt

Thomas Fettiplace, Knt
of East Shefford & Childrey, Berks
(d.ca.1442)

John Fettiplace
of London

Richard Fettiplace
of Besils Leigh

John Fettiplace, Knt
of Besils Leigh, great-grandson of Richard
Inherits on death of Katherine
October 1580 surrenders Ockholt to Crown,
died later that month

Basil Fettiplace

Alice Merbrooke
First wife

John Norreys (d.1466)
Esquire to Henry VI
1450-1454 Built Ockholt
Manor House

Margaret Chedworth (d. 1494)
Third wife
1467 remarried & "living in Bray"

William Norreys Knt (d.1507)

Thomas Fettiplace, Knt,
of Compton Beauchamp
(d.1524 seized of "Okeplace")

Francis Englefield, Knt
1584 Outlawed for treason
1587 Estates attainted; confirmed 1593
(d.1596 in Valladolid, Spain)

Ockholt inherited by grandson **John
Norreys,** but passed to a trustee
married to William's daughter
Elizabeth Norreys

Katherine Fettiplace
(d.1579)

dsp

233

Ownership of Ockwells from the 13th to 18th centuries (2)

Basil Fettiplace

Feb 1581 — Elizabeth I grants him Ockholt Manor for 21 years

May 1581 — Leases Manor to trustees acting for William Day, Provost of Eton, and his son William.

Dec 1582 — Royal Grant

Jan 1583 — Sells Manor to same trustees, who in August enfeoffed it to trustees of Anne, wife of Provost Day, and their son William, not yet of age

William Day

Provost of Eton College 1561 (d.1596)

William Day (son)

1625 — Settles Ockholt Manor on **Thomas Baldwin & Michael Poultney** (son-in-law) who rent it to members of the Day family

Henry Baldwin, of Herts (d.1679)

Settles Ockholt on eldest daughter

Mary Baldwin ══ **Charles Finch**

1786 — Still in ownership of the Finch family when sold to Penyston Portlock Powney MP

1800 — Act in Chancery re. Powney's will states Ockwells is in bad repair

---

Tenanted

Ralph Day (senior)

1661 — Residing in Manor House

Thomas Day (d.1749)

Ralph Day (junior) (d.1772)

And five sisters. Three were unmarried and lived at Ockwells

1786 — Sale document states that Ockwells "were in the occupation heretofore of Thomas Day and now are or late were in the tenure or occupation of **Joan Day**"

Appendix A: Original documents

1.   C13th Grant of Okholt to Richard Norreys; and C15th Religious Foundations in Abingdon, Wokingham, Bray and Maidenhead involving John Norreys Esquire

Early Norreys

<u>Calendar of Patent Rolls 1266-12</u>

Page 190; 1268
Because it appears by inquisition made by Ebulo de Montibus, constable of the castle of Windesore, that the king can give to whom he will a purpesture within the forest of Windesore called **Ocholt**, extended at 40s a year which Godrey de Lifton sometime keeper of the King's manors of Cokham and Braye brought into cultivation; the King grants the same to **Richard le Noreys**, the queen's cook, and his heirs, so that they render 40s a year to the keepers of the said manors for all service and custom

John Norreys Esquire - Guilds & Chantries

<u>Calendar of Patent Rolls 1441-46</u>

Page 36; 1441 October 20 Westminster
License for William , bishop of Salisbury, William, earl of Suffolk, Thomas Bekynton, clerk, John Golafre and **John Noreys, esquire**, Thomas Plesaunce, Philip Ripe, Hugh Mayn and Nicholas Goolde, for the repair of the road which extends from Abyndon, co. Berks towards Dorchestre, co Oxford, and over the water of the Thames through Burford and Culhamford between the said towns, by which road the King's lieges have had carriage and free passage save when it is flooded so that none can attempt it without peril of his life and loss of his goods - to found a perpetual Gild of themselves and others, both men and women in the parish church of St Helen, Abyndon, for thirteen poor, weak and impotent men and women, to pray for the good estate of the King and of the brethren and sisters of the Gild and their benefactors and for the souls of the King and the brethren, sisters and benefactors aforesaid, after death and of their parents , and for two chaplains to celebrate divine service and the church therefor according to the ordinance of the founders; and grant that the members of the Gild may elect four masters for year to year and remove and admit other poor men and women, that they be named the master, brethren and sisters of the gild of the Holy Cross, Abyndon, and be capable of acquiring lands rents, and possessions held in burgage, socage or other service to the value of 40l, and of impleading and being impleaded in any court, and that they have a Common Seal and hold meetings as often as need be.

Page 190; 1443 August 12 Westminster
License to Master Adam Moleyns, dean of the cathedral church of Salisbury, **John Noreys esquire** and John Westende, chaplain to found a perpetual chantry for one chaplain to celebrate divine service daily in honour of the Virgin Mary at the altar of the Virgin within the church of Wokingham in the diocese of Salisbury for the good estates of the King, Adam, John and John........... to be called the chantry of St Mary of Wokyngham.

235

Calendar of Patent Rolls 1446-52

Page 2; 1446 September 9 Westminster

License for William, bishop of Salisbury, **John Norys, esquire** and Thomas Lude , vicar of the parish church of Bray, to found a chantry within the said church of one chaplain to celebrate divine service daily in honour of the Virgin Mary at the altar of the said virgin within the said church, in the diocese of Salisbury for the good estate of the King, the said founders and all others who endow the chantry and for their soules after death; to be called the chantry of St Mary, Bray, and the chaplain to be capable of pleading and of being impleaded in any court and of acquiring in mortmain lands, rents, services and other possessions to the value of 10l a year.

Page 576; 1451 December 20 Westminster

Whereas John Hosbonde, sometime citizen and 'bladere' of London, bequeathed 100l. to buy a sufficient rent for a chantry of one chaplain to celebrate yearly for the souls of him and Richard Bridde and Margery his wife in the chapel of St Andrew and St Mary Magdalene, Maydenhith, co. Berks; and it was agreed between the prior and convent of Hurle and John Reyner, executor of the said John's will, that John Reyner should deliver the 100l. to the prior and convent to find such a chaplain, and they by their writing indented, dated in the their chapter house, Tuesday, SS. Philip and James 26 Edward III, acknowledge the receipt thereof and bound themselves to find a secular chaplain to celebrate daily as above; and Thomas Mettyngham, chaplain of the said chantry , has now made petition that, as well for the establishment of the chantry and the maintenance of the bridge of Maydenhith over the Thames, whereby divers lieges of the king cannot pass without peril at certain times of the year through floods and the weakness of the bridge, the king should confirm the said writing and grant others to the said Thomas and to **John Norys, esquire for the body**, John Pury, esquire, William Norys, Roger Norys, Thomas Babham and Henry Fraunceys:- the king hereby confirms the writing and grants license to the aforesaid to found a gild for themselves and others, men and women, in the said chapel, to find wax lights and other divine necessaries for the daily celebration of the masses of the chaplain; and grant that the members of the gild may elect wardens from year to year, and that the said chaplain and his successors be surveyors of the gild; and that the surveyor, wardens and members be capable of acquiring possessions and of pleading and being impleaded in any court, having a common seal and able to meet to make statutes; grant also that they may acquire lands, rents and possessions not held in chief to the value of 10 marks a year for the repair and maintenance of the bridge and other premises; grant also to them of pontage for ever, and of the whole water under the bridge and for 50 feet on either side thereof on either bank with the soil and fishery thereof

By King etc. and for 11l. 11s. paid in the hanaper

Note: SS. Philip and James 26 Edw III = Tuesday 1 May 1352

## 2.	Ockholt or Ockwells in Bray Court Rolls and Will of John Norreys Esquire

From: Kerry, C, 1861. The History and Antiquities of the Hundred of Bray in the County of Berks, p113-120. Savill & Edwards.

𝔐anor of 𝔒ckholt, or 𝔒ckwells.

The manor of Ocholt, or Ockholt, belonged at an early period to the family of Norreys, ancestors of the Lords Norreys, of Rycote.

Anno 52 Hen. III. (1267), " Rex concessit Ricardo de Norreys, Coco Reginæ, in feodo, perpresturam in Foresta de Windsor, vocat ' Ocholt,' pro annuo reddit' quadragint' solid'." —(*Cal. Rot. Pat.*)	(See p. 120.)

The following Notices of this Family have been gathered from the Court Rolls of Bray (B.), and Cookham (C.).

1305	RICHARD LE NOREYS, paid 3*d.* for the pasturage of his cattle in the Frith (near Ockwells) in 1334. He died in 1337, when it was agreed by the tenants that his executors—viz., JOHN LE NOREYS, Hugo de Braybest,· and Roger de Crosseby, Vicar of Bray, should have the whole of the growing crops, with the use of his lands for a whole year, to pay to the lord his proper dues, according to the custom of the manor of B.—(B.)

1337-8	" WILL'US, filius RICARDI LE NOREYS."—(B.)

1370	ROGER LE NOREYS, in 1376 had 2 calves in " Astcroft," 2*d.* He died in 1422 (B.), seised of lands, &c., in Bray.

1424	THOMAS NOREYS.

1447	JOHN NORRES, " Armig." steward of the manors of Bray and Cookham " for life."—(B.) Fined 3*d.* in 1450 for the improper state of a ditch in " Clenehyrst-lane." He died in 1467, seised of
" Okeholt Maner, voc' ' Noreys Manor.'
Moore's maner.

I

237

Hyndens maner' in Bray.

Spencers maner' et ⎫
Elyngtons maner, ⎭ in Cokeham.

Heyndons maner' in Cokeham.

Bray,   ⎫ multa messuagii, molendina,
Cokeham,   ⎬ terræ, ten', pastur', bosc',
Maydenhithe,   ⎭ prat', reddit', &c."

(*Inquis' post Mort'.*)

1451 WILLIAM NORYS (B.), suitor's fine 12*d.* (C.), 1489. In 1493, W. N. held land in Cookham, called "Cokdoñsee" and "Terrys." — (C.) In 1492, W. N., "milit.," held an estate in Bray called "Erle-land." In 1495 succeeded to the estates of "Moris, Hendonys," "Look Place," and "Ffrench's Tenement," on the death of Margaret, Duchess of Norfolk, relict of John Noreys, Esq., his father. He died in 1507.—(B.)

1455 ROGER NOREYS.—(B.)

1489 R. N., 12*d.*—(C.)

1493 EDMUND N., elected collector for the lands he held, called "Adhelyng." (? Athelyng.—1288, "Joñes Athelyng.")—(B.) Living 1504. 12*d.*

1498 EDWARD NORRES.—(B.)

1504 ROBERT N., "Gent.," Woodward of Altwood. Warrener of Twychene, in 1512.

1507 SIR WILLIAM N., who was commander in the King's army at the battle of Stoke, died seised of Ockwells.

1520 JOHN NORREYS, Esq., held Hendons Manor. "Gent," 1523. "Miles," 1535. In 1540, app^d collector for his lands called "PALMERS." J. N. "de Bray, Gent," suitor, 6*d.* 1537.

1537 It was presented that "SIR LIONEL NORRES died since the Feast of St. Michael last, without lawful male issue, by virtue of which, his estates in Bray descend to Henry Norres, son of Henry Norres, Esq., son and heir of Sir Edward Norres, son of Sir William Norres, as by the last will of the said William fully appeareth."—(B.)

In 1597, HENRY NORRES possessed Chauntry House, in Bray, an estate at Touchen End, called Jenkyn Ewsts, with other lands near "Bray-slade-way."

In 1524, "Sir Thomas Ffetyplas died seised of a certain

tenement called 'OKEPLACE,' lying in Altewoodde. Heriot, a horse; value 26s. Relief, 38s."—(B. C. R.) He married Elizabeth, dau. of Sir Wm. Norres, Knt. (ob. 1507), by Joan, daughter of John de Vere, Earl of Oxford, his second wife.

The family of Finch, of Hertfordshire, became possessed of Ockwells about the year 1679, from whom it was purchased in 1786, by Penyston Portlock Powney, Esq. It is now the property of Charles Pascoe Grenfell, Esq., of Taplow Court.

Mr. Ralph Day resided at Ockwells in 1661. His sons were—

1. Samuel Day (born 1665, died 1670), and
2. Thomas Day, "of Ockwells," bap. 1667, buried 4 July, 1749. By his wife, Sarah (buried 27 Feb. 1759), he had issue, Katherine (died 29 May, 1761), and

Ralph Day, bap. 1707, living 1749; married Sarah . . . ., by whom he had issue (see *Monuments*)—

Mary Day, buried 22 Sept., 1739.—(*Registers and Monuments.*)

The house, which is an excellent specimen of the half-timbered mansions of the Middle Ages, was erected by John Norres, Esq., about the year 1466.

The chapel was not quite completed at his death in 1467.—(See *Will.*)

The fine old heraldic glass which once adorned the windows of the great hall, was removed a few years ago to Taplow Court, the seat of the present owner. The following account of it is from Lyson's *Berks* :—

"These windows are chiefly ornamented with coats of arms having lamberquins, one in each window, on a ground of diagonal stripes, containing flowers and mottoes in text-hand placed alternately. Among the arms are those of Henry VI., with the antelopes his supporters, and of his queen, Margaret of Anjou, with her supporters, the antelope and eagle; also the arms of Norreys, with beavers for supporters; the Abbey of Westminster; Beaufort, Duke of Somerset; Edmund, last Earl of March; Henry, Duke of Warwick; De-la-Pole, Duke of Sussex; Sir Will. Beauchamp, Lord St. Amand; Sir William Laken of Bray, Chief Justice of the King's Bench; the Lord Wenlock [see *Will*]; Sir Richard Nansan, Capt. of Calais; Sir John Pury, Kt. of Chamberhouse Castle, in parish of Thatcham [he held large estates in Bray and Cookham at this time]; and of Bulstrode, quartering Shobingdon."—(See *Will.*)

I 2

The chapel was burnt down about the year 1778. In a compartment of a door-head remaining in the north wall are the Norres arms,—viz., arg. a chev. betw. three ravens' heads, sable; with a beaver for a dexter supporter.

The Will of John Norreys, Esq.

(Extracted from the Principal Registry of H. M. Court of Probate, Doctors' Commons.)

" In the Name of God. Amen. The iiii[th] day of Aprill, the yere of th'incarnaçon of our Lord Jħu Crist M¹cccc.lxv. And the yere of ye reigne of King Edward the iiij[th] aft' ye Conquest, the vth, I JOHN NORREYS, squyer, of the p'issh of Bray in ye Counte of Berks, hoole of mynde and in my goode memorie beying, make and ordeyne my p⁹sent Testament in this maner.

" First. I biqueth and comende my soule to allmyghty God my Maker and to the blissed Virgine Marie his Modir and to all the compayne of heven. And my body to be buried in the Church of Saint Michaell of Bray aforsaid in the North Ile of the said Church. And I woll first and before all thinges, after my body buried, that all the dettes yat I owe of right fully be satisfied and paied.

" It'm. I woll if any p⁹son or p⁹sons can compleyne and verrely prove of any wrong to yat p⁹sone doone by me, and hath not dieuly be satisfied, therfor, I woll that ye same p⁹sone thanne be recompensed and amended of my goodes as conscience and trouth wull require in that behalf, aftre ye discrecōns of myn Executours.

" It'm. I biqueth to the Modir Church of Salesþury to p'y for my soule there vi[s] viij[d].

" It'm. I biqueth to the High Aulter in the Church of Bray aforsaid for my tithes and offerings withdrawen and forgeten. And alsoe that ye Vicarie of the same Church devoutely pray for my soule c[s].

" It'm. I woll yat a M¹ masses with as many placebo' direges and other obs⁹vñces used in mortuaries be song and don for my soule in as hasty time as it may goodely be doone. And at ferdest within xxx daies next suying my decease: and ye cause why I appoint so long a tyme of xxx daies, is, for I would that the moost devoute and vertuous preestes as well religious as seculers that can be goten by the discrecōn of myn Executours as well within the Citee of London as withoute, sing and doo the same masses, placebo', direges, and such other obs⁹vñces. And yat ev⁹ych of ye same preests, doyng such suffragies and obs⁹vñces, for his labo͏ʳ have of my goodes aft⁹ the discrecōn of myn Executours.

" It'm. Yat ye Preestes and Clerkes of the said Church of Bray doo ev⁹y day from my decesse vnto the day of my moneth mynde in ye same church of Bray, for my soule an obite—by note, that is to say with placebo, direge, and laudes in the Eve and comendacōn & masse of Requiem in the morowe. And I woll that the Vicarie of the same church, if he be p⁹sent and helpyng ev⁹y day at the same obite, and not els, haue for his labour xiijˢ iiijᵈ. And that ev⁹ych of the Remenñt of the Preestes aforsaid have for his labo͏ʳ, if he be present & helpyng ev⁹y day at the same obite, and not elles, xˢ. And yat ev⁹ych of the p'issh clerkes of the saide church in semblable wise, if he be present and helpyng, have for his labo͏ʳ vˢ.

" *Furthermore*, I woll in encresing of more Devocion and prayours in this behalf to the honor of all mighty God and p⁹fite of my soule, that all the belles of the said Church of Bray, as sone as my body be buried and the Divine s⁹vice so ther doon, be rong as well by nyght as by day, by the space of xxiiij houres continually to gidres. And that ye Ringers of the same belles have for their labo͏ʳ of ringyng aft⁹ the discrecōn of myn Executours.

" It'm. I woll yat ye grettest belle of the said belles be rong ev⁹y day from my decesse vnto the day of my moneth mynde by an hoole houre continualy to gidres after the sunne goyng downe. And by a nother hole houre to gidres bifore the sonne rising. And that ye Ringers thereof be rewarded for their labo͏ʳ by ev⁹ych of the said houres aft⁹ the discrecōn of my said Executours.

" It'm. I biqueth and woll that y⁹ be gyven and delt e⁹ry day from my decesse unto my moneth mynde aforsaid to the moost pou⁹e and nedy people of the said p'issh of Bray, being in the said Churche or in the same p'issh of my goodes by the hands of myn Executours, or their discrete Depute to p͏ʳy specially for my soule, xxxᵈ.

" It'm. I woll yat myn Executours purvey and ordeyne in as hasty tyme as they can or nowe after my decesse by th'advyse of the p'son of Yatynden, xxx of the moost devout and best named Preestes that can be had, as well as of Religious as of seculers in Redyng and nigh ther aboute in the Countye for to doo an obite, &c., in the P'issh Church of Yattenden.

[He makes the same provision in the parish of Yattenden for the benefit of his soul as above rehearsed in Bray.]

" It'm. I woll and biqueth to ye newe makyng and edefying of the North Ile of ye Church of Bray aforesaid, nowe callid Saint Nicholas Chapell to ye honour of all myghty God, his Modre Sainte Marie, Saint Nicholas, and Saint Kateryn, and for helthe of my soule by the ov⁹sight and discrecōn of myn said Executours or yeir sufficiant Deputees to th'entent yat ye Chauntry Preest aforsaid nowe for tyme beying, and his Successours shall yer sing in p⁹petuite according to the fundacōn of the said Chauntery, in the honour and worship of all mighty God and Lady Saint Marie, and all the Saints above rehersed ; praying for my soule, the soules of my fadir and modre, of Alice, Alianore, and Margarete, somtyme my wifes. And for the soules of all such p⁹sones as hath geve or biqueth in tyme passid, or doth, or biqueth in tyme to come, any landes, rentes, or ten'tes, goodes or catallis, vnto the forsaid Chauntery c. li. [100*l.*]

" Itm. I biqueth to ye Aulter of ye said Ile, to be purveied and ordeigned by th' advyse of y'e forsaid Chauntery preest and the discrecōn of myn said Executours for such ornaments as is moost necessarye for him to ther to syng for my soule and all ye soules aboue rehersed, xx marc.

" Itm. I biqueth to the edifying and making of a tombe and for a marble stone to be laid y⁹ uppon immediately after my decesse within the said Chapell over my bodie yʳ buried, xx marc.

" Itm. I biqueth to ye Rode-light in ye same Churche viˢ viijᵈ.

" Itm. I biqueth to St. Nicholas light viˢ viiiᵈ.

" Itm. I will and biqueth to ye lights of Saint Stephin within the same Church, xx. [*sic.*]

" Itm. I biqueth to ye lights in our Lady Chapell viˢ viijᵈ.

" Itm. I woll and biqueth to ye biyng of a grete belle to be sette and hong in the Steple of Bray aforsaid, for a p⁹petuale Remēbraunce and stering people to more Devocōn in praying for my soule and all cristien soules, L. ħi. [50*l.*]

" Itm. I woll and bequeth c. ħi. to th'entent yat my Executo'ˢ shall finde a covenable preest of good and honest conv⁹sacion to sing in ye Chapell above rehersed within the Church of Bray aforsaid yerely, immediately aft' my decesse for my soule, ye soules of my fadir and modir, of Alice, and Alianor, somtyme my wifes, as long as by the discrecōn of my said Executo'ˢ ye forsaid preest may ther be honestly founde with ye said c. ħi.

" Itm. I biquethe to ye church of Ruscombe, to be had in Remembrance & sp'cially to be praied for yer, c. s.

" Itm. I biqueth to ye making and repairing of ye briggs bytwene the said church of Bray and village called the Wyke, v. marc.

" Itm. I biqueth to the makyng and graveling of ye way bytwene Acroste gate and ye lane called the Freith lane, xl. s.

" Itm. To ye helping and reparing of Maydenhith bridge, xl. s.

" Itm. I woll and biqueth to the full bilding and making uppe of the Chapell with the Chambres ajoynyng with'n my manoir of Okholt in the p'issh of Bray aforsaid not yet finisshed, xl. li.

" Itm. I woll and biqueth to Sir Williā Norreys, my son and heir, all my stuff of houshold being in my manoir of Yatenden and bilongyng to ev⁹y house of office w^tin my said manoir, as halle, p'lour, chambres, Botery, ketchyn, bake-house, and all other to ye same manoir p⁹teynyng.

" Itm. I biqueth to the said Sir Williā, my sonne, in plate to the value of xl. sterling.

" Itm. I woll that my sonne John Norreys th'elder have after my decesse, in money and in plate, c. marc sterling.

" Itm. I biqueth to John, my yonger sonne, in money & in plate, xl. li.

" Itm. I biqueth to Williā, my yongest sonne, c. marc of lawfull money of England.

" Itm. I woll & biqueth to Anne, my eldest daughter, c. li. sterling.

" Itm. I biqueth to Letice, my yongest daughter, in money, cc. marc, and in plate to the value of L marcs.

" Itm. I biqueth to ye mariage of Jene Wales xl. marc of money.

" Itm. I biqueth to Alison Wales, hir suster, in helping to hir mariage, x marc.

" Itm. I woll & biqueth to John Wales, hir Brother, xl. s.

" Itm. I biqueth to Williā Norreys xx marc of sterling.

" Itm. I biqueth to John Norreys, his Brothir, and myn App'tice, x marc.

" Itm. I biqueth to Thomas Merbroke xx s.

" Itm. I biqueth to John Andrewe xxvi^s viii^d.

" Itm. I biqueth to Davy Aprise xx^s.

" Itm. I biqueth to John Winche xx^s.

" Itm. To Rauf Coke xx^s.

" Itm. I will & biqueth, to be distribute and goven by the discrecon of myn Executours unto my Shepherds and meniall s⁹vnts attending my husbandrie, xl. s.

"Itm. I woll yat all ye Remanent of my s⁹v'nts not above rehersed be rewarded after ye discrecon of my said Executours. The residue forsoth of all my goodes, moveable & unmoveable, where suev⁹ they be after my dettes paied, my body buried, my funarie expenses maade, and my biquestes conteyned in this my p⁹sent testament fulfilled, I biqueth & graunte unto Margarett, my wife, if she, after my decesse, take noon husband but lyve soole.   And if so be God fortune hir to be maried after my decesse, yen I woll that the said Margarett, my wife, haue in the name of a Resonable part to hir right belongyng of all maner my goodes and catalles a ᴍ¹ marc, and then moreover the Residue of all my goodes as hir is above specified, I biqueth unto the disposicõn of myn Executoʳs, so that yey the same Residue dispose & distribute for my soule, and for the soules of Alice & Alianor, late my wifes, and of all trieu cristen soules, in werkes of pitee & charitee, as by them may be seen moost pleasaunce to God & p⁹fite to my soule, as they wold I shold doo for their soules in semblable wise.   And of yis my p⁹sent Testament I make & ordeyne myn Executours, yat is to say, the forsaid Margarete, my wife, William Norreys, my Brother, Richard Bulstrode, & Thomas Babham, and I biqueth to ev⁹ych of the same Williā Norreys, &c., for ye:r laboʳ in this behalf to be had, x marc st⁹ling.   Also I make & ordeyne of this my said p⁹sent Testament & Will, my Lord Wenlok sup⁹visʳ to th'assistance and aiding of myn Executours aforsaid, in p⁹fourming and fulfilling of my said Wille. And I biquethe to my said Lorde for his laboʳ in this behalfe to be had, a gilte cuppe cove⁹d, called 'the houswif.'   In wittness wherof, as well to my above said Testament as to this my said Wille, I have put my seale.   These witnessing.

"Probatum fuit suprascript Testaᵐ apud Lamehith quarto die mensis Julii Anno Dn̄i Mil. ccccᵐᵒ lxvijᵐᵒ ac approbat', &c. &c."—(From an Office Copy taken for this work.)

3. Armorial Glass in Yattendon Church in mid-C17th

From: MS Ashmole 850 f173

(Copyright: Bodleian Library)

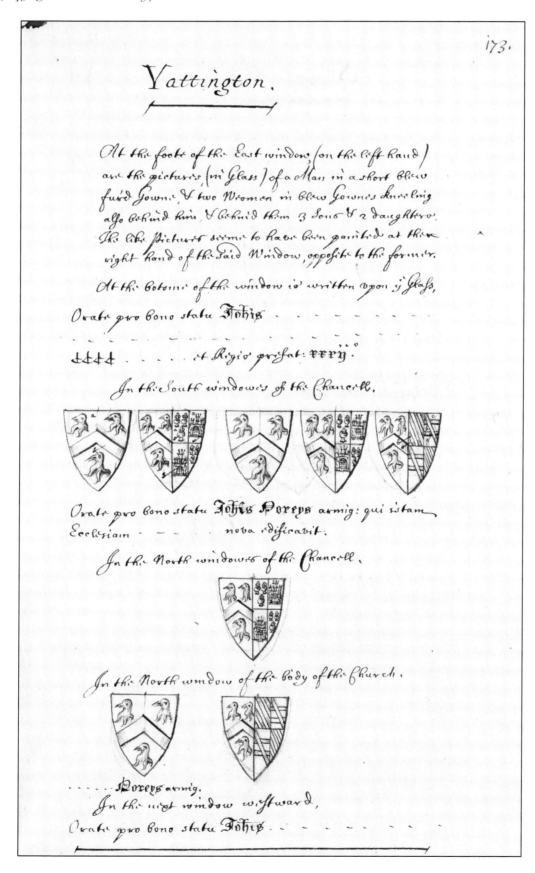

4. Account of the English Embassy in 1444 that led to the Betrothal of Margaret of Anjou to Henry VI, 16 April – 28 May 1444 (22 Henry VI)

From: MSS Digby 196 155v & 156r Bodleian

Translated by Elizabeth Matthew, with additional clarification notes by Ann Darracott. The names of lords underlined are those referred to in 1439 as being among those whose estates would have to be restored to reach peace (see *Proc & Ord of Privy Council of England* vol V p394).

(nb: some details from 156r of this unpublished document are given in Stevenson (vol 2, part 1, xxxvii-xxxviii) who provided a more complete version for Vallet (vol 2, p453- 454)).

1. In the twenty-second year of [the reign of] king Henry VI, the king's ambassadors, namely the marquis of Suffolk and others, crossed the sea and landed in France, and on 16 [26 deleted] April they travelled by water from Blois with the lord duke of Orleans[1] and the bastard of Orleans to Tours in Touraine. [One mile deleted] One league, which was three miles, outside the town, they landed and took horse, and one mile outside the town they met, on horseback, the king of Sicily, the duke of Calabria the son of the same king, the duke of Brittany,[2] the Duke of Alencon,[3] Charles d'Angers,[4] Arthur of Brittany,[5] the count of Vendome,[6] the count of St Pol,[7] the count of Etampes,[8] the count of Tancarville,[9] the

---

[1] Charles, Duke of Orleans was captured at Agincourt in 1415 and his release in 1440 to work for peace is closely entwined with René's release from paying his ransom to Philip the Good and the release of prisoners many captured at Agincourt. Henry V on his deathbed said "You will be careful not to set at liberty our cousin of Orleans, the count d'Eu, the lord de Gaucourt and Sir Guichet de Sisay until our son is of proper age (Monstrelet I, p483). Henry VI began to exercise royal power in July 1436. Hue de Lannoy, Philip's ambassador later that year recommended using Orleans and René to reach a peace between France, England and Burgundy (Vaughn p 105). Of the men mentioned by Henry V, Orleans, Gaucourt and possibly Eu were present at the betrothal ceremony.

[2] Francis I, whose assets had been pledged as part of René's ransom. He had been married to Yolande of Anjou d 1440, René's sister (Merindol, table 1).

[3] John II, who accepted Philip's offer of membership of the Order of the Golden Fleece in 1440 (Vaughn p123). The Privy Council in 1439 noted that this duke's estates would need to be restored, including those held in Normandy by the king (Proc & Ord of Privy Council of England vol V, p394- 395).

[4] Charles of Anjou, brother-in-law to Charles VII (Monstrelet I, p556) and uncle of Margaret of Anjou. As Charles of Maine he married Isabel of Luxembourg, daughter of Peter of Luxembourg, Count of St Pol, in 1444 (Merindol, p53).

[5] Arthur de Richemont, Constable of France, brother of John V Duke of Brittany (d.1442). Captured at Agincourt but released from captivity by Henry V in 1420 to help his brother (Ry.F, p620, p623). Refused to return to captivity after accession of Henry VI. Pro Philip of Burgundy especially before the death of his wife Margaret, Philip's sister in 1442 (Vaughn p123).

[6] Louis de Bourbon captured at Agincourt released in 1424. Actively involved in release of René and peace negotiations between England and France. Gave the Vendome chapel to Chartres cathedral which still has its stained glass.

[7] Louis de Luxembourg, nephew of John de Luxembourg, Count of Ligny, one of Philip of Burgundy's major military men. Louis married Joan of Bar in 1435. Ligny had been in conflict with René, as Duke of Bar, and reached agreement with him in 1432, one of the things discussed was Joan's inheritance (Monstrelet I, 613).

[8] County of Etampes disputed between Charles VII and Duke Philip. Philip had given it to his cousin John of Burgundy (later count of Nevers) though it had been the possession of Richard of Brittany (d.1438) (Richard was brother of John V, Duke of Brittany (d.1442), & Arthur of Richemont who was uncle of Francis I, Duke of Brittany). Charles VII confirmed the county in 1442 to Richard's son Francis (see Vaughn, p115).

[9] Probably William de Harcourt, Earl of Tankerville, and seneschal of Anjou (Lecoy de la Marche I, 392-3). Earls of Harcourt, Tankerville and Aumale among those referred to in Privy Council of 1443 regarding the restoration of estates, all seem to be of the French Harcourts (an English branch dates from the Norman

count of Vee ewe,[10] the lord of Tramayle,[11] the lord of Gawcorte,[12] the lord of Precigny,[13] the lord of Boyle and other honourable escorts who conducted our men into the city to his (i.e. Orleans') inn and thus they rested a whole day and night.

2. On the morrow, the next day following, the said ambassadors of the king were led into the presence of the king of the French a mile outside the city where the said king kept his court. He cheerfully received the letters of our king from the hands of lord Suffolk in the presence of the king of Sicily, the dauphin, the duke of Calabria and the others named above. And thus received by the king and leave taken, they were led by the duke of Orleans into the presence of the queen of France in a certain chamber where the said queen kept her court with the dauphiness and at least forty noblemen and gentlewomen attending on her, together with the count of Vendome, the count of St Pol, the count of Etampes and many others. And thus received, they asked leave to return to his [Orleans] inn [i.e. town house or lodging].

3. Also, on the nineteenth day of the month of May next following, lord [Py deleted] Peter de Brees [?Breze] and others made a compact with the lord of Suffolk and others of our men that they wished to equip men of their parts to shoot with the more skilled of ours for 100 scut'. And at once the earl of Suffolk promised to keep the compact if they wished to shoot for 1000 scut'. And thus of our company were chosen Henry Banaster, John Goolde, Bulley, Thomas Maskare, John Kanlyn and Helias to shoot with those men the same day before noon. Thus, led before the dauphin, the duke of Orleans, the duke of Calabria, the duke of Brittany, the duke of Alencon and others, they shot before those aforesaid once or twice, when suddenly there came in fifteen or sixteen Scotsmen of the chamber of the king of France, well equipped in capes with hoods with gold decoration, and they shot well, far more beautifully than anyone to this date in England, and as the greater archers they were laudably commended and thus they had the honour.

4. Besides this, on the first day of May, the queen of France and the dauphiness and others rode into the country before lunch to get the may [sic], with gallant knights and esquires numbering 300, as it was said, and on the third day of that month the duke of Burbundie [?Burgundy] arrived in the city with 200 men, as was said.

5. Also, on the fourth day of the same month, the queen of Sicily with Margaret her daughter and others came from Angers in Maine to a certain monastery of nuns one mile distant from the aforesaid city and rested there.

---

conquest and is still extant). Christopher de Harcourt, 3rd son of James de Harcourt, lord of Montgomery (Monstrelet I, p633) in embassy involved in obtaining René's release (Lecoy de la Marche I, p106). John, Earl of Aumale son of Earl of Harcourt killed at Verneuil 1424 (Monstrelet I, p511). John VII, Earl of Harcourt (1370-1452) was a prisoner in 1415 at Agincourt. Chateau Harcourt was occupied by the English from 1418-1449. Later inherited by René's grandson also René whose mother was the King of Sicily's eldest daughter Yolande but whose paternal grandmother was Marie Harcourt (Le Chateau Harcourt guidebook p14).

[10] Charles d'Artois, Count of Eu was captured at Agincourt, and released in 1438 in exchange for John Beaufort, Duke of Somerset. (Monstrelet 2, p70).

[11] ?Tremouille, if so for Georges Duc de la Tremouille a leading adviser of Charles VII who had been opposed to Joan of Arc and had helped separate Alencon from her (Sackville West, pp232-233, 255, who. suggested he'd been bribed by Burgundy in 1429; p247).

[12] Raoul de Gaucourt captured at Harfleur in 1415, released in1416 to go to France and return (Ry.F, p591) embassy for his liberation in 1424 (Ry.F, p641).

[13] Bertrand de Beauveau, lord de Precigny, was a counsellor of Charles VII as well as René's confident (Griffiths 1981, p537).

6. Further, on the next day following, the lord of Suffolk and the king's ambassadors went to aforesaid abbey to pay their respects [?text unclear, but this must be the general sense] to the said queen and the lady Margaret her daughter, where they were cheerfully received and made welcome with all their men. Soon after there entered the dauphin and the duke of Borboyne [Bourbon][14] whom the queen, with a curtsey, embraced[?]. Having had some conversation together with them, the said ambassadors returned to their inn.

7. Also, on the twenty-fourth day of the same month, the said lord of Suffolk and [other deleted] all the ambassadors rode to the cathedral church of St Martin in the said city of Tours to contract a betrothal between the most reverend and powerful king of England and France and the said Margaret, daughter of the king and queen of Sicily and Jerusalem. They were not kept waiting long. King Charles entered with the said king of Sicily, clasping their hands together, with the dukes of Brittany and of Alencon and others following. And immediately after, came the queen of France with the queen of Sicily in the same manner as the said kings, with the dauphiness and the duchess of Calabria following them. And quickly the dauphin and Charles d'Angers, leading the aforesaid Margaret between them, presented her to the said king Charles, who took of his hat and led her to the papal legate, who betrothed the lord of Suffolk, in the name of Henry King of England and France, and her together. This accomplished, all the people joyfully shouted "Nowell,...11" and clapped hands. And then the queen of France went to her [Margaret] and put her on the right hand of the queen her mother, both kings and queens going out to the abbey of St Julien in the same city where a great feast was brought forth. There the queen of England kept state with the queen of France on the right hand and the said legate on the left, and the dauphiness and duchess of Calabria with the lord of Suffolk at tables at the side of the hall. In this way those queens were served together with all the courses, one after the other, with subtleties and various disgicionibus [not at all clear what this is – presumably some aspect of the feast, perhaps wine-tasting] between which entered two giants with two great trees in their hands and after them two camels with castles on their backs and similarly [armed] men fighting and hurling lances one to another or by turns. And the queens, lords and ladies dined well into the evening, and then they took their horses, going back to their inns.

8. Hereafter, on the twenty-seventh day of the same month, the said lord of Suffolk and the other ambassadors, getting leave of the king and queen of France and the dauphin together with the dauphiness and other lords and ladies, left for his inn with honour and prepared to ride to England. Also, on the morrow, the next day following, they went to the queen of England and took leave of her and of the King of Sicily and the queen and of all others there present. On the next day, however, all the ambassadors left Tours, the duke of Alencon, the count of Vendome, the lord of Precigny and lord Peter de Bresse [presumably Breze again] leading them out of that city. As they rode to the end of the bridge of the same city, they met the dauphin and other lords who took his [Suffolk's] leave with a friendly farewell, and they went to England with a safe-conduct. And they reported all their deeds and exploits to the king and thus it proceeded to the conclusion as may be seen set out below.

---

[14] Charles, Duke of Bourbon, was reconciled with Philip of Burgundy by 1437 and signed a treaty with him in January 1440 (Vaughn, p123). Bourbon had been involved in the embassy to arrange René's release which occurred before the release of the Count of Eu, (Monstrelet 2, p46, p70). Bourbon was married to Agnes of Burgundy, another of Philip's sisters in 1425 (Vaughn, p123) and the Count of Eu's sister, Bonne, was married briefly to Philip in 1424, dying a year later.

5.   Margaret of Anjou's Escort to England in 1445

From: Add. MSS 23938 f5 & f13 British Library (Compotus de expensis Margareta Reginae, venientis in Angliam, Jul. 1444-Oc. 1446).

The following list of names of those who composed this escort is given in this authentic document of the times and is transcribed in Hookham (vol 1, p246). Hookham only quotes the shorter of two lists in this manuscript. John Wenlock is listed in the longer list.

Thomas Lord Clifford
Ralph Lord Graystock
James de Bomonord (Ormond)
Beatrice Lady Talbot, Baroness
Emma Lady Scales, Baroness
Sir Thomas Stanley
Sir Edward Hall
Sir William Bonville
Sir Richard Roos
Sir Robert Harcourt
Sir John Holland
Sir Hugh Cokesey
Sir Robert Wynchelsey
Sir Robert Hungerford
Lady Elizabeth Grey
Lady Elizabeth Hall
Master Walter Lyzard, the Queen's Chaplain and confessor
William Breust, Clerk
Rose Merston, damsel
Margaret Stanlewe
Henry Quarranto, Clerk and Secretary to the Lady, the Queen
Michael Trigory, the Queen's Chaplain
Henry Trevilean, Chaplain and almsgiver
John Bridd, servant
George Pavier, Master of the Navy, called Christopher of Newcastle

In addition to the retinue who accompanied Margaret from Orleans and Lorraine, the party consisted of the Marquis of Suffolk, three barons, two baronesses, nine knights, two ladies, six damsels, four chaplains, fifty esquires, and 182 valets, or serving men, besides various retainers of inferior rank (Stevenson, vol 2 part 1, p xl).

Another list is cited in Beaucourt (vol 1, p 86-90) who transcribed the *Chronique de Mathieu d'Escouchy* – an account by a contemporary chronicler (nb: names in brackets are Beaucourt's clarifications):

"….Et, pour la recevoir, envoya le Roy Henry pluseurs seigneurs et dames de son pays audit lieu de Rouen, moult haultement et richement habilliez; c'est assavoir:
le duc d'Yorcq   (Richard, duc d'York)
le comte de Suffort   (Suffolk)
le seigneur de Tallebot   (John Talbot, comte de Shrewsbury)
le marquis de Susalby   (Richard Nevill, comte de Westmoreland et de Salisbury)
le seigneur de Clif   (Clifle or Clifton)*
le baron de Graisoit   (Ralph lord Greystock)
Messire Jamet d'Ormont   (James Butler, comte d'Ormond)**
Messire Jehan Belledit   (Bolledit)
Messire Guillaume Bonneclubbe   (Sir William Bonville, senechal d'Aquitaine)
Messire Richard Rioz   (Robert Roos)
Messire Jehan Secalay   (Jehan de Semilly)
Messire Edouart Hoult   (Edward Hull)
Messire Robert de Villeby   (Robert, Lord Willoughby)
Robert de Harcourt,   (Baron de Bosworth, de la branche de la maison de Harcourt etablie en Angleterre)
Messire Huy Coquesin   (Hue Cokeseye)
Comtesse de Suffort   (Alice Chaucer, petite fille du celebre poete de ce nom)***
la dame de Talbot   (Marguerite Beauchamp, fille de Richard Beauchamp, comte de Warwick.)#
la dame de Salsebery   (Alice, fille de Thomas Montagu, comte de Salisbury, tue au seige d'Orleans en 1428)
la dame Marguerite Hoult   (Hull)
la dame de Talbot la jeune   (Elizabeth d'Ormond)##

* Thomas, Lord Clifford.
** Should be James Butler, son of the Earl of Ormond (see Watts 2004b).
*** On entering Rouen, Alice Chaucer, Marchioness of Suffolk, took the place of the Queen as she was unwell.
# Wife of John Talbot, 1st Earl of Shrewsbury and eldest daughter of Richard Beauchamp, Earl of Warwick, by his first wife, Elizabeth d. & h. of Thomas, Lord Berkeley, Viscount Lisle.
Elizabeth of Ormond, daughter of fourth Earl of Ormond, sister of fifth earl, married to John Talbot, son of John Talbot, 1st Earl of Shrewsbury.

6. William de la Pole, Duke of Suffolk - Will and Letter to Son

Will and final letter to his son John written as he is leaving England to go into exile.

Will
(In *North Country Wills*, The Surtees Society, vol VCXVI, 1908, pp50-51)

Having ordered that his body be buried at Charterhouse at Hull, Suffolk (who wrote his will in his own hand) directs:

where y wol my ymage and stone be made and the ymage of my best beloved wyf by me, she to be there with me yf she lust, my said sepulture to be made by her discretion in ye said Charterhouse where she shal thinke best, in caas be yat in my dayes it be not made nor begonne; desiringe, yf it may, to lye so as the masses that y have perpetuelly founded there for my said best beloved wyf and me may be daily songen over me. And also ye day of my funeralx, the day of my beryeng, that ye charge thereof be bysette upon pore creatures to pray for me, and in no pompes nor pryde of ye world. Also y wol yat my londes and goodes be disposed after that that y have disposed them in my last wille of ye date of these presentez, and only ordeyne my said best beloved wyfe my sole executrice, beseching her at ye reverence of God to take ye charge upon her for the wele of my soule, for above al the erthe my singuler trust is moost in her, and y wol for her ease, yf she wol and elles nought, that she may take unto her such on personne as she lust to name, to helpe her in yexecution yerof for her ease, to laboure under her as she wold commande hym. And last of al with the blessing of God and of me, as hertely as y can yeve it to my dere and trew son, y bequethe betwene hym and his moder love and al good accorde and yeve hym her hoolly, and for a remembraunce my gret balays to my said son.

[The "gret balays" seems to have been a ruby. His wife, the sole executor, was Alice Chaucer whose previous husband was Thomas Montacute, Earl of Salisbury (d.1828).]

Letter to son
(From the *Paston Letters*, Ed. Archer-Hind, pp23-24)

My dear and only well-beloved son, I beseech our Lord in Heaven, the Maker of all the World, to bless you, and to send you ever grace to love him, and to dread him, to the which, as far as a father may charge his child, I both charge you, and pray you to set all your spirits and wits to do, and to know his holy laws and commandments, by the which ye shall, with his great mercy, pass all the great tempests and troubles of this wretched world.

And that also, weetingly, ye do nothing for love nor dread of any earthly creature that should displease him. And there as any frailty maketh you to fall, beseech his mercy soon to call you to him again with repentance, satisfaction, and contrition of your heart, never more in will to offend him.

Secondly, next him above all earthly things, to be true liegeman in heart, in will, in thought, in deed, unto the king our aldermost high and dread sovereign lord, to whom both ye and I be so much bound to; charging you as father can and may, rather to die than to be the contrary, or to know anything that were against the welfare or prosperity of his most royal person, but that as far as your body and life may stretch ye live and die to defend it, and to let his highness have knowledge thereof in all the haste ye can.

Thirdly, in the same wise, I charge you, my dear son, alway as ye be bounden by the commandment of God to do, to love, to worship, your lady and mother; and also that ye obey alway her commandments, and to believe her counsels and advices in all your works, the which dread not but shall be best and truest to you. And if any other body would steer you to the contrary, to flee the counsel in any wise, for ye shall find it naught and evil.

Furthermore, as far as father may and can, I charge you in any wise to flee the company and counsel of proud men, of covetous men, and of flattering men, the more especially and mightily to withstand them, and not to draw nor to meddle with them, with all your might and power; and to draw to you and to your company good and virtuous men, and such as be of good conversation, and of truth, and by them shall ye never be deceived nor repent you of.

Moreover, never follow your own wit in nowise, but in all your works, of such folks as I write of above, ask your advice and counsel, and doing thus, with the mercy of God, ye shall do right well, and live in right much worship, and great heart's rest and ease.

And I will be to you as good lord and father as my heart can think.

And last of all, as heartily and as lovingly as ever father blessed his child in earth, I give you the blessing of Our Lord and of me, which of his infinite mercy increase you in all virtue and good living; and that your blood may by his grace from kindred to kindred multiply in this earth to his service, in such wise as after the departing from this wretched world here, ye and they may glorify him eternally amongst his angels in heaven.

Written of mine hand,
The day of my departing from this land.

Your true and loving father

7.   John Norreys Esquire – Inquisition Post Mortem

From: *CIPM*, Henry V – Richard III, Vol IV, 1828, no. 45, page 337 (6 Edw IV), House of Commons.

This is a list of real property (manors, lands, pastures etc) held by Norreys at the time of his death in 1466, and an indication of who granted the properties.

Johannes Noreys Armiger

Okeholt maner voc' Noreys maner
Moores maner
Hyndons maner in Bray*
Sunninghill maner*
Newenham in Warfield maner#
Spensers maner and Elyngtons maner in Cokeham (= Cookham)*
Heyndons maner in Cokeham*
multa messuages, molendine terrae ten' pastur' bofc part' reddit and c. in
Bray*
Cokeham*
Maydenhithe
Binfeld*
Shotesbrooke~
Wargrave#
Reding+
Wyndesor Nova*
Wyndesor Vetus*
Clewer*
Twyford+
Hurst+
Wokyngham~
Wyngefeld~
Ascote~
Warefeld#
Brakenhale~
Purley Parva maner
Le Thele terr'
Foulescote alias Fogelescote maner

Held of: * Queen Elizabeth (Woodville) wife of Edward IV
            # Bishop of Winchester (William Waynflete, sometime Provost of Eton)
            + Abbot of Reading
            ~ Abbot of Abingdon

nb: *Hydons maner in Bray* was sold to Sir Thomas Reeve (d.1777) in 1762 (Kerry, pp122-123). *Heyndons maner in Cokeham* evidently stayed in the family until 1608, when Francis, Lord Norreys, sold *Hindons Farm in Cookham* to Sir Thomas Bodley who in 1612 endowed the University of Oxford with it to found the famous library.

8. Papal Dispensation for the Marriage of Henry VI to Margaret of Anjou

From: Calendar of Papal Registers, vol VIII, 1427-1447, p249; Jan 1444 (14 Eugenius IV*)

To Henry King of England. Dispensation at his petition containing that for the peace and tranquillity of the realms of France and England he had contracted marriage per verba legitima de presenti with Margaret daughter of Rene King of Sicily and for the said reason desires its speedy consummation; and adding that the sea voyage to England is, during the winter, apt to be prolonged by reason of storms and tempests ... to solemnly celebrate the nuptials before the church and consummate the said marriage in days when it is forbidden to do so.

This item is referred to in a contemporary hand as *Liber Secundus Secretus Bullarum inceptus Rome de mense Oct 1443 / Pontificates sanctissi domini nostril domini Eugenius papa quarte anno XIIII.*

* Pope Eugenius IV (1431-1447)

9.   1582 Royal Charter granting Ockwells Manor to Basil Fettiplace

Queen Elizabeth's grant to Basil (Bessel, Besils) Fettiplace[15] exists in two copies:

1. An unimposing "file copy" retained by the state and now in The National Archives among the rolls of letters patent issued by Elizabeth I (TNA reference C66/1223). This version replaces many of the more standard phrases in the V&A copy with "etc". A summary of this version of the document appears as entry 135 in Wilkinson L J (ed), ca. 2001, *Calendar of Patent Rolls 25 Elizabeth I (1582-83) C 66/1223-1236,* vol 286, published by the List and Index Society:

> **135** 31 Dec 1582. Windsor Castle. Grant, in fee simple (by the advice of William [Cecil], baron of Burghley, lord treasurer, privy councillor, and Sir Walter Myldmay, chancellor of the Exchequer, privy councillor), to Basil Fetyplace, son and heir of Sir John Fetyplace of Besselsleigh, Berks (on Sir John's surrender, by indenture 31 Oct 22 Eliz (1580) of his [recited] Exchequer patent 9 Dec 22 Eliz [1579], of the manor of Ockholt in Bray, Berks, with all lands there (late of Sir Thomas Fetyplace, deceased, forfeited by Sir Francis Englefeild [sic], fugitive, and now in the tenure of James Wynche). To hold in socage as of the manor of Bray by fealty. Duty to do suit of court at the manor of Bray every three weeks, and to pay a yearly rent of £75s 7¾d with any other rents and services formerly rendered by Lady Katherine Englefeild, deceased, and a further yearly rent of £8 3s 2d as long as the queen's title to the premises by reason of the above forfeiture shall remain valid. The premises were granted by Exchequer patent 9 Dec 22 Eliz [1579] to the said Sir John Fetyplace (kinsman and heir of the said Lady Katherine Englefeild, late wife of Sir Francis Englefeild and daughter and heir of the said Thomas Fetyplace) for such time as the queen's title thereto should remain valid from Michaelmas last; with reservations, including advowsons; yearly rent £8 3s 2d.
> For £200 paid at the Exchequer.

2. A decorated and finely written copy given to Basil Fettiplace and now held at the National Art Library (within the V&A):
Catalogue record (item (MSL/1916/523). Image ID: 2010EB6758.
https://nal-vam.on.worldcat.org/oclc/1008387837.

The V&A catalogue mistakenly states that the grant is to John Fettiplace (d.1580), and misdates his death. This charter was donated to the V&A by Col. C du Pre Penton Powney, a descendent of Penyston Portlock Powney, once owner of Ockwells. It is illustrated on page 116 and a full translation of this copy is given below, with modern punctuation to aid readability:

> **Elizabeth, by the grace of God queen of England, France and Ireland**, defender of the faith etc, to all to whom the present letters come, greetings.

> Whereas John Fettyplace of Besilsleigh in our county of Berkshire, knight, blood-

---

[15] Spelling of the surname also varies; see ffetyplace, Fetyplace.Fettiplace. The summary gives the original spelling of Fetyplace and also Englefeild. In the full translation the spellings of Fettyplace and Englefeild are given.

relation and nearest heir to Lady Catherine Englefield deceased, gave, granted and confirmed to us, our heirs and successors, through his indenture enrolled in our chancellery and dated the thirty-first day of October in the twenty-second year of our reign,

all that manor, farm, lands, tenements and hereditaments situated, lying and existing in the parish of Bray in our aforesaid county of Berkshire called or known by the name of the manor of Ockeholte alias Ockholt alias Ocole alias Norrys manor alias Fettyplace manor,

and all other lands, tenements, meadows, leasowes, pastures, woods, underwoods, rents, reversions, services and hereditaments pertaining or belonging to the aforesaid manor, farm and other premises or of any of them, or accepted, reputed, held, used or known as a part, parcel, or member of the aforesaid manor, farm and other premises or of any one of them,

and all other lands, tenements, and hereditaments in the parish of Bray aforesaid which once belonged to Thomas Fettyplace knight, deceased — father of Lady Catherine Englefield, lately the wife of Francis Englefield knight — whose heir was the aforesaid Catherine, and now or lately in the tenure of a certain James Wynch or his assigns or someone making a claim through him or under him,

and the whole estate, right, title, interest, possession and claims of the aforesaid John Fettyplace knight, of, in, or to the aforesaid manor, farm and other premises with their appurtenances or to any part or parcel thereof,

for us the afore-stated queen, our heirs and successors, to have and to hold the aforesaid manor, farm, lands, tenements and all and singular the other premises with all and singular their appurtenances recited by the aforesaid indenture;

and whereas we,

on the advice of our dear and faithful councillors William Baron Burghley, our treasurer of England, and Walter Mildmaye, knight, chancellor of the court of our Exchequer, barons of our Exchequer,

in exchange for a fine of two hundred pounds of lawful money of England, [paid] by our dear aforesaid John Fettyplace, knight, into the receipts of our Exchequer for our use,

freely demised and granted through our letters patent under the seal of our Exchequer dated at Westminster on the ninth day of December in the twenty-second year of our reign,

all and singular the premises with all and singular their appurtenances, amongst others by the name or names of all that manor of Ockeholte with all its appurtenances situated lying and existing in the parish of Bray in our said county of Berkshire,

and all the lands, tenements, meadows, feedings, pastures, and profits of reversions, services, and hereditaments whatsoever with all their appurtenances in Ockeholte and Braye aforesaid in the said county of Berkshire lately in the tenure of Catherine Lady Englefield, lately wife of Francis Englefield knight, and also of all and singular the messuages, mills, houses, buildings, structures, barns, stables, dovecots, gardens, orchards, gardens, tofts, crofts, curtilages, lands, tenements, meadows, feedings, pastures, leasows, heaths, commons, wastes, furze, moors, marshes, waters, water courses, pools, banks, stanks, fish-ponds, fisheries, fishings, returns from tenants (both free as well as customary) of the said manor of Ockeholte and Bray, and the rents, reversions, services, court leets and views of frankpledge, perquisites and their profits, fines, amerciaments, heriots, chattels, waifs, strays, and all other profits, commodities, emoluments and hereditaments whatsoever in any way belonging, pertaining, happening or arising to the said manor of Ockeholte or held, known, accepted, used, demised, let, occupied, or enjoyed as being members, part or parcel of the said manor, and a parcel of the lands and possessions of the said Francis Englefield knight and then being in our hands and at our disposal by reason of the forfeiture of the aforesaid Francis Englefield because the said Francis Englefield has gone out of this kingdom of England into foreign and overseas parts and is staying there contrary to the form of the statute issued and provided in such a case,

always however excepted and wholly reserved to us, our heirs and successors all rights of mining and quarrying in the premises and the advowsons of any churches and chapels whatsoever of the premises,

for the afore-stated John Fettyplace, knight, his executors and assigns to have and to hold the manor of Ockeholte, its messuages, mills, cottages, lands, tenements, meadows, feedings, pastures, rents, reversions, services, court leets, views of frank pledge and their profits and all and singular other premises above through the aforesaid letters patent demised and granted with all their rights, members and appurtenances, except those before excepted,

from the feast of St Michael the Archangel then last past for as long as the premises shall remain or ought to remain in the hands of us, our heirs or successors, by reason of the contempt and forfeiture of the said Francis Englefield knight,

by rendering yearly to us, our heirs and successors, in respect of and for the aforesaid manor of Ockeholte with its appurtenances, eight pounds three shillings and two pence of lawful money of England at the feasts of the Annunciation to the blessed virgin Mary and of St Michael the Archangel to the receipts of our Exchequer or into the hands of the bailiffs or receivers of premises existing for the time being, in equal portions to be paid within the aforesaid term, as more fully is clear and appears through the same indenture lately recited and enrolled about the same;

know ye now that we of our especial grace and of our certain knowledge and mere motion, for various good and reasonable causes and considerations specially moving us in this part, on behalf of ourselves, our heirs and successors, have given, granted, and in this our present writing confirmed to Basil Fettyplace esquire son and heir apparent of the aforesaid John Fettyplace knight

the whole of the aforesaid manor, farm, lands, tenements and hereditaments lying and existing in Bray aforesaid called or known by the name of the manor of Ockeholt otherwise Ockholt or Ocole or Norrys manor or Fettyplace manor and all and singular the other premises whatsoever with all and singular their rights, members and all their appurtenances given or granted to us, our heirs and successors through the aforesaid indenture recited above, bearing the aforesaid date the thirty-first day of October, and the whole of our right, estate, title, claim, interest and charges whatsoever concerning or to the aforesaid manor, farm, lands, tenements and other premises and in whatever is part and parcel of it

for the afore-stated Basil Fettyplace, his heirs and assigns

to have the aforesaid manor, farm, tenements, and all other premises with all and singular their appurtenances to the service and use of the aforesaid Basil, his heirs and assigns for ever

to be held of us, our heirs and successors, as of our manor of Bray aforesaid by fealty in free socage and not in chief

and to make to us, our heirs and successors, suit at the court of the said manor of Bray aforesaid every three weeks

and to render and to pay to us, our heirs and successors, annually seven pounds five shillings seven pence and three farthings on two feasts in the year, that is, on the feast of the Annunciation to the blessed virgin Mary and on the feast of Saint Michael the Archangel, in equal portions into the hands of the bailiff or collector of our manor of Bray aforesaid for the time being existing

and to pay and do to us, our heirs and successors, other rents, services and commodities as often and of the same quality and quantity as the aforesaid Catherine was required or accustomed to do to us or our forebears by law for the premises for all services, exactions, and all charges

and further to render to us, our heirs and successors, for the premises for as long as we, our heirs and successors are entitled to the profits of the premises by reason of the contempt and forfeiture of the aforesaid Francis Englefield knight and by virtue of the Act of Parliament concerning fugitives lately issued and provided, eight pounds, three shillings and two pence of lawful money of England, to be paid at the feasts of the Annunciation to the Blessed Virgin Mary and of St Michael the Archangel in equal portions to the receipts of our Exchequer and that of our heirs and successors or into the hands of our bailiffs or receivers existing for the time being in our said county of Berkshire.

And further we will, and through the present [letters patents] we grant on behalf of ourselves, our heirs and successors, to the afore-stated Basil Fettyplace, his heirs and assigns, that these our letters patent and the enrolment of the same shall be firm, valid, good, sufficient and effectual in law in relation to us, our heirs and successors, as much in all our courts as anywhere else whatsoever within our kingdom of England, without the need for any confirmations, licences or tolerations to be procured or obtained from us, our heirs and successors hereafter by the aforestated Basil, his heirs and assigns,

notwithstanding any mis-naming or mis-reciting of, or failure to recite, the aforesaid manor, farm, lands, tenements and other premises or any parcel thereof

and notwithstanding any mis-reciting of, or failure to recite, any inquisition of the premises or of any parcel thereof

258

and notwithstanding any mis-reciting of any demisings or grantings of the premises or of any parcel thereof existing on record or not on record

and notwithstanding any other defects in the correct naming of any town, hamlet, parish, place or county in which the premises or any parcel thereof exist or exists, or in failure to name premises or any parcel thereof in nature, kind, species or quality.

And also we will and by these present [letters patent] grant to the aforenamed Basil Fettyplace that he has and will have these our letters patent made and sealed in due manner under our Great Seal of England without having in any way to render, pay or make a fine or fee, great or small, accordingly to us in our Hanaper or elsewhere to our use;

notwithstanding the fact that no express mention is made in the present [letters patent] of the true annual value or the certainty of the premises or of any of them or of any other gifts or grants thereof made before these times by us or by someone or some of our progenitors to the aforenamed Basil Fettyplace, and notwithstanding any other statute, Act, ordinance, proclamation, provision or restriction to the contrary thereof made, issued, ordained, or provided, or any other matter, case or ground whatsover in another.

In witness of which matter we have had made these our letters patent.

Witnessed by me myself at our castle of Windsor on the thirty-first day of December in the twenty-fifth year of our reign.

By writ of privy seal and on the aforesaid date by authority of Parliament. **Powle**.

N.B. The name of the clerk of the Crown in Chancery was subscribed/printed at the end of all documents as a way of authentication of their having passed through the Crown Office: (https://en.wikipedia.org/wiki/Letters_Patent_(United_Kingdom).
The charter is signed by "Powle" i.e. Thomas Powle (d.1601), clerk of the Crown of England from 1546 till his death:
(https://web.archive.org/web/20180416114917/http://www.history.ac.uk/resources/offi ce/chancery-appt).

10. 1765 drawings made by Sir Thomas Reeve and copied by Charles Kerry in C19th

From: Kerry's notebook Vol II MSS Top Berks 15/2 p118-121 Bodleian
(Copyright: Bodleian Library)

Copies by Charles Kerry of original drawings made in 1765 by Sir Thomas Reeve of Hendon's House, Holyport, Berkshire. According to Kerry, Sir Thomas Reeve was a distinguished herald and antiquary. It is not known what labels Reeve's drawings had but the mention of Lysons on page 120 of Kerry's notebook suggests that he certainly added to them. In the captions below "Light" refers to the corresponding light in the glass in the great hall in which the coat appears.

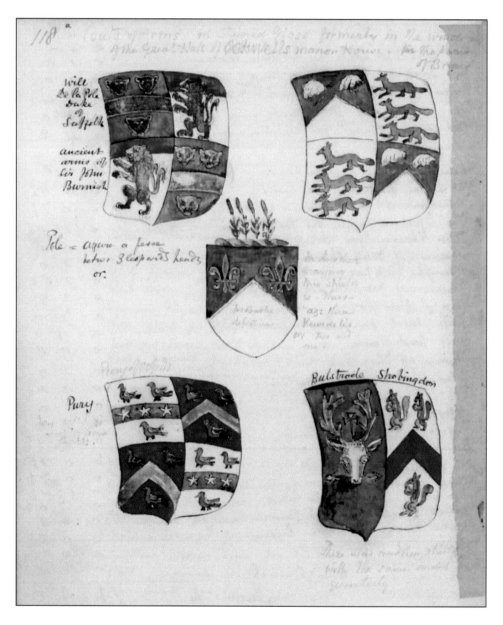

Top left: Light 4, named here as William de la Pole Duke of Suffolk though in his book Kerry (1861, p115) gave de la Pole, Duke of Sussex!
Top right: Light 13, John Nanfan, showing damage.
Middle: Light 11, William Laken, incorrectly said to be "probably defective."
Bottom right: Light 18, William Bulstrode, only upper two quarters drawn.

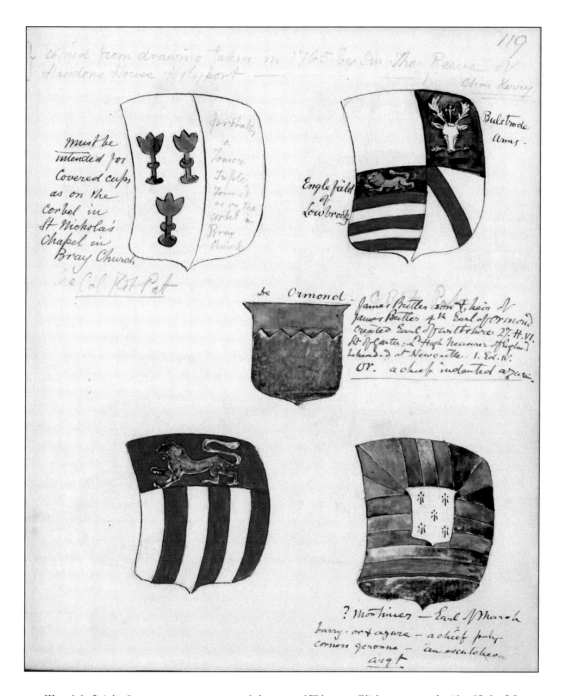

Top left: *Light 9, upper two quarters of the coat of Eleanor Clitheroe, second wife of John Norreys.*
Top right: *Light 16, Edmund Brudenell showing a missing quarter.*
Middle: *Light 6, James Butler fourth Earl of Ormond; incorrect identification by Kerry.*
Bottom left: *Light 15, Edward Langford; colour in chief later changed from red to blue.*
Bottom right: *Light 12 Hugh Mortimer; incorrect identification by Kerry.*

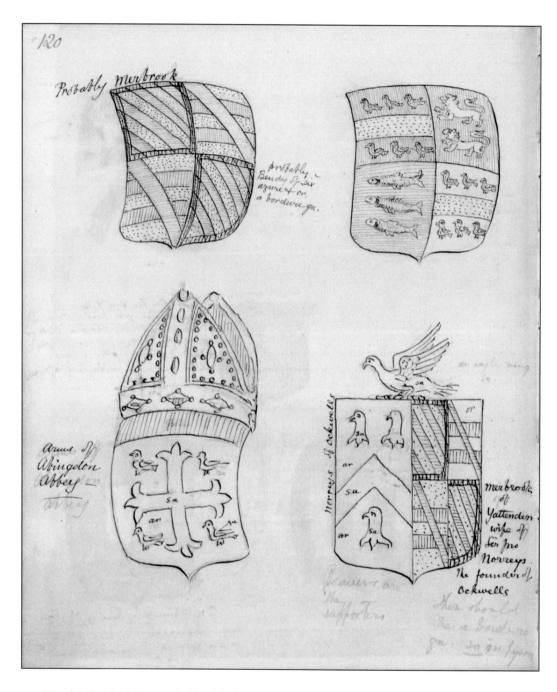

120

Probably Merbrook

probably
Bendy of six
azure & or.
a bordure gu.

Arms of
Abingdon
Abbey—

Norreys of Ockwells

an eagle rising
or

ar

s.a

ar

s.a

ar

s.a

or

Merbrook
of
Yattenden
wife of
Sir Jno
Norreys
the founder of
Ockwells

beavers are
the
supporters

there should
be a bordure
gu — so in Lyson

Top left: *Light 14, coat of Alice Merbrooke, first wife of John Norreys.*
Bottom right: their impaled coats. Kerry cites Lysons (in pencil, bottom right) as source for
adding a bordure to what he identified as the Merbrook (sic) coat, suggesting Reeve omitted it.
Top right: Light 8 Richard Beauchamp, Bishop of Salisbury. Reeve rarely drew the crests; two
occur here: that of Norreys and Abbey of Abingdon, bottom left, Light 7.

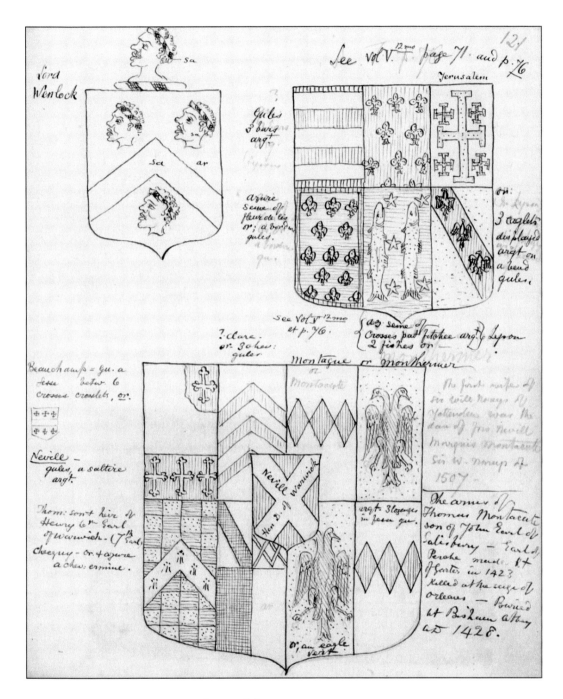

Top left: Light 10, John Wenlock with his crest.

Top right: Light 3, Margaret of Anjou, quarters 2, 3 & 4 were said to be fragments in 1798. Reeve in 1765 does not show damage though may have missed the trace of red label that is extant in quarter 2.

Bottom: Light 1, Henry Beauchamp, said to be defaced in 1798. Reeve in 1765 only shows damage in the Despenser coat (second quarter from left bottom row). This bouché shaped coat, impaling that of his wife Cicely Neville, is complex and was probably drawn here as a heater shape to simplify the drafting. Its complexity may have confused the 1798 observer causing it to be described as "defaced". nb: The pencil note, top right of this coat, is incorrect. It is the widow of John Neville, not his daughter, who married Sir William Norreys as his second wife, not his first wife; see also Appendix C, Tree 1a, (ii).

263

11. 1872 Description of Ockwells Manor when in use as the Farmhouse

From: BRO D/EG T14

(1872 Lease of Ockwells Farm and cottages at Cox Green between the surviving trustees of the will of the late C P Grenfell Esq and Mr Robert Parrott).

MENS ROOM – One forty-inch kitchen range with oven and boiler. Memorandum: no tap and back of grate broken. Two sets of cupboards with shelves under.

BANQUETING HALL – Ancient dining table and side seats on brackets and bearers. A pair of ancient riding boots, saddle, coat of chain armour, sword and buck's head and antlers.

SOUTH SITTING ROOM – One thirty-inch register stove fixed.

KITCHEN – Bacon rack fixed. Three shelves, dresser and drawers. One elm seat fixed to wall. Spit rack and shelves fixed to wall. One old forty-three-inch range not fixed. One ironing stove with doors and bars fixed complete. Deal cupboard with folding doors and three shelves. Three rows of shelving fixed to wall.

WASH HOUSE – A strong two-inch elm shelf on legs and bearers. Old deal dresser with drawers and shelves. Wrought iron oven door and brick oven, lead pump with cheeks and boards fixed complete. Old wooden bottle rack roofed in and covered with tiles.

DAIRY – Four shelves fixed to wall.

SITTING ROOM- One thirty-inch Register stove. One stove fixed to wall.

CELLAR – One shelf fixed to wall.

LARDER – Four shelves fixed to wall. One three-inch brass barrel lift pump, suction tap and rising main complete to water closet. One deal shelf suspended from ceiling. Palisade partition and door to farm. China closets with shelves.

PARLOUR – One forty-inch register stove. Two small hanging brackets at side of fireplace. One brass finger plate.

FRONT ENTRANCE – Looking north. One door knocker, one oil painting and carved frame.

LANDING – Three bells

NORTH EAST BEDROOM – One thirty-inch register stove.

NORTH WEST BEDROOM – One thirty eight-inch Rumford stove and ¾ inch deal cupboard.

WEST BEDROOM – One bell with wires complete.

BEST BEDROOM – One thirty-inch Register stove.

SOUTH BEDROOM – One thirty-inch Romford stove.

MENS BEDROOM – One bell.

12. Correspondence relating to Ockwells at the Society for the Protection of Ancient Buildings (SPAB)

From: Original letters held by the SPAB in the "*Ockwells, Bray*" file

[Transcribed by the author]

SPAB was founded by William Morris in 1877. The state of Ockwells was one of its earliest concerns. This at the time when the tenant was Allport Wilkerson, who used the manor house as a farm house, and W H Grenfell had control of the house. Grenfell built a new farm house for the tenant in 1887.

9 November 1880; **SPAB**, the Secretary – Newman Marks – wrote to **W H Grenfell**, asking to visit the Ockwells to "ascertain its state and condition." It was proposed that a sub-committee consisting of Messrs S W Kershaw, Webb and Vinall should view the house and report.

Their report dated 20 November 1880 read:

"The undersigned members of this committee made their survey on Saturday the 20th Nov & spent some hours in examining all the accessible parts of the building. They have the pleasure of reporting that in spite of the neglect under which it has evidently suffered for many years the natural strength of its materials has resisted decay to a surprising extent & but very modest amount of absolute repair is needed to put the building in a condition to withstand decay for many years to come.

This is due no doubt to the fact that the structure is mainly of timber the greater part of which remains in perfectly sound condition. The date of the building is the early part of the fifteenth century and its plan is we think remarkable for that date. The Hall has an entrance porch and screens passage with the usual cross buildings at the ends but with the unusual addition of a glazed corridor and attached buildings of 2 stories enclosing a small court at the back. This corridor gives access to the offices and more private apartments both upstairs and down.

The entrance porch and hall are practically perfect & the gables of the oriel & cross buildings are also original and unmodernised. The inner court is so far as we are able to see it unaltered but modern chambers have been built within it & has reduced it to a very small dimension. The rest of the building has undoubted marks of originality, but we were not able to examine them except from the outside. Your committee concluded the examination by resolving that such an important example of domestic architecture should not be allowed to remain unmeasured and carefully drawn and hereby beg leave to propose that accurate and complete drawings be made by order of the Society as soon as permission of owner & tenant and weather permits. As regards the necessary repairs these are so few and simple that no great expenditure of money is needed, but they demand immediate [missing word]

We would chiefly recommend that a capable clerk of works should be appointed with definite instructions that he should direct the workmen constantly and cautiously to the end & that the work should not be let by contract. The parts most in need of repair are clearly shown by the fungus growing within the hall and porch, there are three of these places all of them suggesting defects in the gutters above. The condition of the lead gutters demands immediate attention. Possibly it may be found necessary to strip some portion of the [tiling?] & renew the [laths/latter?] but careful examination might show that very little absolute <u>renewal</u> is necessary.

The ivy which has been allowed to grow too freely on the east and west sides should be kept within bounds though not wholly cleared away. It may be now to some extent of a binder & support to the walls. In trimming the ivy & generally in raising ladders to the roof too great care cannot be given to the very delicate carvings of the [cusp?] barge boards & panelled gables. The presence of a watchful clerk of works would be most valuable in protecting the ancient work from the ordinary dangers which attend even the simple operations we have recommended.

Beyond these few really important matters there is nothing to call for expense unless the committee is inclined to suggest that the use of the hall and adjoining offices by the tenant is objectionable. The floor of the hall is much broken, perhaps in wood splitting & though the damage there is not a vital injury the liability to further rough treatment may be a cause of greater mischief. It might be worthy of consideration whether some new building on the east side of the main block might not be more convenient for the tenant & relieve him from the temptation to use the historical portion for the rougher necessities of a farm house.

At the same time it must be observed that the occupation of one part of the building is a real advantage to the other by the constant supervision it ensures & we would not suggest isolation of the more ancient part.

In speaking of the Hall we should have said it is now under ceiled & consequently the timbers of the roof are not visible from below. It might be well considered whether when the repairs are in progress a piece of this ceiling should not be removed for the sake of admitting some light to the roof & allowing its beautiful construction to be seen.

In conclusion we feel bound to say how injurious to the building would be any attempt to restore it either as a dwelling or for show: in its present condition nothing but watchful protection against the weather & violence is needed to preserve it for many years as an authentic and admirable example of our ancient skill in housebuilding [we] think more ambitious repairs, still more what is called restoration would quite destroy its value as an original work without adding one year to its future existence

George Wardle
Philip Webb"

The sub-committee's field notes recorded:

"Roof repair is wanting as the entrance of rain is very marked particularly at the entrance porch and in the big chamber [probably great hall] so the loft above and over bay window of hall another bad place [on?] fire place. At all these points the mischief is of old standing. [Offer?] to supply a clerk of works and a few labourers under him to [...?] repair under proper direction [....?] Floor of hall [is?] to let it remain in foresaid broken condition. Hall is non-ceiled should not one bay of the ceiling be opened to admit air flight, to allow antiquarians to see it and also that repair and care of it might be more easy. Roof timbers fine state of preservation very big [...?] Tiling [only?] repair do not remove the main timbers of present ceiling of Great Hall. Ivy* over front of building near porch. Tiling in many parts is very good ought not to be removed." [*Ivy marked so on little diagram].

1 February 1888; letter to SPAB from Ernest Law, who was interested in buying the lease when the house was in the possession of **Tom Columbus Smith** who had a 99-year lease from Grenfell:

"I have seen the owner and went with him over the house and I think the result of our interview was to impress on him the fact that the more severely he left the house alone, the more value it would have; and so far he has done no irreparable injury, though he has commenced operations.

I have frequent and accurate instructions of all he does (though this is quite in confidence) and I feel pretty sure that all his threats of destroying its archaeological character are therefor made in order to induce some enthusiasts to step forward and make him an extravagant offer in order to save it – He is working the newspapers with this object; and has put an advertisement in the *Morning Post* saying he is ready to treat for sale; or lease of it. His terms however are preposterous – asking thousands where 3 or 4 hundred would be more than a fair price. He is building a factory near the road now, hoping to get as much for the house as though it were not there and then afterwards to be bought at an exorbitant sum.

I fancy that if he finds no one will acquiesce in his preposterous terms that he will then become more reasonable.

He is under strict covenants in his lease from Mr Grenfell not to interfere with the old part of the house, or to remove or destroy any of the oak panelling, staircase or the fireplaces – but this he does not allow to be known – but plays a game of brag as to what he will do and can do.

I am still in hopes he may come round at least to taking £400 or £500 for his lease – whereby he will be relieved from the covenants of having to spend £400 on the premises within the year.

I should be glad to know if you heard of anyone who is willing to offer anything considerable for it. If so I should be anxious to join with him in the hopes that then we might offer enough to rescue the place and perhaps become joint owners.

In the meanwhile I will keep you informed of all I hear as to his processes. He is playing an astute game; but I think he recognises that its value is entirely antiquarian and that if he really succeeds to alter it much, he will kill his goose with the golden eggs.

Yours truly Ernest Law"

1 February 1888; Secretary of SPAB requests *Pall Mall Gazette* to republish a statement from the *Builder* magazine which stated that:

"I understand the present owner of the property (Smith) states that he cannot throw away money in restoring the house, simply as a hobby, but must make it suitable for his requirements. He has decided to build an embattled tower at the back of the house, and has already commenced building a warehouse where the garden wall skirts the high road, but the latter being away from the house does not much injure it, although the picturesqueness of its surroundings will be affected. The proposed alterations to the interior would destroy all its antiquarian and architectural value. The hall (represented in *Nash's Mansions*) would be divided into two storeys containing three rooms and a staircase. An entrance-door would stand where the lovely bay window now is, and the porch would

267

be removed. The owner of the property is very reluctant to do anything which will destroy the interesting character of the house, and would, I believe, surrender it to any antiquarian society, provided they would undertake to properly restore and maintain it."

24 February 1888; letter to **Allan Fea**, who had recently written to the *Standard* (22ⁿᵈ February) regarding Ockwells observing: "the present owner….so as to suit his own requirements, will have to modernise it, and make considerable alterations, which will completely destroy all its ancient characteristics; but, before commencing these "improvements" he has generously offered to hand over the interesting part of the house to any Antiquarian Society that will undertake its restoration. …..But, if some steps are not taken immediately to preserve it, it will be too late, for I understand workmen are now on the spot, ready to pull down and destroy what can never be replaced."

The letter to **Fea** reads:

"I must first say that the Society made a careful report upon the building in 1880 and said what we considered should be done. Since then the owner Mr Grenfell of Taplow Court Maidenhead has given a lease of the building and grounds to a Mr Smith.

A gentleman tried to buy Mr Smith's lease of him in order that he may put the building in repair and so save it but he says Mr Smith wants a fancy price for it.

This piece of information however I fear I must ask you to consider as private by who I mean it must not find its way into print.

Now you say that Mr Smith has "offered to hand over the interesting part of the house to any Antiquarian Soc. that will undertake its restoration."

Does this mean that he would allow such a Society to do the repairs for him at its own cost? or that if the repairs are done he will give up the interesting part of the house to the public.?   …..

signed Thackeray Turner, Sec."

16 March 1888; letter to **Slingsby Smallwood,** Hon. Sec. Berkshire Archaeological Society, commenting on his article about Ockwells in the 6 March 1888 edition of the *Standard.*

18 November 1889; letter from **SPAB** to **Mr G P Boyce**

"My committee is much frightened at the idea of Mr Wade having the building"

25 November 1889; letter to **SPAB** from **Mr G P Boyce**

"I'm afraid that little can be done in the way of influencing Mr L (i.e. Leech) and his architect as regards the proper treatment of the old building."

30 November 1889; Letter to SPAB from **W C Alexander**

"In reply to your letter I find I can [do] nothing further with regard to this building. As soon as I heard it had been purchased by Mr Leech I spoke to Mrs Leech, his mother, of the extreme value of this building and the necessity of giving it into the hands of an architect who would preserve every detail of the of work, naming one who might be

268

trusted to do this. I also wrote to Mr Leech congratulating him on his ownership of such a building and expressing my hope that nothing would be done to decrease its historic value. In reply he thanked me and said he had instructed the work to an architect of whose ability and knowledge there could be no question. I could only hope the work was in good hands as it was quite sure the owner did not wish any advice."

6 December 1889; letter from **SPAB** to **Leech** requesting permission to visit Ockwells and talk to his architect:

"Of course you will understand that I cannot help being interested in knowing how you propose to treat the building although I am fully alive to the rights of private property and should not feel justified in making the matter public or in offering objections in the same manner as I should if it were a church or a town hall."

10 December 1889; letter to **SPAB** from **Stephen Leech** then at the British Embassy, Berlin:

"I have received your letter of the 6th instant with reference to Ockwells and regret that as I am at present abroad I do not see my way to visiting it with you or to putting you in communication with the architect or architects, whom I may employ in the restoration; as, however, you expressed an interest in the place I should be glad for you to go over it any day when it may suit your convenience and the present caretaker will be instructed accordingly."

21 December 1889; letter from **SPAB** to **Stephen Leech** just after the visit:

"The committee of the Society is anxious with all due respect to throw out as a suggestion the possibility of using the latter part of the house for dwelling purposes and of keeping the fifteenth-century portion as lumber rooms and box rooms upstairs and of not trying to make the fine old hall living room as it would be impossible to do so without an undesirable amount of renewal and soon when all was done it could only be fit for summer use."

16 July 1890; letter to **SPAB** from **Felix Wade**, Leech's architect:

"Some little time ago you wrote to Mr Leech the owner of Ockwells Manor for information as to proposed restoration. Would it suit you to meet me at Ockwells early next week when I shall be glad to give you any information I am able to at the present time – not much is decided at the present – as future plans to some extent depend on what we are discovering in the search for old foundations."

25 July 1890; letter from **SPAB** to **Felix Wade**:

Dear Sir

"Re. Ockwells Manor House
At a meeting of this Society held here yesterday I gave a description of this [house?] as I saw it last Tuesday and I also explained what you were contemplating doing.

The Committee of this Society, is aware, from the manner in which you dealt with Acton Burnell Ch:, that you disagree with this Society [.........?] the Committee feels it cannot [....?] express the Society's views, for the building is so well known as one of the finest specimens [....?] of house architecture of that period in this part of England; and many are interested in its fate, that the Committee feels bound to state clearly what are its views, for it could not allow it said that what you are proposing […?] the approval of the Society as [...?] at you request might possibly [...?] unless otherwise contradicted.

The Committee is glad to find that the complete stripping of the building showed it to be in a far sounder condition than had been expected, but it is at a loss to understand why you should have removed [wory?] over the floor boards in the way of covering the floor boards.

Respecting your proposal to put back the [....?] of the porch as you suppose it was at one time, as it probably was, the Committee would suggest that such an alteration would be a mistake because you cannot be certain that it was as you propose and also because the alteration necessitates the discarding of the existing ancient post on the right as you enter.

Your suggestion that the staircase should be removed from the internal court is in the Committee's opinion unfortunate. The staircase is a fine piece of oak work obviously made for its present position. If placed anywhere else most of its interest would be lost, whereas in its present position it is part of the history of the building.

The Committee cannot sympathise with your proposal to jack up the timbers of the big hall so as to bring the wall plates level for it believes such a course will result in straining the ancient work without any corresponding advantage. Neither can the Committee sympathise with the proposal to add a bay window to the right end of the main front or the removal of the brick filling under the hall windows.

The Committee would not advocate any action which would render the house unfit for habitation but it fails to see how the alterations above named in any way render the building more fit for habitation except perhaps in the case of the proposed new bay window and such an addition would not be objectionable from the Society's point of view, provided no attempt was made to imitate the ancient work. This addition or any other addition made should be substantial, [quick?] and not directly imitative in design.

It appears that you consider no harm is done if no actual ancient work in taken away. The Committee considers that the value of the ancient work may be seriously diminished by being overpowered by the large quantity of modern work surrounding it. We must recognise that things cannot last forever and also that the reproduction of a work of art by a man who is not an artist is certainly valueless as a work of art. [And?] you cannot claim that our modern mechanic is an artist. I will not attempt to explain this point of view to you as it is clearly put forward by Ruskin in the extract which I enclose.

I remain Dear Sir
Yours faithfully
Thackeray Turner
Secretary

F B Wade, Esq. ARIBA"

25ᵗʰ July; letter from **SPAB** to **Stephen Leech**, Ockwells Manor House:

"Dear Sir,

The Committee of this Society has desired me to send you a copy of the letter which it is today sending to Mr Wade. I hope you will not consider that I have acted uncourteously in any way towards you or your architect who have been courteous to me. As I was sent down by [the] Committee I necessarily had to make a report. This report was short but it was as distressing to my Committee as my visit to the old house was to me. I felt the whole time that you were completely unconscious of our point of view that you believe in the possibility of bring back the [joust?].

There is no reason whatsoever why the fine old front should not have been so carefully -- repaired as to alter its appearance but little. Even now it is not too late but if the enclosed extracts from Prof. Ruskin's work do not seem to you reasonable it is of course foolish to hope that you should do otherwise than you are doing.

I have said more than I intended but trust that you will pardon me and that you will understand that it is the possible loss of the building which makes me speak.

I remain Dear Sir,
Yours faithfully
Thackeray Turner, Sec."

27 July 1890; Letter to **SPAB** from **Stephen Leech**, then staying at 4, Kensington Palace Gardens:

"Dear Sir,

I have your letter of the 25th inst. and the copy of that sent by you to Mr Wade on the subject of Ockwells.

As Mr Wade will himself answer it I will only say that I regret very much that the Society should disapprove of so many of my proposed alterations. I feel that I am doing as little as possible to the place consistent with keeping it at all and that all additions and alterations will only be carried out where there is sufficient proof to justify me in deciding upon them.

Believe me
Yours faithfully
Stephen Leech"

14 May 1893; letter to **SPAB** from **Powell**, Bisham Vicarage, Great Marlow, Buckinghamshire (probably from Rev Thomas Edward Powell, incumbent at Bisham at that time):

"My Dear Turner,

I wish you could save two glorious old oak barns at Ockwells (Bray) – there's 18 mo. to do it in. Mr Leach the owner intends – if in 18 months the place is not sold – to go and live there and thereupon to pull down these two barns and w. the [...?] make additions to the house itself which means the devil – the barns are very long tie beam and queen posts – fine perspective.

Yrs ever sincerely
[Alpoth?] Powell"

With a note scribbled above: "Leach am told is "a great antiquarian" and appreciates his old garden and in some sort apparently the house. He is connected with Brit. Embassy and principal in the Engi. bank [sic] at Berlin."

Appendix B: The problem connecting the pedigree of the Norreys of Ockwells, Berks, with that of the Norris of Speke, Lancs.

In 1566 Henry Norreys, great-great-grandson of John Norreys Esquire, was knighted, going to France as Ambassador in January 1567.[1] In 1572 he was ennobled as Lord Norreys of Rycote by Elizabeth I. By 1568 Henry had commissioned the heralds to provide him with a pedigree. They connected his ancestral line to the pedigree of the Norris family of Speke drawn up in 1567 in a Visitation of Lancashire, carried out by William Flower Esq, Norroy King of Arms.[2]

This Appendix explains why the claim is unreliable.

The College of Arms hold three sixteenth-century pedigrees of the Norreys/Norris family of Bray (i.e. Ockwells) connecting them with the Norris family of Speke. The pedigrees are:

E8 f51-52: *"The trewe…of the 3 houses of Norreis* [that] *is to say of Speake in Lancashire, of Bray in Barkshire and of Fyffeld in the same shire with all the collaterals of the same three houses 1568."* (**E8 f51**). That the herald at the time was struggling to connect the various Norreys families is evident as the title is crossed out and underneath is written *"This could not be finished for lack of ….but in another book ye shall find it set forth at large"* and a further note: *"This descent agreeth not all together with one taken …by Norrey …of armes."* This pedigree begins with the marriage of Sir Henry Norris and Alice Erneys, and then shows John, second son of Sir Henry, marrying an Elizabeth Ravenscroft. However, this latter marriage is crossed out with instead John's son Roger being married to a Ravenscroft (**E8 f52**). The pedigree terminates with the children of Lord Norreys of Rycote.

E12 f89-f91: *"The Lord Norreis and Norreis of Speke with others of that house."* This attaches all of the pedigree done for the Norris of Speke in 1567 to that of Ockwells via a marriage between John Norris, second son of Sir Henry Norris of Speke, and Alice Erneys to a Millicent Ravenscroft, terminating with the children of Lord Norreys of Rycote.

E12 f96: A third pedigree (untitled) again begins with the marriage of Sir Henry Norris of Speke to Alice Erneys, and then shows John, second son of Sir Henry marrying a Ravenscroft, again Elizabeth. The pedigree, dated 1580, terminates with Francis, grandson of Lord Norreys of Rycote, described as *"now of one year and more".*

The essential problem is that these pedigrees make Sir Henry Norris of Speke (d.1437) the great-great-grandfather of John Norreys of Ockwells Esquire (d.1466).

---

[1] Doran 2021. The previous ambassador, Sir Thomas Hoby, who held Bisham Abbey not far from Ockwells, had also been knighted just before going to France in March 1566 but died the following July (Laoutaris, p49, p67).
[2] Raines 1870, p83-85.

The tree below shows the connection between the two families as given by the College of Arms:

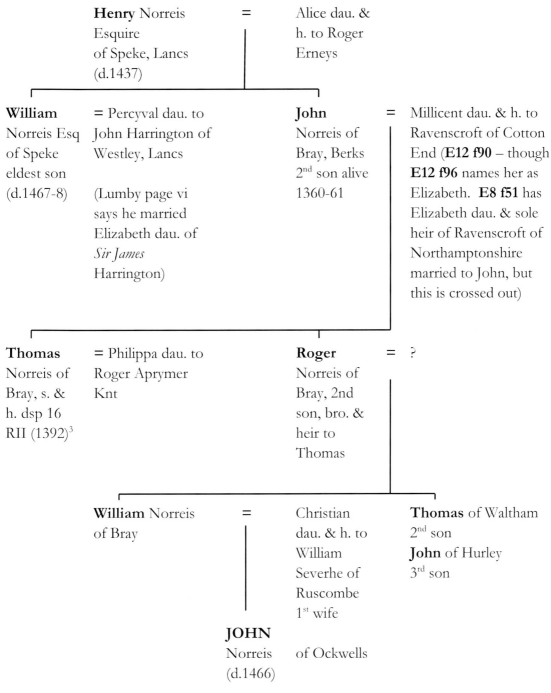

Henry Norreis Esquire of Speke, Lancs (d.1437)	=	Alice dau. & h. to Roger Erneys

| William
Norreis Esq
of Speke
eldest son
(d.1467-8) | = Percyval dau. to
John Harrington of
Westley, Lancs

(Lumby page vi
says he married
Elizabeth dau. of
Sir James
Harrington) | John
Norreis of
Bray, Berks
2nd son alive
1360-61 | = | Millicent dau. & h. to
Ravenscroft of Cotton
End (**E12 f90** – though
E12 f96 names her as
Elizabeth. **E8 f51** has
Elizabeth dau. & sole
heir of Ravenscroft of
Northamptonshire
married to John, but
this is crossed out) |

| Thomas
Norreis of
Bray, s. &
h. dsp 16
RII (1392)[3] | = Philippa dau. to
Roger Aprymer
Knt | Roger
Norreis of
Bray, 2nd
son, bro. &
heir to
Thomas | = | ? |

William Norreis of Bray	=	Christian dau. & h. to William Severhe of Ruscombe 1st wife	Thomas of Waltham 2nd son John of Hurley 3rd son
JOHN Norreis (d.1466)		of Ockwells	

---

[3] In 1392 Thomas Noreys (Norreis) and John Foghlere of Bray granted Thomas Lyllebroke (Lillibroc) and Isabel his wife of the lands and mills etc called Reymills (Raymills) in Cookham, lately held by the grantors of Thomas Gernone, Vicar of Bray, Thomas Lyllebroke and Thomas Cruchefelde (Darby Notebook, vol 6, p103, unpub ms in Maidenhead Library). Lillibrooke manor covers land in Cookham and Bray. The Bray land is immediately adjacent to Ockwells manor held by the Norreys family since C13th. A year earlier, in 1391, Thomas and Roger Noreys were witnesses to the grant of land in Maidenhead (in Bray) to Robert Horn of Cookham (St Georges Chapel Archive SGC XV.58.D.43). This offers some confirmation that the tree is correct, making Thomas Noreys, John's great uncle. He is probably the Thomas Noreys Esq who witnessed a document before the Prior of Bustlesham (Bisham) dated at Cookham in August 1400 (see CCR 1400, pp206 -7, though, according to the tree, John also had an uncle named Thomas). In 1422 Roger Noreys, his brother, granted lands in Bray to Simon Fazakerley which, when they were transferred in 1427 and 1435 included William Noreys as a witness to the transfer (three deeds on one paper St Georges Chapel Archive SGC XV.58.D.58). This William Norys (sic) is probably the father of John Norreys Esquire.

WHY THE LINK IS UNRELIABLE

The Victoria County History of Northamptonshire says *"It is difficult to connect Millicent daughter and heir of Ravenscroft of Cotton End who married John Norris (d.1467, sic) of Bray, Berks"*.[4]

The John Norreis, second son, given in the Lancashire Visitation as Millicent/Elizabeth Ravenscroft's husband, is said to be of Bray and alive in 1360-61. A John Noreys appears in 1337 in the Bray Court Rolls as an executor of Richard le Noreys.[5] This Richard is probably a kinsman of the Richard le Norreys who was granted Ocholt in 1268. It is more likely that John was a kinsman of Richard than of a Norris of Speke. The College of Arms pedigrees make no mention of Richard le Noreys, Coci (cook) to Queen Eleanor, who was given the original grant of Ocholt (now Ockwells).

William Norris of Speke, according to the descent recorded in the College of Arms (see above), was the elder brother of John, second son (alive 1360-61). However, this William was alive in 1445,[6] not dying till 1467-8.[7]

Sir Henry Norris of Speke died in 1437,[8] so there is no way that John Norreys Esquire of Ockwells (d.1466) could be his great-great-grandson. This problem has been pointed out before. Ormerod[9] noted that Dugdale, following E12, had made John Norreys (d.1466) great-grandson of the John of Bray who was alive in 1361, concluding that this would require an earlier Sir Henry than the husband of Alice Erneys. Ormerod hoped for *"future discoveries rather than renouncing the connection between Speke and the noblest of her reputed descendants"*. Earlier Sir Henry Norrises of Speke existed but no link to the Berkshire Norreys family has been found.

The Norris of Speke visitation names a third son of Sir Henry Norris of Speke (d.1437) as Sir William Norrys of *Yatindin, co Barks*.[10] As Sir William Norreys of Yattendon was the eldest son of John Norreys Esquire (d.1466) of Ockwells, who had obtained Yattendon by his marriage to Alice Merbrooke, this makes the descent even more of an impossibility.

There is no reference to Ocholt in the records of the Norris family of Lancashire & Cheshire.[11]

In 1559 the father-in-law of Henry Norreys (later Lord Norreys of Rycote), John, Lord Williams of Rycote and Thame, was buried in St Mary's Church, Thame. His extant tomb bears his armorials at each end and on the sides impaled coats for his sons and daughters. The coat for the marriage of Henry and Williams' daughter, Margery, has Ravenscroft for Norreys quartering Merbrooke because Henry was descended from John Norreys and his first wife, Alice Merbrooke. It does not have the Norris of Speke coat, presumably because the pedigree was not completed till much later.

---

[4] VCH Northamptonshire, vol 4, p256.
[5] Kerry, p113.
[6] See tree in Ormerod.
[7] Lumby, p vi.
[8] Ibid, p vi.
[9] Ormerod, p160.
[10] See Raines, p83.
[11] See Lumby.

Armorial of Henry Norreys and his wife Margery from the monument of her father, John, Lord Williams (d.1559), in St Mary's Church, Thame. Inset: the coat of Norreys of Ockwells quartering Merbrooke

Edward, the brother of Sir Henry Norreys, died age 5 in 1529 and was buried in St Mary's Church, Ewelme. His extant brass plaque again bears Ravenscroft for Norreys quartering Merbrooke (Mountfort) but there is no Norris of Speke coat, as again the pedigree had not yet been created.

The brass of Edward (d.1529), brother of Henry Norreys, with Norreys of Ockwells quartering Merbrooke in quarters 1 and 4, on the floor of the nave in St Mary's Church, Ewelme

Accompanying brass says Edward was 2nd son of Henry Norreys Esquire, which Henry was 2nd son f Sir Edward Norreys, son and heir of Sir William Norreys

Elizabeth Bulstrode, great-granddaughter of Richard Bulstrode (see Appendix C, Tree 5a), died in 1631 at Fawley Court. She was married to Rev James Whitlock (d.1632). Their monument in St Mary's Church, Fawley, Buckinghamshire, put up by their son Bulstrode Whitlock, bears their impaled coat. This coat also appears twice in armorial glass in the church and was originally in Fawley Court ca.1654. In all three coats the Ravenscroft for Norreys coat is next to the Bulstrode coat and the Norris of Speke coat is absent. This is after the Norreys pedigree of ca.1580 claimed descent from the Speke line. The same blazon is found on the monument for Henry Bulstrode, her brother (d.1632) (see page 101). It is possible the Bulstrodes distrusted the claim of descent from the Norrises of Speke.

The impaled armorial of Rev. James Whitlock and Elizabeth Bulstrode from the Whitlock monument in St Mary's Church, Fawley. Inset: Elizabeth's impalement showing the coats of Bulstrode, Norreys of Ockwells and, below right, Shobington (with red squirrels; these should be black)

THE USE OF THE NORRIS OF SPEKE COAT BY THE NORREYS OF OCKWELLS

Pedigree **E12 f96** in the College of Arms, produced for Henry, 1st Lord Norreys of Rycote (d.1601), gives a date of 1580 as when Francis Norreys became heir apparent. The family appear to have started using the Norris of Speke coat shortly after the pedigree was completed.

Jersey (C16th)

Around 1593 Sir Antony Paulet, governor of Jersey, built Mont Orgueil Castle incorporating a stone plaque of his coat impaled with the Norris of Speke coat for his wife, Katherine Norreys, daughter of Lord Henry Norreys of Rycote. Katherine's brother, Maximillian, who died fighting for the King of France in 1591, is buried in St Helier Church, Jersey, under a plaque provided by his brother-in-law which unfortunately has no heraldry.

Stone plaque on Mont Orgueil Castle in Jersey, bearing the coat of Sir Anthony Paulet impaling that of his wife, Katherine Norreys, daughter of Henry, Lord Norreys, using the Norris of Speke coat

276

Westminster Abbey (C17th)

Lord Norreys' grandson Francis, born 1579, is the last family member named in the pedigree with the date 1580 (**E12 f96**). It was Francis who apparently commissioned the enormous monument in Westminster Abbey put up after 1606,[12] which features his grandparents lying on a four-poster bed surrounded by their soldier sons – a monument that features a large shield where the Norris of Speke is in prime position with next to it that of Norreys of Ockwells and then the Montfort coat for Alice Merbrooke, John Norreys Esquire's first wife. It has been suggested that the construction of this monument resulted in the Earl Marshall issuing an order to sculptors to submit designs to the College of Arms so that the heraldry might be checked, also making a strong protest against pretenders to the science of heraldry.[13]

Armorial on the monument to Henry, Lord Norreys of Rycote, with quarters for Norris of Speke, Norreys of Ockwells and Merbrooke (copyright: Dean & Chapter of Westminster)

Bath Abbey (C17th)

An identical coat for Francis, Henry Norreys' grandson and 2nd Lord Norreys, can be found in Bath Abbey in a window recording donors to the Abbey.

Right: Armorial for Francis, grandson of Henry, Lord Norreys, in a window of Bath Abbey. Francis organised the monument to his grandfather in Westminster Abbey that has the same armorial

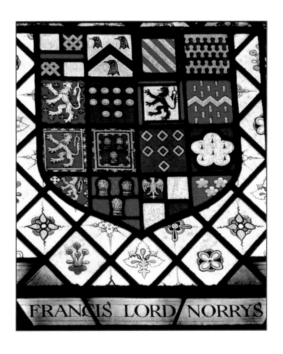

Francis, Lord Norreys, when he sold Hindons Farm in Cookham and other assets to Sir Thomas Bodley in April 1608, assets that in 1612 were given to Oxford University to

---

[12] Esdaile, p464.
[13] Ibid.

found the Bodleian Library, used a seal bearing the Norris of Speke coat affixed below his signature on the agreement (available on the Digital Bodleian website).

The seal of Francis, Lord Norreys of Rycote, bearing the Norreys of Speke coat

St Michael's Church, Weston on the Green (C17th)

Francis' heir, Francis Rose Norreys (d.1669), on his memorial slab of black marble in St Michael's Church, Weston on the Green, Oxfordshire, bore the Norris of Speke coat differenced with an engrailed bordure indicative of his illegitimacy. His crest is certainly a bird with upraised wings but could equally well represent the eagle of the Norris of Speke as the raven of the Norreys of Ockwells. Memorials for his wife and descendants in the same church show the same Speke coat though after a while the bordure was omitted.

Coat of Francis Rose Norreys, heir of Francis, Lord Norreys, on his memorial at east end of St Michaels Church, Weston on the Green

Mallow in Ireland (C19th)

Sir Thomas Norreys, one of the sons of Henry, Lord Norreys of Rycote, was Vice President of Munster where he rebuilt an Irish castle tower at Mallow, Cork County, to make a suitable residence for the Lord President of Munster, his elder brother Sir John (who died in the castle in 1597). As Sir John was for many years away fighting Elizabeth I's wars, Thomas administered Munster, and, as Mallow was being developed as a plantation town, accumulated land there.

Thomas's daughter Elizabeth Norreys married Sir John Jephson (see Appendix C, Tree 1a iv) and the family remained in Mallow, Elizabeth and her husband later building a new mansion on the site of the stables. By the nineteenth century this building needed restoration and it was rebuilt by their descendent Denham Jephson. In July 1838 Denham was created a baronet of Mallow in the County of Cork and later that month assumed by royal licence the additional surname of Norreys, becoming Sir (Charles) Denham Orlando Jephson-Norreys, 1st Baronet. In his rebuilt house, he evidently put up two armorial achievements to celebrate his ancestors.

Armorials put up by Sir (Charles) Denham Orlando Jephson-Norreys in the nineteenth century when he rebuilt the mansion at Mallow, apparently celebrating his descent from both Norris of Speke and Norreys of Ockwells

The first armorial shows the Norris of Speke coat quartering that of the Norreys of Ockwells showing that the myth of descent from the Norris family of Speke was still current in the nineteenth century. The second is that of John Norreys Esquire and his first wife, Alice Merbrooke, the original of which is in Ockwells Manor House, Berkshire. This Mallow armorial was almost certainly copied from the illustration in Lysons' *Magna Britannia*. Other features of the Ockwells armorial, Norreys badge of three golden distaffs and his motto, *ffeythfully serve*, are replicated at Mallow.

279

HOW THE TWO NORREYS FAMILIES <u>ARE</u> CONNECTED

Edward Norreys (grandson of John Norreys Esquire of Ockwells) and William Norris of Speke (d.1506) were both knighted at the battle of Stoke in 1487 and would have met. William's father, Thomas Norris Esquire of Speke (d.1487), had married a Norris of the West Derby branch (see Appendix C, Tree 1b) so may have seen an opportunity to marry a son to another Norreys family.

However it happened, Edmund, younger brother of William, came south to marry Alice Fowler, daughter of John Fowler of Fifield, not far from Ockwells, whose wife was Agnes, daughter of William Norreys of Winkfield, younger brother of John Norreys Esquire (see College of Arms Pedigree **E8 f28** verso, on which Kerry based his Norreys pedigree, and Appendix C, Tree 1b). The marriage of the great-niece of John Norreys Esquire (d.1466) to a younger son of Thomas Norris Esquire (d.1487) linked the two families and almost certainly took place before Henry, Lord Norreys of Rycote, commissioned his pedigree.

Edmund's grandson, William Norris Esquire of Fifield (d.1591), is buried in the Norreys Chapel of St Michael's Church, Bray. 1591 is after Henry Norreys' pedigree was completed by the College of Arms. William thought he was being buried in the family chapel, witness the phrase on his monument *is interred with his ancestors* and the use of the motto *Faithfully Serve*, seen in the Ockwells glass, but he could only claim descent from William Norreys of Winkfield, younger brother of John Norreys Esquire. Possibly he was aware of this as the armorials on his monument clearly show his descent from a cadet line of the Norris family of Speke. The Norreys of Ockwells coat is absent.

The impaled coat of William Norris, Esquire, of Fifield and his wife on his monument in St Michaels Bray showing the Norris of Speke coat in the first quarter and using the "Faithfully Serve" motto of the Norreys of Ockwells

Extant seventeenth-century armorial glass in Speke Hall, Lancashire, possibly put up by Edward Norris (d.1606) show the Norris of Speke family believed they were related.

Armorial glass in the windows of Speke Hall, Lancashire, possibly put up by Edward Norris (d.1606). Left: cadet line of the Norris of Speke. Right: Norreys quartering Merbrooke for Norreys of Ockwells

When the College of Arms was creating Henry Norrys' pedigree (1568-1580), Henry was ambassador to France (1566-70); keeper of the armoury and porter of the outer gate, Windsor castle (1578); and high steward, Abingdon (c.1580).[14] During that period and later, the descendants of William Norreys of Winkfield, younger brother of John Norreys Esquire, had become prominent in court. John Norris (d.1577) was Gentleman Usher of the Black Rod and the Order of the Garter, and Comptroller of the Works at Windsor Castle as was his son William (d.1591) whose splendid monument, as noted above, is extant in St Michaels Church, Bray. His son John was also Comptroller at Windsor Castle and was knighted by Elizabeth I in 1601, the same year that Henry, Lord Norreys of Rycote, died. This cadet branch was certainly connected to the Norris family of Speke (Appendix C, Tree 1b). Perhaps Lord Norreys was happy to feel part of a larger family, particularly if they had influence at court.

FINAL COMMENTS

There is no reliable evidence that John Norreys Esquire of Ockwells was a descendent of the Norris family of Speke – a view held by a writer to the Athenaeum magazine in 1867 who evidently took a poor view of the heralds saying: *"If the heralds are right, the descent from the cook is an heraldic myth; but I distrust the heralds, and have reason to believe that the most noted and most noble branch of the Norreys family – that of Ockwells, Yattendon and of Ricote, did really descend from Richard de Norreys, cook to the Queen of Henry the Third, and that the separation of this branch from that of Speke – if they were ever connected – must have taken place prior to 1257; but this belief involves another, viz.: that heralds in ancient days "cooked" their visitations and family pedigrees as thoroughly as the directors of our days do their accounts, and that, unless where fortified by charters, wills, deeds, or other instruments, or by historical facts, they are not to be relied on."*[15] Although the present author had not seen this source, in 2005, whilst writing an account entitled *The Norris family of Ockwells, Speke, and Fifield – are they related?*, the same conclusion was reached.[16]

---

[14] Fuidge. Doran says he was ambassador to France 1567-1570.
[15] "D.J.N." in *Athenaeum* 1867 no 2045, p 19.
[16] *MCS News* Jan 2005, pp7-10.

Unfortunately, the herald's pedigree has led to the use the wrong coat for the Norreys of Ockwells that has persisted over centuries, even until the present day. For example, mid nineteenth-century armorial glass in windows of the eleventh-century St Botoph's Church, Swyncombe (near Ewelme), illustrates the history of the manor of Swyncombe and includes coats for Henry Norreys Esquire (ex.1536) and Anne Broke (née Bulstrode) widow of Thomas Broke Esquire (d.1518) who were both granted Swyncombe in 1519.[17] However, the Norreys coat used is the incorrect Speke coat.

Left: Thomas Broke, Esquire, and Anne Bulstrode; and right: Henry Norreys Esquire

Similarly, the parish church at Yattendon, a manor acquired by John Norreys of Ockwells from his first wife, Alice Merbrooke, has the Norris of Speke coat in one of its windows.

A modern Norris of Speke coat in a window of St Peter & St Paul, Yattendon – a church restored in the mid-fifteenth century by John Norreys Esquire of Ockwells

---

[17] Napier, pp338-9.

Finally, Rycote Chapel, near Thame, Oxfordshire, has been decorated with banners of past owners one of which wrongly includes the Norris of Speke coat for Henry Norreys, 1st Lord Norreys of Rycote, who had commissioned the pedigree that claimed he descended from the Norris family of Speke.

Banners in Rycote Chapel (banner in foreground is for Norris of Speke)

At the beginning of the seventeenth century there was an attempt to create a new line of Norreys when Edward Norreys, Knight of Englefield (d.1603), the only son of Henry, Lord Norreys (d.1601) to outlive his father and so a descendent of John Norreys Esquire of Ockwells, married Elizabeth Norreys (d.1621), the last heir of the Norreys of Fifield, who had Speke blood in her veins (see Appendix C, Trees 1a & b). Unfortunately, no children were forthcoming.

Appendix C: Family trees

Note: d.s.p. = died without issue
        d.v.p. = died before parents

Tree 1a: Norreys Family from C15th to C16th [1]

(i)

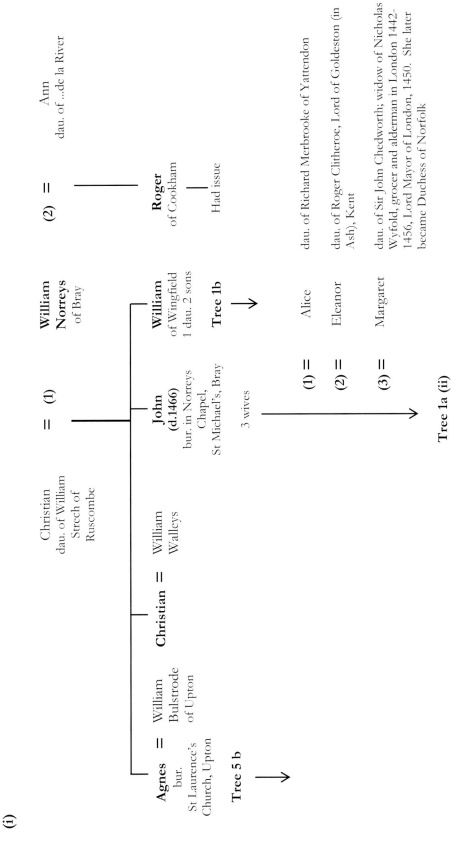

Christian
dau. of William
Strech of
Ruscombe

(2) =

Ann
dau. of ...de la River

**William
Norreys**
of Bray

= (1)

Roger
of Cookham

Had issue

William
of Wingfield
1 dau. 2 sons

Tree 1b →

John
(d.1466)
bur. in Norreys
Chapel,
St Michael's, Bray

3 wives

(1) =   Alice   dau. of Richard Merbrooke of Yattendon

(2) =   Eleanor   dau. of Roger Clitheroe, Lord of Goldeston (in
Ash), Kent

(3) =   Margaret   dau. of Sir John Chedworth; widow of Nicholas
Wyfold, grocer and alderman in London 1442-
1456, Lord Mayor of London, 1450. She later
became Duchess of Norfolk

Tree 1a (ii)

Christian = William
Walleys

Agnes =
bur.
St Laurence's
Church, Upton

William
Bulstrode
of Upton

Tree 5 b →

285

(ii)

John Norreys Esquire [2]
(d.1466)

Married

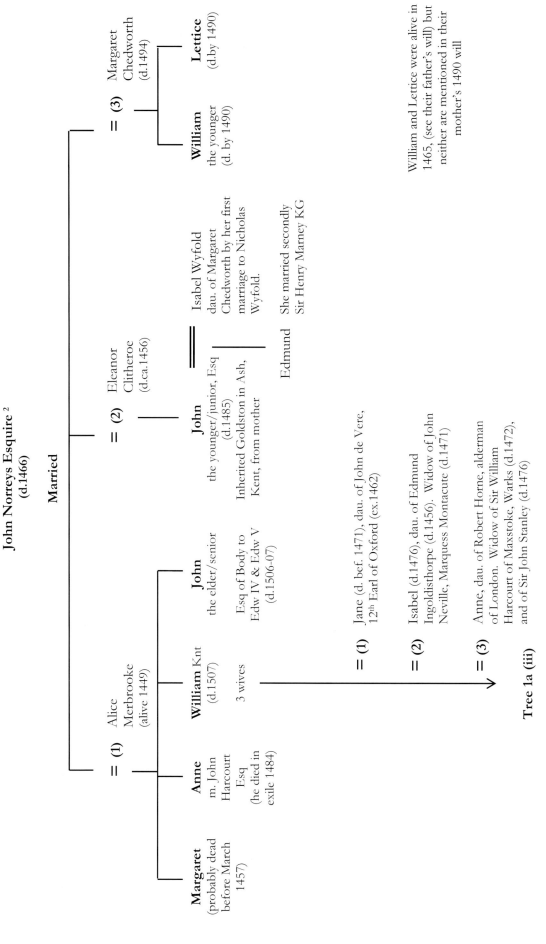

= (1) Alice Merbrooke (alive 1449)

= (2) Eleanor Clitheroe (d.ca.1456)

= (3) Margaret Chedworth (d.1494)

Margaret (probably dead before March 1457)

Anne m. John Harcourt Esq (he died in exile 1484)

William Knt (d.1507) 3 wives

John the elder/senior Esq of Body to Edw IV & Edw V (d.1506-07)

John the younger/junior, Esq (d.1485) Inherited Goldston in Ash, Kent, from mother

Edmund

William the younger (d. by 1490)

Lettice (d.by 1490)

Isabel Wyfold dau. of Margaret Chedworth by her first marriage to Nicholas Wyfold.

She married secondly Sir Henry Marney KG

= (1) Jane (d. bef. 1471), dau. of John de Vere, 12ᵗʰ Earl of Oxford (ex.1462)

= (2) Isabel (d.1476), dau. of Edmund Ingoldisthorpe (d.1456). Widow of John Neville, Marquess Montacute (d.1471)

= (3) Anne, dau. of Robert Horne, alderman of London. Widow of Sir William Harcourt of Maxstoke, Warks (d.1472), and of Sir John Stanley (d.1476)

Tree 1a (iii)

William and Lettice were alive in 1465, (see their father's will) but neither are mentioned in their mother's 1490 will

286

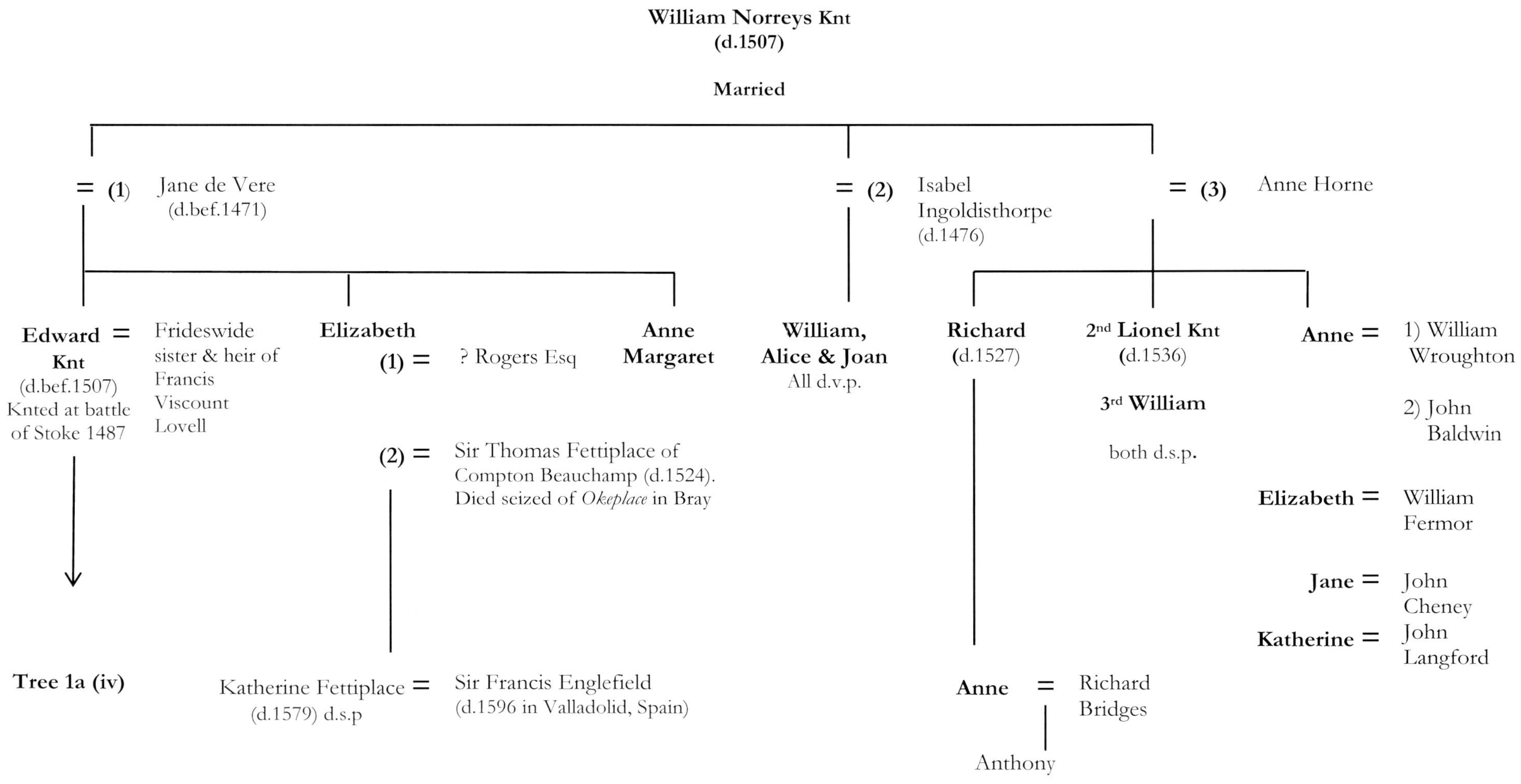

William Norreys Knt
(d.1507)

Married

= (1) Jane de Vere
(d.bef.1471)

= (2) Isabel
Ingoldisthorpe
(d.1476)

= (3) Anne Horne

Edward =
Knt
(d.bef.1507)
Knted at battle
of Stoke 1487

Frideswide
sister & heir of
Francis
Viscount
Lovell

Elizabeth

(1) = ? Rogers Esq

(2) = Sir Thomas Fettiplace of
Compton Beauchamp (d.1524).
Died seized of *Okeplace* in Bray

Anne
Margaret

William,
Alice & Joan
All d.v.p.

Richard
(d.1527)

2ⁿᵈ Lionel Knt
(d.1536)

3ʳᵈ William

both d.s.p.

Anne = Richard
Bridges

Anthony

Anne = 1) William
Wroughton

2) John
Baldwin

Elizabeth = William
Fermor

Jane = John
Cheney

Katherine = John
Langford

Katherine Fettiplace =
(d.1579) d.s.p

Sir Francis Englefield
(d.1596 in Valladolid, Spain)

Tree 1a (iv)

287

(iv)

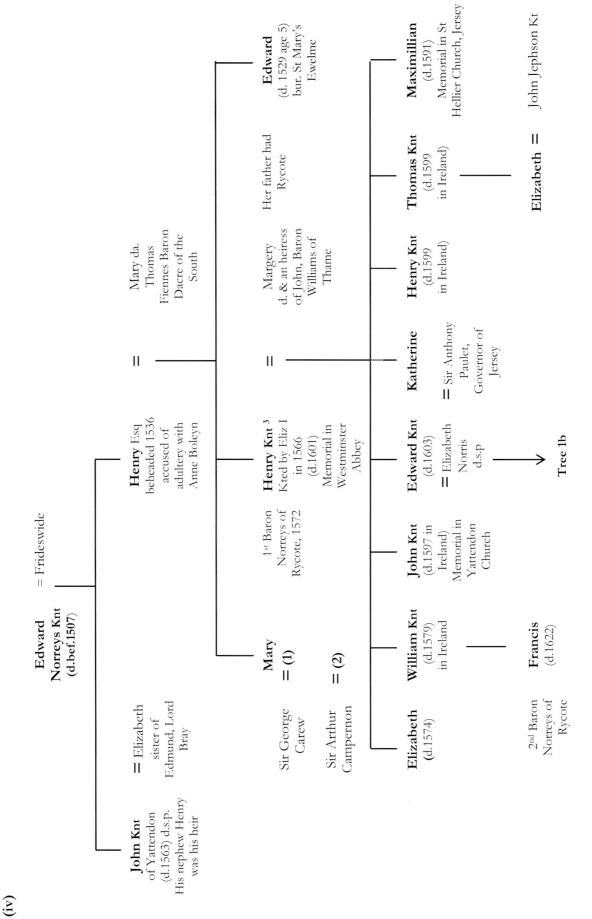

Edward
Norreys Knt
(d.bef.1507) = Frideswide

John Knt
of Yattendon
(d.1563) d.s.p.
His nephew Henry
was his heir

Henry Esq
beheaded 1536
accused of
adultery with
Anne Boleyn = Mary da.
Thomas
Fiennes Baron
Dacre of the
South

Edward
(d. 1529 age 5)
bur. St Mary's
Ewelme

Mary
= (1)

= (2)

Sir George
Carew

Sir Arthur
Campernon

Henry Knt [3]
Kted by Eliz I
in 1566
(d.1601)
Memorial in
Westminster
Abbey

1st Baron
Norreys of
Rycote, 1572

= Margery
d. & an heiress
of John, Baron
Williams of
Thame

Her father had
Rycote

Elizabeth
(d.1574)

William Knt
(d.1579)
in Ireland

John Knt
(d.1597 in
Ireland)
Memorial in
Yattendon
Church

Edward Knt
(d.1603)
= Elizabeth
Norris
d.s.p

Katherine
= Sir Anthony
Paulet,
Governor of
Jersey

Henry Knt
(d.1599
in Ireland)

Thomas Knt
(d.1599
in Ireland)

Maximillian
(d.1591)
Memorial in St
Hellier Church, Jersey

Francis
(d.1622)

2nd Baron
Norreys of
Rycote

→

Tree 1b

Elizabeth = John Jephson Kt

288

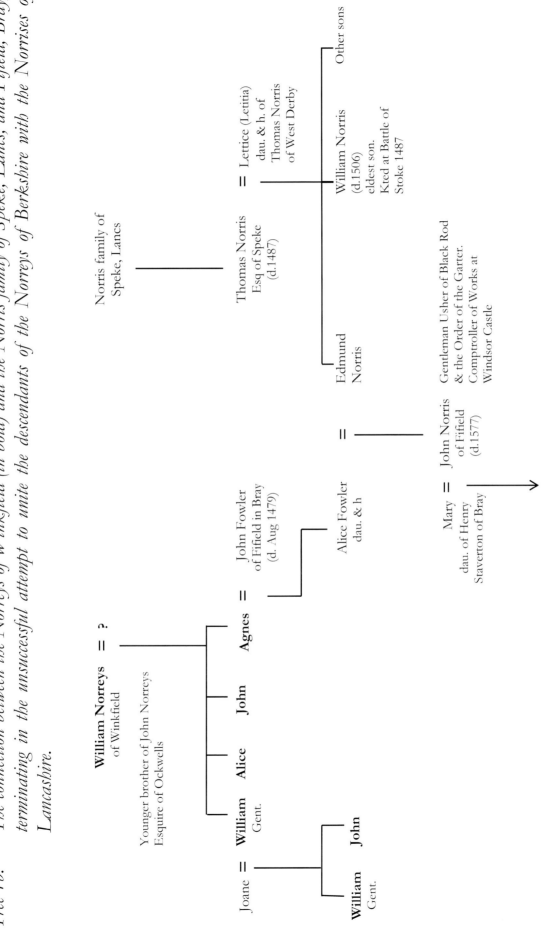

Tree 1b: The connection between the Norreys of Winkfield (in bold) and the Norris family of Speke, Lancs, and Fifield, Bray, terminating in the unsuccessful attempt to unite the descendants of the Norreys of Berkshire with the Norrises of Lancashire.

Norris family of Speke, Lancs

William Norreys = ?
of Winkfield

Younger brother of John Norreys
Esquire of Ockwells

Thomas Norris
Esq of Speke
(d.1487)

= Lettice (Letitia)
dau. & h. of
Thomas Norris
of West Derby

William   **Alice**   **John**   **Agnes** =   John Fowler
Gent.   of Fifield in Bray
                                   (d. Aug 1479)

Edmund
Norris

William Norris
(d.1506)
eldest son.
Kted at Battle of
Stoke 1487

Other sons

Joane =

William   **John**
Gent.

Alice Fowler
dau. & h

=

John Norris
of Fifield
(d.1577)

Gentleman Usher of Black Rod
& the Order of the Garter.
Comptroller of Works at
Windsor Castle

Mary =
dau. of Henry
Staverton of Bray

289

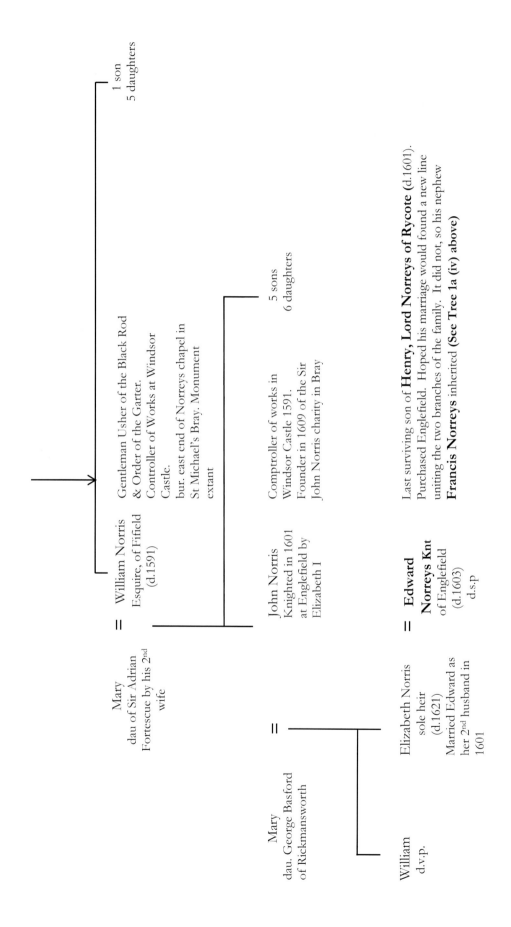

1 son
5 daughters

William Norris
Esquire, of Fifield
(d.1591)

Gentleman Usher of the Black Rod
& Order of the Garter.
Controller of Works at Windsor
Castle.
bur. east end of Norreys chapel in
St Michael's Bray. Monument
extant

=

Mary
dau of Sir Adrian
Fortescue by his 2nd
wife

5 sons
6 daughters

John Norris
Knighted in 1601
at Englefield by
Elizabeth I

Comptroller of works in
Windsor Castle 1591.
Founder in 1609 of the Sir
John Norris charity in Bray

=

Mary
dau. George Basford
of Rickmansworth

Elizabeth Norris
sole heir
(d.1621)
Married Edward as
her 2nd husband in
1601

=

**Edward
Norreys Knt**
of Englefield
(d.1603)
d.s.p

Last surviving son of **Henry, Lord Norreys of Rycote** (d.1601).
Purchased Englefield. Hoped his marriage would found a new line
uniting the two branches of the family. It did not, so his nephew
Francis Norreys inherited **(See Tree 1a (iv) above)**

William
d.v.p.

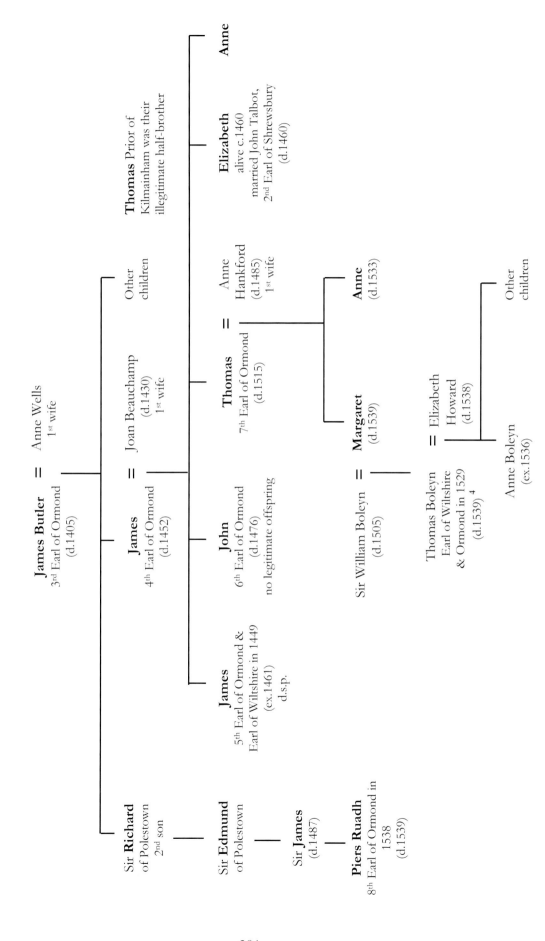

Tree 2: The descent of the Butler earls of Ormond and the temporary transfer of the earldom to the Boleyns

James Butler = Anne Wells
3rd Earl of Ormond   1st wife
(d.1405)

Sir **Richard**
of Polestown
2nd son

James = Joan Beauchamp
4th Earl of Ormond   (d.1430)
(d.1452)   1st wife

Thomas Prior of
Kilmainham was their
illegitimate half-brother

Other
children

Sir **Edmund**
of Polestown

James
5th Earl of Ormond &
Earl of Wiltshire in 1449
(ex.1461)
d.s.p.

John
6th Earl of Ormond
(d.1476)
no legitimate offspring

Thomas = Anne
7th Earl of Ormond   Hankford
(d.1515)   (d.1485)
1st wife

Sir **James**
(d.1487)

Sir William Boleyn = **Margaret**
(d.1505)   (d.1539)

Anne
(d.1533)

Piers Ruadh
8th Earl of Ormond in
1538
(d.1539)

Thomas Boleyn = Elizabeth
Earl of Wiltshire   Howard
& Ormond in 1529   (d.1538)
(d.1539) [4]

Elizabeth
alive c.1460
married John Talbot,
2nd Earl of Shrewsbury
(d.1460)

Anne

Anne Boleyn
(ex.1536)

Other
children

291

Tree 3:   Clitheroe [5]

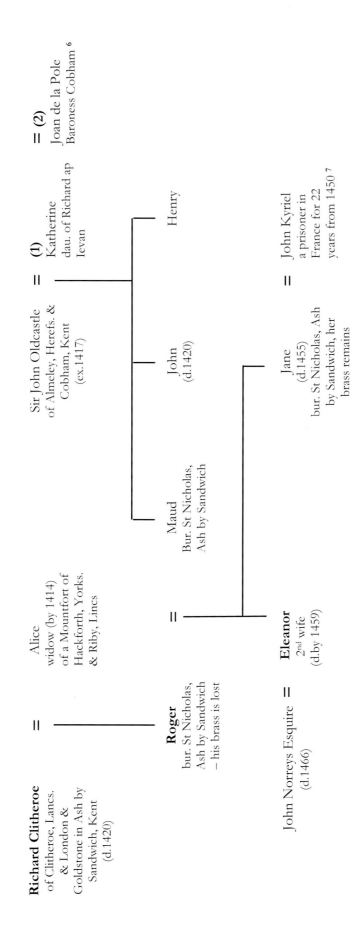

Richard Clitheroe
of Clitheroe, Lancs.
& London &
Goldstone in Ash by
Sandwich, Kent
(d.1420)

=

Alice
widow (by 1414)
of a Mountfort of
Hackforth, Yorks.
& Riby, Lincs

Sir John Oldcastle
of Almeley, Herefs. &
Cobham, Kent
(ex.1417)

= **(1)**
Katherine
dau. of Richard ap
Ievan

= **(2)**
Joan de la Pole
Baroness Cobham [6]

Roger
bur. St Nicholas,
Ash by Sandwich
– his brass is lost

Maud
Bur. St Nicholas,
Ash by Sandwich

John
(d.1420)

Henry

John Norreys Esquire
(d.1466)

=

Eleanor
2ⁿᵈ wife
(d.by 1459)

Jane
(d.1455)
bur. St Nicholas, Ash
by Sandwich, her
brass remains

= John Kyriel
a prisoner in
France for 22
years from 1450 [7]

292

Tree 4: Mountfort (Montfort)

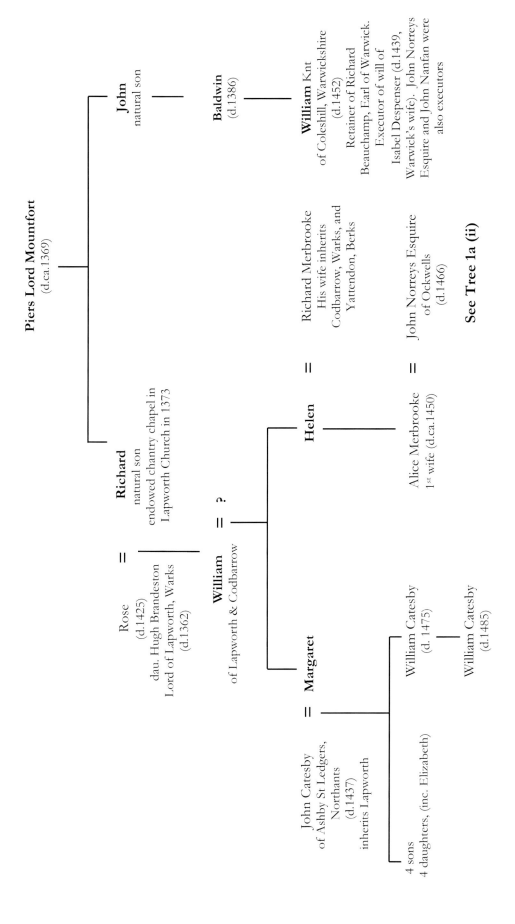

Piers Lord Mountfort
(d.ca.1369)

Richard
natural son
endowed chantry chapel in
Lapworth Church in 1373

John
natural son

Rose =
(d.1425)
dau. Hugh Brandeston
Lord of Lapworth, Warks
(d.1362)

Baldwin
(d.1386)

William
of Lapworth & Codbarrow

= ?

Helen

William Knt
of Coleshill, Warwickshire
(d.1452)
Retainer of Richard
Beauchamp, Earl of Warwick.
Executor of will of
Isabel Despenser (d.1439,
Warwick's wife). John Norreys
Esquire and John Nanfan were
also executors

=

Richard Merbrooke
His wife inherits
Codbarrow, Warks, and
Yattendon, Berks

Margaret

=

Alice Merbrooke
1st wife (d.ca.1450)

=

John Norreys Esquire
of Ockwells
(d.1466)

See Tree 1a (ii)

John Catesby
of Ashby St Ledgers,
Northants
(d.1437)
inherits Lapworth

William Catesby
(d. 1475)

William Catesby
(d.1485)

4 sons
4 daughters, (inc. Elizabeth)

293

Tree 5a: Bulstrode [8]

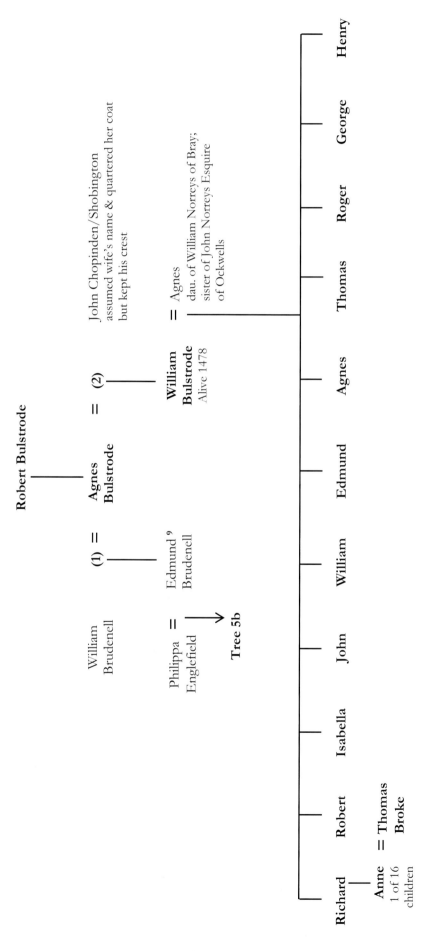

John Chopinden/Shobington
assumed wife's name & quartered her coat
but kept his crest

Robert Bulstrode

William Brudenell   (1) =   **Agnes Bulstrode**   = (2)   **William Bulstrode** Alive 1478

= **Agnes** dau. of William Norreys of Bray; sister of John Norreys Esquire of Ockwells

Edmund [9] Brudenell

Philippa = Englefield   →   **Tree 5b**

Richard   Robert   Isabella   John   William   Edmund   Agnes   Thomas   Roger   George   Henry

Anne 1 of 16 children   = **Thomas Broke**

Tree 5b: *Brudenell*

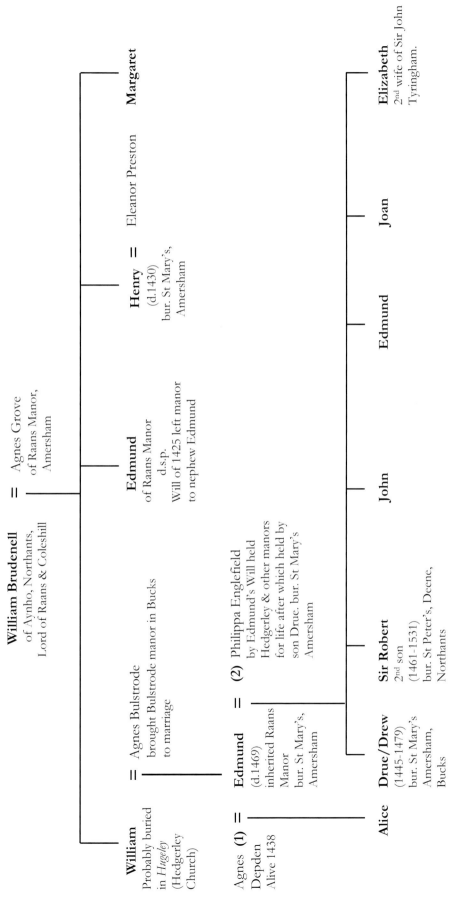

William Brudenell
of Aynho, Northants,
Lord of Raans & Coleshill

= Agnes Grove
of Raans Manor,
Amersham

William
Probably buried
in *Hageley*
(Hedgerley
Church)

= Agnes Bulstrode
brought Bulstrode manor in Bucks
to marriage

Edmund
of Raans Manor
d.s.p.
Will of 1425 left manor
to nephew Edmund

Henry =
(d.1430)
bur. St Mary's,
Amersham

Eleanor Preston

Margaret

Agnes (1) =
Depden
Alive 1438

Edmund =
(d.1469)
inherited Raans
Manor
bur. St Mary's,
Amersham

(2) Philippa Englefield
by Edmund's Will held
Hedgerley & other manors
for life after which held by
son Drue. bur. St Mary's
Amersham

Alice

Drue/Drew
(1445-1479)
bur. St Mary's
Amersham,
Bucks

Sir Robert
2nd son
(1461-1531)
bur. St Peter's, Deene,
Northants

John

Edmund

Joan

Elizabeth
2nd wife of Sir John
Tyringham.

Tree 6:   *Connecting the Fettiplace, Horne and Norreys families*

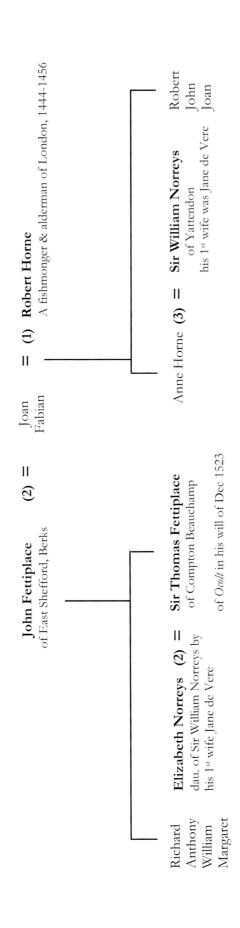

John Fettiplace   **(2)**   **=**   Joan   **=**   **(1)**   **Robert Horne**
of East Shefford, Berks   Fabian   A fishmonger & alderman of London, 1444-1456

Elizabeth Norreys   **(2)**   **=**   **Sir Thomas Fettiplace**   Anne Horne **(3)**   **=**   **Sir William Norreys**   Robert
dau. of Sir William Norreys by   of Compton Beauchamp   of Yattendon   John
his 1st wife Jane de Vere   of *Ocolt* in his will of Dec 1523   his 1st wife was Jane de Vere   Joan

Richard
Anthony
William
Margaret

296

Tree 7: Partial descent of the Englefields from C14th to C17th [10]

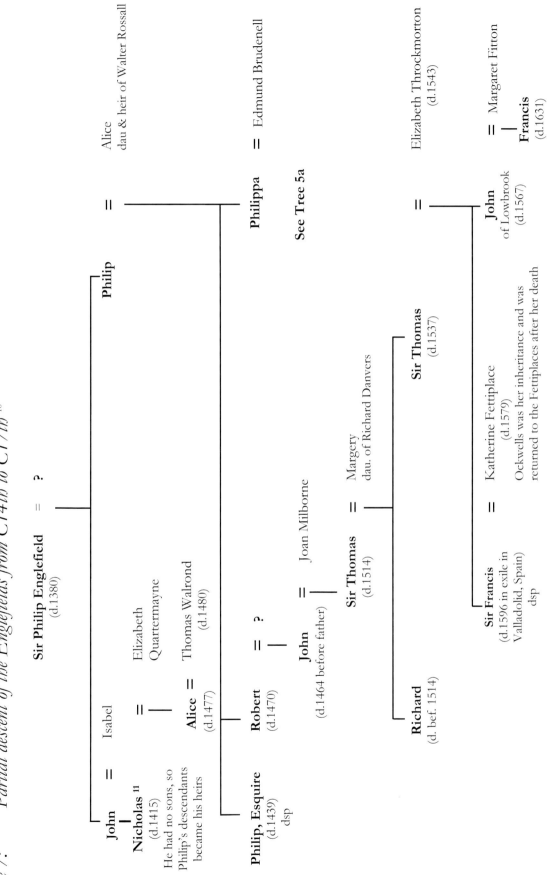

Notes to accompany family trees

[1] Principal sources for Trees 1a and 1b: College of Arms Norris pedigrees E8 & E12; Harding, 1981a & 1981b; Virgoe; *Pedigree of the family of Norreys of Ockwells, Moores and Hindens in Bray*, and details of the Sir John Norris charity, p164 et seq. in Kerry 1861; Begent & Chesshyre, pp337, 391; Lumby pvi; Clark 2020b, p679.

[2] John Norreys Esquire (d.1466) had three daughters: Margaret, Anne and Lettice. No source so far discovered definitely links the daughters with a particular mother. However, it is likely that Margaret was his daughter by Alice Merbrooke, who was lady-in-waiting to Margaret of Anjou, and probably named for the queen. Margaret Norreys was alive in 1454, when a marriage contract was being arranged for her, but was probably dead by 1457 (Clark 2020a, p673; Clark 2020f, p296). Only Anne ("my eldest daughter") and Lettice ("my youngest daughter") are mentioned in his 1465 will (Appendix A, No 2). John (junior) his son by Eleanor Clitheroe died in 1485 and left a son Edmund aged 3 or more (*CIPM* Henry VII, Vol 1, 1898, p43, no. 106). Wedgwood & Holt p639 says Edmund was son of John (senior), Norreys' son by Alice (who died 1506/7) citing CPR 1494-1509, p542. This citation refers to Edmund having in 1507 a license of entry without proof of age to his father's lands. As in 1507 Edmund, son of John (junior), would be at least 25, this most likely refers to the latter's son.

[3] Married to Margery Williams by 1544, he was protected by her father Sir John during Mary's reign, when he would have met Princess Elizabeth. In 1565 he secured Yattendon, his uncle's property, becoming Elizabeth's Ambassador to France from 1567 to 1570 (Doran 2021). All Henry, Lord Norreys' sons distinguished themselves as soldiers. Only Edward outlived his father. A very young Francis was the heir apparent in 1580 – the last date quoted in the pedigree compiled for Lord Norreys; his father, William, had died the year before (College of Arms pedigree E12 f96). See Appendix B for details of the monument to his grandfather that Francis had put up in Westminster Abbey with its incorrect heraldry. Francis is said to have committed suicide in 1622 at Rycote.

[4] After daughter Anne was executed, her father lost posts and revenue from crown estates given to him. In 1538 Piers Butler, the great-grandson of Sir Richard Butler of Polestown, (younger brother of the fourth earl), was recognised as the eighth Earl of Ormond. Thomas Boleyn lost all but his English earldom (of Wiltshire) before his death in March 1539 (Hughes J 2004).

[5] Tree in part from Woodger (*Richard Clitherow*) & Kightly (*Sir John Oldcastle*).

[6] Seemingly a distant kinsman of William de la Pole, Duke of Suffolk.

[7] Historical Guide of the Church of St Nicholas, Ash. Kyriel was a Knight of the Shire for Kent in 39 Henry VI (1460-61) with Robert Horne of Kinardington & Horne's Place, Appledore, Kent, who was Sheriff in 1452 (Cave-Browne). It is unclear whether this Horne was the father of the third wife of Willam Norreys, Anne Horne.

[8] Source for trees: Clark 2020c, p633 & memorial inscription for Agnes Bulstrode née Norreys, once in St Laurence's Church Upton by Chalvey – cf Bulstrode trees in Lipscomb p572 and Ashmole 852 f31 in the Bodleian Library. For Brudenell tree cf Lipscomb, p447.

[9] Edmund's will of 1457 (Nicolas 1826 pp282-4) refers to William Bulstrode *my brother* (half-brother) and has a Richard Bulstrode as his executor, probably his nephew. Agnes's marriage to William Brudenell led to the Brudenells inheriting the manor of Bulstrodes in Chalfont St Peter (Clark 2020c, p633).

[10] VCH Berkshire, vol 3, Englefield, pp405-412.

[11] MacNamara, facing p171, gives Nicholas (d.1415) as another son of Sir Philip Englefield (d.1380).

Appendix D: Notes on Ordnance Survey (OS) maps 1875 to 1932

By 1875 the fifteenth-century Ockwells Manor house had been tenanted for years with latterly the tenant farmer using it as his farm house. The stages by which the house, in 1875 in a desperate state, was gradually restored, gentrified and modernised to survive today is reflected in the illustrations below, abstracted from OS maps. These also show how the manor house and the neighbouring farm buildings of Ockwells farm, initially functioning as somewhat separate entities, gradually became one with the farm, evolving into providing attractive amenities for a country house.

Plan 1: OS 1875 before Victorian restoration when owned by William Henry Grenfell

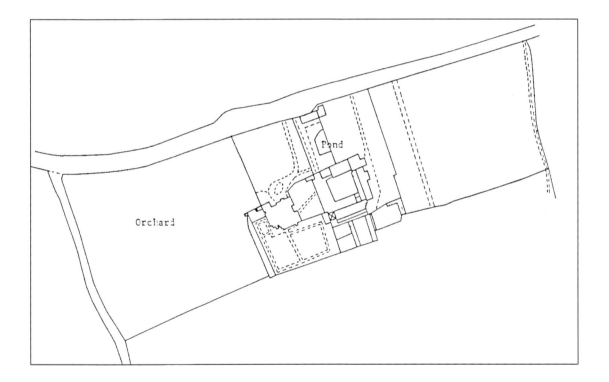

By 1875:

- Carriage sweep and drive from entrance on north front of house put in by the Days still existing.
- A wall connects the fortified wall with the northeast corner of the house and other walls separate the house from the farm.
- Two drives to access farm buildings, one connected to a building(s) next to road.
- Farm buildings on the north side of the outer court and a building at the northeast end of the chapel site still there.
- Two single-storey wooden buildings, possibly sheds, are located on the northwest corner of the house adjacent to a brick wall (see Roland Paul's 1887 drawing). These buildings were lost by 1897.
- Evidence of a building at the east end of the chapel wall, next to the priest's house/gateway.

Plan 2: OS 1897 after Victorian restoration when owned by Sir Edward Barry

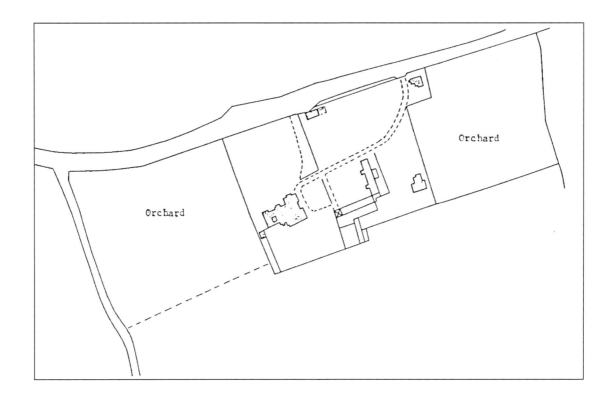

By 1897:

- The drive from the north front has disappeared; the single line in its position suggests it was a footpath (see more detailed map on page 168). However, the later 1910 map shows a double line here so its function is unclear. Other drives from Ockwells Road have also gone, though the building served by one of them remains near the road and a nearby wall remains.
- New carriage sweep on east front and new drive from there to a new lodge, put in once the farm buildings on the north side of the outer court were down.
- Farmhouse built by Grenfell in 1887; farmhouse is that seen to east of south end of tithe barn.
- Extension on the west front added by Stephen Leech when he restored the house in 1889-1891, still existing.
- Chapel wall not shown but was still there. Building at northeast end of chapel site presumably lost. Perhaps this was when the rumoured box containing a man's skull was found.

Plan 3: OS 1910 still in the ownership of Sir Edward Barry

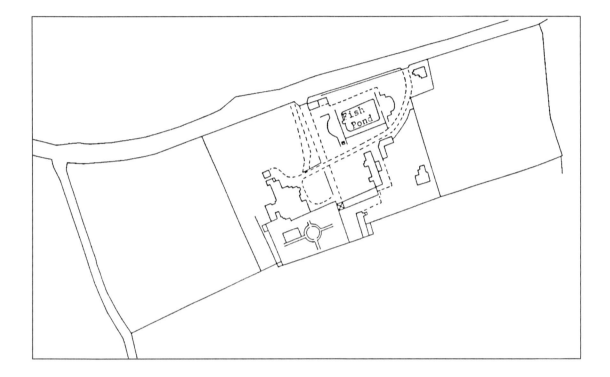

By 1910:

- New drive to road nearer house created; the building at the roadside seen in the OS 1875 map appears now to be used as a lodge. The wall nearby, although not drawn in this map, was there in 1932 so may have been omitted accidentally.
- Unclear what the function was of what appears to be another drive parallel to the new one. This, and the building it seems to lead to, lost by 1932.
- The earlier drive to the new lodge further east still there.
- Extension on north front and garage added.
- Ornamental fish pond created from old farm pond.
- New buildings added to the east of the tithe barn.
- Leech's extension on west front still there.
- Farm house to east of tithe barn built by Grenfell still there.
- Italian style garden created south of manor house.

Plan 4: OS 1932 still in the ownership of Sir Edward Barry

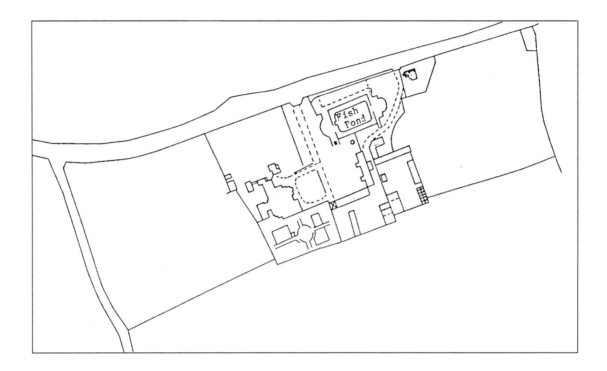

By 1932:

- At the end of the new drive the building formerly near the roadside, there since 1875, is lost.
- The drive parallel to the new one is lost. Garage built.
- Section of drive on north side of outer court lost. The rest still connects to the lodge further east.
- Dovecote added.
- Leech's extension on west front still there.
- Grenfell's farm house to east of tithe barn demolished to allow more buildings including stables to be built.

Appendix E: Authenticity of the armorial glass at Ockwells

INTRODUCTION
Remarkably, there are eighteen lights exhibiting armorial achievements still in the great hall of Ockwells Manor House. Some repairs have been made over the years and some losses have occurred:

One coat has been lost, possibly for the Abbot of Reading, though its crest, a mitre, has been transferred, sometime before 1838, to Light 8 (Richard Beauchamp, Bishop of Salisbury) that was missing its crest in 1798 (see page 306). The crests of two other achievements have been lost, from Light 4 (William de la Pole, Duke of Suffolk) and Light 17 (Edmund Brudenell).
The names of the persons represented, once at the base of each light, have all now also been lost.

In 1798 the *Gentleman's Magazine* printed a letter which read *"The Society of Antiquaries should know that, at an old farm house in the parish of Bray, in Berkshire, called Ockwells, is a hall in which are* **preserved entire some beautifully painted windows of a very ancient date**, *hitherto undescribed by any author. They escaped the notice of the famous Thomas Hearne, though the place of his nativity is within an easy walk of this retired spot. A future volume of Archaeologia might be enriched with a minute account of them, were a person, qualified to give such account, employed to inspect and examine them."*[1]

That these windows still survive is incredible but how much of it dates from the fifteenth century?

HOW AUTHENTIC IS THE STAINED GLASS?
Everard Green described the armorial glass in 1899 after it had been returned to Ockwells following the Victorian restoration. He indicated that in some cases modern glass had been added and his comments may have influenced Greening-Lamborn who in 1949 observed:

"Berkshire has lost much armorial glass since Ashmole made his record of its shields at his Visitation in 1665.[2]   Its best-known collection is probably the secular glass of the late fifteenth century in the hall at Ockwells, described by Mr Everard Green in *Archaeologia*, lvi, 323-36. *But this glass has been very much renovated* and is, in fact, *less interesting* than the early shields at Buckland and Stanford-in-the-Vale or the Tudor heraldry at Aldermaston or even the enamelled shields at Bisham."[3]

However elsewhere he says "The Norreys shields at Ockwells, Berks, and the Cheney shields at Chesham Bois and Drayton Beauchamp, Bucks, illustrate the best work of the fifteenth century."[4]

As no details of the *renovations* were given, early descriptions of the glass were studied to assess what damage had occurred and to evaluate his assessment. Neither Everard Green

---

[1] *Gentleman's Magazine,* Vol LXVIII January 1798 Pt 1, p30. It took another 100 years to fulfil this author's wish to see the windows described in *Archaeologia.*
[2] Ashmole MSS 850 in the Bodleian.
[3] Greening Lamborn E A 1949, p1.
[4] Ibid, p. xxviii.

nor Greening Lamborn appear to have seen the copies, made in the nineteenth century by Charles Kerry, of drawings of the armorial glass made in 1765 by Sir Thomas Reeve of Hendons House, Holyport, Berkshire, which are shown below.[5] Reeve's drawings of the armorial glass are the earliest known but unfortunately the whereabouts of the originals is not known. Kerry's copies indicate that Reeve did not draw the whole achievement, concentrating on the coats and only adding the crests in a few cases.

Greening Lamborn's assessment of the Ockwells glass as "very much renovated and less interesting" can be queried for the following reasons:

As shown below, the present-day armorials are recognisable in the drawings of 1765. These drawings certainly show some damage had already occurred by the eighteenth century (see below for details) but there is no evidence that they are *very much renovated*.

That much of the Ockwells armorial glass is fifteenth-century is supported by comparison with an extant fifteenth-century armorial achievement in St Martin's Church, Holt, Worcestershire, for Sir Walter Scull/Skull (d.ca.1472) that has a similar helm to those at Ockwells.[6]

The crest and helm from the armorial for Sir Walter Scull (d.ca 1472) in St Martin's Church, Holt, Worcestershire. Note the helm similar to those at Ockwells

Clarifying the scheme John Norreys Esquire put up gives an insight into the politics of the mid-fifteenth century, particularly the role of William de la Pole, Duke of Suffolk, and those who Norreys wished to record as his friends and relatives – Everard Green's *liber amoricum*. The Ockwells glass is therefore historically interesting.

---

[5] In some cases, parts of the achievement are drawn; examples include Bulstrode impaling Shobington, which doesn't occur at Ockwells, noting that *there was another shield with the same arms quarterly* (which does occur) and similarly part of the quartered coat for, Eleanor Clitheroe. Ockwells' achievements apparently not drawn by Reeve include those for Norreys impaling Clitheroe, Henry VI and Edmund Beaufort. Drawings of crests were limited to those of Laken, Norreys, Wenlock and Abingdon Abbey.

[6] As at Ockwells, some jewelling (insertion of small pieces of glass to resemble jewels) occurs in the robe of the Virgin Mary in the light below the Skull armorial at Holt. Skull was married to Margaret Beauchamp, daughter of Sir John Beauchamp of Holt (d.1420), kinsman of Richard Beauchamp, Earl of Warwick. Their impaled coat occurs on a tile in the church there. The Beauchamp connection suggests the glazier at Holt was John Prudde who glazed Warwick's chapel in St Mary's Church, Warwick.

C18th Records

1765 drawings made by Sir Thomas Reeve and copied by Charles Kerry in C19th[7]

Three of the four coats below showed possible evidence of damage by 1765.

Light 11 for William Laken

The 1765 drawing by Reeve, copied by Kerry, showed the lower part of the shield as blank and states this area to be *probably defective*. Was this because of multiple fleur de lis? Kerry notes that another drawing had *Az fleur de lis or 2 & 1*. This is the usual modern coat for France. In 1899 Everard Green described the shield as "mended".

Light 13 for John Nanfan

In 1765 this had damage to the lower parts of quarters 1 and 4. These two quarters appear to have been renewed entirely as the wings instead of being horizontal are now vertical. Everard Green in 1899 did not mention any damage or repair but it had been done by then.

Light 15 for Edward Langford

No damage is apparent but there has been a change. If no-one made a mistake, at some point, since 1765, the colour of the field in chief in this coat has changed from red to blue.[8] Blue is the usual colour. The coat of Sir Thomas Langford in a fourteenth-century Roll in the Society of Antiquaries (MS 136 pt 1) has a blue field in chief.

Light 16 for Edmund Brudenell

In 1765 quarter 1 was missing; quarter 2 is the Bulstrode coat; quarter 3 is for Englefield; quarter 4 unidentified. In 1899 Everard Green noted that the shield had been renewed by which time the Bulstrode coat had been lost, the Englefield quarter had lost the sable colour in chief, and quarters 1 and 2 had been replaced by the glass restorer by replicating quarters 3 and 4. The painting made of the hall at Ockwells by Charles Knight and published in *Olde England* in 1847 shows that this achievement had the crest of a bird with slightly upswept wings, presumably lost when the glass was removed to Taplow Court for safe keeping (see Light 16 in main text).

---

[7] See MSS Top Berks 15/2 f118a-121vol II; copyright: Bodleian Library. It does not have vol V which according to f121 has relevant information on pages 71 & 76. According to Kerry, Sir Thomas Reeve was a distinguished herald and antiquary. He made his will in 1767, proved 1777 (TNA PROB 11/1031/269), which unfortunately does not mention anything useful in locating the drawings. See also Appendix A, No. 10.
[8] This may have occurred when the colour of mantling was changed.

None of the coats showing evidence of damage in 1765 (see above) is mentioned in the 1798 statement, below, which only lists twelve coats, noting a different three coats as being defaced.

Mr. URBAN,   *August* 28.

AT the farm called Ockwells, near Maidenhead, lately enquired after in your Magazine, and belonging to the representatives of Penyston Powney, esq. deceased, is a very large old house, probably the manor-house. In the great hall is a window of six bays, containing the following coats of arms:

1. Defaced.

2. The arms of England. Crest, a lion on a cap of maintenance.

3. Quarterly, the arms of England, impaling, 1. three bars Gules; 2. 3. 4. are fragments; 5. Sable, 3 fishes hauriant. The shield is surmounted by a crown: supporters, an antelope and an eagle.

4. 1st and 4th. Az. a fess between 3 leopards faces Or. 2d and 3d. Gu. a lion double queué of the second.

5. The arms of England. Supporters, two antelopes.

6. Arms defaced. Crest, an eagle.

In a side window of three bays are,

1. Quarterly, 1st and 4th. Gules, a fess between 6 martlets Or. 2 Gules, 2 lions Argent. 3. Az. 3 fishes naiant Argent.

2. Arms defaced. Crest, a mitre.

3. A cross patonce between 4 martlets Sable. Crest, a mitre. The arms of the abbey of Abingdon.

In another window are the arms of *Mortimer*; crest, a ducal coronet: and the following coats.

1. Argent, a chevron between 3 blackmoors heads Sable.

2. Quarterly, 1 and 4. Sable, a stag's head Or, holding an arrow in its mouth. 2 and 3. Argent, a chevron between 3 squirrels.

The motto, *feythfully serve*, is repeated diagonally, forming the ground-work of the windows. The motto, *humble et loiall*, occurs in a few places.

If this sketch, which was hastily taken, and in which may be some errors, should excite any ingenious Antiquary to examine the building more accurately, it will give great pleasure to

Yours, &c.   S. C.

The armorial glass in the oriel window, nine coats in all (nos. 1-6 & 7, 7a and 8), was described together with the coats of three achievements out of the ten (nos. 10, 12 and 18) occurring in the side wall of the hall.[9] The following were described as defaced:

In the oriel:
(Following the numbering on the original article)

1. Defaced (no details are given). This is Light 1, for Henry Beauchamp, Duke of Warwick, impaling the coat of his wife Cicely Neville (the impalement is for her mother, Alice Montacute, with the small central shield for her father, Richard Neville).

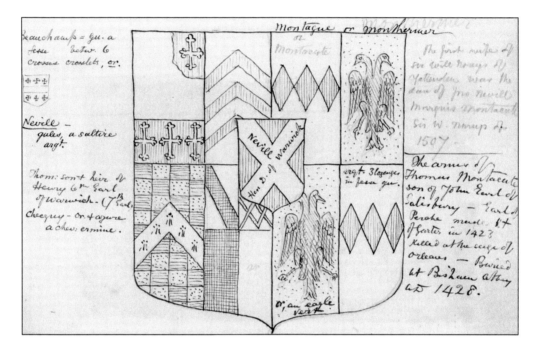

In 1765 when the armorial glass was drawn by Sir Thomas Reeve (*above*) the achievement was drawn as a heater shape, presumably to facilitate the drafting of this complex achievement, though it is actually bouché, (i.e. with a curved notch cut out to simulate where a lance would rest). The missing part of the Beauchamp coat (top left hand quarter) in the drawing shows the position where the simulated notch would have been. The only quarter missing in 1765 was the lower part of the Despenser coat.   All the other quarters were as now, including the impalement. Everard Green in 1899 describes the shield as *much broken and mended with fragments of old glass and the impalement is modern*.[10] Unfortunately no corroborative evidence of this is given. Was he influenced by the 1798 description? The achievement is certainly more complex than the others and the lower part of the Despenser coat has been renewed but the quality of the diapering in the supposed modern impalement suggests it is indeed original glass. If it is modern it must have been created by a master glazier, such as Thomas Willement.

3. This is Light 3, for Margaret of Anjou, Queen of Henry VI.

Quarters 2, 3 and 4 (for Naples, Jerusalem and Anjou) of the impaled coat were said to be fragments. The quarter for 6 (Lorraine) was not mentioned. In the 1765 drawing all the quarters appeared intact though, as now, the three-point label was missing from the Naples quarter. A touch of red indicates it was once there. Lysons drawing published in 1806 of

[9] Gomme, pp116-117; and *The Gentleman's Magazine* vol LXVIII, September 1798 pt II, p762.
[10] Everard Green, p325.

this achievement does not show any damage and Everard Green in 1899 did not report any.

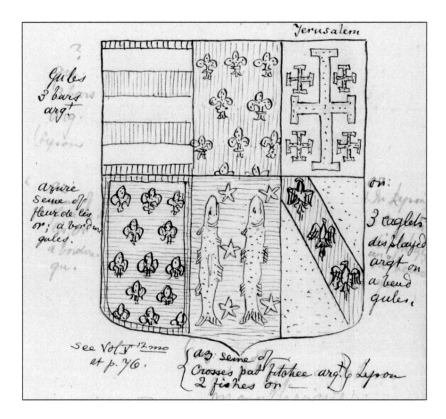

Coat of Margaret of Anjou; showing that quarters 2, 3, and 4 were intact in 1765

6: Arms Defaced, crest an eagle (no details given). This is Light 6, for James Butler fourth Earl of Ormond.

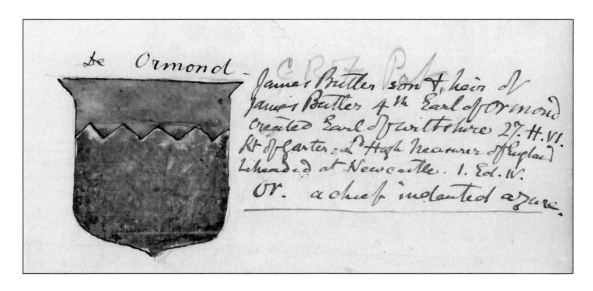

The coat of James Butler, fourth Earl of Ormond, not his son as identified in the caption

In the 1765 drawing, (*above*), the coat is shown intact. Everard Green in 1899 did not report any damage or that it had been restored. Certainly, now there is a line of horizontal leading across the coat in the light in the great hall which could indicate that the shield had been damaged but the diapering over the whole shield appears to be of the same date. Again, if this was modern it must have been done by a master glazier.

308

In the side window of three bays:

1. This is Light 7 for Richard Beauchamp, Bishop of Salisbury, – without a mitre.

2. Arms defaced. This is Light 7a – with a mitre.

3. This is Light 8 for the Abbey of Abingdon, with a mitre.

Reeve's 1765 drawings show the Abbey of Abingdon coat with a mitre and the Bishop of Salisbury's coat without one. Reeve does not appear to have drawn the *defaced coat with a mitre* presumably because it was unidentifiable, though evidently the mitre was still there.

The Ockwells glass was taken out by Charles Pascoe Grenfell in the mid-nineteenth century and kept at Taplow Court until it was returned to the great hall in 1890/1891. Before the armorial glass was taken out a drawing of the hall was made and published in Charles Knight's *Olde England* in 1847 (see Chapter 4 in main text). The armorial achievements are recognisable in the drawing and confirm that they had been put back in their original positions. Unfortunately, this is not true of those in the side windows of the oriel. Lights 7 and 8 have been swapped over and the mitre from the defaced arms in Light 7a added to the coat of Richard Beauchamp, Bishop of Salisbury. As Thomas Willement, glazier to Queen Victoria, appears to have drawn the bishop's coat with the mitre in 1838,[11] before the glass was taken out by Grenfell, some restoration of the glass seems to have already been done (*see right*).

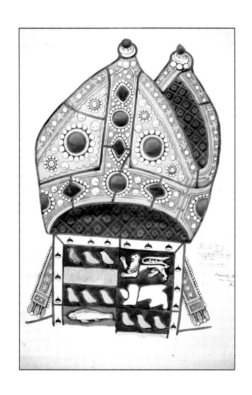

Records of Changes to the Armorial Glass

1899 Comment by Everard Green
Light 17 for John Pury: Everard Green says quarters 2 & 3 for Ate More of Cookham are renewed and inaccurate. The 1765 drawings show that the Ate More quarters bore the same tinctures as now. The only evidence that the quarters have been renewed is that in 1765 the moorcocks on the Ate More coat had stumps similar to those of the martlets in the Pury coat, but by 1838, when drawn by Thomas Willement, had acquired feet. This again indicates these quarters were renewed prior to the glass being taken out and stored at Taplow court.[12] If restoration occurred prior to 1838 it was most likely to have been commissioned by Provost William Day or his son before 1625 as from then on Ockwells was tenanted.

---

[11] Thomas Willement - Ancient Stained Glass vol III, BL Add Ms 34868 pp195-6. This volume contains most of Willement's own drawings of Ockwells glass. Only one drawing is dated - the "Mortimer" coat, which bears a pencilled "1838" (Ibid, p198). Probably the other drawings were done at the same time. All copyright British Library.

[12] Ibid, p200. Willement does not identify the achievement. See also Winston C 1867 vol 2, pp16-17 plate 50 for a black & white drawing.

Ate More and Pury coats: left from Kerry; right: from Willement

Other Changes to the Armorial Glass

Changes in the Colour of Mantling

Colour illustrations in Lysons' *Magna Britannia* of achievements for Edmund Beaufort and John Norreys and his first wife Alice Merbrooke, show that in the early nineteenth century the mantling for both was red.

Lysons original caption: "Arms of Norreys and of Beaufort, Duke of Somerset, painted on glass in the Hall Windows of Ockwells House, Berks"

310

This is confirmed by Knight's drawing published in 1847 (see page 42), which shows red mantling in the achievements for Beaufort, both Norreys and Butler.[13] In each case red has been replaced by blue mantling.

Red is usually flashed onto white glass and possibly the flashing had become damaged. In addition, the change to the mantling on the Norreys-Clitheroe achievement may have been aesthetic to make it conform to the blue mantling of that set of lights, but then why change the Norreys-Merbrooke achievement to blue while all the other achievements in that set of lights had red mantling? Changes to the colour of the mantling must have been effected while the glass was at Taplow Court.

Loss of Names at Base of Achievements

Originally the name of the person represented in each light was depicted in stained glass at the base of the light. Lysons' illustrations show the names *Norrys* at the base of the Light 9 for John Norreys and his wife Alice Merbrooke (*see illustrations below and above*). Also, one of the drawings of Ockwells glass probably made in 1838, by Thomas Willement, was of the name *Langford* (Light 15), see below.[14] All these names are now lost.

Close-up of "Norrys" from Lysons

Close-up of "Langford" from a drawing by Thomas Willement (copyright: BL)

---

[13] Knight, opposite p108.
[14] Willement T, Add. MSS 34868, p145.

Recent Changes

At some point since 1924, work on the achievement of William de la Pole (Light 4) has been carried out. A *Country Life* article of that year shows a helmet-shaped piece of coloured glass in the position of the crest which is no longer there.[15] Presumably this happened during Sir Edward Barry's ownership but no further details have so far emerged.

The Original Glazier

The quality of the Ockwells glass including the presence of "jewelling" indicates an expert glazier which in the fifteenth century is likely to have been John Prudde, king's glazier to Henry VI, and who Norreys would have known both through his work at Windsor Castle but also because both were linked to Richard Beauchamp, Earl of Warwick (d.1439). Prudde did the glazing of this earl's chapel in St Mary's Church, Warwick.[16] Although Hussey attributes the quarries and heater-shaped achievements at Ockwells to the English glaziers, John Prudde or John Grayland, he suggests the others (the bouche coats) are the work of Flemish or German glaziers.[17] However, Richard Marks has identified Prudde as the glazier, based on the jewelling but also the characteristic "moue" (shape) on the mouth of the boy crest of Edward Langford.

CONCLUSION

The evidence does not support Greening Lamborn's dismissal of the armorial glass *as very much renovated* and *less interesting*. However, some repair and renovation clearly has taken place prior to 1838 when drawn by Thomas Willement and again later when the armorial glass was taken out in the mid-nineteenth century by Charles Pascoe Grenfell, who stored it at Taplow Court. This probably was when the crest on the achievement of Edmund Brudenell (Light 16) was lost.[18]

The repaired glass was returned to the manor house by Charles Pascoe's grandson, William Henry Grenfell, later Lord Desborough, during the restoration of the house by Stephen Leech in 1889-1891. The glazier, who probably did the work while it was at Taplow Court, was Thomas Willement (1786-1871), glazier to Queen Victoria.[19] As noted in Chapter 10 he made copies in stained glass of the Ockwells achievements.

Even if only parts of these achievements have been replaced, it has been done to accurately replicate the original armorial as evident in the similarity of today's armorials and the 1765 drawings by Sir Thomas Reeve. Thus in the twenty-first century we still can see this magnificent display of armorial glass as envisaged by John Norreys Esquire in the mid-fifteenth century.

---

[15] See Hussey, I, p95.

[16] Britton, p11. Prudde's indenture for the glazing was in 1447.

[17] Hussey, II, pp94-95. John Grayland, glazier, was paid for making two *armes of the kynges* for the church at Eton in 20th year of Henry VI (1441/1442) (Tighe & Davis, vol 1, p338.)

[18] The crest was still there in Knight's *Olde England* drawing of 1847, so before the glass was removed to Taplow Court.

[19] As noted in Chapter 10, he made copies of the Ockwells achievements for sale to other churches and also drew inspiration from those for Henry VI and his queen when he glazed the south choir aisle window in St George's Chapel that is next to the tomb of Henry VI. See also *MCS News* Feb 2018, pp16-17, which also records contemporary copies in Durham cathedral (C15th) and modern copies in Akron, Ohio (C20th) and explains why they are there).

Appendix F: *Ockwells – additional evidence for the existence of the gable and wing at the east end of the north front*

This gable and wing has lost, or did not have, the carved bargeboards or panelling present in gables of the rest of the east front (see below). However, the presence of herringbone-patterned brickwork on the wing (see the Poynter and Twopeny drawings on page 314) similar to that on the entrance porch suggests the gable and wing were part of the original build and connected with the fortified wall, a remnant of which exists.

1815   Buckler drawing BM Add MS 36356 f220-221

This enlargement of John Buckler's 1815 drawing shows the gable without bargeboards and the wing. There appears to have been an entrance to the wing and there is an indication of slats at the end of the wing, behind the tree on the right

See Twopeny's 1827 drawing below for confirmation of slats

1814-1818   Poynter drawing, RIBA drawing collection[1]

A drawing (*above*) showing the lost gable and wing was made by Ambrose Poynter, who, between 1814 and 1818, was a pupil in the office of John Nash. Nash is said to have used Ockwells for inspiration when designing the Royal Lodge at Windsor for George IV.[2] Poynter's drawing, with correction marks, is in the RIBA drawing collection. He went on to be chiefly an architect of churches and country houses: his best-known London work is the Tudor Gothic-style hospital and chapel of St Katharine in Regent's Park (in 1827).[3]

1827   Twopeny drawing, later published by Parker in 1859

[1] *Notes and sketches of English Gothic Buildings* RIBA Drawing Collection f 92. Copyright: RIBA.
[2] Hughes G M, p376. Most of the Royal Lodge was pulled down by William IV, the brother of George IV (Hibbert p343).
[3] Cust & Bradley 2010. He provided illustrations for *Olde England* edited by Charles Knight, also writing articles. Possibly he did the illustration of the great hall at Ockwells in that book.

In 1827 William Twopeny made a very similar drawing to that by Poynter, containing the same error: in both, the chapel wall is missed out so that a chimney breast can be seen reaching to ground level but following the correction marks on Poynter's drawing. Possibly Poynter attempted a drawing that was corrected by Twopeny. Twopeny's drawing is in a volume of his drawings of ancient architecture in the British Library.[4] He also made drawings of the bargeboards and panelled gable, evidence that he visited Ockwells (illustrated on page 30). This means the gable and wing were still standing in 1827. The two drawings were published by Parker in 1859 by which date both the gable and wing were down.[5]

Twopeny's drawing shows a slatted end to the wing – the end is cut off in Poynter's drawing. In the 1815 drawing by Buckler there is an indication of slats behind the vegetation. It is possible that the wing had been damaged in the past and the remains of it repaired, hence the slats. It is likely that the wing originally connected with the fortified wall further east. If so, this could have been the part of Ockwells mansion that was reportedly burnt down in ca.1778, by a beggar shaking out the ashes of his pipe in the straw of the farmyard.[6] Certainly the arrow slits in the fortified wall that would have been near to this wing show evidence of soot. However, it is also said that it was the chapel that was destroyed by fire.[7]

Hughes notes this northern gable *must have been pulled down after Mr Twopeny made his drawing for the "Domestic Architecture" in 1827*. He also suggests that there was once another gable at the south end of the east front, commenting that *In the large upper chamber of the great gable a doorway still appears which must have opened into this lost wing; it is now blocked up, and a chimney stack was subsequently erected in the garden against the outer wall.*[8] If such a gable/wing existed it would have led to the chapel that was still under construction when John Norreys Esquire died in 1466. However, no drawings of it have been found. By 1832 the northern gable and wing had gone, as depicted in the 1834 drawing by Brayley (*below*) which he based on Delamotte's drawing of 1832 (see Chapter 7).

[4] Twopeny W *Drawings of Ancient Architecture: Domestic – Fifteenth Century* vol IVA pages 11-14 BM Print Room, Books of Prints case 290 b4.
[5] Parker.
[6] *Gentleman's Magazine* 1798 vol LXVIII Part II, December, p1007.
[7] Brayley, p373.
[8] Hughes G M, p376.

Appendix G: Summary of the changes to the floor plans of Ockwells Manor house 1864 – 2019

The following floor plans show how the house was altered during the nineteenth and twentieth centuries, over which time the house was restored twice:

Fig 1: Floor plans from the Maidenhead Civic Society exhibition
Fig 2: 1864 Floor plans by the architect W E Nesfield
Fig 3: 1892 Floor plans from the Sale Catalogue
Fig 4: 1924 Floor plan from VCH Berkshire, vol 3, p94
Fig 5: 1984 Floor plans by the architect David Mansfield Thomas
Fig 6: 2019 Floor plans from the Sale Catalogue

Fig 1: Floor plans from the Maidenhead Civic Society exhibition

These plans, drawn by the late Brian Sanderson based on information supplied by the author, were made for the Maidenhead Civic Society exhibition on the history of Ockwells Manor House staged in 1990. The 1864 floor plan was discovered later and any changes incorporated into the display.

I summarised these changes in the exhibition text as:

A north façade which ebbs and flows
A stair which hops from place to place
Extensions to the west and north
A room on the south east corner which comes and goes

Grey words indicate earlier use of room; cream words indicate current use when plan drawn.
Grey lines indicate structures lost; cream lines indicate current structures.

a) Ground Floor Plan when Ockwells in use as the Farm House

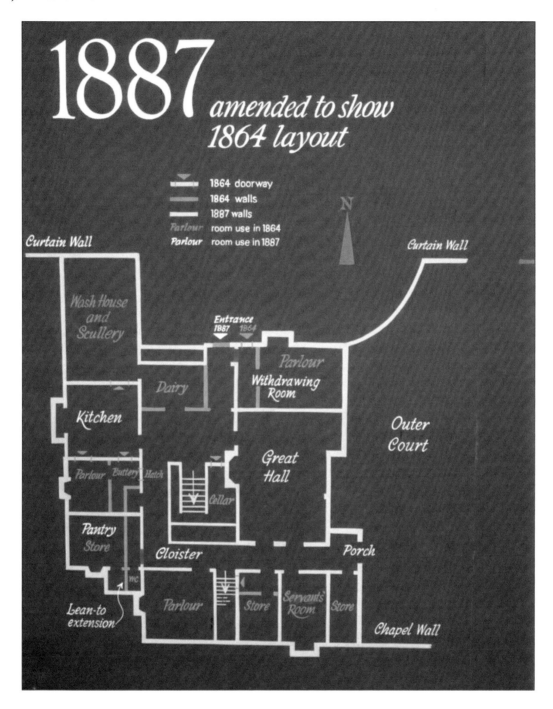

1864 plan from W E Nesfield's drawing (RIBA Drawing Collection).
1887 plan from *Builder Magazine*.

This plan shows:
- The staircase inserted into the central courtyard in the seventeenth century.
- The dairy in 1864, described by Nesfield as a modern lean-to, probably blocked the seventeenth-century entrance necessitating the creation of an alternative entrance.
- The insertion of a WC by 1864 appears to be the origin of a room connecting the south and west fronts which in the past has come and gone.
- A curved wall probably connected the fortified wall with the house, where earlier there had been another gable and wing projecting eastwards.

b) Ockwells after Tom Columbus Smith began "restoration"

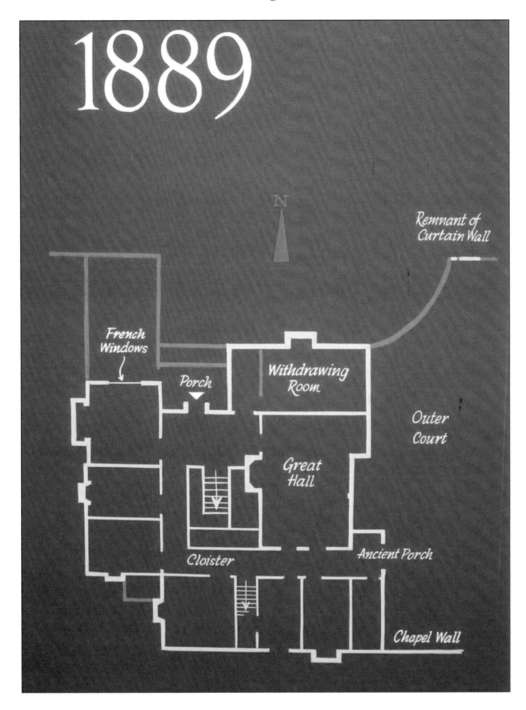

1889 plan – tentative plan – based on a photo in the Historic England collection which shows the north façade and outline of house in the 1889 Sale Catalogue (when the lease on Ockwells was sold by Tom Columbus Smith).

The major changes:
-   Demolition of the single storey wash house and scullery and insertion of french windows in the north wall of the old kitchen (see photo on page 145).
-   The replacement of the dairy with a new porch, beginning the process of turning Ockwells from the farm house into a gentleman's residence.
-   Curved wall connecting with north east corner of the house lost.

c) Ockwells after the main restoration done for Stephen Leech by Felix Wade

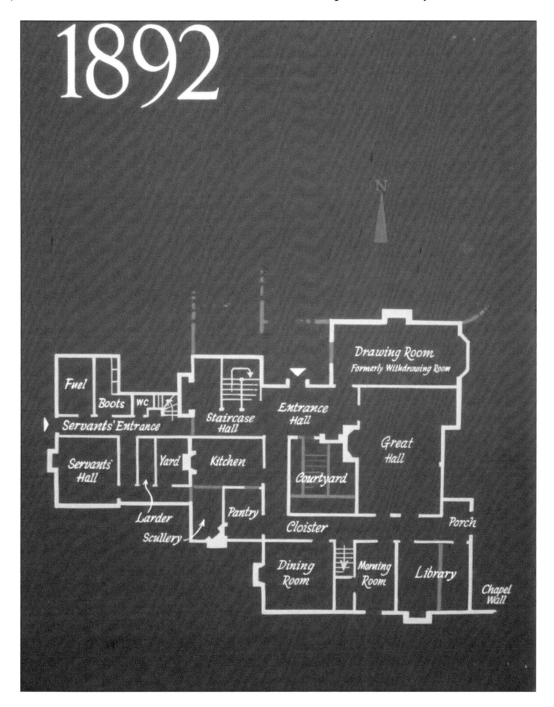

1892 Plan from the 1892 Sale Catalogue

Many changes took place during this restoration but the main ones visible on the plan are:
- The staircase once in the courtyard was moved to the old kitchen.
- An extension was built on the west front with access through the old kitchen.
- The withdrawing room had a new bay window.
- Lean-to room on southwest corner was lost.
- A new wall created a scullery and pantry causing the chimneypiece to be re-orientated/altered.

d) The restored Ockwells is changed by its owner Sir Edward Barry

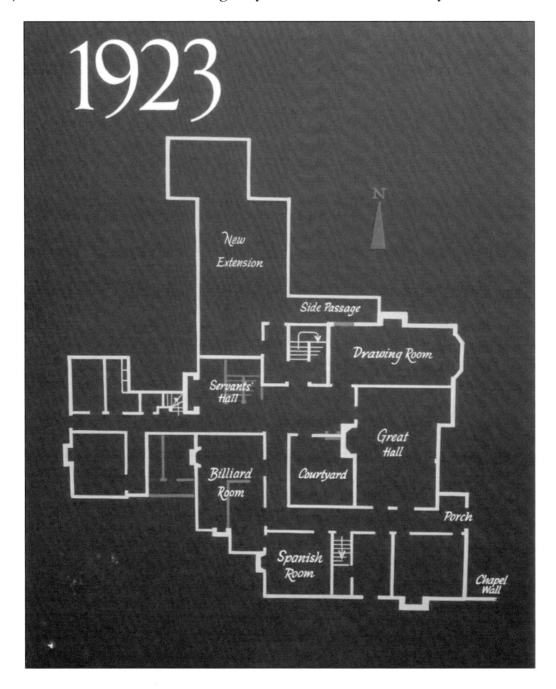

1923 Floor plan from an article in VCH for Berkshire

The changes include:
-   The addition of a new extension to the north façade which necessitated moving the staircase from the old kitchen to a new position outside the north façade.
-   The erection of a side passage to connect the extension with the drawing room.
-   Removal of walls to create a billiard room (formerly his library) which is probably when the pantry fireplace was replaced.
-   Lean-to room on the southwest corner rebuilt to connect room on south and west fronts.

e) Ockwells after restoration for Brian Stein by David Mansfield Thomas

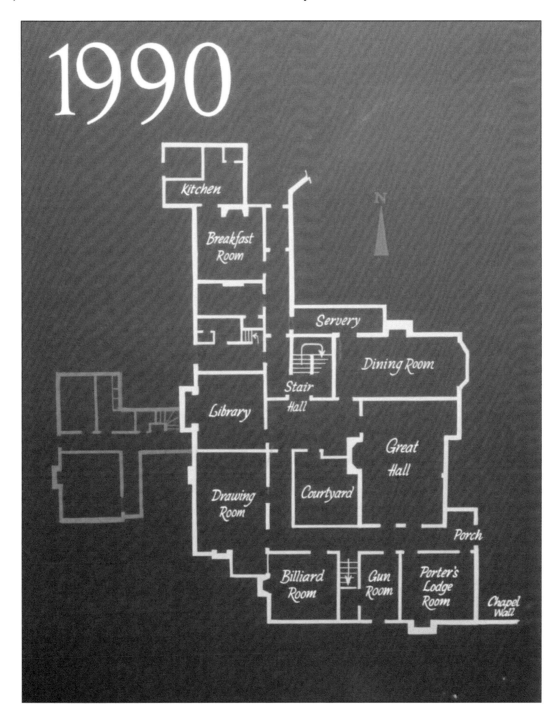

1990 Floor Plan from architect's drawing of 1984

Changes prior to 1984:
- Leech's extension on the west front taken down by Barry ca.1936; former passageways become windows.
- The old buttery fireplace is blocked in.

Changes after 1984:
- Barry's removal of the dividing walls in the old buttery and pantry lead to the ceiling sagging requiring the insertion of a supporting pillar (Samson pillar).

Fig 2: 1864 Floor plans by W E Nesfield
(Copyright: RIBA)

a) Ground floor

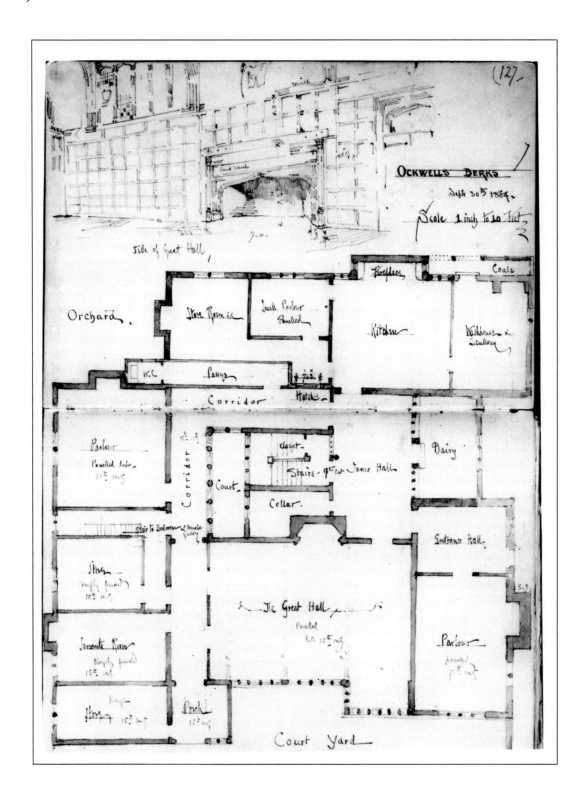

b) Upper floor

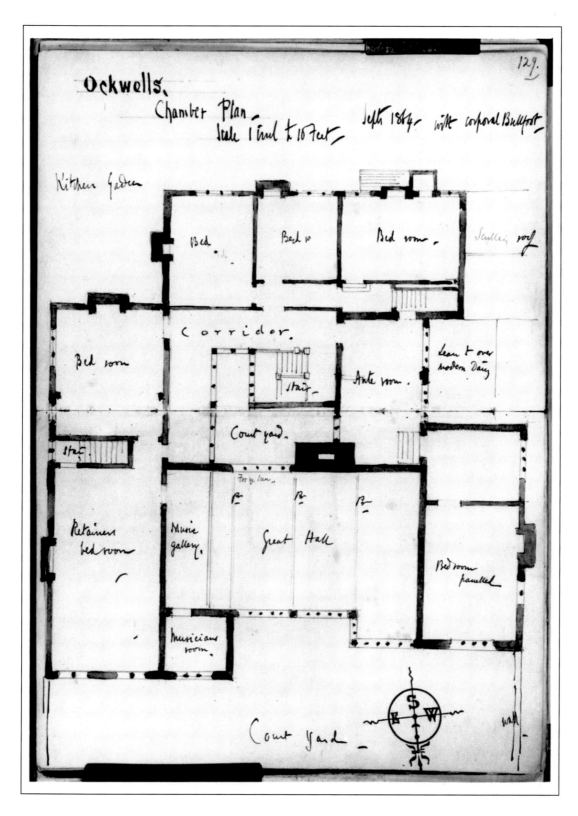

The compass rose on the first-floor plan is inaccurate. The great hall faces east not north.

Fig 3: 1887 Floor Plan from the *Builder*

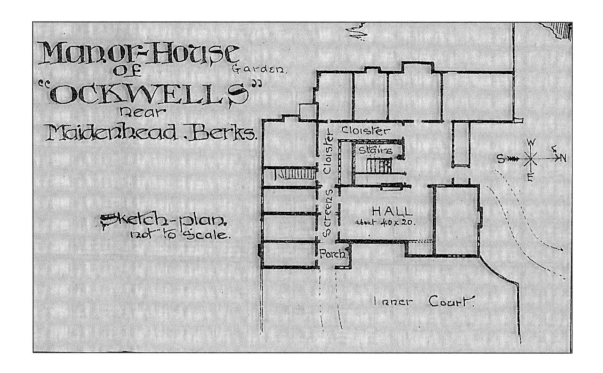

324

Fig 4: 1892 Floor plans from the Sale Catalogue

a) Ground floor

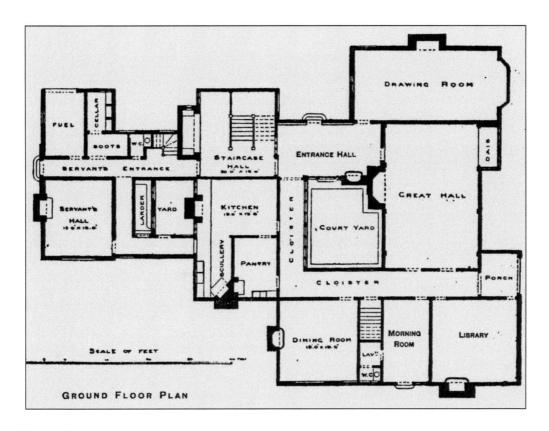

b) Upper floor

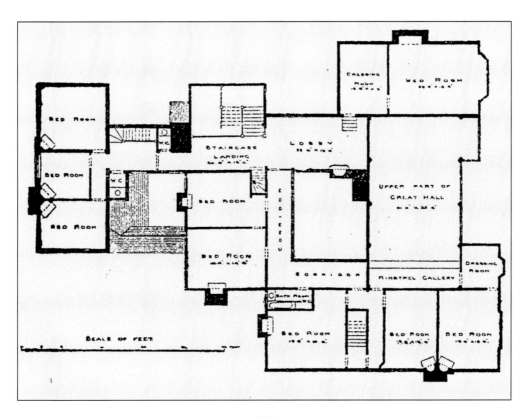

Fig 5: 1924 Floor plan from VCH Berkshire, vol 3, p94

Ground floor

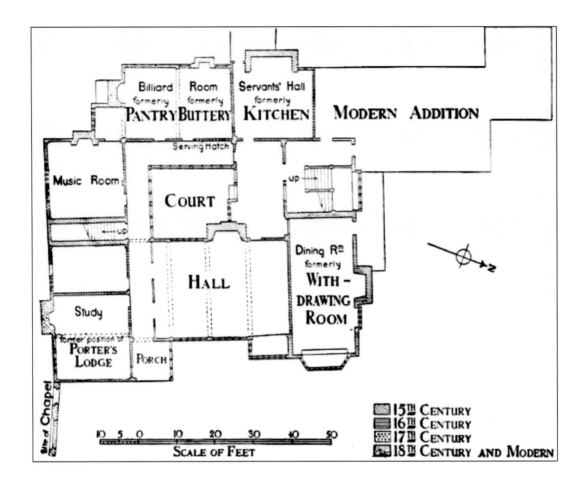

Fig 6: 1984 Floor plans by the architect David Mansfield Thomas

a) Ground floor

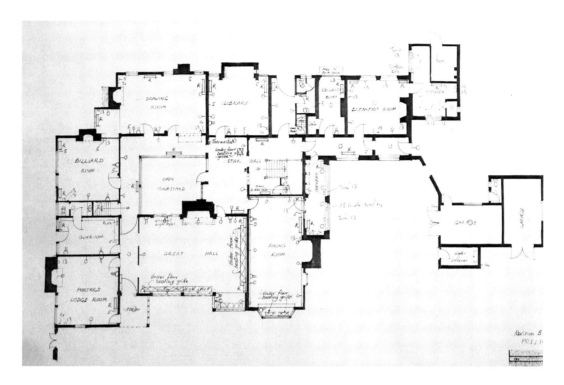

b) Upper floor

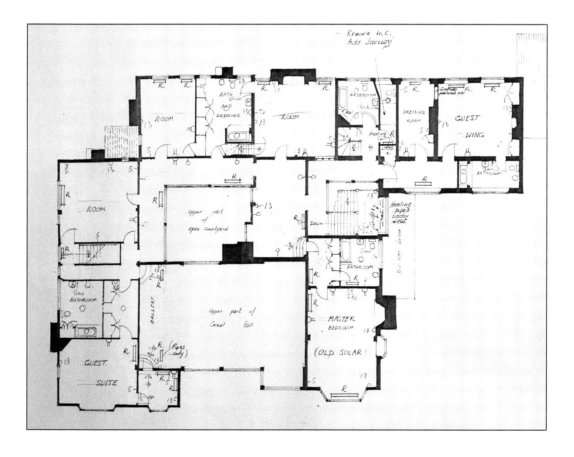

Fig 7: 2019 Floor plans from the Sale Catalogue

a) Ground floor

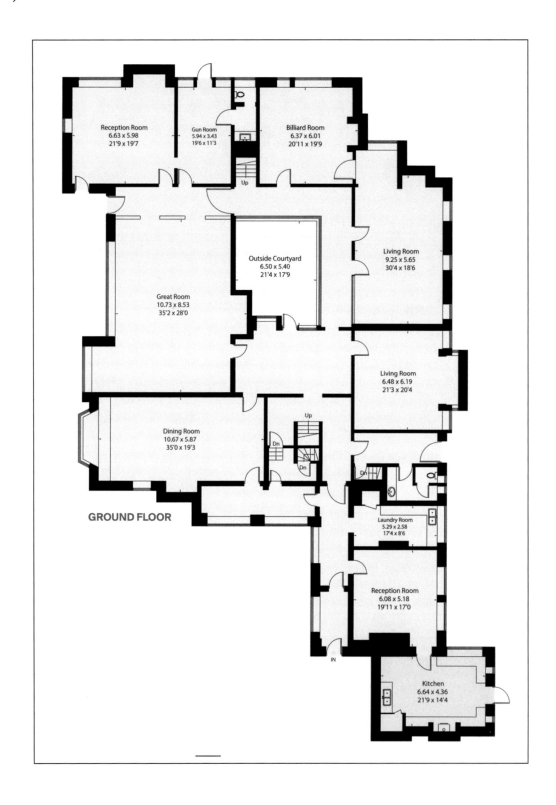

b) First floor

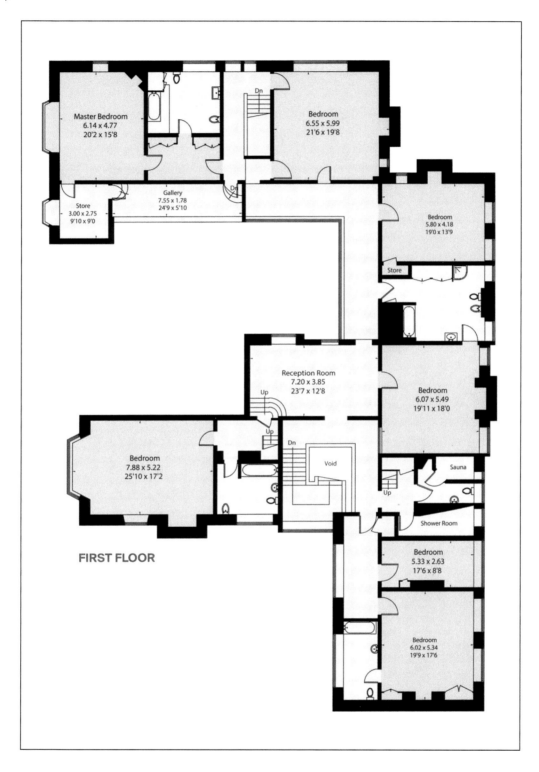

Abbreviations, References and Sources

ABBREVIATIONS

BL	British Library
CCR	Calendar of Close Rolls, HMSO
CFR	Calendar of Fine Rolls, HMSO
CIPM	Calendar of Inquisitions Post Mortem
CPR	Calendar of Patent Rolls, HMSO
HEA	Historic England Archive
M.Ad	*Maidenhead Advertiser*
MCS	Maidenhead Civic Society (*www.maidenheadcivicsoc.org.uk*)
NT	National Trust
ODNB	Oxford Dictionary of National Biography
RBWM	Royal Borough of Windsor & Maidenhead
RIBA	Royal Institute of British Architects
Ry.F	Rymer's Foedera
TNA	The National Archives
VCH	Victoria County History

UNPUBLISHED ORIGINAL AUTHORITIES

Arundel Castle Archive (seat of the Duke of Norfolk)
Lilly H, 1637. *The Genealogie of the Princelie familie of the Howards.*

Berkshire Record Office (BRO)
1918 Sale of Outlying Farms D/EG/E11/29/2

Deeds relating to Ockwells D/EG/T6 & D/EG/T14

Map ca.1800 Ockwells Farm D/EG/P8.

(The documents above were among those deposited in 1952 at the Record Office by Viscountess Gage, daughter of William Henry Grenfell; they are part of the manorial documents, deeds and estate papers relating to the Bray portion of the estate of the Grenfell family, Barons Desborough of Taplow Court, Bucks).

Deeds once in the possession of the Powney family D/EZ97.
(These were purchased by the BRO via eBay in 1994. They complement the Grenfell deeds).

Bodleian Library, University of Oxford
Ashmole 850. Notes made by Elias Ashmole on heraldry in Berkshire in the mid-seventeenth century.

Digby MSS 155-6. Account of the embassy led by William de la Pole, Marquess of Suffolk, in 1444 to arrange the marriage of Henry VI to Margaret of Anjou.

MSS Top Berks d.15/1; d.15/2, and d.15/3. Charles Kerry's notebooks, Vols I-III.

- Notebook Vol II, d.15/2, p118-121: copies made of drawings of Ockwells armorial glass taken in 1765 by Sir Thomas Reeve of Hendon's House, Holyport.
- Notebook Vol III, d.15/3: extracts from the Court Roll of Bray (including notices of the Norreys family) and the Court Roll of Lowbrook.

British Library
Add. MSS 23938 f5 and f13. *Compotus de expensis Margareta Reginae, venientis in Angliam*, July 1444 - October 1446.

Add. MSS 36356 ff220-221. John Buckler, 1815. Original drawing of Ockwells farm house, vol 1 Bedford – Berks.

Add. MSS 34868. Thomas Willement. Ancient Stained Glass vol III; p145 inscription Langford; p195-6 coat of Bishop Richard Beauchamp; p198 coat of Mortimer; p200 no identity given, but was coat of John Pury.

Harleian MSS 14581. Heraldry – coat of Richard Beauchamp, Bishop of Salisbury f100 R.

William Twopeny. Drawings of Ancient Architecture: Domestic – Fifteenth Century, vol IVA, pp11-14.

College of Arms
- Pedigree *The Lord Norreis and Norreis of Speke with others of that House*, E12 f 89-91.
- Pedigree, untitled, E12 f 96.
- Pedigree *The trewe… of the three houses of Norreis [that] is to say of Speake in Lancashire, of Bray in Berkshire and of Fyffeld in the same shire with all the collaterals of the same three houses 1568*, E8 f 51-52, f28.28.
- Pedigree of Norris of Fyfield in C. Barks (sic), E8

Historic England Archive (formerly the National Monument Record Collection)
Ockwells Photographic Archive.

Maidenhead Library
Darby's Notebooks. Unpublished manuscripts by Stephen Darby, 19 vols plus index B.C 94.

St Georges Chapel, Archives, Windsor Castle
SGC XV.21.83 & 84: Staines, Middlesex. Conveyance of Land and Power of Attorney.
SGC XV.25.56 &57: Leighton Buzzard Manor, Bedfordshire. Concord in the King's Court and Agreement concerning conveyance of lands.
SGC XV.45.140: New Windsor, Berks. Grant of a messuage in Peascod Street.
SGC XV.45.197: New Windsor, Berks. Grant of a tenement in Peascod Street.
SGC XV.54.65 & 66: Sandleford Priory, Berkshire. Surrender of lands.
SGC XV.54.67: Sandleford Priory, Berkshire. Inquisition into duty to celebrate mass.
SGC XV.58.D.43: Grant of land in Maidenhead, Bray.
SGC XV.58.D.58: Grant of lands in Bray (three deeds).

The National Archives, Kew
Birmingham Collection, NRA 28607, HMC 10 vols.

E150/784/11 William Norris, knight: Exchequer, Kings Remembrancer, Escheators' Files, Inquisitions Post Mortem, Series II and other inquisitions, Henry VII to Elizabeth I.

C142/24/76 William Norris, knight: Chancery, Inquisitions Post Mortem, Series II and other inquisitions, Henry VII to Charles I.

Reading Public Library
C R B Barrett. A copy of a set of six signed prints of drawings of Ockwells made in 1887; Slocock Collection, vol 1, ff77-79.

Royal Armouries
(Material deposited by Sir James Gow Mann FSA)
MANN 5/2 16, 1938, 44 pages. Manuscript catalogue of arms and armour in the possession of Sir Edward Barry, Bt, DL, JP at Ockwells Manor, Bray, Berkshire, by James G Mann FSA.

MANN 5/2 17, 1939, 59 pages: Manuscript catalogue of the furniture and pictures in the possession of Sir Edward Barry, Bt, DL, JP at Ockwells Manor, Bray, Berkshire, by James G Mann FSA.

MANN 5/2 12, 1949: Inventory and schedule of the 16/18 Century furniture and effects made at Ockwells Manor, Maidenhead, the property of the late Sir Edward Barry.

MANN 5/2 18, 1950: Ockwells Manor Estate, Maidenhead, Berks: schedule of the contents of the manor house included in the sale to S H Barnett.

Royal Institute of Architects (RIBA)
William Eden Nesfield, 1864. Drawings Collection – Ockwells floor plans, Sketchbook II, folio 127 – ground floor; folio 129 – first floor.

Ambrose Poynter (undated). Notes and Sketches of English Gothic Buildings – drawing of east front by folio 92 (see page 96 of the RIBA catalogue).

Walter Peart. Drawings of Ockwells Manor – east front f143, oriel window f144, gable of guest chamber f145; hall fireplace f146; east gable of solar f147; lintels and spandrels to porch and entrance doorway f148, latter dated 1879. (See page 43 of the RIBA Catalogue).

Society of Antiquaries
Drawings of Ockwells made by Roland Paul in 1887 (Shelf mark UM 249 c-d).

Society for the Protection of Ancient Buildings (SPAB)
Letters concerning the proposed restoration of Ockwells in the nineteenth century including correspondence with Stephen Leech and Felix Wade, his architect.

Victoria and Albert Museum.
Letters Patent granting the manor of Ockholt to Basil Fettiplace, given at Windsor 31 December 1582 (donated by Col. C du Pre Penton Powney).

UNPUBLISHED REPORTS & THESES

COX GREEN COMMUNITY ASSOCIATION, 1983. *Ockwells Manor; the campaign to save Ockwells Manor and surrounds for the community*, 4p.

DARBY S, 1899. *Place and Field Names Cookham Parish, Berks*. Privately printed.

DARBY S, (undated). Handwritten notebooks, vols 1-19. Maidenhead Library.

DARRACOTT A, 2014. *An account of the personalities once represented in the armorial glass of the C14th St John the Baptist Church, Shottesbrooke*, 46pp. Maidenhead Civic Society, www.maidenheadcivicsoc.org.uk.

DARRACOTT A, 2015. *A history trail of Bisham Abbey and All Saints Church, Bisham*, 36pp. Maidenhead Civic Society, www.maidenheadcivicsoc.org.uk.

DARRACOTT A, 2018. *Armorial Glass for John Norreys, Esquire of the Body of Henry VI and Margaret of Anjou, Queen of England, in the Galilee Chapel of Durham Cathedral*, Maidenhead Civic Society, www.maidenheadcivicsoc.org.uk.

DARRACOTT A, 2019. *Heraldry used on Roof Bosses in St George's Chapel – Badges of York & Lancaster*. Maidenhead Civic Society, www.maidenheadcivicsoc.org.uk.

DARRACOTT A, 2022. *The Medieval Stained Glass of Holy Trinity Church, Long Melford, Suffolk, and its link with the Howard family and Ockwells Manor House, Berkshire*. Maidenhead Civic Society, www.maidenheadcivicsoc.org.uk.

RUTHERFORD S, 2019. *Ockwells Manor, Berkshire Historic Setting Analysis*. Unpub. report for RBWM.

SALE CATALOGUES

- 1889. *"Ockwells", Maidenhead – Medieval Manor House for sale by auction 4th June 1889*. Auctioneers Walton & Co. Also at BRO, ref D/EG/E11/2.
- 1892. *"Ockwells" Estate including the celebrated and historical ancient manor house together with Ockwells Farm, for sale by auction 12th July 1892*. Auctioneers Debenham, Tewson, Farmer; and Bridgewater, Burnham & Son. Also at BRO, ref D/EG/E11/3; also D/EG/E11/4.
- 1950. *Ockwells Manor near Maidenhead Berks – the historic residential, agricultural and sporting estate for sale by public auction 12th July 1950*. Auctioneers Cyril Jones & Clifton, Maidenhead; and John W Wood & Co. London.
- 1983. *Ockwells Manor Maidenhead, Berks* For sale by private treaty with vacant possession Simmons & Lawrence and Hampton & Sons.
- 2019. *Ockwells Manor Nr Maidenhead, Royal Berkshire*. Savills & Knight Frank.

SILK C, 1989. *The lifestyle of the gentry in the later middle ages with special reference to John Norreys of Ockwells Manor, Berkshire*. Unpub. dissertation for University of Southampton.

VAN SICKLE W H H, 1987. *Ockwells Manor house, Berkshire: a history of ownership, occupancy and alterations*. Prepared for Mr Brian Stein.

PUBLISHED WORKS

ALDIN C, 1923. *Old Manor Houses*. William Heinemann Ltd.

ALLEN T, 2015. *The Lost Abbey of Abingdon*. Friends of Abbey Gardens (available from Abingdon Town Council).

AMIN N, 2017. *The house of Beaufort – the bastard line that captured the Crown*. Amberley.

ANDENMATTEN B & DE RAEMY D, 1990. *La Maison de Savoie en Pays de Vaud*. Editions Payot, Lausanne.

ANDREWS H C, 1918. *Ockholt, alias Ockwells Manor, and its owners*. Berks, Bucks and Oxon Archaeological Journal, vol 24, nos 1&2, p19-28.

ASTILL G, 2002. *Windsor in the context of medieval Berkshire*. pp1-14. In: *Windsor – Medieval Archaeology, Art and Architecture in the Thames Valley*; eds. Laurence Keen and Eileen Scarff.

BAGLEY J J, 1948. *Margaret of Anjou*. Jenkins.

BAGGS, A P, BLAIR W J, CHANCE E, COLVIN C, COOPER J, DAY C J, SELWYN N & TOWNLEY S C, 1990. *Stanton Harcourt: Manors and other estates*. In: *A History of the County of Oxford Volume 12, Wootton Hundred (South) including Woodstock*; eds. Alan Crossley and C R Elrington. Victoria County History, London.

BAKER J H, 2004, *Robert Brudenell*. ODNB.

BAKER T F T, 1982a. *Sir Francis Englefield (1521/22-1596)*. In: *The History of Parliament: the House of Commons 1509-1558*, 3 vols, ed. S T Bindoff. Boydell and Brewer.

BAKER T F T, 1982b. *John Fettiplace (1526/7-1580)*. In: *The History of Parliament: the House of Commons 1509-1558*, 3 vols, ed. S T Bindoff. Boydell and Brewer.

BANKS T C, 1808. *The Dormant & Extinct Baronage of England*. London.

BARFIELD S, 1901. *Thatcham, Berks, and its manors*, 3 vols. James Parker & Co.

BARRY S L, 1928. *The pedigree of the Barrys of Eynsham, Oxon*. Deane & Son Ltd.

BAUDIER M, 1737. *A history of the memorable and extraordinary calamities of Margaret of Anjou, Queen of England*. Reprinted by Gale Ecco, 2010.

BEAUCOURT G, du FRESNE de, 1863. *Chronique de Mathieu d'Escouchy*. Libraire de la Societe de l'Histoire de France.

BEGENT P J & CHESSHYRE H, 1999. *The Most Noble Order of the Garter – 650 years*. Spink.

BELTZ G F, 1841. *Memorials of the most noble Order of the Garter*. William Pickering, London.

BENNETT M, 1987. *Lambert Simnel and the battle of Stoke*. Alan Sutton.

Berkshire Feet of Fines Part II Fines 1400-1509 & Index (Ed. M. Yates) 2017 vol 24. Berkshire Record Society.

BLOORE P & MARTIN E, 2015. *Wingfield College and its patrons – piety and patronage in medieval Suffolk*. The Boydell Press.

BOULAY F R H, 1957. *Registrum Thome Bourgchier, Cantariensis Archiepiscopi, 1454-1486*. Oxford University Press.

BRAYLEY E W, 1834. *The graphic and historical illustrator*. J Chidley, London.

BRITTON J, 1814. *Some account of the Beauchamp Chapel at Warwick*. Architectural. Antiquities, pt XXXI, vol IV, p7-18. Longman, Hurst, Rees, Orme & Browne.

BROOKS F W, 1939. *A medieval brickyard at Hull*. Journal of the British. Archaeological. Association, 3rd Series, vol IV.

BROWN R, COLVIN H M, & TAYLOR A J, 1963. *The History of the King's Works*, vol 1 – *The Middle Ages*. HMSO.

BRUCE J (Ed), 1853. *Letters and Papers of the Verney family down to the year 1639*. Camden Society.

BURKE B, 1871. *History of the Landed Gentry of Great Britain and Ireland*. Harrison.

BURKE B, 1883. *Dormant, Abeyant, Forfeited and Extinct Peerages of the British Empire*. Harrison.

Calendar Inquisitions Post Mortem. Henry V, Henry VI, Edward IV and Richard III, Vol IV, 1828. House of Commons.

Calendar Inquisitions Post Mortem. Henry VII, Vol 1, 1898; Vol 2, 1915. HMSO.

CARTE T, 1851. *The life of James Duke of Ormond*, vol 1. Oxford University Press.

CAVE-BROWNE J, 1895. *Knights of the Shire for Kent from AD 1275 to AD 1831*. Archaeologica. Cantiana, vol 21.

CHUNG P W, 1967. *The World of Pat Chung*. Merkle Press Inc, Washington DC.

CLARK K L, 2016. *The Nevills of Middleham*. The History Press.

CLARK L S, 2020a. *John Norris (d.1466)*. In: *Vol V, The History of Parliament: the House of Commons 1422-1461*, 7 vols, ed. L S Clark. Cambridge University Press.

CLARK L S, 2020b. *William Norris (bef.1441-1507)*. In: *Vol V, The History of Parliament: the House of Commons 1422-1461*, 7 vols, ed. L S Clark. Cambridge University Press.

CLARK L S, 2020c. *Richard Bulstrode (d.1502)*. In: *Vol III, The History of Parliament: the House of Commons 1422-1461*, 7 vols, ed. L S Clark. Cambridge University Press.

CLARK L S, 2020d. *Edward Langford (1417-1474).* In: *Vol V, The History of Parliament: the House of Commons 1422-1461,* 7 vols, ed. L S Clark. Cambridge University Press.

CLARK L S, 2020e. *John Pury (d.1484).* In: *Vol VI, The History of Parliament: the House of Commons 1422-1461,* 7 vols, ed. L S Clark. Cambridge University Press.

CLARK L S, 2020f. *Robert Rademylde (1425-1457).* In: *Vol VI, The History of Parliament: the House of Commons 1422-1461,* 7 vols, ed. L S Clark. Cambridge University Press.

COBBE H, 1899. *Luton Church – historical and descriptive.* George Bell & Sons.

COOKE A H, 1925. *The early history of Mapledurham.* Oxford Record Society.

COUNTESS of WARWICK, 1903. *Warwick Castle & its Earls,* 2 vols. Hutchinson & Co.

COLE C, 1950. *New lights on old lights.* Coat of Arms, no 1, p21-24.

COLE C, 1952-3. *Sisters in Arms.* Coat of Arms, vol II, pp149-153; pp183-188; pp217-219.

COX M, 1989. *The story of Abingdon – Part II Medieval Abingdon 1186-1556.*

CRAM L, 1988. *Reading Abbey.* Reading Museum & Gallery.

CRON B M, 1994. *The Duke of Suffolk, the Angevin marriage, and the ceding of Maine, 1445.* Journal of Medieval History, vol 20 pp77-99.

CUST L, 1899. *A history of Eton College.* Duckworth & Co.

CUST L H, revised by BRADLEY S, 2004 *Ambrose Poynter (1796-1886) architect.* ODNB.

DARBY S, 1909. *Chapters in the history of Cookham.* Privately printed.

DARRACOTT A, 2005. *The rebuilding of the quire of Great Malvern Priory in the 15th Century – and its link with Richard Beauchamp, Earl of Warwick, his wife Isabel Despencer, Richard, Duke of York, and John Carpenter, Bishop of Worcester*, 104pp. ABD Titles.

DAVIES R G, 2004. *Richard Beauchamp, Bishop of Salisbury.* ODNB.

DEVRIES K, 1999. *Joan of Arc a military leader.* Sutton Publishing.

DORAN S, 2021 *Norris [Norreys], Henry, first Baron Norris (c. 1525–1601).* ODNB.

DRYSDALE P, 2011. *Faith and heraldry –the stained glass in the Church of St James the Great, Radley.* Radley History Club.

DUGDALE W, 1656. *The Antiquities of Warwickshire.* Thomas Warren.

DUNN D E S, 2001. *Margaret of Anjou, chivalry and garter.* In: *St George's Chapel, Windsor, in the late Middle Ages* (eds: C Richmond & E Scarff). Historical Monographs relating to St Georges Chapel, vol 17. Dean and Canons of Windsor.

DUNNING R W, ROGERS K H, SPALDING, P A SHRIMPTON C, STEVENSON J H & TOMLINSON M, 1970. *Parishes: Wootton Bassett.* In: *A History of the County of Wiltshire*, Volume 9, (ed. Elizabeth Crittall), pp86-205. London.

DUKE E, 1837. *Prolusiones historicae: or essays illustrative of the halle of John Halle.* W B Brodie & Co.

DURRANT P & PAINTER J, 2018. *Reading Abbey and the Abbey Quarter.* Two Rivers Press.

EAVIS A, 2019. *Urbs in rure: A metropolitan elite at Holy Trinity, Long Melford, Suffolk,* pp82-106. In: *The urban church in late medieval England.* Proceedings of the 2017 Harlaxton Symposium (eds Harry D & Steer C). Shaun Tyas.

ELLIS R H, 1978. *Catalogue of Seals in the Public Record Office – Personal Seals*; vol I 1978; vol II 1981. HMSO.

EMERY A, 2006. *Greater medieval houses of England and Wales, 1300-1500, vol 3: Southern England.* Cambridge University Press.

ESDAILE K A, 1950. *A Westminster Abbey puzzle – the Norris monument traced to Isaac James.* In: *Country Life*, February 17.

ETON COLLEGE RECORDS, 1988. Vol 63: *Miscellaneous Estate Rolls.*

EVERARD GREEN, 1899. *The identification of the eighteen worthies commemorated in the heraldic glass in the hall windows of Ockwells Manor house, in the parish of Bray, in Berkshire.* Archaeologia vol 56, Issue 2, pp323-336. Also published online by Cambridge University Press, 2012.

FEA A, 1902. *Picturesque old houses.* S H Bousfield & Co.

FOSTER J, 1989. *The Dictionary of Heraldry.* Bracken Books.

FUIDGE N M, 1981. *Sir Henry Norris I (c.1525-1601), of Rycote, Oxon. and Bray, Berks.* In: *The History of Parliament: the House of Commons 1558-1603,* ed. P W Hasler. Boydell & Brewer.

GAIRDNER J, (ed) 1880. *Three fifteenth century chronicles with historical memoranda by John Stowe.* Camden Society, n.s. xxvll, pp 148-163 (notes of occurrences under Henry VI & Edward IV).

GIBBS R, 1885. *The History of Aylesbury.* Reprinted by Paul P B Minet, 1971.

GIBSON J M, (undated). *Cobham College.* President & Trustees of the New College of Cobham.

GILBERT J T, 1865. *History of the Viceroys of Ireland.* Dublin.

GILL L, 1999. *Richard III and Buckingham's rebellion.* Sutton Publishing.

GOMME G L (ed), 1891. *The Gentleman's Magazine Library – chief contents from 1731 to 1868 English Topography*, pp112-119. Elliot Stock, Bray.

GOODALL J A, 2001. *God's House at Ewelme – life, devotion and architecture in a fifteenth century almshouse.* Ashgate.

GOODALL J A, 2002. *Henry VI's court and the construction of Eton College*, pp 247-263. In: *Windsor – Medieval Archaeology, Art and Architecture in the Thames Valley;* eds. Laurence Keen and Eileen Scarff. British Archaeological Association, Conference Transactions XXV.

GORHAM G C, 1838. *An Account of the Chapel, Chauntry and Guild of Maidenhead, Berkshire.* Extracted from: The Collectanea Topographica et Genealogica, Vol VI.

GRANT J C, 2000. *St Peter's Church, Martley – a History.* Severnside Printers Ltd.

GREENING LAMBORN E A, 1949. *The armorial glass of the Oxford Diocese 1250-1850.* Oxford University Press.

GRIFFITHS R A, 1972. *The principality of Wales in the later Middle Ages – the structure and personnel of government: I, South Wales 1277-1536.* University of Wales Press.

GRIFFITHS R A, 1981. *The reign of King Henry VI.* University of California Press.

GRIFFITHS R A, 2004. *Henry VI.* ODNB

HABINGTON T, 1895. *A survey of Worcestershire.* 2 vols, (ed. J Amphlett), Worcestershire Historical Society.

HAMPTON W E, 1979. *Memorials of the Wars of the Roses.* Richard III Society.

HARDING A, 1981a. *Edward Norris (ca.1550-1603) of Rycote, Oxon. and Englefield, Berks.* In: *The History of Parliament: the House of Commons 1558-1603,* ed. P W Hasler. Boydell & Brewster.

HARDING A, 1981b. *John Norris (ca.1550-Dec. 1612 or Jan 1613), of Fifield and Bray, Berks. and Woodwicks, Herts.* In: *The History of Parliament: the House of Commons 1558-1603,* ed. P W Hasler. Boydell & Brewster.

HARDY T D, 1873. *Rymer's Foedera,* vol II 1377-1654. Longman & Co and Trubner & Co, London.

HASTED E, 1797. *General History: Sheriffs of Kent.* In: *The History & Topographical Survey of the county of Kent,* vol 1, pp177-213.

HARVEY L S, 1957. *The De La Pole family of Kingston upon Hull.* East Yorkshire Local History Society.

HIBBERT C, 1973. *George IV.* Allen Lane.

HILLABY J & C, 2006. *Leominster Minster Priory and Borough c660-1539.* The Friends of Leominster Priory with Logaston Press.

HOOKHAM M A, 1872. *The life and times of Margaret of Anjou,* 2 vols. Tinsley Bros.

HORROX R, 1983. *The De La Poles of Hull.* East Yorkshire Local History Society.

HORROX R, 1993. *The Government of Richard III.* In: *Richard III – A Medieval Kingship,* ed. J Gillingham. Collins & Brown.

HUGHES G M, 1890. *A History of Windsor Forest, Sunninghill and the Great Park.* Ballantyne, Hanson & Co.

HUGHES J, 2004. *Boleyn, Thomas, Earl of Wiltshire and Earl of Ormonde.* ODNB.

HURRY J B, 1901. *Reading Abbey.* Elliot Stock.

HUSSEY C, 1924. *Ockwells Manor, Bray: I pp52-60; II pp92-99, III pp130-137.* In: *Country Life.*

Illustrated guide to the heraldic roof bosses in the roof vault of St George's Chapel, Windsor Castle, 2016. Dean & Canons of Windsor.

Illustrated guide to woodwork in the quire of St George's Chapel, Windsor Castle, 2017. Dean & Canons of Windsor

INGRAM M E, 1948. *Our Lady of Hull – being the history of the church and parish of St Mary the Virgin, Kingston upon Hull.* A Brown & Son.

JAMES M R, 1933. *St Georges Chapel – The woodwork of the choir.* Oxley & Son.

JESSE E, 1847. *Favorite haunts and rural studies.* John Murray.

JOHNSON P A, 1988. *Duke Richard of York 1411-1460.* Clarendon Press, Oxford.

JONES M, 1981. *John Beaufort Duke of Somerset and the French Expedition of 1443.* In: *Patronage, the Crown and the Provinces in Later Medieval England,* ch 4, ed. R A Griffiths. Alan Sutton.

JONES M, 2004. *Edmund Beaufort.* ODNB.

KEKEWICH M L, 2004a. *William Aiscough, Bishop of Salisbury.* ODNB.

KEKEWICH M L, 2004b. *John Wenlock.* ODNB.

KEMP B R (ed), 1986. *Reading Abbey Cartularies: I General documents and those relating to English Counties other than Berkshire:* 1987; *II Berkshire Documents, Scottish Charters & Miscellaneous documents* Camden Fourth Series, vols 31 & 33. Royal Historical Society.

KENDALL P M, 1973. *Richard the Third.* George Allen & Unwin.

KERRY C, 1861. *The history and antiquities of the hundred of Bray in the county of Berks.* Savill & Edwards.

KIGHTLY C, 1993. *Sir John Oldcastle (ca.1370-1417) of Almeley, Herefs. and Cobham, Kent.* In: *The History of Parliament: the House of Commons 1386-1421,* eds. J S Roskell, L Clark & C Rawcliffe. Boydell & Brewer.

KINGSFORD C L, 1977. *Chronicles of London.* Alan Sutton.

KIRBY K L, 1986. *Wiltshire Feet of Fines relating to 1377-1509 (abstracts).* Wiltshire Record Society.

KIRWAN J, 2018. *The chief Butlers of Ireland and the house of Ormond.* Irish Academic Press.

KLEINEKE H, 2020. *John Nanfan (d. ca.1462)*. In: vol V, *The History of Parliament: the House of Commons 1422-1461*, 7 vols, ed. L S Clark. Cambridge University Press.

KNIGHT C, 1847. *Old England a Pictorial Museum*. Vol I (published in 1845) & Vol II (published in 1847. James Sangster. Also two volumes bound together, reprinted 1987 by Bracken Books.

LAKING G F, 1905. *Mr Edward Barry's collection of arms and armour at Ockwells Manor, Bray*. In: *The Connoisseur*, vol XI, no 42, pp67-76.

LAMBRICK G & SLADE C F, 1989. *Two cartularies of Abingdon Abbey*. Vol 32, Oxford Historical Society.

LAOUTARIS C, 2014. *Shakespeare and the Countess*. Fig Tree - imprint of Penguin Books.

LEASK H G, 1971. *Irish churches and monastic buildings – medieval gothic the last phases*, vol 3. Dundalgan Press, W Tempest Ltd.

LECOY De La MARCHE A, 1875. *Le Roi Rene – sa vie, son administration, ses travaux artistiques et litteraires*. 2 vols. Librairie de Firmin-Didot Freres, Fils et Cie.

LEES-MILNE J H, 2007. *Diaries 1942-1954* (ed. M Bloch). Hachette UK.

LEES-MILNE J H, 2011. *Diaries 1971-1982* (ed. M Bloch). Hachette UK.

LEWIS D, 2010. *St Georges Chapel and the medieval town of Windsor*. In: *St Georges Chapel – History and Heritage*, eds. N Saul & T Tatton-Brown, pp57-62. The Dovecote Press.

LEWIS D, 2015. *Windsor and Eton*. In: *The British Historic Towns Atlas*, Vol IV, eds. M Biddle & C Barron. The Historic Towns Trust.

LIPSCOMB G, 1847. *The history & antiquities of the county of Buckingham*, vols 1-4. J & W Robins, London.

LIVERSIDGE M J M, 1989. *Abingdon's "Right Goodly Cross of Stone"*. In: Abingdon Essays, eds. W J H Liversidge & MJH Liversidge p42-57.

LONG E T, 1941. *Medieval Domestic Architecture in Berkshire, Part III*. Berkshire Archaeological Journal, vol. 45, Part 1, pp28-36.

LOOMIE A J, 2013. *Sir Francis Englefield*. ODNB.

LOS P G & LOS W A, 1997. *Brick & Tile Making*. In: *An Historical Atlas of East Yorkshire*, (eds. S Neave & S Ellis). University of Hull Press.

LUMBY J H, 1939. *Calendar of Norris Deeds (Lancashire)*. Vol 93, Record Society of Lancashire & Cheshire.

LYSONS D AND LYSONS S, 1806. *Magna Britannia, Vol. 1: Bedfordshire, Berkshire and Buckinghamshire*, 743pp. T Cadell and W Davies, London.

LYSONS D AND LYSONS S, 1813. *Magna Britannia, Vol. 1, Part II: Berkshire*, 502pp. T Cadell and W Davies, London. (The 1813 edition has all the text and illustrations from the Berkshire section of the 1806 edition together with additions and corrections on pages 447-473).

MACLEAN J, 1886. *Notes on the manors and advowsons of Birts Morton and Pendock*. Transactions of the. Bristol and Gloucester Archaeological. Society., vol X pp186-225.

MACNAMARA F N, 1895. *Memorials of the Danvers family (of Dauntsey and Culworth)*. Hardy & Page.

MANCINI D (translated by Armstrong C A J), 1989. *The usurpation of Richard III*. Alan Sutton.

MARKS R, 1993. *Stained glass in England during the Middle Ages*. Routledge.

MARKS R, 2004. *John Prudde*. ODNB.

MARR L J, 1982. *A History of the Bailiwick of Guernsey*. Phillimore.

MATTHEW E, 2004. *James Butler 4th Earl of Ormond*. ODNB.

McLEOD E, 1969. *Charles of Orleans – Prince and Poet*. Chatto & Windus.

MERINDOL C, 1987. *Le Roi Rene et la seconde maison d'Anjou*. Le Leopard d'Or.

METCALFE W C, 1885. *A book of knights banneret, knights of the bath and knights batchelor*. Mitchell & Hughes.

MIDDLETON T, 1975. *The Book of Maidenhead*. Barracuda Books Ltd.

MONSTRELET E De, 1840. *The chronicles of Enguerrand de Monstrelet* (translated by T Johnes), 2 vols. William Smith, London.

MORLEY H T, 1924. *Monumental brasses of Berkshire*. Reading.

MORETON C E, 2020. *John Wenlock (d.1471)*. In: vol VI, *The History of Parliament: the House of Commons 1422-1461*, 7 vols, ed. L S Clark. Cambridge University Press.

MYERS A R, 1985. *Crown, Household and Parliament in Fifteenth Century England*. Hambledon Press.

NAPIER H A, 1858. *Historical notices of the parishes of Swyncombe and Ewelme in the county of Oxford*. James Wright.

NASH J, 1839. *The mansions of England in olden time*. Vol 1. Henry Sotheran, London. (Also published in 1840, 1841 and 1849 by Thomas McLean, Haymarket, London).

NASH J, 1849. *Description of the plates of the mansions of England in olden time*. Thomas McLean, London.

NICOLAS H (ed), 1826. *Testamenta Vetusta*. 2 vols. Nichols & Son, London.

NICOLAS H (ed), 1837. *Proceedings & Ordinances of the Privy Council of England*, vol VI, Henry VI, 1443-1460, HMSO.

NOLAN J S, 1997. *Sir John Norreys and the Elizabethan Military World.* University of Exeter Press.

O'REILLY B M, 1909. *The curios of Ockwells Manor.* In: The Ladies Field, pp14-15.

ORMEROD G, 1850. *A memoir of the Lancashire house of Le Norreis or Norres and on its Speke branch in particular, &c., with notices of its connection with military transactions at Flodden, Edinburgh and Musselburgh.* Transactions of the Historical Society of Lancashire & Cheshire, vol 2, pp138-182.

OTWAY RUTHVEN A J, 1980. *A history of Medieval Ireland.* Barnes & Noble.

PARKER J H, 1859. *Some account of Domestic Architecture in England from Richard II to Henry VIII*, Part II. John Henry and James Parker, Oxford.

The Paston Letters (ed. Archer-Hind), 1924. 2 vols. Everyman's Library no 752. Dent & Sons.

The Paston Letters (ed. J Warrington), 1924, revised 1956. Everyman's Library no 753, vol 2. Dent & Sons.

PAYLING S J, 2020a. *John Catesby (d.1437).* In: *Vol III, The History of Parliament: the House of Commons 1422-1461,* 7 vols, ed. L S Clark. Cambridge University Press.

PAYLING S J, 2020b. *William Lacon I (ca.1408-1475).* In: *Vol V, The History of Parliament: the House of Commons 1422-1461,* 7 vols, ed. L S Clark. Cambridge University Press.

PEVSNER N, 1966., reprinted 1988. *Buildings of England – Berkshire*, p187. Penguin Books.

POLLARD A J, 2004. *Robert Neville, Bishop of Durham.* ODNB.

PRESTON A E, 1929. *Christ's Hospital Abingdon – the almshouses, the hall and the portraits.* Reprinted with an addendum in 1994. University Press, Oxford.

RADFORD L B, 1908. *Henry Beaufort Bishop, Chancellor, Cardinal.* Pitman & Sons.

RAINES F R (ed), 1870. *The visitation of the county palatine of Lancaster made in the year 1567 by William Flower Esq.* Vol 81, Chetham Society.

ROBINSON J M, 1995. *The Dukes of Norfolk.* Phillimore.

ROSKELL J S, 1954. *The Commons in the Parliament of 1422 – English Society and Parliamentary representation under the Lancastrians.* Manchester University Press.

ROSKELL J S, 1958. *John Lord Wenlock of Sommeries.* Vol 38, Bedford Historical Record Society.

ROSKELL J S, CLARK L, & RAWCLIFFE C (eds), 1993. *The History of Parliament: the House of Commons 1386-1421.* Boydell & Brewer.

ROSS C, 1981. *Richard III.* Eyre Methuen.

RYLANDS W H (ed), 1907. *The four visitations of Berkshire.* 1532 visitation: Norrys of Yattendon, vol I, p10; 1566 visitation: Norris of Fyfield and Yattendon, vol II, p184-186. The Harleian Society, vol LVI.

RYLANDS W H (ed), 1909. *The visitation of Buckinghamshire, 1634.* The Harleian Society, vol LVIII.

Rymer's Foedera (ed HARDY T D), 1873. Vol II 1377-1654. Longman & Co.

SACKVILLE-WEST V, 1936. *Saint Joan of Arc.* Cobden-Sanderson.

SAUL N & TATTON BROWN T (eds), 2010. *St George's Chapel, Windsor: History and Heritage.* Dovecote Press.

SEARLE W G, 1867. *The Queen's College of St Margaret and St Bernard.* Cambridge Antiquarian Society, vol 1, 1446-1560.

SHAW W A, 1971 (original ed. 1906). *The Knights of England.* Two vols. Heraldry Today.

SHORTT H De S, 1970. *The Hungerford and Beauchamp Chantry Chapels.* Friends of Salisbury Cathedral.

SHUFFREY L A, 1912. *The English Fireplace.* B T Batsford.

SLADE C F, 1963-64. *Reading Records (4): Documents concerning relations between town and abbey c.1500 AD.* Berkshire Archaeological Journal, vol 61, pp48-62.

SLADE C F, 2002. *Reading Gild Accounts 1357-1516.* Pt I: *Introduction and accounts 1357-1448* vol 6; Pt II: *Accounts and Index 1450- 1516,* vol 7. Berkshire Record Society.

SMITH E F, (no date). *Tewkesbury Abbey.* Society for the Promotion of Christian Knowledge.

SOMERVILLE R, 1953. *History of the Duchy of Lancaster. Vol 1, 1265-1603.* The Chancellor and Council of the Duchy of Lancaster.

SOTHEBY & CO, 1965. *Catalogue of important early armour formerly in the collection of the late Sir Edward Barry Bt., of Ockwells Manor, Bray, Berkshire. The property of S.H. Barnett Esq removed from Claverdon Hall, Warwickshire.*

ST JOHN HOPE W H, 1901. *Stall plates of the Knights of the Order of the Garter 1348-1485.* Archibald Constable & Co Ltd, London.

ST JOHN HOPE W H, 1913. *Windsor Castle an architectural history.* Country Life.

STEVENSON J (ed), 1861-1864. *Letters and papers illustrative of the wars of the English in France during the reign of Henry the Sixth, King of England.* Vol 1, 1861, Longman, Green, Longman and Roberts; vol 2, pt 1 and vol 2, pt 2, 1864, Longman, Green, Longman, Roberts and Green.

TAYLOR M, 2017. *Charters – the making of Hull.* Hull Culture & Leisure Ltd.

THOMAS R S, 2004. *Edmund Tudor.* ODNB.

TIGHE R R & DAVIS J E, 1858. *Annals of Windsor - a history of the castle and town*, 2 vols. Longman, Brown, Green, Longmans and Roberts.

TOWNSEND J, 1910. *A History of Abingdon.* Henry Frowde, London.

TYACK G, BRADLEY S & PEVSNER N, 2010. *Buildings of England – Berkshire.* Yale University Press.

USHER B, 2004. *William Day, Bishop of Winchester.* ODNB.

VALLET M A, 1862-. *Histoire de Charles VII roi de France et son époque 1403-1461.* 3 vols. Paris.

VAUGHAN R, 1970. *Philip the Good.* Longman.

VCH Berkshire. Vol 1, 1906; vol 2, 1907; vol 3 1923 (eds. P H Ditchfield & W Page); vols 3 & 4 (eds. P H Ditchfield, W Page & J Hauteville Cope). University of London. Reprinted 1972.

VCH Buckinghamshire, 1925. Vol 3 (ed. W Page). Constable & Co. Ltd.

VCH Northamptonshire 1937. Vol 4 (ed. L F Salzman). Oxford University Press.

VCH County of York East Riding, 1969. Vol 1, *The City of Kingston upon Hull* (ed. K J Allison). *Medieval Hull.* Oxford University Press.

VCH Warwickshire, 1949 vol 5, Kington Hundred (ed. L F Salzman). Oxford University Press.

VCH Worcestershire, 1913. Vol 4 (eds. W Page & J W Willis-Bund). Constable & Co. Ltd.

VILLENEUVE BARGEMONT F L, 1825. *Histoire de Rene d'Anjou*, vol 1: 1408-1445; vol 2: 1446-1476; vol 3: 1476-1481. J J Blaise, Paris.

VINEY E, 1965. *The Sheriffs of Buckinghamshire from the eleventh century to the present day.* Hazell Watson & Viney Ltd.

VIRGOE R, 1982. *John Norris (by 1502-1577), of Fifield, Berks.* In: *The History of Parliament: the House of Commons 1558-1603,* ed. S T Bindoff. Boydell & Brewer.

Visitation of Buckinghamshire 1634. The Harleian Society, vol LVIII, 1909. (ed

WAKE J, 1953. *The Brudenells of Deene.* Cassell & Co Ltd.

WATTS J, 2004a. *William de la Pole, 1ˢᵗ Duke of Suffolk.* ODNB.

WATTS J, 2004b. *James Butler, 5ᵗʰ Earl of Wiltshire and Ormond.* ODNB.

WEDGWOOD J C & HOLT A (eds), 1936. *History of Parliament: Biographies of the members of the Commons House, 1439-1509.* HMSO.

WEDGWOOD J C (ed), 1938. *History of Parliament: Register of the Ministers and of the members of both Houses 1439-1509.* HMSO.

WENTWORTH DAY J, 1946. *Harvest Adventure*. George G Harrap & Sons.

WETHERED F T, 1903. *St Mary's, Hurley, in the middle ages based on Hurley Charters and Deeds*. Bedford Press, London.

WETHERED F T, 1909. *Lands and Tythes of Hurley Priory 1086-1535*. Charles Slaughter & Co, Reading.

WINSTON C, 1867. *An inquiry into the difference of style observable in ancient glass paintings especially in England* (part I – text; part II – plates). James Parker & Co.

WOODGER L S, 1993. *Richard Clitheroe I (d.1420), of Clitheroe, Lancs. and London and Goldstone in Ash-next-Sandwich, Kent*. In: Roskell J S, Clark L, & Rawcliffe C (eds), 1993. *The History of Parliament: the House of Commons 1386-1421*. Boydell & Brewer.

WOLFFE B, 1983. *Henry VI*. Methuen Ltd, London.

WRATHALL A E, 2021. *Helsfell Hall – Not just an old Lakeland barn*. Titus Wilson, Kendal.

WRIGHT T (ed), 1861. *Political poems and songs relating to English History, from the accession of Edward III to the reign of Henry VIII*. 2 Vols. Longman, Green, Longman & Roberts.

Acknowledgements and photo credits

As noted in the Preface, the initial impetus for this study came from a request in 1988 from Mr Brian Stein, the current owner, for further information about the house to supplement a useful report on its history prepared for him by Mr Harvey Van Sickle. He and his wife Jill have extended almost unfettered access to the house and grounds over the years enabling photography of rooms and artefacts and also visits by interested groups. Mr Stein has also allowed me to copy his own Ockwells related documents and photos. Without this contribution the foregoing history could not have been written.

During the course of the research for this book, a great many individuals – unfortunately too numerous to record – have given assistance and guidance and I am most grateful for this. However, I should like to thank, in particular, Dr Linda Clark for her advice over a sustained period of time, for always answering my queries, allowing me to see drafts of the biographies of John Norreys Esquire and his son Sir William, as well as other Members of Parliament connected with Norreys which were in preparation for *The History of Parliament – Commons 1422 to 1461*, and then sending me copies of the finished biographies during the Covid pandemic lockdown period of 2021.

The identification of those represented by their armorial achievements in the Ockwells great hall, and therefore the scheme devised by John Norreys Esquire, gradually unfolded over the years. A major breakthrough was the identification of who was represented by the Mortimer of Chirk coat at Ockwells. This emerged from my study of fifteenth-century tiles and armorial glass in Great Malvern Priory, and I thank John MacGregor, former Custos of the Priory, for his help.

The following people have made significant contributions to specific parts of the work:

Dr Elizabeth Matthews for translating a vital handwritten document in Medieval Latin relating to the 1444 betrothal ceremony in France;

Jenny Harper for assistance with translations from Latin, and in particular for alerting me to documents related to the 1582 Elizabethan Charter granting Ockwells to Basil Fettiplace;

Dr Anne Curry and Professor Ralph Griffiths for advice on medieval history; and the late Peter Begent for advice on heraldry during the early stages of this research;

and my husband, Dr Brian Darracott, who took most of the photographs, designed and laid out the text and illustrations, and whose copious editing has improved this book immeasurably.

Descendants of Sir Edward Barry have been very kind in allowing me access to various family archives in their possession. In particular I should like to thank:

the present Sir Edward Barry (5th baronet) for discussions and use of the illustrations on pages 179, 181, 182, and 187;

the late David Muspratt, grandson of Sir Edward Barry (2nd baronet), for discussions and use of the illustrations on pages 134, 151, 159 (lower), 165 (upper), 166 (upper), 167 (upper), 170 (lower), and 176 (upper left);

and Sara Poore, of New Zealand, great-granddaughter of Sir Edward Barry (2nd baronet) for use of the illustrations on pages 160, 166 (lower), 167 (lower), 169 (upper left), 171 (upper), 176 (upper right), and 177 (upper, and lower left).

The late Peter William Cannon, former estate manager at Ockwells had preserved for many years important heritage material relating to Ockwells that he had rescued when the house was sold and vacated by Sidney Barnett in 1960 and subsequently during the Pandemic of 2020 entrusted the material to my care. I have used some of this in the illustrations on pages 144, 152, 153, 161, 165 (lower) and 175.

Martin Little, former head gardener at Ockwells, has been able to enlighten me on recent changes in ownership of neighbouring land formerly part of the Ockwells estate. He also provided the illustrations of the gardens on pages 204 and 205.

Margaret A Tramontine, then Curator of Collections at Stan Hywet Hall, sent me the illustrations of the glass on page 184 (lower) and 221. Illustrations of Stan Hywet Hall and F A Seiberling on pages 183 and 185 (upper) can be found at https://seiberlingvisualhistory.org, and that on page 184 (upper) at https://www.stanhywet.org/manor-house.

I am also grateful to the following:

Estate agents Messrs Savills & Knight Frank for permission to reproduce photographs from the 2019 Ockwells Sale Catalogue taken by photographer Ed Kingsford. These are on pages 1, 2 (upper), 3, 201, 207 (lower), 208, 212 (lower), 328 and 329.

At my request, Mr David Noonan, of Cork County Council, kindly took the photographs of the armorial glass at Mallow Castle, Ireland, on pages 221 and 279.

The late Brian Sanderson – a graphic designer and long-time member of Maidenhead Civic Society – drew the sketch depicting the Ockwells lights shown on page 44 and also the several floor plans in Appendix G, Fig 1.

Local historian, the late Elias Kupfermann, who loaned me his microfiche of Charles Kerry's notebook from the Bodleian Library that led to the discovery of Kerry's copies of drawings of Ockwells armorial glass done in 1765 by Sir Thomas Reeve of Hendon's House, Holyport. Elias also alerted me to Ockwells documents being sold on eBay, subsequently purchased by Berkshire Record Office.

Robert Yorke, Archivist at the College of Arms library, for making available the Norreys pedigrees and bringing to my attention relevant references.

The late Peter Begent FSA, FHS, who at the start of this work advised me to visit Ewelme and was a constant support.

Local buildings Eton College, Taplow Court and St Michael's Church, Bray, and St George's Chapel, Windsor, have close links to Ockwells Manor. The late Eric Anderson, former Headmaster of Eton; Andrew Mackenzie, the then Estate Manager of NSUK at Taplow

Court; Jim Tucker, Church Warden at St Michael's, and Eileen Scarff, former Head Archivist at St George's Chapel, Windsor, helped with visits and information.

The initial printing of this work has been enabled through generous grants from The Prince Philip Trust Fund; the Louis Baylis Charitable Trust; the Kidwells Park Trust; and the Shell Community Kindness Grant fund, to all of which I am extremely grateful.

Many libraries, archives, record offices and societies have given permission for copies of their records to be quoted and reproduced and these have been specifically acknowledged in the main text where appropriate. Every effort has been made to trace other potential copyright holders and to obtain their permission for the use of copyrighted material. The publisher apologises for any errors or omissions and would be grateful to be notified of any corrections that should be incorporated in future reprints or editions of this book.

Index to People and Places

* Indicates an armorial achievement at Ockwells

Langford* Edward, 12, 14, 15, 20, 24, 44, 47, 90-91, 94-95, 97, 104, 124, 149, 158, 190, 261, 305, 311-312

Lapworth, 9, 88-89, 293

Lavington, Thomas, 14-16, 68, 94

Law, Ernest, 139-140, 267

Leech, Sir Stephen, 119, 137, 146-158, 162-165, 168, 171, 182, 190, 201, 204-5, 207, 218, 229-230, 268-271, 300-302, 312, 319, 321

Leech, Ethel, sister of Sir Stephen Leech, 148

Leech, Helen, aunt of Sir Stephen Leech, mother of Beatrix Potter, 148

Lees-Milne, James, 180-82, 218

Lillibrooke Manor, see Lowbrooks Farm

Lodge Edward, estate manager of William Henry Grenfell, 156

Lorraine, Isabella of, Queen of Sicily, 53-54, 247-248

Lowbrooks Farm, 114, 129, 179, 187

Lucas, John Seymour, RA, 138, 180, 182-3, 190

Lucas, Robert, 123, 227

Lucas, Tom L, 190, 194

Luxembourg, Isabel de, daughter of Peter, Count of St Pol, 246

Luxembourg, John de, Count of Ligny, 246

Luxembourg, Louis de, son of Peter, Count of St Pol, 246

Luxembourg, Peter de, Count of St Pol, brother of John, Count of Ligny, 246

Maidenhead, Guild (Gild) of SS Andrew & Mary Magdalene, 6, 17, 18-19, 21, 94, 97, 100, 236

Maine, Charles Count of, brother of Rene of Anjou, 16, 61, 246

Mann, Sir James Gow, 176, 179

Mallow Castle, Cork, 221, 279-280

Martley, 80 82

Merbrooke, Alice 1st wife of John Norreys, 9, 13, 15, 16, 19-21, 24, 44, 47, 54, 62, 87-89, 94, 105, 221, 262, 274-75, 277, 279, 281-282, 285-286, 293, 310-311

Merbrooke, Richard, father of Alice Merbrooke, 15-16, 94, 285, 293

Montacute, Alice, daughter of Thomas Montacute, Earl of Salisbury, 49, 51, 58, 91, 96, 222, 307

Montacute, Thomas, Earl of Salisbury, 9, 49, 57-58, 91, 96, 251

Montacute, William, Earl of Salisbury, 49, 91, 222

Mortimer*, Sir Hugh, 44, 47, 80-82, 104

Mortimer, John (aka Jack Cade), 16

Mortimer, Roger, 1st Baron Mortimer of Chirk, 81, 104, 123

Mortimer, Roger 1st Earl of March, 81, 222

Morris, William, founder of the SPAB, 135, 138, 228, 265

Nanfan* John, 10, 12, 16, 44, 47, 50, 83-86, 104, 260, 305

Nanfan, Sir Richard, son of John, 84, 104

Neville Cicely, wife of Henry Beauchamp, Duke of Warwick, 16, 49-50, 84, 105, 263, 307

Neville, John, Marquess Montagu/Montacute, 21, 81, 263, 286

Neville, Richard, Earl of Salisbury, 15, 20, 49, 51, 58, 91, 222, 307; for wife of, see Alice Montacute

Neville, Richard, Earl of Warwick, 20, 84

Neville, Robert, Bishop of Durham, 15, 54

Taylor, Elizabeth, actress, 190-191
Taylor, Elizabeth Jane, 138-139
Taplow Court, 80, 83, 92, 103, 129-130, 132-133, 139, 141, 156-157, 218, 227-228, 268, 305, 309, 311-312, 347; estate office, 156
Tedstone Wafre, 80

Tewkesbury, manor of, 84; Abbey, 50, 84; battle of, 54 61, 75
Thatcham, 96-97, 99
Thomas, David Mansfield, architect, 200, 232, 321, 327
Tremouille, Georges, Duc de la, 247
Trethewell, 83
Turne, Thackeray, Secretary, SPAB, 268-271

Upton, 98-99, 285; St Laurence's Church, 99-101, 123, 285, 298

Valladolid, English College of, 113-114, 233, 297

Wade, Felix, architect, 148-150, 154, 157, 218, 229, 268-271, 319
Warwick, St Mary's Church, 24, 50-52, 304, 312
Wenlock*, Sir John, 16, 22, 44, 47, 74-77, 94-95, 104, 249, 263
Wentworth Day, James, 182, 223
Westminster Abbey, 54, 108, 277, 298
Weston on the Green, 278
Whitlock, Rev James, 275-276; for wife of, see Elizabeth Bulstrode
Wilkerson, Allport, 132, 135, 137, 228, 265
Willement, Thomas, Queen Victoria's glazier, 124, 218-220, 307, 309-312
Williams, Sir John of Rycote, 274-275, 288, 298
Windsor, 1, 12-13, 17, 19-20, 24, 61, 79, 94, 96, 121, 128, 141, 158, 160, 162, 211, 223, 226; Royal Lodge, 141, 314; Castle, 10, 12-13, 20, 24, 46, 52, 60, 79, 109, 158, 190, 196, 220, 255, 259, 281, 289-290, 312; St George's Chapel, 12, 19, 46, 69-70, 108, 220; Forest, 3, 5, 41
Windsor, Guild (Gild) of the Holy Trinity, 12
Winch, James, 116-118, 225-226
Wokingham, All Saints Church, 13, 235

Yattendon, 88; manor of, 1, 9, 12, 15, 21, 24, 47, 88, 91, 105, 109-110, 274, 281, 285, 288, 293, 296, 298; parish church of St Peter & St Paul 19, 21, 68, 88, 105, 110, 245, 282, 288
Young, Thomas, 123, 227